Environmental Activism on the Ground

CANADIAN HISTORY AND ENVIRONMENT SERIES

SERIES EDITOR: Alan MacEachern

ISSN 1925-3702 (Print) ISSN 1925-3710 (Online)

The Canadian History & Environment series brings together scholars from across the academy and beyond to explore the relationships between people and nature in Canada's past.

Alan MacEachern, Founding Director
NiCHE: Network in Canadian History & Environment
Nouvelle initiative canadienne en histoire de l'environnement
http://niche-canada.org

UNIVERSITY OF CALGARY
Press

ENVIRONMENTAL ACTIVISM ON THE GROUND

Small Green and Indigenous Organizing

Edited by Jonathan Clapperton and Liza Piper

Canadian History and Environment Series
ISSN 1925-3702 (Print) ISSN 1925-3710 (Online)

University of Calgary Press
2500 University Drive NW
Calgary, Alberta
Canada T2N 1N4
press.ucalgary.ca

LIBRARY AND ARCHIVES CANADA CATALOGUING IN PUBLICATION

Environmental activism on the ground : small green
and Indigenous organizing / edited by Jonathan Clapperton
and Liza Piper.

(Canadian history and environment series ; 9)
Includes bibliographical references and index.
Issued in print and electronic formats.
ISBN 978-1-77385-004-7 (softcover).—ISBN 978-1-77385-006-1
(PDF).—ISBN 978-1-77385-007-8 (EPUB).—ISBN 978-1-77385-008-5
(Kindle).—ISBN 978-1-77385-005-4 (open access PDF)

  1. Environmentalism—Case studies. 2. Indigenous peoples—
Politics and government—Case studies. 3. Case studies. I. Piper, Liza,
1978-, editor—II. Clapperton, Jonathan, 1981-, editor III. Series: Canadian
history and environment series ; 9

GE195.E58 2019   333.72   C2018-906251-7
                                        C2018-906252-5

The University of Calgary Press acknowledges the support of the Government of Alberta through the Alberta Media Fund for our publications. We acknowledge the financial support of the Government of Canada. We acknowledge the financial support of the Canada Council for the Arts for our publishing program.

This book has been published with the help of a grant from the Canadian Federation for the Humanities and Social Sciences, through the Awards to Scholarly Publications Program, using funds provided by the Social Sciences and Humanities Research Council of Canada.

Alberta Government   Canada   Canada Council for the Arts   Conseil des Arts du Canada

Cover image: First Nations raising a traditional welcome figure at the legislature during the Meares Island protest in October 1984. *Victoria Times Colonist* file photo.
Copyediting by Peter Enman
Cover design, page design, and typesetting by Melina Cusano

CONTENTS

ILLUSTRATIONS

Figures

Tables

ACKNOWLEDGEMENTS

Foremost, we wish to thank the participants at the original Edmonton workshop in 2014, including especially the contributors to this volume, who continued to be supportive of the long, and sometimes winding, road that this project took from its inception.

Special gratitude is given to Melanie Marvin, formerly with the Department of History and Classics at the University of Alberta, for doing much of the organizational work for the workshop in 2014. We also thank Hereward Longley for his work as a research assistant on this book. We are thankful to the family of Tobasonakwut Peter Kinew, and Marcia Ruby at *Alternatives*, for allowing us to reprint Kinew's article (Chapter 7).

We also gratefully acknowledge the generous financial support from the Social Sciences and Humanities Research Council, the Rachel Carson Center for Environment and Society, the Network in Canadian History & Environment, and both the Department of History and Classics and the Department of Sociology at the University of Alberta.

In the Shadow of the Green Giants: Environmentalism and Civic Engagement

Jonathan Clapperton & Liza Piper

In 1970, three women living in Edmonton, with shared social and en-vironmental concerns and alert to the belching refineries of east Edmon-ton, established a group called STOP: Save Tomorrow, Oppose Pollution. STOP engaged broadly with the environmental issues of the day, from air and water pollution in urban areas to the implications of the Mackenzie Valley Pipeline Inquiry. They put on puppet theatres for children, issued press releases, organized letter-writing campaigns, and generally engaged in the diverse practices and small-scale strategies possible with limited re-sources that characterize grassroots activism. Louise Swift, one of STOP's founders and later also a Raging Granny, described their tactics to the magazine *Alberta Views*. To raise awareness of the issue of phosphates in household detergents, for example, a seemingly prosaic but nevertheless pivotal environmental issue in Canada in the 1970s, Swift described how members "would stuff shopping carts full of groceries at Safeway and pro-ceed to the longest checkout line, then make a loud scene when they 'dis-covered' they were buying a product with phosphates."[1] That 2004 issue of *Alberta Views* was dedicated to activism in Alberta: part celebration and part encouragement to Albertans to become involved in social and environmental issues and to "challeng[e] apathy head on."[2] The editorial board described environmental activists, in particular, as fighting "an up-hill battle every day"—a feeling no doubt experienced even more acutely three decades earlier by those of STOP in big-oil country.[3]

Edmonton is the capital of Alberta: current home to the oil (or "tar") sands, long-standing centre of Canada's oil industry, and widely perceived as barren ground for environmentalism. For our purposes, the creation of STOP is the exception that proves the rule: a wave of environmental consciousness transformed North America and places beyond in the 1970s, including supposed environmentalist backwaters like Edmonton and the rest of Alberta. STOP was by no means the only Alberta organization agitating for greater attention to environmental issues in this period. University of Calgary students came together in the wake of the first Earth Day to form the Calgary Eco-Centre Society. Funded by such diverse entities as the Alberta Fish and Game Association (a long-standing advocate for environmental protection across the province) and Dome Petroleum (a Calgary-based oil company), the Eco-Centre worked to disseminate ecologically minded educational materials among the wider public.[4]

The rise of environmentalist organizations in the 1970s provoked significant backlash in Alberta, as elsewhere. Industry lobby organizations, such as the Coal Association of Canada, might have been expected to dismiss what they called "the emotional desires" of advocates for more ecologically minded approaches to resource development.[5] But opposition was expressed even in seemingly more sympathetic quarters. W. H. (Wally) Hanson, the chief forester with the Eastern Rockies Forest Conservation Board (ERFCB) (a joint federal-provincial management board that sought to protect the ecologically sensitive Eastern Slopes of the Rocky Mountains), criticized the "environmentalist cult" and contrasted its provocations to his own and the ERFCB's arguably more effective, and certainly more moderate, approach to conservation.[6] Both STOP and the Calgary Eco-Centre Society folded in the early 1980s, in part because the emergent professionalism of the environmental movement of that period left less room, and created at least the perception that there was less need, for the kind of amateur, grassroots activism so prevalent across different locales in the 1970s. Other organizations founded in the same period nevertheless endured. The Alberta Wilderness Association, founded in 1965, espoused a more explicitly preservationist ideology that harkened back to

Jonathan Clapperton & Liza Piper

early twentieth-century conservation efforts. It is now the oldest wilderness conservation group in Alberta. The Lubicon Lake Nation initiated its contemporary struggle with oil and gas development on their lands in northern Alberta in 1976, when the Nation, along with other affected groups, formed the Alberta Isolated Communities and filed a caveat against the Alberta government in an effort to forestall further industrial development.[7] It was not until October 2018, that the Lubicon Lake Band agreed to a final land claim settlement with the federal and provincial governments.

Edmonton is where the workshop from which this book originated was hosted in 2014, and this snapshot of late twentieth-century environmentalism in Alberta highlights some of the core elements of our volume and its contribution to the wider literature on the history of North American environmentalism.[8] As the chapters here collectively argue, the efflorescence of small activist groups in the late 1960s, and into the 1970s, focused on local issues but attuned to national, continental, and global dynamics, served as more than just the building blocks from which larger, more powerful environmentalist organizations emerged. Rather, they represent a strand within the history of North American environmentalism, one in which workers, women, small businesspeople, Indigenous activists, and other often marginalized groups feature more prominently as compared to their roles in the largest green organizations: Greenpeace, the Sierra Club, the National Audubon Society, Earth First!, and the World Wildlife Fund. This volume focuses on the experiences of small-scale, localized environmental activists, including Indigenous activists, from the late twentieth into the twenty-first century, to emphasize the contributions and significance of these forms of small green activism within the larger movement as a whole. Readers will observe that the authors in this volume use a variety of terms to refer to Indigenous people in those instances where a collective noun is more appropriate than identifying the specific nation or group to which people belong. The different collective nouns (Indigenous peoples, Native peoples, American Indians) reflect the fact that the scholarship here is drawn from Canada, the United States, and elsewhere in the Americas where the normal terms are different. Although it is less consistent, the editors and authors felt it important that each chapter use the language meaningful to its specific context.

The first part of *Environmental Activism on the Ground* explores the processes and possibilities of small-scale and Indigenous environment- al activism. The five chapters here consider the different ways in which Indigenous and non-Indigenous activists have worked from the ground up to achieve significant change in resisting exploitative and damaging resource development and in building parks, heritage sites, and protected areas that recognize the indivisibility of cultural and natural resources and work to protect both. This part also includes a methodological inves- tigation of how historians can better probe the experiences of ordinary people (in contrast to scientists, politicians, and other elites) in the history of environmentalism. The second part of the volume then takes us more fully into the past and the era from the late 1960s into the 1990s, when the modern environmental movement flourished, to consider the character of small-scale environmentalism in this period. These chapters contextualize and deepen our understanding of some of the processes described in Part 1, "Processes and Possibilities," and adopted by small green and Indigen- ous activists, and their consequences in Canadian history in particular.

Environmental history, a discipline that informs many of the chap- ters in this volume, is attuned to matters of scale. Typically this attention focuses on geographic scale, or scales of production and consumption; in this instance we have redirected the question of scale back on to the so- cial movement of environmentalism itself. When it comes to evaluating the efficacy of environmental organizations and groups, studies of the environmental movement's last six decades remain enthralled by those traditionally seen as prime history makers: the larger, (supposedly) more successful and powerful "Green Giants." Implicit in such focus is the idea that the bigger the rock thrown in the pond, the greater the splash it cre- ates. While the most renowned environmental organizations have been integral to the spread of the environmental movement, these organiza- tions nevertheless represent but a fraction of the interests that shaped, and continue to shape, that movement and are far outnumbered by localized, often grassroots, environmental organizations that tend to fly below both academic and public radars. While small-scale and Indigenous organ- izations and collectives do not garner as many, or as sensational, media headlines, boast internationally renowned celebrities, or have financial pockets and political connections as deep as the "Green Giants," they do, by weight of mass, form a powerful transformational force; toss enough small rocks into the pond, and they, too, cause a significant stir. Using anthropological, historical, and sociological approaches to measure the splash of such environmental organizations, groups, and associations is a central objective of this book.

Environmentalist leaders, as part of the environmental justice movement, have recognized the importance of "everyday" and "non-elite" peoples who are pushing forward the broader environmental movement's agenda.[9] Popular books intended for a lay audience also encourage individuals to become "everyday environmental activists" without necessarily becoming members of environmental organizations.[10] Indigenous peoples struggling to resist enduring colonial pressures, and to protect their rights to cultural preservation and self-determination, have also acted as crucial participants in environmental struggles. In Canada and the United States, treaty rights have served as barriers to persistent and intense industrial pressures, even as other forms of legal protections for the environment have weakened. By bringing together research on Indigenous activism with insights into the role that ordinary members of society have played and continue to play in the environmental movement's unfolding drama, this edited collection seeks to open new avenues for scholarship into small-scale activism and its successes.

The question of scale animates *Environmental Activism on the Ground* in two ways. First, it offers a central organizing principle, in that each chapter explores small green activism in a different context. From parks and protected areas across the Americas (Evans) to the rural landscapes of Nova Scotia (Leeming), each chapter offers insight into the diversity of organizations and the historical contexts in which small-scale activism appeared. Each chapter also illuminates common themes that run through the historical experiences of such activism: the need to make and maintain alliances with other groups, the struggles over objectives particularly where environmental degradation has followed from larger imbalances of power, and the connections between immediate, local concerns and wider, even global, changes.

Second, several of the chapters (particularly Clapperton and Zelko) engage with the question of whether the shift to larger environmentalist organizations represents a significant change over time. In this regard,

Environmental Activism on the Ground undermines more linear narratives of the environmental movement, such as Robert Gottlieb's *Forcing the Spring*, Adam Rome's *The Genius of Earth Day*, and, especially, Kirkpatrick Sale's *The Green Revolution*, among others, which create a fairly standard periodization of the environmental movement's progression over time.[11] Rather, our volume collectively shows that the environmental movement's growth was unevenly felt across time and space.

Recent scholarly works on the nineteenth- and early twentieth-century North American environmental movement have characterized it as initiated as much by lower- and middle-class people as the powerful elite. From either side of the Canada-US border, Tina Loo and Chad Montrie respectively have sought to emphasize the crucial role of individuals and smaller organizations, such as union locals, in articulating an earlier environmentalist ethos.[12] Although much scholarly attention on the later, better-known environmentalism of the 1960s and 1970s remains focused on larger organizations or on state initiatives, such as Michael Bess's *Light-Green Society*, there is a growing body of work (some of which has been authored by contributors to this present collection), such as the recent edited collection *Canadian Countercultures and the Environment*, that examines local activism and its effects.[13] While every environmental campaign is local in a sense, and even large environmental organizations are headquartered in different local contexts, these are not what is intended by this book. Rather, we follow in the same vein as *Countercultures and the Environment* by identifying local activism as being that which involves people who are local/residents to a particular space/place. While a focus on local activism was one variable used to delimit the study, the other was a focus on those organizations that were small-scale.

Historical interpretation of twentieth-century environmentalism as a social movement has drawn attention to its social and cultural origins in suburban natures, youth activism, and late twentieth-century media cultures, and away from key figures who led major environmentalist organizations or state-based initiatives.[14] Some attention has been focused on the place of relationships between historically marginalized groups, such as Indigenous peoples and African Americans and Canadians, and their involvement in environmental activism, particularly within the environmental justice literature.[15] This volume pays attention to local and small-scale activities, with particular attention to North American Indigenous experiences. This is an integration that rarely makes a substantial appearance in collections or histories of environmental activism. And it is an important aspect of how we aim to build on and further articulate a reappraisal of the environmental movement as a small-scale, ordinary activity as much as a large-scale and elite-driven one.

What is readily apparent from the contributions to this volume, as well as in present-day environmental activism in North America, is the role of Indigenous people as activists, and of Indigenous rights in enabling greater environmental protection than might otherwise be possible. Similarly, one of the fastest-growing bodies of literature on Indigenous peoples concerns their relationship to the environment; included in this is a growing literature on the popularized connection between Indigenous peoples and environmentalism, most notably epitomized, and to some extent sparked, by Shepard Krech's *The Ecological Indian: Myth and History*.[16] It should go without saying that Indigenous peoples are not uniform, and that while some individuals might also identify as environmentalists, arguably the majority seek to balance environmental stewardship with resource and industrial development. A case in point is the ongoing controversy in British Columbia and Alberta over the Kinder Morgan Trans Mountain Pipeline expansion. While many First Nations along the pipeline's proposed path are opposed to the project, many others have signed on to benefit agreements and support the project.[17]

Unlike much of this discussion, however, our purpose in this volume is not to debate the extent to which Indigenous peoples are, or are not, conservationists or ecologists; nor, of course, is it to reduce all Indigenous peoples to automatic environmentalists. Rather, chapters in this volume highlight the diverse interactions Indigenous peoples have had in environmental activism, relationships—both cooperative and confrontational—with environmentalists or initiatives labelled as such, and developing and maintaining local power, as well as highlighting the possibilities for future activism and partnership. Chapters in this collection contribute to work done by E. Richard Atleo (Umeek), Raymond Pierotti, Daniel Wildcat, and others in showing the intertwined cultural and environmental heritage of Indigenous peoples, and the history of Indigenous rights in enabling and ensuring heritage and environmental protection of valued places.[18] They also contribute to the ongoing conversation around Indigenous worldviews and how they affect Indigenous lifeway struggles, especially as they relate to Indigenous activism. Vine Deloria Jr.'s grounding book *The Metaphysics of Modern Existence* describes the changes in how people thought about the environment as cultures moved from small, localized tribal groups to globalized, western European political forms.[19] Likewise, Emma S. Norman's article on Indigenous-led activism to protect water rights connects to Indigenous thought and leadership, and calls for reform in colonial governance mechanisms and structures.[20] Timothy Leduc's exploration of Inuit views on climate change shows that climate change (and environmental change more broadly) is inextricably linked to cultural change as well.[21] In this fashion, attention to environmental activism and understandings of environmental change that is taking place outside the Western mainstream likewise draws attention to themes that fall outside the mainstream of the historiography.

This volume is interdisciplinary, as it presents different kinds of scholarship—from history, public history, anthropology, geography, and sociology—to assess the past, present, and future. In this regard, we aim not only to engage with scholarly debates about the character of late twentieth-century environmentalism but also to draw on a range of disciplinary perspectives to better understand the ongoing evolution of environmental activism and the role of small green organizations in how this takes shape. The chapters present analyses of late twentieth- and early twenty-first century environmentalism from Canada and the United States (and, in Evans' chapter, comparison with Latin America), with particular attention to the local and small-scale, with the aim of understanding historical interconnections between geographically diverse initiatives. While the environmental movement (as with the environment itself) transcends national boundaries, the overwhelming majority of studies on it persist in using the nation-state as the principal analytical lens through which to frame important events and processes. Our central methodological strategy, therefore, was to approach the topic from different geographical perspectives. In particular, almost all of the chapters in the first part of this volume compare case studies across regions, from Anna Willow (British Columbia and Ontario, Canada) to Zoltán Grossman (the Pacific Northwest), Jessica DeWitt (Canada and the US), and Sterling Evans (the Western

Jonathan Clapperton & Liza Piper

Hemisphere). Otherwise, most chapters focus on a single province, region, or even environmental feature, including those by John Welch (the White Mountain Apache's land in Arizona, USA), Tobasonakwut Peter Kinew (northern Ontario, Canada), Jonathan Clapperton (southwestern British Columbia, Canada), Mark Leeming (Nova Scotia, Canada) and Mark McLaughlin (New Brunswick, Canada). With the exception of Frank Zelko's chapter, which starts local but moves internationally, following on the growth of Greenpeace as an organization, the place-based approach shared by the chapters in this volume serves to highlight both the importance of the local to small-scale organizations, and the important comparisons that can nevertheless be drawn between—at times—geographically very distant places.

Most of the chapters adopt a transnational analytical frame, drawing in similar issues and mapping the connections between environmentalism and environmentalists from myriad places, in effect considering the perspectives and sensibilities of recent debates in transnational and global history.[22] That is, each author recognizes and makes the connections between the fact that the movements of people, ideas, and non-human nature flow across multiple boundaries, and that *global* and *local* are always intimately entwined. However, our book also collectively weighs the degree to which globalizing processes do not necessarily erase the local but rather local efforts resound on varying geographical scales. There are themes common to historical experiences in Canada and the United States especially, but the Americas more broadly (and with which Evans, in particular, engages), that emerge clearly in this collection. Put another way: this book seeks to emphasize local diversity and uniqueness without forgoing identifying general principles, common forces, and shared experiences that have made environmentalism appealing around the world to peoples separated by radically different backgrounds. The real strength of the environmental movement, as noted elsewhere, lay in its diversity.[23]

We sought to provide new forays into the topic of small green activism by addressing a number of critical questions, and the chapters are connected by providing answers to each of the following questions: How have the dynamics of environmental organizations changed or remained the same over time and space? What pressures, both internal and external, have shaped and directed their policies, and how did they make themselves heard among the many voices claiming to speak for the environment, including the much louder national or international environmental organizations, or "Green Giants"? How have these environmental organizations recruited and kept members and how has their support changed over time? Such issues are all currently underdeveloped within the existing literature on the environmental movement in North America and even more so across the rest of the globe. In addressing these questions, individual chapters also make important contributions to the more specific literatures within which each can be situated.

The Chapters

The chapters in "Processes and Possibilities" use, for the most part, comparative case studies to dissect important processes that shape small green activism, and to assess the possibilities for change that are thereby enabled. Anna Willow's opening chapter, "Strategies for Survival: First Nations Encounters with Environmentalism," helps to frame some of the key dynamics that animate other chapters in the collection. Willow draws on her own, long-term experience of working with Indigenous communities, in this case with the Grassy Narrows First Nation, Ontario, and West Moberly First Nation, British Columbia. She focuses on partnerships between First Nations residents of Canada's boreal forest and environmentally concerned non-Indigenous peoples—a thread also picked up by Grossman, Welch, and Evans—in highlighting the relationship of Indigenous environmental activism to broader efforts at social and political change. Much of Willow's contribution appraises the important lessons that both First Nations and environmentalists have learned in collaborating with one another, and she concludes with insights into what those of us who study environmentalists and environmentalism can take from them. Grossman similarly examines alliances of Indigenous peoples with a diverse mix of environmental and climate activists, farmers, and even ranchers ("cowboys") in their opposition to the extraction and movement of fossil fuels in North America. He contends that these interconnected and numerous Indigenous/non-Indigenous alliances function as a "thin green line" between North American fossil fuel basins—the Alberta Tar Sands, the Powder River Coal Basin, and the Bakken Oil Shale Basin—and

Asian markets. Grossman's discussion has important similarities to John Welch's chapter, where he finds how tribal sovereignty can be strengthened by, rather than diminished through, partnerships between Indigenous and non-Indigenous activists.

The next three chapters in Part 1, from John Welch, Sterling Evans, and Jessica DeWitt, focus on parks and heritage conservation in Canada and the United States, with Evans also considering Costa Rica and Brazil. In particular, these chapters pay attention to the role of Indigenous peoples (Evans and Welch), small businesspeople (DeWitt), and tourists (all three authors) in shaping parks and their environmental objectives. By turning attention away from the best-known, iconic national parks to smaller, local heritage organizations and state and provincial parks, these chapters deepen our understanding of the enduring place of nature and heritage conservation and preservation within the wider environmental movement. Parks history, at this scale, is not just about symbolism, policy, and standards of management but about the negotiations that shape the protection of local places, and by extension the diversity—natural and cultural—that they enshrine. In his chapter, "Conserving Contested Ground: Sovereignty-Driven Stewardship by the White Mountain Apache Tribe and the Fort Apache Heritage Foundation," Welch draws on his three decades of experience working for, and with, the White Mountain Apache Tribe in Arizona. Welch reveals how the Western Apache, partnering with other small-scale bodies—Indigenous nations, non-profit organizations, and local citizens—gained control of the buildings that were previously the base for colonizing Western Apache lands and peoples—Fort Apache and the Theodore Roosevelt School—and retooled them to advance conceptions of their sovereignty while simultaneously protecting the environment.

Evans' geographically diverse case studies in chapter 4, "From Southern Alberta to Northern Brazil: Indigenous Conservation and the Preservation of Cultural Resources," illustrate a changing relationship between states and nature whereby historical and contemporary Indigenous rights are reflected in acknowledging an Indigenous sense of place and the importance of Indigenous access to land regardless of its protected status. Protected places are likewise at the heart of chapter 5, "Parks For and *By* the People: Acknowledging Ordinary People in the Formation, Protection, and Use of State and Provincial Parks." DeWitt demonstrates how—by drawing on diverse historiography and both conventional and innovative source materials—historians can study the role of ordinary people in the management of state and provincial parks in the United States and Canada respectively. This is a methodological chapter that identifies a process for bringing the history of small green activist organizations (and their conservationist allies) to light and, in so doing, to better understand their influence within green activism.[24]

The first three chapters in Part 2, "Histories," focus on the relationships between environmental and Indigenous activism in Canada's past. Piper's chapter analyzes the magazine *Alternatives* in the 1970s as a forum from which it is possible to discern how Indigenous concerns and perspectives intersected with mainstream environmentalism in Canada, and Ontario in particular. Piper's chapter serves to introduce Kinew's chapter on the Marmion Lake Generating Station, which is reprinted from *Alternatives* and was originally published in 1978. Kinew was Chief of the Sabaskong Reserve at the time and wrote about efforts by Treaty 3 chiefs to resist resource development and its damaging environmental impacts. Clapperton's chapter on Clayoquot Sound illuminates the complex character of Indigenous-environmentalist advocacy in the 1990s. These three chapters taken together highlight the central significance of conflicts over natural resource development in providing the occasions for environmentalists and Indigenous activists in Canada to work together and to come into conflict, a point also made recently by Lianne Leddy.[25] These chapters historicize the role of Indigenous rights in providing leverage for environmental activism: they demonstrate that there was nothing inevitable or automatic about these alliances in Canada, and that they rather were contingent on debates, legal decisions, and the evolution of political rights and discourse in the 1970s and 1980s in particular.

Each chapter in the second part of the volume presents a different historical episode, primarily drawn from Canadian examples, that sheds light on the processes identified by the authors in the first part, and applies some of the approaches suggested by DeWitt, to deepen our understanding of how small green activism changed and influenced change over time. Mark Leeming's study of rural environmentalism, "Local Economic Independence as Environmentalism: Nova Scotia in the 1970s," draws on the insights of Ramachandra Guha and Juan Martinez-Alier, who focused on the "environmentalism of the poor" in Peru, Ecuador, Indonesia, and India, and applies these insights to the Canadian province of Nova Scotia. Leeming gives particular attention to the economic dimensions of environmental activism, particularly as rural economies declined relative to urban ones. He demonstrates the diverse roots of rural environmentalism, as well as the alliances, including with Indigenous activists, necessary to achieve shared objectives. These themes resonate closely with the case studies presented earlier by Willow and Grossman.

The final three chapters offer insights into the tensions around size, scale, and impact that shaped histories of environmental activism and activist groups from the late 1960s into the 1980s. McLaughlin's chapter keeps attention on the east coast of Canada. He examines the history of the Conservation Council of New Brunswick (CCNB), that province's first and foremost environmentalist group, founded in 1969. He notes that the "Holy Grail" for many environmentalists (of any scale) is meaningful engagement with government officials, but, of course, officials are not always receptive, and environmentalist groups have at times been ineffective in building such ties. Welch's study offers one perspective on these struggles. McLaughlin's chapter provides another. Here we have a case study that highlights how figures within government and individual personalities can make the difference between effecting change or being pushed aside and becoming irrelevant. Clapperton's chapter, "The Ebb and Flow of Local Environmentalist Activism: The Society for Pollution and Environmental Control (SPEC), British Columbia," moves to a highly urban setting on the west coast of Canada. His case study examines the internal and external politics of SPEC, traces how it got big, then shrunk, and how it maintained relevance by returning to its roots as a smaller, much more localized environmental organization that continues to be active in Vancouver. One of Clapperton's key insights is to reveal that many of the practices that contemporary environmental proponents point to as new kinds of environmentalism predicted to revitalize the current environmental movement actually have historical antecedents with small green activist groups. Although SPEC rose up to be, within a few years, the largest environmental organization in the province, and, likely, the country, it has received scant scholarly attention, in part because of another Vancouver-based organization, Greenpeace, and its rise to prominence shortly thereafter. Zelko's study of Greenpeace, "From Social Movement to Environmental Behemoth: How Greenpeace Got Big," is fittingly the subject of the final chapter of this collection. While many of those in SPEC, such as Bill Darnell and Bob Hunter, went on to be involved in Greenpeace, Zelko asks how a small band of Vancouver-based anti-nuclear protesters created such a high-profile organization, and focuses on the genesis and early years of the organization before it "got big." Zelko not only traces the path that Greenpeace took to become big but also points out that there were many other possibilities: Greenpeace could have become simply a social movement rather than a professional organization, and could have easily been one more failed environmental organization after its first campaign.

Cautious Optimism for our Environmental Futures

Stories of decline are a persistent feature of both environmental activist rhetoric and of environmental history. Indeed, the very nature of environmentalism—concern for the natural world and a heightened awareness of threats to it—seems to demand a declensionist narrative. Environmental movements were born out of the identification of past and present environmental ruination, along with the prediction of future catastrophe. George Perkins Marsh, in *Man and Nature: Or, Physical Geography as Modified by Human Action* (1864), explained the collapse of Mediterranean civilizations as the result of environmental degradation, and warned his nineteenth-century American contemporaries that the same trend was perceivable in the United States. Marsh's ideas are widely considered to have inspired the subsequent conservation movement, with David Lowenthal labelling him a "prophet of conservation," and the US National Park Service identifying him as the "father of the American conservation movement."[26] Nearly a century later Rachel Carson, in *Silent Spring* (1962), documented the widespread, damaging impacts of pesticides in the environment, industrial deception about the harm pesticides caused, and government complicity in ignoring clear signs of environmental degradation. A groundswell of public outrage followed thereafter, and Carson, oftentimes referred to in popular discourse as the "mother" of environmentalism, is credited for sparking the modern environmental movement.[27] Such tragic narratives as those told by Marsh and Carson no doubt served as catalysts to galvanize otherwise apathetic or indifferent publics into action. It is unsurprising that the activists hoping to achieve the same success as the above two progenitors would employ their own environmental narratives using the same trope.

Yet, after warnings of catastrophic environmental decline for decades, challenges to the continued relevance and effectiveness of such stories have emerged. All of these refutations claim that "doom-and-gloom" narratives are no longer inspiring public activism to the same degree as they once did, or, even worse, that they are actually counterproductive and now produce a general public that is desensitized, hopeless, indifferent, burnt out, and at times even hostile to such messages.[28] Indeed, a central feature of Ted Nordhaus and Michael Shellenberger's 2004 essay, and subsequent book, on "the Death of Environmentalism" was its unfavourable comparison of environmentalists, for their apocalyptic and complaint-based approach, with Martin Luther King Jr.'s positive "I have a dream" vision. Nordhaus and Shellenberger called on environmentalists to "replace their doomsday discourse with an imaginative, aspirational, and future-oriented one."[29] The "old politics," the authors polemically claimed, "has taken us as far as it can."[30] Hyperbole, we might add, is not helpful either, though such critique is useful for strategically thinking about how to reframe the environmental movement.

Negative campaigning continues to influence efforts to forestall ecologically harmful developments, such as the Dakota Access Pipeline, and warnings of extinction-level catastrophe as a result of climate change undoubtedly motivated delegates at the 2015 UN Climate Change Conference in Paris to produce concrete results. Nevertheless, the authors in this collection agreed during the workshop from which this volume emerged that a hopeful and optimistic book was not only more welcome as a contribution to larger debates but was also a more accurate reflection of the recent history of small green and Indigenous activism than a book that measured their failures. As the chapters here detail, small green activism (perhaps a misnomer considering the role it has played in shaping history) has been, and continues to be, relevant—possibly now more than ever.

Notes

1   For the importance of laundry detergent to the history of Canadian environmentalism, see Jennifer Read, "'Let Us Heed the Voice of Youth': Laundry Detergents, Phosphates and the Emergence of the Environmental Movement in Ontario," *Journal of the Canadian Historical Association* 7, no. 1 (1996): 227–50; and Ryan O'Connor, *The First Green Wave: Pollution Probe and the Origins of Environmental Activism in Ontario* (Vancouver: UBC Press, 2014). The interview with Swift appears in Dan Rubinstein, "Activists Among Us," *Alberta Views*, March/April 2004, 37–43.

2   Editorial board, "Activism in Alberta 2004: Justice Politics Environment Peace," *Alberta Views*, March/April 2004, 16.

3   Editorial board, "Activism in Alberta," 18.

4   For long-standing environmental advocacy of fish and game clubs in Alberta, see George Colpitts, *Fish Wars and Trout Travesties: Saving Southern Alberta's Coldwater Streams in the 1920s* (Edmonton: AU Press, 2018).

5   Coal Association of Canada, "Submission to Public Hearings Conducted by the Environment Conservation Authority," p. 2, 21 December 1971, File M-8393-1361, Coal Association of Canada fonds, Glenbow Archives.

6   W. R. Hanson, *History of the Eastern Rockies Forest Conservation Board* (Calgary: Eastern Rockies Forest Conservation Board, 1973), n.p., section 9.8.

7   Darlene Abreu-Ferreira, "Oil and Lubicons Don't Mix: A Land Claim in Northern Alberta in Historical Perspective," *Canadian Journal of Native Studies* 12, no. 1 (1992): 12.

8   This edited book emerged from papers presented at a three-day interdisciplinary workshop titled "Environmentalism from Below: Appraising the Efficacy of Small-Scale and Subaltern Environmentalist Organizations," held in August 2014. Although narratives of decline are prevalent in environmental history, one of the themes that emerged from this workshop was that this is not the whole story. We read papers and heard from presenters who provided numerous success stories and were (cautiously) optimistic about our collective environmental futures. Additionally, these chapters form one of two outlets, designed to complement each other, for the discussions held at the workshop; the other is a collection of articles in the Rachel Carson Center's *Perspectives* journal, published in 2016.

9   Douglas Bevington, *The Rebirth of Environmentalism: Grassroots Activism from the Spotted Owl to the Polar Bear* (Washington, DC: Island Press, 2009); and David Suzuki and Holly Dressel, *Good News for a Change: How Everyday People are Helping the Planet* (Vancouver: Greystone Books, 2003).

10 Michael Norton, *The Everyday Activist: 365 Ways to Change the World* (Oxford: Pan Macmillan, 2007).

11 Robert Gottlieb, *Forcing the Spring: The Transformation of the American Environmental Movement* (Washington, DC: Island Press, 1993); Adam Rome, *The Genius of Earth Day: How a 1970s Teach-In Unexpectedly Made the First Green Generation* (New York: Hill & Wang, 2014); Kirkpatrick Sale, *The Green Revolution: The American*

Environmental Movement 1962–1992 (New York: Hill & Wang, 1993); Philip Shabecoff, *A Fierce Green Fire: The American Environmental Movement* (New York: Hill & Wang, 1993); Hal K. Rothman, *The Greening of a Nation? Environmentalism in the United States Since 1945* (New York: Harcourt Brace, 1998).

12   Chad Montrie, *A People's History of Environmentalism in the United States* (New York: Continuum, 2011); and Tina Loo, *States of Nature: Conserving Canada's Wildlife in the Twentieth Century* (Vancouver: UBC Press, 2006).

13   Michael Bess, *The Light-Green Society: Ecology and Technological Modernity in France, 1960–2000* (Chicago: University of Chicago Press, 2003); Colin M. Coates, ed., *Canadian Countercultures and the Environment* (Calgary: University of Calgary Press, 2016); Robert D. Lifset, *Power on the Hudson: Storm King Mountain and the Emergence of Modern American Environmentalism* (Pittsburgh: University of Pittsburgh Press, 2014); O'Connor, *The First Green Wave*; Pradyumna Karan and Unryu Suganuma, *Local Environmental Movements: A Comparative Study of the United States and Japan* (Lexington: University Press of Kentucky, 2008); Marco Armiero and Lise Sedrez, eds., *A History of Environmentalism: Local Struggles, Global Histories* (London: Bloomsbury Academic, 2014); Mark McLaughlin, "Green Shoots: Aerial Insecticide Spraying and the Growth of Environmental Consciousness in New Brunswick, 1952–1973," *Acadiensis* 40, no. 1 (2011): 3–23; and Mark Leeming, "The Creation of Radicalism: Anti-Nuclear Activism in Nova Scotia, c. 1972–1979," *Canadian Historical Review* 95, no. 2 (2014): 217–41.

14   See, for examples: Christopher Sellers, *Crabgrass Crucible: Suburban Nature and the Rise of Environmentalism in Twentieth-Century America* (Chapel Hill: University of North Carolina Press, 2012); Rome, *The Genius of Earth Day*; Finis Dunaway, *Seeing Green: The Use and Abuse of American Environmental Images* (Chicago: University of Chicago Press, 2015).

15   See, for examples: Julian Agyeman et al., eds., *Speaking for Ourselves: Environmental Justice in Canada* (Vancouver: UBC Press, 2009); Ronald D. Sandler and Phaedra C. Pezzullo, *Environmental Justice and Environmentalism: The Social Justice Challenge to the Environmental Movement* (Cambridge, MA: MIT Press, 2007); Anna J. Willow, "Re(con)figuring Alliances: Place Membership, Environmental Justice, and the Remaking of Indigenous-Environmentalist Relationships in Canada's Boreal Forest," *Human Organization* 71, no. 4 (2012): 371–82; Anna J. Willow, "Collaborative Conservation and Contexts of Resistance: New (and Enduring) Strategies for Survival," *American Indian Culture & Research Journal* 39, no. 2 (2015): 29–52; M. Paloma Pavel, ed., *Breakthrough Communities: Sustainability and Justice in the Next American Metropolis* (Cambridge, MA: MIT Press, 2009); W. Malcolm Byrnes, "Climate Justice: Hurricane Katrina, and African American Environmentalism," *Journal of African American Studies* 18, no. 3 (2014): 305–14.

16   Shepard Krech III, *The Ecological Indian: Myth and History* (New York: W. W. Norton, 1999). See also Michael Eugene Harkin and David Rich Lewis, eds., *Native Americans and the Environment: Perspectives on the Ecological Indian* (Lincoln: University of Nebraska Press, 2007); Kimberly TallBear, "Shepard Krech's *The Ecological Indian*: One Indian's Perspective," *International Institute for Indigenous Resource Management*

(September 2000): 1–5, http://www.iiirm.org/publications/Book%20Reviews/Reviews/ Krech001.pdf.

17   Mike Smyth, "Not All First Nations Oppose Kinder Morgan Pipeline Expansion," *Vancouver Province*, 18 April 2018.

18   See E. Richard Atleo (Umeek), *Tsawalk: A Nuu-chah-nulth Worldview* (Vancouver: UBC Press, 2006); E. Richard Atleo, *Principles of Tsawalk: An Indigenous Approach to a Global Crisis* (Vancouver: UBC Press, 2011); Raymond Pierotti, *Indigenous Knowledge, Ecology, and Evolutionary Biology* (New York: Routledge, 2011); Daniel Wildcat, *Red Alert! Saving the Plant with Indigenous Knowledge* (Golden, CO: Fulcrum, 2009); Julie Cruikshank, *Do Glaciers Listen? Local Knowledge, Colonial Encounters, and Social Imagination* (Vancouver: UBC Press, 2005); David Neufeld, "Kluane National Park Reserve, 1923–1974: Modernity and Pluralism," in *A Century of Parks Canada, 1911–2011*, ed. Claire E. Campbell (Calgary: University of Calgary Press, 2011), 235–72; Jonathan Clapperton, "Desolate Viewscapes: Sliammon First Nation, Desolation Sound Marine Park and Environmental Narratives," *Environment and History* 18 (2012): 529–59; Jocelyn Thorpe, *Temagami's Tangled Wild: Race, Gender, and the Making of Canadian Nature* (Vancouver: UBC Press, 2012); David Rich Lewis, "Skull Valley Goshutes and the Politics of Nuclear Waste," in Harkin and Lewis, *Native Americans and the Environment*, 304–42; Hans Carlson, *Home is the Hunter: The James Bay Cree and Their Land* (Vancouver: UBC Press, 2008); Richmond L. Clowe and Imre Sutton, eds., *Trusteeship in Change: Toward Tribal Autonomy in Resource Management* (Boulder: University of Colorado Press, 2001); and Jeanette Wolfley, "Reclaiming a Presence in Ancestral Lands: The Return of Native People to the National Parks," *Natural Resources Journal* 56, no. 1 (2016): 55–80.

19   Vine Deloria Jr., *The Metaphysics of Modern Existence* (San Francisco: Harper & Row, 1979).

20   Emma S. Norman, "Standing Up For Inherent Rights: The Role of Indigenous-Led Activism in Protecting Sacred Waters and the Way of Life," *Society & Natural Resources* 30, no. 4 (2017): 537–53.

21   Timothy B. Leduc, *Climate, Culture, Change: Inuit and Western Dialogues with a Warming North* (Ottawa: University of Ottawa Press, 2011). For further reading see: Mario Blaser, ed., *Indigenous Peoples and Autonomy: Insights for a Global Age* (Vancouver: UBC Press, 2010); Isabel Altamirano-Jiménez, ed., *Indigenous Encounters with Neoliberalism: Place, Women, and the Environment in Canada and Mexico* (Vancouver: UBC Press, 2013); Leanne Simpson, "Indigenous Education for Cultural Survival," *Canadian Journal of Environmental Education* 7, no. 1 (2002): 13–25.

22   Bernhard Gissibl, Sabine Höhler, and Patrick Kupper, "Introduction: Towards a Global History of National Parks," in *Civilizing Nature: National Parks in Global Historical Perspective*, ed. Bernhard Gissibl, Sabine Höhler, and Patrick Kupper (New York: Berghahn Books, 2012), 2; and Warren Magnusson and Karena Shaw, eds., *Political Space: Reading the Global Through Clayoquot Sound* (Minneapolis: University of Minnesota Press, 2002).

23   Patrick F. Noonan, "Foreword," in *Voices from the Environmental Movement: Perspectives for a New Era*, ed. Donald Snow (Washington, DC: Island Press, 1992), ix.

24 For brief examinations of the similarities and differences between conservationists and environmentalists, see: Thomas Dunlap, "Conservationists and Environmentalists: An Attempt at Definition," *Environmental Review* 4, no. 1 (1980): 29–31; Robert Gottlieb, "The Next Environmentalism: How Movements Respond to the Changes that Elections Bring – From Nixon to Obama," *Environmental History* 14, no. 2 (2009): 298–308.

25 Lianne C. Leddy, "Intersections on Indigenous and Environmental History in Canada," *Canadian Historical Review* 98, no. 1 (2017): 91–93; See also work by Daniel Sims, "Ware's Waldo: Hydroelectric Development and the Creation of the Other in British Columbia," in *Sustaining the West: Cultural Responses to Canadian Environments*, ed. Liza Piper and Lisa Szabo-Jones (Waterloo, ON: Wilfrid Laurier University Press, 2015), 303–24.

26 David Lowenthal, *George Perkins Marsh: Prophet of Conservation* (Seattle: University of Washington Press, 2015); "George Perkins Marsh," National Park Service, last modified 11 March 2015, https://www.nps.gov/mabi/learn/historyculture/gpmarsh.htm.

27 Mark Hamilton Lytle, *The Gentle Subversive: Rachel Carson,* Silent Spring, *and the Rise of the Environmental Movement* (New York: Oxford University Press, 2007); Patricia H. Hynes, "Ellen Swallow, Lois Gibbs and Rachel Carson: Catalysts of the American Environmental Movement," *Women's Studies International Forum* 8, no. 4 (1984): 291–98; and Eliza Griswold, "How 'Silent Spring' Ignited the Environmental Movement," *New York Times Magazine*, 21 September 2012, http://www.nytimes.com/2012/09/23/magazine/how-silent-spring-ignited-the-environmental-movement.html.

28 Benjamin Kline, *First Along the River: A Brief History of the U.S. Environmental Movement* (Toronto: Rowman & Littlefield, 2007), 129–46; Eddie Yuen, "The Politics of Failure Have Failed: The Environmental Movement and Catastrophism," in *Catastrophism: The Apocalyptic Politics of Collapse and Rebirth*, ed. Sasha Lilley, David McNally and Eddie Yuen (Oakland, CA: PM Press, 2012), 15–43; Jamie Horgan, "Doom and Gloom Environmental Scenarios Have Led to Apathy," *New York Times,* 8 May 2014, http://www.nytimes.com/roomfordebate/2014/05/08/climate-debate-isnt-so-heated-in-the-us/doom-and-gloom-environmental-scenarios-have-led-to-apathy. Paul Sabin's *The Bet: Paul Ehrlich, Julian Simon, and Our Gamble over Earth's Future* (New Haven, CT: Yale University Press, 2013) offers an interesting exploration of the competing pull of optimistic versus pessimistic visions of the future.

29 Ted Nordhaus and Michael Shellenberger, *Break Through: From the Death of Environmentalism to the Politics of Possibility* (New York: Houghton Mifflin, 2007), 2.

30 Ibid., 5.

PART 1

PROCESSES AND POSSIBILITIES

1

Strategies for Survival: First Nations Encounters with Environmentalism

Anna J. Willow

Although I have proudly called myself an environmentalist for many years, I have lately found myself hesitating before making this claim. It is not because I value environmental protection any less than I used to; unlike some gloomy folks who have abandoned the quest in anticipation of planetary doom, I see caring for the earth as more essential than ever. Nor is my apprehension underlain by a belief that environmentalism has failed in its mission.[1] Instead, my reservations arise from an increasing awareness of how environmentalism is envisioned and utilized by environmental protectors who do not define themselves as environmentalists, who have not directed the mainstream movement's trajectory, and who do not share the cultural assumptions of most of its proponents.

This chapter is about how Canadian First Nations citizens' motives and strategies intersect with the predominantly non-Indigenous societal phenomenon that bears the *environmentalism* label. Drawing on two examples—one from Ontario and one from British Columbia—of recent alliances between boreal forest First Nations communities and environmentally concerned non-Natives, I propose that Indigenous participants approach such alliances as components of comprehensive ongoing struggles for survival. By extension, this chapter is a call to rethink environmentalism as we know it, to complement fine-grained organizational histories with big-picture cross-cultural analyses that make it possible to imagine environmentalism not just as a trajectory of movements and beliefs but also as a rich assemblage of tools and processes. In other words, the case studies explored here suggest that environmentalism can be a means by which to achieve ends that are more diverse and more enduring than standard academic interpretations imply. This chapter offers a chance to reflect on the lessons that First Nations encounters with environmentalism contain for the environmental movement, for those of us who participate in and study it, and for humanity's long-term prospects.

When I began my graduate training in environmental anthropology, I was an idealistic student with a middle-class Euro-American background that I did not yet recognize as privileged. I wanted to make a positive difference in the world, to study something that really mattered. That came to mean figuring out why some people are willing to take dramatic action to protect the environment while others eagerly exploit non-human entities and interactions for profit or (more commonly) seem indifferent to the destruction that surrounds them. I was intrigued by my readings about American Indian ways of knowing, being, and living and not yet troubled by "ecological Indian" images that I now view as deeply problematic.[2] I fell in love with *Anishinaabemowin* (the Anishinaabe language) in the classroom, was drawn into the Sokaogon Chippewa Community's struggle to protect a critical portion of their northern Wisconsin homeland from sulfide mining in 2001, and travelled to northwestern Ontario in May 2003 when I learned that the people of Grassy Narrows First Nation had initiated a blockade to protest the industrial clearcutting that was ravaging their traditional land use area.[3]

Once I began working with Indigenous activists, I quickly realized the ethnocentric impossibility of comprehending environment, culture, and politics as separate entities. I have worked ever since to understand how the ultimate goal of land-based self-determination is woven into First Nations peoples' efforts to protect Canada's boreal forest.[4] I have never claimed neutrality regarding the struggles I describe. Using ethnography (which rapidly becomes history) to document unfolding events, and constructing academic interpretations inspired by my observations, I take encouragement from J. K. Gibson-Graham and Gerda Roelvink, who declare that "to understand the world *is* to change it."[5] By exposing settler colonialism's unjust foundations and enduring legacies and by telling stories that stimulate readers' reconsiderations of taken-for-granted histories and cultural constructs, I write with the mission of inspiring not only new understandings but also the more environmentally sustainable and socially just futures that these understandings might ultimately make possible.

Encounters with Environmentalism

Why do some First Nations people choose to work with non-Native environmentalists? After all, more than a few Native groups have deliberately avoided these kinds of collaborations.[6] And their misgivings are not without reason. The North American environmental movement has a well-documented history of excluding Indigenous peoples—conceptually as well as physically—from the places it protects. The forcible expulsion of Indigenous people from Yellowstone and Yosemite National Parks in the United States and from Banff, Riding Mountain, and Quetico National Parks in Canada epitomized the colonial mindset, with Indigenous residents removed from lands subsequently entrusted to management by non-Native "experts."[7] The anti-fur campaigns of the 1970s and 1980s, which stripped trappers of a viable land-based livelihood, further damaged environmentalism's reputation among Native northerners.[8]

Over the course of three decades, environmental protection paradigms have gradually moved beyond exclusionary "fortress conservation" models to embrace community-based and collaborative approaches that support the sustainable use of protected areas and the inclusion of Indigenous peoples and their knowledge.[9] In North America, this shift has inspired the creation of ad hoc alliances (like those documented by Grossman in this volume and elsewhere) as well as formal co-management bodies, both which have offered valuable new vehicles for broadcasting Native voices and concerns.[10] Still, critics contend that these partnerships empower Indigenous people only within an inherently inequitable (post) colonial social system. Anthropologist Paul Nadasdy, for example, argues that because such arrangements take existing political and economic relations for granted, "the form and nature of 'participation' is shaped by those relations and the assumptions underlying them. To be 'empowered,' local people must first agree to the rules of the game, rules that they had no role in creating and that constrain what it is possible to do and think."[11] Global observers of Indigenous inclusion in natural resource management and conservation projects have noted similar structural asymmetries.[12] As a result, even collaborations that have resulted in productive public pressure and withdrawals of resource development plans frequently see Indigenous interests misinterpreted by environmentalists.[13] With very different objectives, and agendas that are only partially compatible, relationships that succeed in the short term rarely stand the test of time.[14]

Why, then, do it? It's absolutely *not* naïveté. On the contrary, my experiences with First Nations environmental leaders have revealed that most of the individuals who make this choice are well aware of the inherent paradoxes and potential pitfalls. And, while relationships with environmentalists do offer some obvious immediate benefits (such as funding and publicity), these cynical explanations address First Nations activists' proximate, rather than ultimate, aims and are incapable of accounting for relationships that endure over time. I propose that environmental alliances can be more constructively comprehended as strategic choices made by astute leaders seeking to retain or regain control of customary lands and thereby promote their peoples' physical, cultural, and political survival. In the following pages, I share two brief case studies in order to demonstrate that although the forms Indigenous-environmentalist alliances take and the circumstances that inform them vary, First Nations participants share an understanding of environmental protection as one key component of multi-dimensional—and multi-generational—campaigns to ensure the continuance of the land-based subsistence on which their survival as culturally distinct and politically autonomous peoples depends.

Struggles and Strategies I: Grassy Narrows First Nation

Located eighty kilometres north of Kenora, Ontario, Grassy Narrows First Nation is a semi-remote community with an on-reserve population of nearly one thousand.[15] Recent generations of Grassy Narrows residents have faced a long line of uninvited changes to their local environment. By the 1950s, the English-Wabigoon River, which flows through Grassy

Narrows' 4,000-square-kilometre traditional land use area as well as the 41-square-kilometre contemporary reserve, had been dammed to facilitate hydroelectric power generation. With the dam came the inundation of near-shore sites (including traditional burial grounds) and unpredictable fluctuations in water level. Then, in the early 1960s, community members were forced to abandon extended family dwellings scattered along the river's tangled peninsulas and islands for a more consolidated parcel of land accessible via a newly constructed road. The federal government argued that the move would expedite the delivery of education and health care services, but with customary living arrangements and kinship patterns disrupted and the new road granting easy access to alcohol and other damaging substances, the negative social consequences of relocation were severe.[16] In the following decade, high levels of methylmercury were detected in the English-Wabigoon River, the result of dumping (to a tune of ten tonnes of the substance) by a pulp and paper mill located in far-upstream Dryden, Ontario.[17] Beyond the contamination's detrimental health consequences, the region's wage economy—largely supported by commercial fishing and guiding for the tourist industry—collapsed.[18]

As if the combined impacts of dam construction, relocation, and mercury contamination were not enough, the closed canopy boreal forest surrounding Grassy Narrows saw a surge in industrial logging in the 1990s. As the clearcuts grew larger and drew closer, areas essential to the practice of land-based subsistence were irrevocably altered. After several years of letter writing and conventional protest—not to mention a lawsuit filed in 2000 by three Grassy Narrows trappers against the Ontario Ministry of Natural Resources—Grassy Narrows youth and activists acted independently of their chief and council to initiate a blockade on a logging road just north of their reserve community on 3 December 2002.[19]

When I first travelled to Grassy Narrows as a supporter and student-researcher, the blockade was still in full swing.[20] I initially assumed that the protest was primarily about protecting the environment. I quickly learned that there was much more to it. As a young Anishinaabe activist explained in a 2004 public statement, "We grew up hunting and fishing and just living off the land. We still have our culture and beliefs. That's what we wanted to save that day. Laying those logs on the road wasn't just against clearcutting, it was for *everything* that affects Anishinaabeg negatively today."[21] People at Grassy Narrows *do* talk about their close relationship to the land; they talk about the fact that Indigenous inhabitants of northern Canada have often been dealt with in ways that appear oddly analogous to wildlife management techniques, and about the need to protect Mother Earth. But their concern for the environment is not abstract. It flows from tangible experiences of being in the boreal forest and from their determination that Anishinaabe people continue to have opportunities to live and learn their culture out on the land.

At Grassy Narrows, I also learned that the landscape of the blockade is a deeply political one: the fact that clearcutting has impeded Anishinaabe land-based subsistence is viewed as a blatant violation of Treaty 3 of 1873, which promised that the descendants of Native signatories would "have right to pursue their avocations of hunting and fishing throughout the tract surrendered."[22] Oral historical understandings of the agreement further hold that the treaty was an agreement to share—not give away—the land.[23] By taking direct action, people at Grassy Narrows were not only protesting the ongoing clearcutting but were simultaneously making a strong statement about their right to make decisions concerning their homeland and its resources.

At the Grassy Narrows blockade and at blockade-related events in Kenora and in Winnipeg, Manitoba, non-Anishinaabe individuals were a constant source of support for Grassy Narrows activists. Among the most notable of the partnerships that developed was an alliance between Anishinaabe activists and a San Francisco–based environmental NGO called Rainforest Action Network (RAN).[24] Both parties acknowledged that the other's comprehensive agenda was not identical to their own: RAN's overarching goal was to protect global forest ecosystems, while Anishinaabe activists sought to protect their own homeland, rights, and way of life. By 2006, however, both agreed to a shared short-range goal of stopping clearcutting within Grassy Narrows' traditional land use area. As one former RAN campaigner told me,

> At first RAN's goals and Grassy blockaders' goals were not the same, but had some important overlap. Both wanted to hurt [the company responsible for the logging]. Both wanted to stop clearcutting in Grassy Narrows' territory, or stop

industrial logging all together on the Territory. Both wanted to increase public awareness of the impacts of industrial logging on communities and ecosystems.[25]

RAN was able to offer Anishinaabe activists funding, logistical assistance, and solidarity to support local gatherings, trainings, and direct action events (such as the blockade that stopped traffic on the Trans-Canada Highway in July 2006 and made national news in Canada).[26] Bolstered by positive personal relationships between RAN campaigners and Grassy Narrows residents, the partnership also generated international media attention and support from a broader RAN campaign targeting a key corporate purchaser of wood from the contested area.

After two years of joint campaigning, the company authorized to log in the area voluntarily relinquished its licence in June 2008, indicating an important (if temporary) victory.[27] Grassy Narrows activists embraced the alliance with RAN because of its potential to help them realize their immediate objective of stopping industrial clearcutting within their territory, which, in turn, promoted their ultimate goal of cultural and political survival through land-based self-determination. The alliance offered a new means to achieve an enduring end.

Struggles and Strategies II: West Moberly First Nations

Ten years and one month after I began my quest to understand the complex factors that converged to inspire the Grassy Narrows blockade, I sat with Roland Willson, chief of West Moberly First Nations (WMFN), in his office near Chetwynd, British Columbia. "We're trying to preserve our culture. We're trying to preserve who we are as a people," he told me. We want "our grandchildren and their grandchildren to be able to know what it is to be Dane-zaa."[28] I was 2,400 kilometres from Grassy Narrows, but his words sounded familiar. First Nations citizens in northeastern British Columbia have struggled against outsiders' attempts to control the rich resources of *Dane-zaa nané?*—the Dane-zaa homeland—for generations. It was the desire for non-renewable resources—reported petroleum reserves in northeastern British Columbia itself and the Klondike gold sought by passing prospectors—that motivated the Canadian government to initiate negotiations for Treaty 8 in 1899.[29] Eager to ensure hunting, fishing, and trapping rights in the face of Euro-Canadian encroachment, Dane-zaa leaders refused to sign until commissioners promised they would be "as free to hunt and fish after the treaty as they would be if they never entered into it."[30] Contemporary Treaty 8 citizens argue that industrial activities and environmental degradation now prevent them from fully exercising their land-based subsistence rights, thereby violating the treaty agreement.[31] This, too, sounded familiar.

Although agricultural settlement in the Peace River's fertile valleys began in the early 1900s, it was the construction of the Alaska Highway in 1942 that opened the region to significant resource-extractive industry. Additional cultivation, logging, and conventional oil and gas production followed the highway, fragmenting wildlife habitat and progressively undermining Dane-zaa subsistence opportunities. In recent years, oil and gas extraction has increased exponentially with the introduction of high-velocity horizontal hydrofracturing (commonly called *fracking*) technology that makes it possible and profitable to extract fossil fuels from the deep shale layers that underlie much of *Dane-zaa nané?*. WMFN has taken a stand against unrestrained shale energy production by participating in a joint position paper critiquing the industry's profligate use of water, flawed consultation framework, and general lack of attention to cumulative impacts.[32]

Northeastern British Columbia also supplies southern energy demands with two massive hydroelectric dams along the Peace River. A controversial third dam (referred to as Site C) is now under construction, although legal cases opposing the project are still ongoing. WMFN has actively opposed the Site C dam and is collaborating with environmental groups to publicize its detrimental potential.[33] Compounding the devastating impacts of hydroelectric power generation on caribou and other species, recent decades have brought massive metallurgical coal mines to the surrounding area. Hopeful that their people will once again be able to hunt caribou within their customary land use area, WMFN took legal action against proposed mining exploration in a critical caribou habitat zone and collaborated with conservation biologists to develop an action plan for the Moberly caribou herd.[34]

Dane-zaa people now face direct impacts from two large hydroelectric dams (and the additional dam at Site C), eleven mines, 8,000 oil and gas well sites, 10,000 pipelines, eight wind farms, and an untold number of powerlines and support facilities as well as ongoing forestry, agriculture, and sports hunting outfitter operations.[35] Yet provincial agencies and industrial decision makers refuse to acknowledge the impacts of these developments in any cumulative manner.[36] This is the set of circumstances that motivated WMFN to begin working with the Boreal Leadership Council (BLC), a 21-member coalition composed of environmental NGOs, environmentally concerned resource and investment companies, and First Nations organizations committed to working collectively toward "solutions-based dialogue on issues affecting the boreal region of Canada."[37] This, in fact, was what had brought me to British Columbia: I was exploring the BLC as a collaborative conservation model and conducting multi-sited research with participating First Nations groups in order to better understand how cultural and political differences contour and complicate environmental alliances.[38]

Environmental leaders at WMFN are optimistic that working with the BLC will offer new opportunities for taking high-profile, national action on matters of urgent local concern. Specifically and directly, they hope the BLC will be able to stimulate broader awareness of the cumulative impacts associated with many years of industrial activity on *Dane-zaa nané?*. When their decision is examined through a comprehensive historical lens, however, it becomes obvious that they choose to partner with the BLC not primarily for these immediate gains but for the same reason their forbearers insisted on land-based subsistence rights before agreeing to Treaty 8—the same reason that compels their recent positions on shale gas, hydroelectric dams, and problematically sited coal mining. Their ultimate goal, so clearly articulated by Roland Willson, has not changed over time. In a twenty-first-century context of extreme extraction and resource colonialism, partnering with environmental groups may help them reach it.

Environmentalism as a Survival Strategy

The goal of survival—in the conjoined physical, cultural, and political sense I'm evoking here—is widely shared among First Nations citizens in Canada and among others around the world who live with comparable colonial legacies.[39] As Taiaiake Alfred (Mohawk) and Jeff Corntassel (Cherokee) state,

> The struggle to survive as distinct peoples on foundations constituted in their unique heritages, attachments to their homelands, and natural ways of life is what is shared by all Indigenous peoples, as well as the fact that their existence is in large part lived as determined acts of survival against colonizing states' efforts to eradicate them culturally, politically and physically.[40]

The word *survival* in this context does not imply that Indigenous people are content to merely make do. This is not the case. They want to *thrive* as individuals, communities, and political entities, and they want to do it according to standards that they themselves set. Wherever boreal landscapes are rearranged by extractive industrial activities, transformed worlds thus stand as symbols of distant outsiders' political and economic power to sacrifice local environments in order to promote national ambitions and global capital.[41] It is not only the physical conditions and consequences of environmental degradation that contemporary First Nations activists oppose but also the balance of power that permits it.

The year before I met Roland Willson in northeastern British Columbia, my project on collaborative boreal forest conservation and the BLC had taken me to Labrador, where I spoke with employees of the environmental branch of Innu Nation (the governing body that represents Innu citizens in Labrador). Their main message was simple: although the actions they take and the decisions they make may sometimes seem unrelated, "the central pillar of the Innu Nation is ensuring the survival of the Innu people."[42] The project had also taken me back to Anishinaabe country, to the eastern shores of Lake Winnipeg, where Poplar River First Nation environmental leader Sophia Rabliauskas discussed her community's decision to work for decades to document—and eventually gain legal authority to manage—its customary land. It was for the children and the future, she said, so their traditions and way of life would survive.[43] I suspect, too, that White Mountain Apache members of the Fort Apache Heritage Foundation, who enact heritage and historic presentation as a form of environmental protection, would agree with this overarching ambition (see Welch, this volume).

Partnering with an environmental NGO to combat emplaced impacts of externally imposed resource extraction (as in the case of the Grassy Narrows-RAN alliance) and contributing to a national multi-sector coalition (like the BLC) demand very different kinds of interactions and activities. On-the-ground protest events, direct action, and media campaigning appear to have little in common with semi-annual meetings, diplomatic engagement, and topical working groups. Yet in the juxtaposition of these unique relationships sits an underlying similarity: First Nations people who work with non-Native environmentalists are thinking strategically. They are acknowledging environmental encounters as a potential path toward continued access to customary lands and, ultimately, toward the long-term well-being of their people. If we hope to make sense of Indigenous-environmentalist alliances, we need to begin here, with a clear acknowledgment that the roots of environmentally protective action often extend much deeper and much wider than most non-Native environmentalists originally supposed.

What (Some) Environmentalists Have Learned

If First Nations people approach environmentalism as a valuable tool—one of many—that can be used to advance land-based self-determination agendas, we must recognize that non-Indigenous partners in environmental alliances also gain from collaborating with First Nations individuals and organizations. Some of the immediate benefits are obvious to attentive observers: Working with Indigenous groups is a public image asset that can augment funding opportunities and promote positive media attention. It can enhance local legitimacy and open access to contested sites.[44] However, it is worth considering the possibility of benefits that are both more enduring and more profound.

In the case of the Grassy Narrows–RAN alliance, working with Anishinaabe activists allowed RAN to argue that a targeted corporation was not only practising environmentally destructive clearcutting but simultaneously violating Indigenous land rights. With the approval of their Grassy Narrows partners, RAN activists were able to broadcast this message to consumers of wood products across the United States and Canada.[45] Although they were careful not to speak *for* the region's Anishinaabe residents, the partnership made it possible for RAN campaigners to speak *from* an impacted location and to call on supporters to help them "Save Grassy Narrows Boreal Forest."[46] The alliance built bridges between human rights advocates who came to appreciate the environmental dimensions of a social struggle and environmental activists who were moved in the opposite direction. It put a human face on an environmental catastrophe and demonstrated that environmental degradation has devastating social and cultural consequences.[47] Taken together, these qualities made the case against clearcutting more compelling and were instrumental in pressuring a multinational corporation to adopt more sustainable logging practices.

Even more significant, the alliance extended an institutional trajectory that was already primed to accept environmental and social issues as inextricably intertwined. Unlike most North American environmental NGOs, RAN has a history of incorporating local and Indigenous people into its campaigns and has often articulated an organizational mission that includes supporting forest inhabitants and their fundamental rights.[48] According to an individual who worked on RAN's old-growth campaign during the group's active partnership with Grassy Narrows First Nation, the collaboration was especially valuable because it "helped RAN re-root its work in grassroots community level struggles and [helped] re-inject a focus on Indigenous rights into the leadership priorities and dialogue of the organization."[49] Working closely and conscientiously with First Nations activists reminded RAN staffers and supporters that the "natural" environments they work to protect necessarily include a wide variety of human activities and concerns.

Non-Native BLC participants share similar benefits of alliance despite the fact that the BLC developed intentionally rather than organically and devotes its attention to carefully chosen proactive projects rather than issue-driven, action-oriented campaigning. In the eyes of Indigenous Canadians and socially conscious environmentalists, the inclusion of First Nations representatives gives the group's statements on topics ranging from caribou conservation to informed consent an otherwise unattainable level of legitimacy. It makes it impossible to dismiss the BLC's recommendations as those of a detached interest group. For an entity with a national audience composed of First Nations citizens and others sympathetic to Indigenous land and resource rights, including First Nations perspectives means respectability and relevance. It means that the BLC's collective voice emanates not from the urban-industrial centres of southern Canada but from across the 3.5 million square kilometres of the Canadian boreal. This, in turn, enables the BLC to function as an effective and influential entity, consequently increasing its appeal to prospective supporters and funders.

Critically, the incorporation of First Nations individuals and ideas makes it unlikely that discussions about environmental protection will proceed as though the boreal forest is an uninhabited wilderness or a vacant resource frontier. This is especially significant in light of the historical construction of Canadian wilderness as an empowering destination for white (and usually male) tourists and the concomitant pejorative reconstitution of First Nations inhabitants as fixed in time and place.[50] As Arn Keeling and John Sandlos suggest, the conceptual erasure of Indigenous inhabitants to produce pristine "wilderness" for protection (on one hand) and entrepreneurial calls to develop Canada's vast northern regions (on the other) have long stood as two sides of the same developmentalist coin.[51] Challenging this colonial legacy, Indigenous participation obliges BLC members to always abide by the council's founding commitment to "respect the lands, rights and ways of life of Aboriginal people" and to acknowledge First Nations cultural and political concerns as central to the future of conservation in Canada and beyond.[52]

What We (All) Can Learn

What do these cases imply for environmentalism as a way of perceiving the world? And what lessons can environmentalists (and those who study them) take from all of this? In an overview of the accomplishments and challenges of community-based conservation, Fikret Berkes suggests that broader conservation constituencies will only be built when we put aside Western-centric perspectives and develop a "cross-cultural pluralistic definition of conservation."[53] This is essential for reasons that are both practical and profound. If environmental organizations want to increase (or at least retain) their membership and influence—if, in short, they want to remain viable—they must find ways to speak to wider audiences and broaden their bases of support. On a deeper level, if we hope to leave future generations with a world that resembles the bounty and beauty we inherited, we have to convince more people in more places that protecting the environment is an essential and achievable task as well as a valid and vital way of being in the world.

Albeit in very different ways, both the Grassy Narrows–RAN alliance and the BLC coalition signify a paradigmatic shift away from visions of an uninhabited and untouched wild nature toward a more inclusive comprehension that admits humans as an integral part of the environment. Whether or not they affiliate themselves with the environmental justice movement's international network, Indigenous allies in Canada (like environmental justice activists elsewhere) direct non-Native environmentalists' attention to the ties that bind environmental issues to social turmoil and political inequity. They implicitly call for a definitional expansion that acknowledges "social justice, local economic sustainability, health, and community governance as 'environmental issues.'"[54] Working with, listening to, and learning from First Nations citizens compels environmentalists to accept people as part of worlds worth protecting. From environmental alliances, we learn that our own future is intertwined with the future of the non-human world.

Far beyond the small but growing network of scholars who see environmentalism as a complex cultural phenomenon worthy of concerted attention, realizations catalyzed by the global climate crisis are leading others to strikingly similar conclusions. In 2002, atmospheric chemist Paul Crutzen coined the term *Anthropocene* to underscore the predominant human influence on global climate, landforms, and ecosystems.[55] The Anthropocene idea has subsequently influenced physical, biological, and social scientists, with recent analysts arguing that long-standing Western categorical divisions between human/cultural and environmental/natural realms are being challenged by the changing reality of life on earth. "In the Anthropocene," social/ecological researcher Egon Becker observes, "it is impossible to understand nature without society, and society without nature."[56] To some, these connections may ring of revelation, but many who exist outside of Western conceptual traditions have recognized them all along. Environmental injustice permeated Canadian policy makers' once-standard disregard for First Nations' territorial interests and intentional ignorance of Indigenous citizens' concerns about resource-extractive undertakings' potential impacts.[57] First Nations people have been fighting for generations to achieve an accessible and un-degraded environment and for justice in its environmental forms—the very things the rest of us now realize are required if our social structures (and perhaps even our species) are to survive into the future.

I have often wondered if the prominent First Nations activists I know see themselves as environmentalists, and I have had several occasions to ask this question. Although First Nations activists often *accept* environmentalism (for reasons outlined above), it is neither their own project nor their lives' work. For people like Judy DaSilva of Grassy Narrows First Nation (who has been nominated for the Goldman Environmental Prize) and Sophia Rabliauskas of Poplar River First Nation (who won that prize in 2007), environmentalism is a *label* used by outsiders to describe what Indigenous people have been doing all along.[58] This insight forces us to reconsider how we think, talk, and write about environmentalism. First Nations people encounter environmentalism in the context of struggles they perceive as (and that occasionally quite literally become) matters of life and death.[59] For them, environmentalism is not merely an identity or lifestyle card pulled from the deck of an over-optioned post-industrial society. It is neither a charitable crusade nor a professional commitment. It is, instead, a strategic opportunity that may be accepted, adapted, or rejected as circumstances warrant. Understanding environmental protection not as an end in itself but as a means to an even more important ultimate goal—survival—encourages us to reflect on the enormous task that lies ahead. For people like me who have contributed to environmentalist causes for many years, this expanded perspective is both humbling and inspiring.

Viewing environmentalism as "others" see it opens space for a new kind of dialogue; stepping back to appreciate environmentalism from the outside in, as I have attempted to do here, encourages us to envision environmental protection as a small part of a much larger process. Identifying tangible links—and forging conceptual ones—between environmental and social predicaments, First Nations activists and those who have heeded their message recognize that social injustice often appears in environmental guises and that holistic well-being demands environmental integrity. Perhaps First Nations environmental leaders (accompanied by others who, to return to the title of the workshop that inspired this edited collection, come to environmentalism "from below") will carry us beyond environmentalism as we now know it toward the more collective, integrative struggles that are certain to follow. Perhaps, environmental alliances will give rise to an environmental protection paradigm capable of embracing humans as part of "nature" and human rights as a legitimate conservation concern. If we are willing to embrace the heartening possibility that understanding the world and changing it can constitute a unified project, it is likely that this repositioning will engender exciting new thinking about what environmentalism means and, in turn, stimulate constructive new conversations to guide what it might someday become.

Notes

The research described in this chapter was supported by a J. William Fulbright Foreign Scholarship Award (2004–2005), a Canadian Embassy Graduate Research Fellowship (2004–2005), and by the Wenner-Gren Foundation for Anthropological Research (2012–2013). I am grateful for the comments of those who participated in the Environmentalism from Below workshop (particularly the insights offered by John Welch), which encouraged and guided me in improving this work.

1   Jonathan Clapperton discusses various perspectives regarding the alleged failure—even the "death"—of environmentalism at the outset of his chapter (Chapter 11, this volume). For a well-known example of this viewpoint, see Michael Shellenberger and Ted Nordhaus, "The Death of Environmentalism: Global Warming Politics in a Post-Environmental World," *Geopolitics, History, and International Relations* 1 (2009): 121–63.

2   On the ecological Indian stereotype and its consequences, see Shepard Krech III, *The Ecological Indian: Myth and History* (New York: W. W. Norton, 1999). See also Paul

Nadasdy, "Transcending the Debate over the Ecologically Noble Indian: Indigenous Peoples and Environmentalism," *Ethnohistory* 52, no. 2 (2005): 291–331.

3   See Larry Nesper, Anna J. Willow, and Thomas F. King, *The Mushgigagamongsebe District: A Traditional Cultural Property of the Sokaogon Ojibwe Community* (Mole Lake, WI: Sokaogon Chippewa Community, 2002). The terms *Chippewa* and *Ojibwe* (along with various spellings) are frequently utilized in historical, ethnographic, and legal records to refer to the people who call themselves *Anishinaabe*.

4   In previous work, I have used the phrase *land-based self-determination* to describe the ability to independently make key decisions concerning land, livelihood, and opportunities available to future generations. See Anna J. Willow, "Doing Sovereignty in Native North America: Anishinaabe Counter-Mapping and the Struggle for Land-Based Self-Determination," *Human Ecology: An Interdisciplinary Journal* 41, no. 6 (2013): 871–84.

5   J. K. Gibson-Graham and Gerda Roelvink, "An Economic Ethics for the Anthropocene," *Antipode* 41, S1 (2009): 320–46. More recently, Brian Burke and Boon Shear have echoed this point, suggesting that "to describe the world in a compelling way is to change it, and to change the world requires compelling new descriptions." Brian Burke and Boone Shear, "Introduction: Engaged Scholarship for Non-Capitalist Political Ecologies," *Journal of Political Ecology* 21(2014): 130.

6   While most unrealized collaborations are never documented, David McNab describes Teme-Augama Anishnabai activists' 1988 decision to *avoid* working with a non-Native environmental group that opposed the same road extension. In this case, First Nations activists were worried that their land rights issues would be overshadowed by environmentalists' better-publicized concerns. David T. McNab, "Remembering an Intellectual Wilderness: A Captivity Narrative at Queen's Park in 1988–9," in *Blockades and Resistance: Studies in Actions of Peace and the Temagami Blockade of 1988–89*, ed. Bruce Hodgin, Ute Lischke, and David T. McNab, 31–53 (Waterloo, ON: Wilfred Laurier University Press, 2003), 49.

7   On the history of American Indians and National Parks in the United States, see Mark Dowie, *Conservation Refugees: The Hundred-Year Conflict between Global Conservation and Native Peoples* (Cambridge, MA: MIT Press, 2009); Robert H. Keller Jr. and Michael Francis Turek, *American Indians and National Parks* (Tucson: University of Arizona Press, 1999); Mark D. Spence, *Dispossessing the Wilderness: Indian Removal and the Making of the National Parks* (New York: Oxford University Press, 1999). For examples from Canada, see Theodore Binnema and Melanie Niemi, "'Let the Line be Drawn Now': Wilderness, Conservation, and the Exclusion of Aboriginal People from Banff National Park in Canada," *Environmental History* 11, no. 4 (2006): 724–50; Erin E. Sherry, "Protected Areas and Aboriginal Interests: At Home in the Canadian Arctic Wilderness," *International Journal of Wilderness* 5, no. 1 (1999): 17–20. See also Jonathan Clapperton, "Stewards of the Earth? Aboriginal Peoples, Environmentalists, and Historical Representation" (PhD diss., University of Saskatchewan, 2013).

8   George Wenzel, *Animal Rights, Human Rights: Ecology, Economy and Ideology in the Canadian Arctic* (Toronto: University of Toronto Press, 1991). An additional source to consider on this subject is Teale Phelps Bondaroff and Danita Catherine Burke, "Bridging Troubled Waters: History as Political Opportunity Structure" *Journal of*

Civil Society 10, no. 2 (2014): 165–83, which explores the impact of the anti-sealing movement on environmental organization relations directly.

9   As Evans (this volume) demonstrates, circumstances vary enormously, but comparative studies of relationships between Indigenous communities and protected areas seem to suggest improvements in integration and indigenous control. For a critical history of fortress conservation, see Dan Brockington, *Fortress Conservation: The Preservation of the Mkomazi Game Reserves, Tanzania* (Bloomington: Indiana University Press, 2002). On community-based conservation, see Fikret Berkes, "Community-Based Conservation in a Globalized World," *Proceedings of the National Academy of Sciences* 104, no. 39 (2007): 15188–93; Marshall W. Murphree, "Protected Areas and the Commons," *Common Property Resource Digest* 60 (2002): 1–3.

10   On informal alliances, see Zoltán Grossman, *Unlikely Alliances: Native Nations and White Communities Join to Defend Rural Lands* (Seattle: University of Washington Press, 2017); and Zoltán Grossman, "Unlikely Alliances: Treaty Conflicts and Environmental Cooperation Between Native American and Rural White Communities," *American Indian Culture and Research Journal* 29, no. 4 (2005): 21–43. On formal co-management arrangements, see Paul Nadasdy, *Hunters and Bureaucrats: Power, Knowledge, and Aboriginal-State Relations in the Southwest Yukon* (Vancouver: UBC Press, 2003); David C. Natcher, Susan Davis, and Clifford G. Hickey, "Co-Management: Managing Relationships, Not Resources," *Human Organization* 64, no. 3 (2005): 240–50.

11   Paul Nadasdy, "The Anti-Politics of TEK: The Institutionalization of Co-Management Discourse and Practice," *Anthropologica* 47, no 2 (2005): 220. See also Nadasdy, *Hunters and Bureaucrats.*

12   Based on a study of joint forest management in India, for example, Hildyard et al. argue that merely sitting around the same table is not sufficient so long as access to the tangible and intangible resources that constitute power remain uneven. In order to empower formerly marginalized groups, they propose that "participation requires wider processes of social transformation and structural change to the system of social relations through which inequalities are reproduced." Nicholas Hildyard et al., "Pluralism, Participation and Power: Joint Forest Management in India," in *Participation: The New Tyranny?* ed. Bill Cooke and Uma Kothari (London: Zed Books, 2001), 69. Similarly, Howitt and Suchet-Pearson draw on evidence from wildlife management in Australia to declare that employing "naïve or simplistic accommodations of diversity in ways that deny the embeddedness of power and privilege in social, economic and environmental relations at all scales will reproduce the problems in new forms rather than open up new possibilities." Richard Howitt and Sandra Suchet-Pearson, "Rethinking the Building Blocks: Ontological Pluralism and the Idea of 'Management,'" *Geografiska Annaler* 88, no. 3 (2006): 331.

13   See, for example: J. Peter Brosius, "Endangered Forest, Endangered People: Environmentalist Representations of Indigenous Knowledge," *Human Ecology* 27, no. 1 (1997): 47–69; Beth A. Conklin and Laura R. Graham, "The Shifting Middle Ground: Amazonian Indians and Eco-Politics," *American Anthropologist* 97, no. 4 (1995): 695–710.

14   Indigenous activists' goals tend to include political empowerment, self-determination, human health, and economic development in addition to the environmental protection viewed as paramount by most non-Native environmentalists. See William H. Fisher, "Megadevelopment, Environmentalism, and Resistance: The Institutional Context of Kayapó Indigenous Politics in Central Brazil," *Human Organization* 53, no. 3 (1994): 220–32.

15   Indigenous and Northern Affairs Canada lists a registered population of 1,587, with 970 living on the reserve as of December 2017. "First Nation Profiles," http://fnp-ppn.aandc-aadnc.gc.ca/fnp/Main/Search/FNRegPopulation.aspx?BAND_NUMBER=149&lang=eng.

16   On the horrific consequences of relocation and subsequent mercury contamination, see Anastasia M. Shkilnyk, *A Poison Stronger than Love: The Destruction of an Ojibwa Community* (New Haven, CT: Yale University Press, 1985).

17   Ibid. Also see Warner Troyer, *No Safe Place* (Toronto: Clarke, Irwin, 1977); and Kai Erikson and Christopher Vecsey, "A Report to the People of Grassy Narrows," in *American Indian Environments*, ed. Christopher Vecsey and Robert W. Venables (Syracuse, NY: Syracuse University Press, 1990), 152–61.

18   On the health effects of mercury at Grassy Narrows, see Masazumi Harada et al., "Long-term Study on the Effects of Mercury Contamination on Two Indigenous Communities in Canada (1975–2004)," trans. Tadashi Orui, *Research on Environmental Disruption* 34, no. 4 (2005), http://freegrassy.net/wp-content/uploads/2012/06/Harada-et-al-2011-English.pdf.

19   The lawsuit argued that the hunting and trapping rights guaranteed by Treaty 3 were federally protected under the 1982 Constitution Act and, therefore, that the Province of Ontario had no legal power to grant forestry permits to logging companies. In 2014, the Supreme Court of Canada ruled against the Grassy Narrows trappers *(Grassy Narrows First Nation v. Ontario (Natural Resources), 2014 SCC 48 [referred to as Keewatin]).*

20   As noted above, I arrived in northwestern Ontario in May 2003. A constant presence at the blockade site was maintained from its inception through the fall of 2003. It subsequently remained standing in a symbolic sense, with community members present at the site for occasional organized events and frequent impromptu gatherings. The blockade at Grassy Narrows went on to become the longest-standing anti-logging protest in Canadian history. My experience and understanding of the Grassy Narrows blockade are summarized in Anna J. Willow, *Strong Hearts, Native Lands: Anti-Clearcutting Activism at Grassy Narrows First Nation* (Winnipeg: University of Manitoba Press, 2012).

21   From a 2004 public statement entitled "No More!" http://www.friendsofgrassynarrows.com (accessed 6 October 2004, site discontinued).

22   Canada, Treaty No. 3 between Her Majesty The Queen and the Saulteaux Tribe of Ojibbeway Indians at The Northwest Angle on the Lake of The Woods with Adhesions (Ottawa: Queens Printer, 1966 [1871–74]).

23   An alternate version of the Treaty 3 agreement based on notes taken during the negotiations by a Métis man employed by one of the attendant chiefs to record the event is known the Paypom Treaty and is available online at http://caid.ca/paypom010208.pdf.

24   See http://ran.org for more information on Rainforest Action Network. For information on the Grassy Narrows partnership and anti-clearcutting campaign, see http://freegrassy.net. This was not the only partnership important to the Grassy Narrows blockaders. Friends of Grassy Narrows, a grassroots support group founded in Winnipeg, was instrumental in the early period of the blockade. A faith-based witness group called Christian Peacemaker Teams was also a critical ally (see http://cpt.org more information on this organization's current activities).

25   Personal communication with former RAN staff member, 9 May 2011.

26   "Environmentalists Block Highway Near Kenora to Protest Logging," *CBC News Manitoba,* 13 July 2006, http://www.cbc.ca/news/canada/manitoba/environmentalists-block-highway-near-kenora-to-protest-logging-1.581630; Rainforest Action Network, "Grassy Narrows Activists Blocking Trans-Canada Highway to Stop Weyerhaeuser Destruction," Press Release Issued 13 July 2006, http://freegrassy.net/2006/07/13/grassy-narrows-activists-blocking-trans-canada-highway-to-stop-weyerhaeuser-destruction/.

27   While logging has been suspended in the area since 2008, ending clearcutting remains on ongoing struggle for the Grassy Narrows community. The Ontario Ministry of Natural Resources' 2012–2022 forest management plan and an adverse Supreme Court decision in July 2014 mean that logging—and direct action protest—may resume in the near future. For more information and updates on the current situation at Grassy Narrows, see http://freegrassy.net.

28   Interview, 17 June 2013. With a population of just under 250, West Moberly First Nations is a predominantly Dane-zaa (Beaver Indian) community with a significant Cree minority. For additional information, see http://www.westmo.org/. Cree people arrived with the fur trade in the late 1700s and have since been incorporated into Dane-zaa families and communities.

29   René Fumoleau, *As Long as This Land Shall Last: A History of Treaty 8 and Treaty 11, 1870–1939* (1975, repr., Calgary: University of Calgary Press, 2004); Robin Ridington and Jillian Ridington, *Where Happiness Dwells: A History of the Dane-zaa First Nations* (Vancouver: UBC Press, 2013).

30   Fumoleau, *As Long as This Land Shall Last*, 87–88. See also Hugh Brody, *Maps and Dreams: Indians and the British Columbia Frontier* (Prospect Heights, IL: Waveland Press, 1981); David Leonard, *Delayed Frontier: The Peace River Country to 1909* (Calgary: Detselig Enterprises, 1995); Ridington and Ridington, *Where Happiness Dwells*; West Moberly First Nations Land Use Department, *I Want to Eat Caribou before I Die*, Initial Submissions for the Proposed Mining Activity at First Coal Corporation's Goodrich Property (2009).

31   Fieldnotes, 17 June 2013.

32 British Columbia First Nations Energy and Mining Council, Treaty 8 Tribal Association, and West Moberly First Nations, *Shale Gas, Cumulative Impacts and Reforming the Current Consultation Process* (Position Paper, 2012).

33 These groups include the Yellowstone to Yukon Initiative, David Suzuki Foundation, and the more local Peace Valley Environmental Association. See http://paddleforthepeace.ca/ for more information.

34 On the legal challenge initiated by West Moberly First Nations, see Bruce R. Muir and Annie L. Booth, "An Environmental Justice Analysis of Caribou Recovery Planning, Protection of an Indigenous Culture, and Coal Mining Development of Northeast British Columbia, Canada," *Environment, Development, and Sustainability* 14 (2012): 455–76. See also West Moberly First Nations Land Use Department, *I Want to Eat Caribou Before I Die*. Those interested in the caribou conservation plan should see R. Scott McNay, Debbie Cichowski, and Bruce Muir, *Action Plan for the Moberly Herd of Woodland Caribou (Rangifer tarandus caribou) in Canada* [Draft] (West Moberly First Nations, Species at Risk Act Action Plan Series, 2012).

35 Annie L. Booth and Norm W. Skelton, "You Spoil Everything": Indigenous Peoples and the Consequences of Industrial Development in British Columbia," *Environment, Development and Sustainability* 13, no. 4 (2011): 685–702.

36 Annie L. Booth and Norm W. Skelton, "'We are Fighting for Ourselves': First Nations' Evaluation of British Columbia and Canadian Environmental Assessment Processes," *Journal of Environmental Assessment Policy and Management* 13, no. 3 (2011): 367–404.

37 Boreal Leadership Council, "Free, Prior and Informed Consent in Canada." (September 2012), http://borealcouncil.ca/wp-content/uploads/2013/09/FPICReport-English-web.pdf. Uniting First Nations members who want to practise traditional land-based lifeways and determine their homelands' future, environmentalist members who hope to protect as much of the boreal forest as possible, and corporate members who would like to develop the region's resources for sustainable profit, the BLC was established with the goal of identifying commonalities and encouraging constructive conversations concerning environmental use and protection. For more information on the group and its activities, see http://borealcouncil.ca/.

38 While not an official BLC member, WMFN has attended BLC meetings as an observer since 2010 and contributes to working groups focusing on caribou conservation, shale gas, and FPIC (free, prior, and informed consent). The BLC's recent work on FPIC is part of a growing international discussion and is based on the premise that Indigenous peoples have the right to "participate in decisions affecting their lands and resources" Boreal Leadership Council, "Free, Prior and Informed Consent in Canada," 3.

39 Works by contemporary Indigenous authors make this case in a variety of ways. See, for example, contributions to volumes edited by Leanne Betasamosake Simpson, *Lighting the Eighth Fire: The Liberation, Resurgence, and Protection of Indigenous Nations* (Winnipeg: Arbeiter Ring, 2008); Gerald Vizenor, *Survivance: Narratives of Native Presence* (Lincoln: University of Nebraska Press, 2008).

40 Taiaiake Alfred and Jeff Corntassel, "Being Indigenous: Resurgences against Contemporary Colonialism," *Government and Opposition* 40, no. 4 (2005): 597.

41   John Sandlos and Arn Keeling, "Claiming the New North: Development and Colonialism at the Pine Point Mine, Northwest Territories, Canada," *Environment and History* 18, no. 1 (2012): 5–34.

42   Innu Nation forester Guy Playfair, fieldnotes, 25 June 2012.

43   Fieldnotes, 3 August 2012. For more on Poplar River First Nation's conservation history, see Willow, "Doing Sovereignty in Native North America."

44   See, for example, Brosius, "Endangered Forest, Endangered People"; Conklin and Graham, "The Shifting Middle Ground"; Fisher, "Megadevelopment, Environmentalism, and Resistance."

45   Rainforest Action Network, "American Dream, Native Nightmare: A Report on Weyerhaeuser," (2006), https://www.ran.org/wp-content/uploads/2018/06/weyerhauser_report_(1).pdf.

46   Rainforest Action Network, "Grassy Narrows Activists Blocking Trans-Canada Highway to Stop Weyerhaeuser Destruction."

47   See, for examples of putting a human face to the environment: Susan Burgerman, *Moral Victories: How Activists Provoke Multilateral Action* (New York: Cornell University Press, 2001); and Margaret E. Keck and Kathryn Sikkink, *Activists Beyond Borders: Advocacy Networks in International Politics* (Ithaca, NY: Cornell University Press, 1998).

48   Rainforest Action Network, "Catalyzing A Movement," *Greatest Hits, 1985–2010: Rainforest Action Network 2010 Annual Report* (San Francisco: Rainforest Action Network, 2010), 4.

49   Personal communication, 9 May 2011.

50   Jocelyn Thorpe, "Temagami's Tangled Wild: The Making of Race, Nature, and Nation in Early-Twentieth-Century Ontario," in *Rethinking the Great White North: Race, Nature, and the Historical Geographies of Whiteness in Canada,* ed. Andrew Baldwin, Laura Cameron, and Audrey Kobayashi (Vancouver: UBC Press, 2011), 193–210.

51   Arn Keeling and John Sandlos, "Environmental Justice Goes Underground? Historical Notes from Canada's Northern Mining Frontier," *Environmental Justice* 2, no. 3 (2009): 117–25.

52   Boreal leadership Council, "Canadian Boreal Forest Conservation Framework," n.d., http://borealcouncil.ca/wp-content/uploads/2015/03/Framework-2015ENG.pdf.

53   Fikret Berkes, "Rethinking Community-Based Conservation," *Conservation Biology* 18, no. 3 (2004): 621–630.

54   Joni Adamson, *American Indian Literature, Environmental Justice, and Ecocriticism: The Middle Place* (Tucson: University of Arizona Press, 2001), 77. Although concerns related to environmental justice have a long history, the organized movement began in the early 1980s when African American protesters in the southern United States opposed the construction of a toxic-waste landfill (Robert Bullard, *Dumping in Dixie: Race, Class, and Environmental Quality* [Boulder, CO: Westview Press, 1990]). The movement subsequently expanded throughout North America and around the

world to encompass multi-ethnic grassroots groups united by their demands for full participation in decisions that impact their communities' health, livelihoods, and immediate surroundings.

55   Paul J. Crutzen, "Geology of Mankind," *Nature* 415, no. 6867 (2002): 23. See also Will Steffen, Paul J. Crutzen, and John R. McNeill, "The Anthropocene: Are Humans Now Overwhelming the Great Forces of Nature?" *Ambio: A Journal of the Human Environment* 36, no. 8 (2007): 614.

56   Egon Becker, "Social-Ecological Systems as Epistemic Objects," in *Human-Nature Interactions in the Anthropocene,* ed. Marion Glaser et al. (New York: Routledge, 2012), 39.

57   Keeling and Sandlos, "Environmental Justice Goes Underground."

58   Fieldnotes, 17 April 2005 and 5 August 2012.

59   Navajo activist Leroy Jackson, for example, died under suspicious circumstances in 1993 during his organization's struggle to protect the Navajo Nation's forests from overzealous logging. See John W. Sherry, *Land, Wind, and Hard Words: A Story of Navajo Activism* (Albuquerque: University of New Mexico Press, 2002).

Native/Non-Native Alliances Challenging Fossil Fuel Industry Shipping at Pacific Northwest Ports

Zoltán Grossman

> *The natural resources we all depend upon must be protected for future generations . . . to bring us to a place where there is a quality of life, and where Indians and non-Indians are to understand one another and work together.*
>
> — Billy Frank Jr. (Nisqually), 1931–2014

Despite the enormous scale and reach of energy corporations, their top-heavy operations are actually quite vulnerable to social movements that creatively use spatial strategies and tactics.[1] Operating in a local context, small-scale climate justice alliances in the Pacific Northwest are increasingly coordinating their efforts to make a large-scale impact on the fossil fuel industry. The climate justice movement has identified one likely Achilles heel of the energy industry: shipping. The industry needs to ship equipment from ports into its oil, gas, and coal fields, and to ship the fossil fuels via rail, barge, and pipeline to coastal ports for access to the US market and shipment to global markets, particularly in Asia.[2]

The three growing fossil fuel sources in North America are in the middle of the continent: the Alberta Tar Sands, the Powder River Coal Basin, and the Bakken Oil Shale Basin. Every step of the way, small-scale alliances of environmental and climate justice activists, farmers and ranchers, and Native peoples are combining their forces to block plans to ship carbon and the technology to extract it. All three of these sources need outlets to global markets, via ports in the Pacific Northwest states of Washington and Oregon, so both states (along with British Columbia) are functioning as chokepoints for the fossil fuel industry. The region's Native/non-Native alliances are functioning as a "Thin Green Line" between North American fossil fuel basins and the growing Asian market and, as locally based frontline alliances, are successfully targeting the role of port terminals in fossil fuel shipping and equipment networks.[3]

In recent years, the climate-conscious US Pacific Northwest, along with British Columbia, has become a region on the cutting edge of curbing carbon emissions. But any efforts to mitigate greenhouse gases, adapt to climate change, or switch to renewable energies will become moot if the fossil fuel industry continues to expand in Alberta, the Great Plains, and beyond. The alliances of Native and non-Native communities are using their geographic advantages to roll back the growth of the fossil fuel industry, and in the process are building new bonds with each other across regional and racial divides.

Although they have not been covered in national media until very recently, such alliances are not necessarily a new phenomenon. Since the 1970s, small-scale unlikely alliances have joined Native communities with their rural non-Native neighbours to protect their common lands and waters, with little or no involvement by the "Big Green" environmental organizations. These unique convergences have confronted mines, dams, logging, powerlines, nuclear waste, military projects, and other threats to resource-based livelihoods. My main training has been as a community organizer in such alliances in South Dakota and Wisconsin, and I studied these alliances in my doctoral dissertation, conducting interviews with more than one hundred twenty alliance leaders and members, tracking common themes and strategies from their experiences.[4] These alliances not only joined Natives and non-Natives to confront an outside threat as a common enemy but also shifted the consciousness and actions of the non-Native participants, as they learned about the continuity of Indigenous cultural traditions, legal powers, and environmental resilience.[5]

In South Dakota in the late 1970s, Lakota communities and white ranchers were often at odds over water rights and the tribal claim to the sacred Black Hills.[6] Yet despite the intense Indian-white conflicts, the two groups came together against coal and uranium mining, which would endanger the groundwater. The Native activists and white ranchers formed the Black Hills Alliance (where I began my activism four decades ago) to halt the mining plans, and later formed the Cowboy and Indian Alliance (or CIA), which has since worked to stop a bombing range, coal trains, and an oil pipeline.[7]

In roughly the same era of the 1960s and 1970s, a fishing rights conflict had torn apart Washington State. A federal court recognized treaty rights in the 1974 Boldt Decision, and by the 1980s the tribes began to use treaties as a legal tool to protect and restore fish habitat. The result was state-tribal "co-management," with the 1989 Centennial Accord recognizing that the tribes have a seat at the table on natural resource issues outside the reservations. The Nisqually Tribe, for instance, is today recognized in its watershed as the lead entity in creating salmon habitat management plans for private farm owners, and state and federal agencies. The watershed is healing because the tribe is beginning to decolonize its historic lands.[8]

Another treaty confrontation erupted in northern Wisconsin in the late 1980s, when crowds of white sportsmen gathered to protest Ojibwe treaty rights to spear fish. Even as the racist harassment and violence raged, tribes presented their treaty rights as legal obstacles to mining plans, and formed alliances such as the Midwest Treaty Network.[9] Instead of continuing to argue over the fish, some white fishing groups began to cooperate with tribes to protect the fish, and won victories against the world's largest mining companies.[10] After witnessing the fishing war, seeing the 2003 defeat of the Crandon mine gave tribal members some real hope.

In each of these cases, Native peoples and their rural white neighbours found common cause to defend their mutual place and unexpectedly came together to protect their environment and economy from an outside threat and a common enemy. They knew that if they continued to fight over resources, there might not be any left to fight over. Some rural whites began to see Native treaties and sovereignty as better protectors of common ground than their own governments. Racial prejudice is still alive and well in these regions, but the organized racist groups are weaker because they have lost many of their followers to these alliances.[11]

Successful alliances challenge the idea that "particularism" (such as Native identity) is always in contradiction to "universalism" (such as environmental protection). The assertion of Indigenous political strength does *not* weaken the idea of joining with non-Natives to defend the land, and can even strengthen it with the power of tribal sovereignty. The stories of these small-scale alliances identify ways to reconcile differences between cultures with the goal of finding common-ground similarities between them. They offer possible lessons on how to weave together the politics of unity and identity.

In the process, small-scale rural environmental groups are partnering with neighbouring Indigenous nations that can "jump scales" by bringing national and international attention to seemingly local and isolated environmental concerns.[12] Although Native reservations exist at a small scale geographically, their political and economic power extends outward into neighbouring non-Native communities. In the treaties, they retained the right to hunt, fish, and gather outside reservation boundaries, and their tribal sovereignty establishes a nation-to-nation relationship between their tribal governments and federal agencies. Local-scale environmental campaigns can be "supersized" into larger-scale campaigns when and if tribal nations get involved, without sacrificing local decision making. Tribal sovereignty, rather than diminishing the power of neighbouring non-Native communities, can strengthen both communities' universalist goals of protecting the land and water for everyone.

Spatial Strategies

The place-based small green alliances opposing fossil fuel shipping are developing new ways to think globally, but act locally, to help roll back carbon pollution. Geographic strategies to stop equipment from reaching the oil fields, or to block fossil fuels from being shipped via rail or pipeline, can be more effective if they are coordinated continent-wide. The goal is to make the expansion of energy projects more costly and risky, and ultimately to downsize them.

Zoltán Grossman

A 2014 study titled "Conflict Translates Environmental and Social Risks into Business Costs" spells out how social movement opposition raises costs for resource extraction companies. As the authors write: "High commodity prices have fuelled the expansion of mining and hydrocarbon extraction. These developments profoundly transform environments, communities, and economies, and frequently generate social conflict. Our analysis shows that mining and hydrocarbon companies fail to factor in the full scale of the costs of conflict."[13] In a Harvard Kennedy School study, Rachel Davis and Daniel Franks (two of the authors of the 2014 study) further observed that "the greatest costs of conflict . . . were the opportunity costs in terms of the lost value linked to future projects, expansion plans, or sales that did not go ahead. The costs most often overlooked by companies were indirect costs resulting from staff time being diverted to managing conflict—particularly senior management time."[14]

By blocking shipping plans, small-scale climate justice forces can combine efforts to help to prevent the rapid expansion of the energy industry, by keeping more of the fossil fuels in the ground and by delaying projects, thereby costing companies money, further hindering their ability to execute future projects. The energy companies can also play a geographical "shell game" to shift burdens around the landscape, and pit communities against each other, such as Native and non-Native communities. The most effective rural alliances have been those (such as in the Pacific Northwest) that have crossed cultural lines and created relationships and collaboration that corporate planners had not anticipated.[15] In the process, they become less vulnerable to corporate divide-and-conquer tactics and begin to find common ground beyond the environmental concern that initially brought them together.

Important alliances have brought together tribal members and large-scale environmental organizations—such as Greenpeace—as evidenced by the 2015 actions of "kayaktivists" and tribal canoes against Shell oil drilling rigs headed from the Pacific Northwest to Alaska.[16] But it is often easy for corporations to portray "Big Green" urban-based environmental groups as "outsiders" who do not care about rural jobs or people. The strongest alliances are those established in defence of a common place, and a local alliance of tribes and non-Native residents may be more able to defeat environmental threats as a legitimatized force of "insiders" than an alliance only between rural tribes and urban environmental activists who can be successfully be portrayed as "outsiders" (when the real outsiders are the corporations themselves).

In the Pacific Northwest, if the 1974 Boldt Decision had gone the other way, or if the tribes had not used their treaty rights to protect and restore fish habitat, the Pacific Northwest would be more industrialized and damaged than it already is.[17] The legal power of the treaties enables the tribes to co-manage the natural resources, and tribal sovereignty enables them to put up barriers to damaging projects, and seize opportunities to heal and decolonize the landscape.

As author Naomi Klein notes,

> One of the most exciting parts of the emergence of this fossil fuel resistance . . . is the way in which it is building really powerful ties between non-Native and Native communities. . . . I think what more and more of us are starting to understand is that Indigenous First Nations, treaty rights, and aboriginal title, are the most powerful legal barrier to the plans to just flay this continent. And those rights become more powerful when there are mass movements defending them, and when they are embraced by whole societies.[18]

The leading role of tribal nations and First Nations is most evident in the growing movements to keep fossil fuels in the ground and challenge the shipping of oil and coal from interior basins to coastal ports. These basins include the Alberta Tar Sands, the Powder River Coal Basin of Montana and Wyoming, and the Bakken Oil Shale Basin centred on North Dakota.

Alberta Tar Sands

Oil industry opponents describe the Alberta Tar Sands as the "Mordor" of the industry, with some northern tracts of the province turned into a wasteland, air quality degraded to the level of Beijing, and Cree and Métis communities contaminated with toxic chemicals in their water.[19] The fights to block two proposed tar-sands pipelines, against the Keystone XL pipeline in the Great Plains, and the Enbridge Northern Gateway pipeline across northern British Columbia, led by Native peoples, are by now well known.[20]

But lesser known in the United States is that tar-sands oil is now pumped through the Kinder Morgan Trans Mountain pipeline to Burnaby, near Vancouver, British Columbia, to the Ferndale refinery on former Lummi land in Washington, and to the Anacortes refinery on former Swinomish land—the latter two taken by White House executive orders in the 1870s.[21] The pipeline has ruptured at times, but the company has proposed a second, parallel pipeline along the existing route, opposed by many First Nations and allies.[22] The proposal for a second, parallel pipeline would vastly increase oil tanker traffic in the narrow inter-island straits of the Salish Sea, which is an already risky environment for salmon and orcas. First Nations in British Columbia and Washington tribal governments joined to intervene against the second pipeline.[23] Indigenous nations on both sides of the border united together in 2014 in the Nawtsamaat Alliance to sign an International Treaty to Protect the Sacredness of the Salish Sea, and sought endorsements from allies fighting fossil fuel shipping.[24]

Oil companies are also engaged in "heavy hauls" of gargantuan mining equipment, called "megaloads," *from* Pacific Northwest ports to northern Alberta. Direct actions by Nez Perce tribal council members and other Idaho residents forced the 2013 cancellation of a proposed heavy haul along winding river roads through Lolo Pass. Members of the Umatilla and Warm Springs tribes have more recently been confronting the "megaloads" off-loaded from barges in eastern Oregon.[25] But the main sources of fossil fuel shipping in Pacific Northwest ports are from two lesser-known basins.

Powder River Coal Basin

The Powder River Coal Basin, in Wyoming and Montana, has been a fossil fuel frontier since the early 1970s and produces 42 percent of US coal.[26] Strip-mining machines the size of a twenty-storey building ravage the landscape, removing the "overburden" topsoil and leaving behind a sterile "hardpan" surface where nothing can grow. In coal boom towns (such as Gillette, Wyoming), trailer parks have colonized the hillsides, as the local community extends its public services for the influx of miners, leading to an inevitable "boom-and-bust" effect.

In the late 1970s, Northern Cheyenne allied with white ranchers to curb the proliferation of coal plants, with the tribe declaring its air to be Class I (the highest quality) under EPA "Treatment As State" non-degradation rules.[27] The alliance marked one of the first times that the "cowboys" supported the "Indians" in protecting their common environment and livelihood, despite continuing differences between the communities.

Given the widespread success of environmental alliances in rolling back the coal industry in the United States in the twenty-first century, the industry is turning toward exports to growing Asian economies as the key to future profits.[28] The energy industry is now proposing to ship Powder River Basin coal to Asia through northwest ports. Environmentalists, farmers, ranchers, and tribes fear the coal dust from the trains (up to a ton of dust from each of 150 rail cars) would endanger waterways along the routes and the health of local people and livestock.[29]

Only one west coast port, in Tsawwassen, British Columbia, currently has a coal-export terminal.[30] In 2013 to 2015, local opponents defeated coal terminals proposed in Aberdeen, Washington, and St. Helens, Coos Bay, and Boardman/Turkey Point, Oregon. By 2016, the Gateway Pacific Terminal project at Cherry Point, near Bellingham, and the Millennium Bulk Terminal, near Longview on the Columbia, were the two remaining Washington proposals. The Affiliated Tribes of Northwest Indians took a strong stand against all the proposed coal and oil terminals.[31]

The Columbia River Inter-Tribal Fish Commission opposed plans for coal barges along the Columbia Gorge as a threat to the treaty salmon fishing of four tribes, as did tribal members along the coal train route.[32] Thousands of people attended scoping hearings on the projects in the two states, and dozens of towns and cities passed resolutions against the plans, with local governments questioning the traffic tie-ups, noise, and delays in other rail shipments. Although some labour union members supported the plan for jobs, others opposed it as helping to export jobs to China, and for contributing to climate change.

Cherry Point would be the largest coal terminal on the west coast, exporting 48 million metric tons a year. But Cherry Point (Xwe'chi'eXen, in the Lummi dialect of the Lushootseed Salish language) is the site of a

3,500-year-old village and its sacred burial ground, which the company has already desecrated. The rail trestle would be built 300 feet out into a historic reef-net salmon fishing area, where ancient anchors have been found. The area has historically hosted one of the few herring spawning grounds in the northwest United States.[33] The Lummi saw the coal plan as a violation of the 1855 Point Elliott Treaty, which guarantees the tribes' access to fish in their "usual and accustomed grounds."

In 2012, the Lummi Tribal Council symbolically burned a $1 million check, to make the statement that no amount of company money will convince them to back the project.[34] The tribe was able to lend its powerful voice to assist local coal terminal opponents and attract the attention of federal agencies and national media. Even though the non-tribal fishing fleet in the Cherry Point area was five times larger than the tribal fleet, the Lummi had to assist non-Indian fishers to have their voices heard. During the crab harvest opening that year, the Whatcom Commercial Fishermen's Association (led by a non-Native president and a Lummi vice-president) organized tribal and non-tribal boats in a protest flotilla, in which the twenty fishing and crabbing vessels displayed signs with slogans such as "Our Goal: No Coal."[35]

Just as the Lummi are leading the movement to stop the coal terminal in Washington, Northern Cheyenne tribal members came to the forefront of the movement to stop the proposed Otter Creek coal mine and Tongue River Railroad at the other end of the rail line.[36] They see stopping the coal export terminals as key to stopping new Montana coal mining operations. As such, they testified at Northwest hearings, again in conjunction with white ranchers from the Tongue River Valley around Colstrip, Montana.[37]

Montana tribes and ranchers had previously united in the 1970s to slow coal mining and in the 1990s to stop gold mining.[38] But now we see strong Native/non-Native alliances at both ends of this coal shipping route, which have expanded the scale of conflict. Northern Cheyenne organizer Vanessa Braided Hair observes of the company, "what Arch Coal doesn't understand is community. . . . They don't understand the fierceness with which the people, Indian and non-Indian, in southeastern Montana love the land."[39] Rancher Roger Sprague says of the Northern Cheyenne, "we're neighbors with these people, and we're proud to work with these people. We don't want this mine in here. . . . It's our life. We've fought hard to put it together, and we'd like to keep it that way."[40] In 2013–17, Lummi carver Jewell James led a series of totem pole journeys, taking his poles between the Northern Plains and the Northwest to demonstrate the unity of many Indigenous peoples and allies along fossil fuel train and pipeline routes.[41] In March 2016, the Otter Creek coal mine and Tongue River railroad were defeated.[42]

Oglala Lakota anti-coal activist Krystal Two Bulls observed that a true alliance

> is a relationship. It's like a family. . . . I think because of these alliances being built, I think it's going to set precedents for other relationships. . . . These farmers and ranchers are going to be leading the way in paving the road for other farmers and ranchers to be able to see we can work together. . . . I think that's the role of a true ally. In looking at historically these Big Green organizations coming into Indigenous communities and parachuting in, and just doing whatever their framework says they should do and then leaving, that's been the precedent for so long. Now you're looking at these alliances where these people are working together on a common ground, so they're actually showing and exhibiting true allyship, where they're coming in and meeting them at the same level as opposed to coming in and saying this is how we're going to do it, you can be a part of it.[43]

Using their treaty rights, sovereign powers and federal trust responsibility, some US tribes can draw federal agencies and courts into the fray in a way that local and state governments cannot. In Washington State, federal court decisions have recognized Native rights to fish, hunt, and gather outside the reservations, and to "co-manage" the fishery with the state government.[44] Because harm to streams and rivers would violate these treaty rights, Washington tribes have a role in protecting and restoring fish habitat.[45] In 2007, a federal court even used the treaties to order the state to protect salmon from poorly constructed culverts.[46] Tribes cannot move away from risks or shift their treaty harvesting areas, because they are fixed in place. Because of their commitment to stay in the place, tribes can offer a strong cultural anchor to place-based environmental movements that makes them less willing to compromise.

In May 2016, the Army Corps of Engineers backed the Lummi treaty case against the coal terminal, effectively dooming the project.[47] By increasing the costs for the industry, opponents are increasing the costs of shipping and (even if they lose a battle or two) severely limiting the bulk volume of coal that can be shipped for export. By making fossil fuel shipments more socially and economically costly, they are bringing closer the day when the energy economy is forced to convert to renewable fuels. As long as subsidized fossil fuels remain cheaper, the needed conversion to renewables will never take place.

Bakken Oil Shale Basin

The Bakken oil shale formation in North Dakota is a growing fossil fuel frontier zone, around the new boom town of Williston.[48] The process of *fracking* (described by Willow in this volume) has recently made the state number two in US oil production, after Texas. Fracking has been an environmental concern, lowering water tables and contaminating water with chemicals, gases, and oil spills, yet under the "Halliburton Loophole," the process is exempt from the Safe Drinking Water Act. The oil boom has been a social scourge, with housing shortages, drug use, prostitution in "man camps," and endless traffic of chemical and water trucks.[49]

Although the Fort Berthold tribal government originally supported the fracking for development, some tribal members have been displaced, and others fear an increase in cancers that they claim have been climbing as a result of previous oil and coal development.[50] Tribal members have pressured tribal leadership to roll back their approval for fracking.[51] Tribal member Kandi Mossett of the Indigenous Environmental Network testified that "several community members, including myself, are tired of being sick. . . . We are taking a stand and fighting back, not only for our own lives but for the lives of those who cannot speak for themselves, and we will not stop fighting until we have a reached a true level of environmental and climate justice in our Indigenous lands."[52] In North Dakota, the shipment of Bakken oil sparked the resistance to the construction of the

Dakota Access Pipeline on treaty lands next to the Standing Rock Sioux Reservation in 2016–17.[53]

Because the companies only care about profitable oil, the natural gas is flared off, making the Bakken glow like a city, visible from Earth's orbit. Bakken crude is more volatile than other oil, so when oil trains derail they erupt in huge explosions, like the 2013 fireball that killed forty-seven people in Quebec. There were more oil train spills in 2013 than in the thirty-seven years prior.[54] Rail safety concerns have led many Northwest communities to grow concerned about increasing Bakken oil rail traffic.

Washington ports propose to receive rail shipments of fracked crude oil from North Dakota. According to the Sightline Institute, if all Northwest oil, coal, and gas projects proceeded, they would cumulatively ship the carbon equivalent of five Keystone XL pipelines.[55] A Tesoro oil terminal planned for Vancouver, Washington, across the Columbia from Portland has met strong local opposition.[56] Up to fifty oil trains a month, each 1.5 miles long, would supply three oil terminals in Aberdeen, where Bakken oil would be loaded into enormous tankers, next to key migratory bird habitat.[57] A lawsuit by the Quinault Nation and environmental groups, who are also concerned about the effects of an oil tanker spill on local fisheries and shellfish beds, convinced the state to revoke permits for the oil terminals, pending an Environmental Impact Statement.[58]

Nearly unanimous public opposition emerged in 2014–16 during a series of Department of Ecology hearings along the proposed oil train route.[59] On the morning he passed, Northwest Indian Fisheries Commission Chairman Billy Frank Jr. posted his last blog, supporting the Quinault Nation's position. He wrote, "It's clear that crude oil can be explosive and the tankers used to transport it by rail are simply unsafe. . . . Everyone knows that oil and water don't mix, and neither do oil and fish. . . . It's not a matter of whether spills will happen, it's a matter of when."[60]

The Grays Harbor community in Washington State has historically been hostile to outside large-scale mainstream environmental groups, whom they blame for the closure of local timber mills when the Northwest "spotted owl wars" pitted logging jobs against endangered species protection.[61] But the new small-scale alliances are able to frame themselves as "insiders" in the local area, tied to the ancient Indigenous presence on the land. As Quinault Vice President Tyson Johnston commented, some local residents "will lump us in too with a lot of the environmental groups and we do carry a lot of those values, but we're in this for very different reasons such as sovereignty, our future generations."[62]

The Quinault Nation had traditionally been at odds with the Washington Dungeness Crab Fishermen's Association, which has challenged Quinault treaty-backed crab harvests. But as Association Vice President Larry Thevik pointed out, the oil terminal proposals have "united us in the preservation of the resource that we bicker over. It has also kind of created a new channel of communication because . . . those of us at the bottom of the food chain, the actual fishers, have been able to talk somewhat directly to another nation."[63] Joe Schumacker, the Quinault Nation Marine Resources Scientist, agreed that "with no resource, there's no battle . . . we have to maintain what's out there. Those people, those local crabbers out here are almost as place-based as the tribes. I will never say that they are as place-based, but they feel so deeply rooted here and it's part of their lives. . . . We find ourselves working together on these matters."[64]

Quinault President Fawn Sharp (also President of the Affiliated Tribes of Northwest Indians) was born in 1970 "at the height of the fishing rights conflict. I was a young child, but was very impressionable. At eight years old, I understood what treaty abrogation meant, that there were others trying to wipe out the entire livelihood of not only my family, but my larger Quinault family."[65] Sharp reflected that "part of the relationship that we have today arose out of generations of disputes. Through those disputes, whether they liked us . . . didn't like us . . . they came to know and understand Quinault and our values, and where we are and what we're about. . . . For us, a lot of the relationships we have with our neighbors arose out of a relationship of much division, strife and conflict, but through that . . . they've come to know who we are. That, to me, is a foundational bit of understanding."

Sharp was later impressed in meeting Larry Thevik and other local crabbers when they worked for a renewable energy project and against a coal terminal and agreed to work together with the Quinault even as they disagreed about crab harvest allocation. When the oil terminal issue emerged, Sharp noted that she "thought we need to develop these partnerships because this oil issue is so much larger than Quinault Nation." She added a "footnote of hope" that "the cooperation that we're seeing now is going to provide another sort of step of maturity and good faith and alliance and looking beyond special interest or individual interest to the greater good. Perhaps today's generation and younger people growing up in this political climate will come to understand that it is so much better to work together with neighbors."

By August 2017, all three of the Grays Harbor oil terminal projects had been defeated, and by January 2018 the State of Washington also rejected an application for an even larger oil terminal at Vancouver, on the Columbia River.[66] Despite the Trump administration's increased push for the fossil fuel industry, Pacific Northwest citizens have effectively defeated nearly all of the proposed oil and coal terminals. The attention of Washington tribes has turned toward Liquefied Natural Gas (LNG), as the Puyallup Tribe led opposition to an LNG plant in Tacoma.[67]

Alliances in the Fossil Fuel Wars

Similar "unlikely alliances" of Native peoples and their rural white neighbours are standing strong against fossil fuel and mining projects elsewhere in the continent. In Nebraska and South Dakota, grassroots coalitions of Native peoples and white ranchers and farmers are fighting the Keystone XL pipeline.[68] The aptly named "Cowboy and Indian Alliance" (CIA) originated in a cross-border treaty between tribes, First Nations, and their allies against the pipeline from the Alberta Tar Sands.[69] The pipeline company tried to buy off some farmers by moving the pipeline route away from their lands—but those farmers have not given up the fight, and continue to work with others who are still directly affected, including Native communities.[70]

In 2014, the "CIA" erected a *tipi* encampment on the National Mall and held a horse procession in Washington, DC.[71] Freelance journalist Kristin Moe observed:

> The environmental movement has long come under criticism for being led by the so-called Big Greens—largely white, middle class membership groups whose interests don't often represent those actually living in the frontline communities where the pipeline will be built. But the coali-

       Zoltán Grossman

tion of cowboys and Indians offers a radical departure from this history. Moreover, it is a model of relationship-based organizing, rooted in a kind of spirituality often absent from the progressive world, and—given the role of indigenous leaders—begins to address the violence of colonization in a meaningful way.[72]

Farmers and ranchers oppose eminent domain by stressing their right to private property, which in their case, of course, was originally land stolen from the tribes. So tribes insist that their allies not only fight damaging projects but also become stewards of the land and help to protect sacred sites on their property. As Yankton Nakota elder Faith Spotted Eagle states, "We come from two cultures that clashed over land, and so this is a healing for the generations."[73]

In the Maritimes, Mi'kmaq and Maliseet are confronting shale gas fracking, joined by Acadian and Anglophone neighbours.[74] Climate change enables the expansion of the scope of conflict to encompass a wide range of rural and urban communities. The climate justice movement's focus on regional and global climate change enables a wider scale of collaboration than purely localist approaches that can succumb to corporate "divide-and-conquer" tactics.

In the Great Lakes, Bad River Ojibwe and Menominee are leading the fight to stop metallic mining, drawing on past anti-mining alliances of Ojibwe and white fishers, and Ho-Chunk and other local residents are protesting frac sand mining.[75] The key to any successful environmental strategy is to turn it from a Not In My Back Yard struggle to a Not In Anybody's Back Yard struggle. Alliances have to anticipate and respond to wedge issues that may racially divide an alliance, such as geographically moving the burden of negative environmental effects away from white communities and toward Native communities, in the hopes that the white residents will abandon their opposition.[76]

The Idle No More movement that emerged in Canada in 2012–13 similarly connects First Nations' sovereignty to the protection of the Earth for all people—Native and non-Native alike. Idle No More co-founder Sylvia McAdam states, "Indigenous sovereignty is all about protecting the land, the water, the animals, and all the environment we share."[77] Gyasi Ross observes that Idle No More (or the Indigenous Nationhood Movement) "is about protecting the Earth for all people from the carnivorous and capitalistic spirit that wants to exploit and extract every last bit of resources from the land. . . . It's not a Native thing or a white thing, it's an Indigenous worldview thing. It's a 'protect the Earth' thing."[78] Leanne Simpson sees Idle No More as

> an opportunity for the environmental movement, for social-justice groups, and for mainstream Canadians to stand with us. . . . We have a lot of ideas about how to live gently within our territory in a way where we have separate jurisdictions and separate nations but over a shared territory. I think there's a responsibility on the part of mainstream community and society to figure out a way of living more sustainably and extracting themselves from extractivist thinking.[79]

Cooperation Growing from Conflict

It would make logical sense that the greatest Native/non-Native cooperation would develop in the areas with the least prior conflict. Yet a recurring irony is that cooperation more easily developed in areas where tribes had most strongly asserted their rights, and the white backlash had been the most intense. Treaty claims in the short run caused conflict but in the long run educated whites about tribal cultures and legal powers, and strengthened the commitment of both communities to value the resources. A common "sense of place" extended beyond the immediate threat, and it redefined their idea of "home" to include their neighbours. As Mole Lake Ojibwe elder Frances Van Zile said, "This is my home; when it's your home you try to take as good care of it as how can, including all the people in it."[80]

This is not to say that all tribal nations have treaty rights, or that they all use treaties for environmental protection. Tribal governments are under the same economic pressures to accept corporate development as are other governments. In fact, the Crow and Navajo tribal councils have promoted their own coal mines, and the tribal governments on the Fort Berthold and Uintah-Ouray reservations have allowed fracking, over the objections of some tribal members. But when tribal nations do support environmental protection, they have powerful legal tools and can use tribal sovereignty within reservation boundaries, and treaty rights in ceded territories outside the reservations. Native nations in the Pacific Northwest use their treaty rights not to romanticize an idyllic vision of an Indigenous past but to safeguard their cultural revitalization and resource-based economic livelihood into the future.

Of course, not all treaty conflicts have led to environmental cooperation, mainly because some white neighbours of the tribes do not support environmental protection in the first place. In places such as Alberta and Arizona, many white communities and governments are hostile to both Indigenous sovereignty and environmentalists. The formation of alliances presupposes willing partners in both the Native and non-Native communities, who aim to protect land and water as necessary for their well-being. Even when the conditions exist for an alliance, it takes conscious leadership to put it into motion. The initial bridges are usually built by Native and non-Native neighbours who have some prior contact with the other community.

Alliances based on "universalist" similarities are vulnerable to failure if they fail to respect "particularist" differences. The idea of "why can't we all just get along" (like "United We Stand" or "All Lives Matter") is sometimes used to suppress marginalized voices, asking them to sideline their demands in the interest of the "common good." This overemphasis on unity makes alliances more vulnerable, since authorities may try to divide them by meeting the demands of the (relatively advantaged) white members. A few alliances—such as against low-level military flights in southern Wisconsin—floundered because the white "allies" declared victory for their particular demands and went home, and did not keep up the fight to also win the demands of their Native neighbours. "Unity" is not enough when it is a unity of unequal partners; Native leadership needs to always be involved in the decision-making process.[81]

But successful alliances can go beyond temporary "alliances of convenience" to building more durable, lasting connections. In the course of working together with Native neighbours for short-term self-interest, initially using tribal rights for their own benefit, many non-Natives learn in the long term about the historical continuity of tribal cultures and legal powers, and develop collaborations and friendships that last beyond the resolving of the immediate environmental issue. For example, farmers and ranchers learn about sacred sites located on their property, and then open access to tribal members.[82] In other cases, the cooperation recedes after the alliance fades away, but the next alliance is much easier to form around another environmental threat, in a "two steps forward, one step back" pattern.

In Washington State, local tribal/non-tribal cooperation to restore salmon habitat provides a template for collaboration in response to climate change. The Tulalip Tribes, for example, are cooperating with dairy farmers to keep cattle waste out of the Snohomish watershed's salmon streams, by converting it into biogas energy.[83] The Tulalip are also exploring collaborative plans to store glacial and snowpack runoff to lessen spring floods and summer droughts that have been exacerbated by warming temperatures.[84] Local governments who had battled the Swinomish Tribe over water rights are now collaborating to prevent coastal flooding and sea level rise.[85] The Nisqually Tribe and City of Olympia agreed to shift their main source of freshwater from the sacred McAllister Springs to wells on higher ground, out of the reach of future sea level rise.[86] Many other stories of local and regional collaboration for resilience are being told in the Pacific Northwest.[87]

Non-Native Responsibilities

The continued existence of Native nationhood today undermines the claims of settler colonial states to the land.[88] Unlikely alliances can help chip away at the legitimacy of colonial structures, *even among some of the settlers themselves,* when they begin to realize that Native sovereignty has become a more effective guardian of their own land, water, and livelihood than their own non-Native governments. Rancher Paul Seamans, of Dakota Rural Action, told me the Lakota "feel the government should step up and do what's right by them on the 1868 Treaty. . . . They're not after the deeded land. They would like the government to recognize that they've been screwed, and . . . to have the federal and state lands back. . . . After being around them and listening to their point of view, I get to thinking, 'hey, if I was Indian I would be doing the same exact damn thing that they're doing.'"[89] Through the process of common opposition to a harmful project, white communities often find out about other past and present Native grievances.

Many rural whites, who at first pragmatically "exploited" tribal powers for their own short-term self-interest, learned in the long term about the continuity of tribal cultures and nationhood, and came to realize the value of those powers on their own merits. Naomi Klein asserts, "It has to be more than an extractive relationship to those rights: 'those rights are useful to us, because they help us protect our water, so we want to use those rights'—that's exactly the wrong way of thinking about this. These are rights that come out of a vision of how to live well, that were hard-won and hard-protected, and they point us towards a non-extractive regeneration-based way of living on this planet. That is the most hopeful and exciting part of this new wave of activism."[90]

To stand in solidarity with Indigenous nations is not just to "support Native rights" but to strike at the very underpinnings of the Western social order that de-indigenized Europeans before the colonization of North America even started, and begin to free both Native and non-Native peoples from that order for the sake of our collective survival. As Vancouver activist Harsha Walia writes, "I have been encouraged to think of human interconnectedness and kinship in building alliances with Indigenous communities. . . . Striving toward decolonization and walking together toward transformation requires us to challenge a dehumanizing social organization that perpetuates our isolation from each other and normalizes a lack of responsibility to one another and the Earth."[91]

By asserting their treaty rights, Indigenous nations are benefiting not only themselves but also their treaty partners. Since descendants of the original European settlers in North America are more separated in time and place from their indigenous origins, they benefit from respectfully working together with Native nations to help find their own path to what it means to be a human being living on the Earth—without appropriating Native cultures. The non-Native role is not to look at oneself merely as an individual "ally," and fail to take any action until we have cleansed ourselves of all personal racism, but to become *part of an alliance*, to collectively take on racist institutions as we work on ourselves.

Our role is not simply to learn from Native peoples, and extract knowledge that can serve non-Native purposes, but to recognize that the tribal exercise of power can serve Native and non-Native people alike. It is not the role of non-Natives to dissect Native cultures but to study Native/non-Native relations, and white attitudes and policies. The responsibility of non-Natives is to help remove the barriers and obstacles to Native sovereignty in their *own* governments and communities.

As the current "fossil fuel wars" show, non-Native neighbours can begin to look to Native nations for models to make North America more socially just, more ecologically resilient, and more hopeful. As Red Cliff Ojibwe organizer Walt Bresette once told non-Natives fighting a proposed mine, "You can all love this land as much as we do."[92]

Notes

1 Bill McKibben, "Fossil Fuel Resistance," *Rolling Stone*, 11 April 2013, https://www.rollingstone.com/politics/news/the-fossil-fuel-resistance-20130411.

2 Zoltán Grossman, "The Achilles Heel of the Fossil Fuel Monster," *Works in Progress* (March 2013), http://olywip.org/the-achilles-heel-of-the-fossil-fuels-monster/.

3 Eric de Place, "The Thin Green Line: The Northwest Faces Off Against Titanic Coal and Oil Export Schemes," *Sightline*, 20 March 2014, http://www.sightline.org/2014/03/20/the-thin-green-line/.

4 Zoltán Grossman, "Unlikely Alliances: Treaty Conflicts and Environmental Cooperation Between Rural Native and White Communities" (PhD diss., University of Wisconsin, 2002).

5 Zoltán Grossman, "Unlikely Alliances: Treaty Conflicts and Environmental Cooperation between Native American and Rural White Communities," *American Indian Culture and Research Journal* 29, no. 4 (2005): 21–43.

6 Edward Lazarus, *Black Hills, White Justice: The Sioux Nation versus the United States, 1775 to the Present* (New York: HarperCollins, 1991); and Jeffrey Ostler, *The Lakotas and the Black Hills: The Struggle for Sacred Ground* (New York: Penguin, 2010).

7 Zoltán Grossman, *Unlikely Alliances: Native Nations and White Communities Join to Defend Rural Lands* (Seattle: University of Washington Press, 2017), 139–69.

8 Nisqually River Council, *Nisqually Watershed Stewardship Plan*, May 2011, https://www.slideshare.net/Nisqually/nisqually-watershed-stewardship-plan; Lara Evans,

Zoltán Grossman et al., "Nisqually Watershed Podcasts," 2009, http://blogs.evergreen. edu/nativeplace.

9   *Midwest Treaty Network*, last updated 2013, http://treaty.indigenousnative.org/content. html.

10   Ibid.

11   Grossman, *Unlikely Alliances*, 205–72.

12   Ibid., 47.

13   Daniel M. Franks et al., "Conflict Translates Environmental and Social Risk into Business Costs," *Proceedings of the National Academy of Sciences* 111, no. 21 (May 2014): 7576–81, https://doi.org/10.1073/pnas.1405135111.

14   Rachel Davis and Daniel M. Franks, "Costs of Company-Community Conflict in the Extractive Sector," *Corporate Social Responsibility Initiative Report No. 66* (Cambridge, MA: Harvard Kennedy School, 2014), http://www.hks.harvard.edu/m-rcbg/CSRI/ research/Costs%20of%20Conflict_Davis%20%20Franks.pdf.

15   Grossman, *Unlikely Alliances*, 104–5, 287–90.

16   Sydney Brownstone, "Why Descendants of Chief Leschi Led the Protest Against Shell on Saturday," *The Stranger*, 18 May 2015, http://www.thestranger.com/blogs/ slog/2015/05/18/22234185/why-descendants-of-chief-seattle-led-the-protest-against-shell-on-saturday.

17   Grossman, *Unlikely Alliances*, 45-61.

18   "Talk by Naomi Klein author of *This Changes Everything: Capitalism vs. The Climate*," Town Hall Seattle, TalkingStickTV, 28 September 2014, https://www.youtube.com/ watch?v=4b2B-ys3N1o.

19   Toban Black, Stephen D'Arcy, Tony Weis, and Joshua Kahn Russell, eds., *A Line in the Tar Sands: Struggles for Environmental Justice* (Oakland, CA: PM Press, 2014).

20   "Native Energy," *Indigenous Environmental Network*, last updated May 2017, http:// www.ienearth.org/category/tar-sands/.

21   Briana Alzola, "Swinomish want historic reservation reinstated," *Anacortes American*, 14 December 2016; and Jay Taber, "Cherry Point Ownership," *Intercontinental Cry*, 26 November 2013.

22   Grant Granger, "The day oil rained down on Burnaby," *Burnaby Now*, 21 July 2017. http://www.burnabynow.com/news/the-day-oil-rained-down-on-burnaby-1.21287293; and Nawt-sa-maat Alliance, https://www.facebook.com/groups/nawtsamaat/.

23   Yvette Brend, "Oil vs orcas: Trans Mountain opponents tell federal court tanker traffic endangers whales," CBC News, 4 October 2017; and "Kinder Morgan Pipeline Threatens Ecology and Economy of Salish Tribes," Earthjustice, 13 February 2014, https://earthjustice.org/news/press/2014/kinder-morgan-pipeline-threatens-ecology-and-economy-of-salish-tribes.

24   David Ball, "Cross-border Indigenous Treaty Takes on Kinder Morgan Pipeline,"*The Tyee*, 23 September 2014, http://m.thetyee.ca/News/2014/09/23/Cross-Border-Pipeline-

Pact; Jeremy Shepherd, "Coastal First Nations sign treaty to stop Kinder Morgan pipeline," *Business Vancouver*, 24 September 2014, http://www.biv.com/article/2014/9/coastal-first-nations-sign-treaty-stop-kinder-morg/.

25   Winona LaDuke, *The Winona LaDuke Chronicles: Stories from the Front Lines in the Battle for Environmental Justice* (Ponsford, MN: Spotted Horse Press, 2016), 76–81; All Against the Haul, https://www.facebook.com/AllAgainstTheHaul; Naomi Klein, *This Changes Everything: Capitalism vs. the Climate* (New York: Simon & Schuster, 2014), 319.

26   Douglas Fisher, "Rising Coal Exports Prompt Fears from Rail Communities," *The Daily Climate*, 6 May 2012, http://www.climatecentral.org/news/partner-news/rising-coal-exports-prompt-fears-from-rail-communities.

27   Grossman, *Unlikely Alliances*, 144–45.

28   Eric de Place, "The Thin Green Line: The Northwest Faces off against Titanic Coal and Oil Export Schemes," *Sightline Daily*, 20 March 2014.

29   "Power Past Coal: Communities Against Coal Export," last updated 4 January 2018, http://www.powerpastcoal.org/; and Western Organizations of Resource Councils, *Heavy Traffic Ahead: Rail Impacts of Powder River Basin Coal to Asia by Way of Pacific Northwest Terminals* (July 2012), http://www.beyondtoxics.org/wp-content/uploads/2012/07/REPORT-Heavy-Traffic-Ahead-7-2012.pdf.

30   Valerie Volcovici, "Coal Firms Plead to Courts, Trump for West Coast Export Terminals," Reuters, 29 January 2018.

31   Affiliated Tribes of Northwest Indians, "Oppose the Proposals for the Transportation and Export of Fossil Fuels in the Pacific Northwest," Resolution no. 13-47, 16 May 2013, http://www.atnitribes.org/sites/default/files/res-13-47.pdf.

32   Northwest Tribal Coal Summit, "Northwest Tribes say No Shortcuts for Coal Export Proposals," Columbia River Inter-Tribal Fish Commission, 27 September 2012, http://www.critfc.org/press/northwest-tribes-say-no-short-cuts-for-coal-export-proposals/.

33   Floyd McKay, "Coal Port Faces Huge Obstacle in Lummi Opposition," *Crosscut*, 19 August 2013, http://crosscut.com/2013/08/mckay-lummi-corps/.

34   Floyd McKay, "Lummi Tribe joins the opposition to Whatcom coal port," *Crosscut*, 21 September 2012, https://crosscut.com/2012/09/lummi.

35   Kirk Johnson, "Tribes Add Potent Voice Against Plan for Northwest Coal Terminals," *New York Times*, 12 October 2012, www.nytimes.com/2012/10/12/us/tribes-add-powerful-voice-against-northwest-coal-plan.html; Brandi Montreuil, "Protest held at Xwe'chi'eXen (Cherry Point)," *Tulalip News*, 15 October 2012, http://www.tulalipnews.com/wp/2012/10/15/protest-held-at-xwechiexen-cherry-point/.

36   Alexis Bonogofsky (National Wildlife Foundation Tribal Lands Partnerships Project), interview by author, 26 March 2014.

37   Amber Cortes, "Treaty Rights and Totem Poles: How One Tribe is Carving out Resistance to Coal," *Grist*, 15 August 2014, http://exp.grist.org/lummi.

38 "History," Northern Plains Resource Council, last modified 2018, https://www.northernplains.org/history/.

39 Vanessa Braided Hair, "Why the Otter Creek Coal Mine Will Never be Built," *National Wildlife Federation's Blog*, 10 April 2013, http://blog.nwf.org/2013/04/why-the-otter-creek-coal-mine-will-never-be-built/.

40 John S. Adams, "Mont., Wash. tribes join ranchers to fight coal mine," *USA Today*, 23 September 2013.

41 Jewell James, *Protecting Treaty Rights, Sacred Places, and Lifeways: Coal vs. Communities,* booklet (August 2014), https://content.sierraclub.org/creative-archive/sites/content.sierraclub.org.creative-archive/files/pdfs/0777-Lummi-Report_07_web.pdf; see also www.totempolejourney.com.

42 Nick Engelfried, "How Montanans Stopped the Largest New Coal Mine in North America," *Yes!*, 28 March 2016, http://www.yesmagazine.org/planet/how-montanans-stopped-the-largest-new-coal-mine-in-north-america-20160328.

43 Krystal Two Bulls (Oglala Lakota, organizer against coal mining at Northern Cheyenne), interview by author, Missoula, MT, 6 November 2015.

44 Centennial Accord between the Federally Recognized Indian Tribes in Washington State and the State of Washington, 4 August 1989, https://goia.wa.gov/relations/centennial-accord; Sara Singleton, *Constructing Cooperation: The Evolution of Institutions of Comanagement* (Ann Arbor, MI: University of Michigan Press, 1998), 73–98.

45 Northwest Indian Fisheries Commission, last modified 2016, http://www.nwifc.org.

46 Craig Welch, "Tribes Take Salmon Battle into State's Road Culverts," *Seattle Times*, 20 October 2009, https://www.seattletimes.com/seattle-news/tribes-take-salmon-battle-into-states-road-culverts/.

47 Tim Ballew II, "Cherry Point Victory Shows Treaty Rights Protect Us All," *Bellingham Herald*, 14 May 2016.

48 Edwin Dobb, "The New Oil Landscape," *National Geographic*, March 2013, http://ngm.nationalgeographic.com/2013/03/bakken-shale-oil/dobb-text.

49 Bakken Watch, last updated 2011, http://bakkenwatch.blogspot.com/; Earthworks, last access 2018, Hydraulic Fracturing 101, https://earthworks.org/issues/hydraulic_fracturing_101/.

50 Pratap Chatterjee, "North Dakota Oil Boom Displaces Tribal Residents," *Corpwatch*, 25 April 2012, http://www.corpwatch.org/article.php?id=15713; Curt Brown, "While North Dakota Embraces the Oil Boom, Tribal Members Ask Environmental Questions," *Minneapolis Star Tribune*, 29 November 2013.

51 Angela Parker, "Sovereignty by the Barrel: Indigenous Oil Policies in the Bakken," presentation to the Native American and Indigenous Studies Association [NAISA], Austin, TX, 30 May 2014.

52 Indigenous Environmental Network, "Obama's Visit to Canada Must Address Dirty Oil from the Tar Sands in Northern Alberta," Press Release, 19 February 2009.

53   Grossman, *Unlikely Alliances*, 188–92.

54   Curtis Tate, "More Oil Spilled From Trains in 2013 than in Previous 4 Decades, Federal Data Show," *McClatchy DC*, 20 January 2014, http://www.mcclatchydc. com/2014/01/20/215143/more-oil-spilled-from-trains-in.html.

55   Eric de Place, *The Northwest's Pipeline on Rails* (Seattle: Sightline Institute, June 2013), http://www.sightline.org/research/the-northwests-pipeline-on-rails/; Eric de Place, *Northwest Fossil Fuel Exports* (Seattle: Sightline Institute, September 2014), http://www. sightline.org/research/northwest-fossil-fuel-exports-2/.

56   "Our Work Fighting Fossil Fuels: Oil," *Columbia Riverkeeper*, last updated 2018, https:// www.columbiariverkeeper.org/our-work/fighting-fossil-fuels.

57   Citizens for a Clean Harbor, last updated 2017, http://cleanharbor.org.

58   David Haviland, "Quinault and Earthjustice Hope to Shine Light on Crude by Rail," *KBKW Local News,* 23 April 2013, http://kbkw.com/modules/news/article. php?storyid=5400; David Haviland, "Quinault Indian Nation Urges Opposition to Oil Transport and Shipment Through Grays Harbor," *KBKW Local News*, 23 April 2014, http://kbkw.com/local-news/139970.

59   Brad Shannon, "State Oil Trains Run Into Heavy Opposition," *The Olympian*, 4 May 2014.

60   Billy Frank Jr., "Keep Big Oil Out of Grays Harbor," *Being Frank* (blog), Northwest Indian Fisheries Commission, 5 May 2014, https://nwifc.org/keep-big-oil-grays-harbor/.

61   William Dietrich, *The Final Forest: Big Trees, Forks, and the Pacific Northwest* (Seattle: University of Washington Press, 2011).

62   Tyson Johnston (vice president, Quinault Indian Nation), interview by author, Taholah, WA, 8 October 2015.

63   Larry Thevik (vice president, Washington Dungeness Crab Fishermen's Association), interview by author, Ocean Shores, WA, 8 October 2015.

64   Joe Schumacker (marine resources scientist, Quinault Indian Nation), interview by author, Taholah, WA, 8 October 2015.

65   Fawn Sharp (president of Quinault Indian Nation and Affiliated Tribes of Northwest Indians), interview by author, Taholah, WA, 29 October 2015.

66   Angelo Bruscas, "Crude oil no longer in plans, Port of Grays Harbor officials say," *Spokesman-Review*, 30 August 2017, http://www.spokesman.com/stories/2017/aug/30/ crude-oil-no-longer-in-plans-port-of-grays-harbor-/; Rick Anderson, "How forces combined again in Washington state to reject yet another oil terminal," *Los Angeles Times*, 4 February 2018, http://www.latimes.com/nation/la-na-washington-state-oil-terminal-20180204-story.html.

67   Hal Bernton and Lynda V. Mapes, "Puyallup Tribe leads protest against liquefied-natural-gas plant at Tacoma Port," *Seattle Times*, 18 December 2017, https://www. seattletimes.com/seattle-news/environment/puyallup-tribe-leads-protest-against-lng-plant-at-tacoma-port/.

68   Bold Nebraska, last updated 2018, http://boldnebraska.org.

69   International Treaty to Protect the Sacred from Tar Sands Projects, 25 January 2013, https://puc.sd.gov/commission/dockets/HydrocarbonPipeline/2014/HP14-001/tarsands.pdf.

70   Jane Kleeb (Bold Nebraska Executive Director), interview by author, Hastings, NE, 20 March 2014.

71   Reject and Protect, last updated April 2014, http://rejectandprotect.org/.

72   Kristin Moe, "When Cowboys and Indians Unite – Inside the Unlikely Alliance that is Remaking the Climate Movement," *Waging Nonviolence*, 2 May 2014, http://wagingnonviolence.org/feature/cowboys-indians-unite-inside-unlikely-alliance-foretells-victory-climate-movement/.

73   Faith Spotted Eagle (Ihanktonwan Nakota/Dakota), interview by author, Yankton, SD, 20 March 2014.

74   Sam Koplinka-Loehr, "Protectors *vs.* Destroyers—Canadians Unite to Stop Fracking in New Brunswick," *Waging Nonviolence*, 14 October 2013, http://wagingnonviolence.org/feature/protectors-vs-destroyers-canadians-unite-stop-fracking-new-brunswick/.

75   Penokee Hills Information Directory (2014), http://www.penokees.org/; The Water's Edge, last updated 2014, http://www.savethewatersedge.com; Rich Kremer, "Ho-Chunk Members Call for Coalition Against Frac Sand Mining," *Wisconsin Public Radio*, 21 November 2013, http://www.wrpc.net/articles/672/.

76   Grossman, *Unlikely Alliances*, 131–34, 145, 241–43.

77   Sylvia McAdam, Idle No More Co-Founder (lecture, South Puget Sound Community College, Olympia, WA, 14 March 2013).

78   Gyasi Ross, "Still Don't Know What #IdleNoMore Is About? Here's a Cheat-Sheet,' *Huffington Post*, 16 January 2013, http://www.huffingtonpost.ca/gyasi-/what-is-idle-no-more-_b_2486435.html.

79   Naomi Klein, "Dancing the World into Being: A Conversation with Idle No More's Leanne Simpson," *Yes!*, 5 March 2013, http://www.yesmagazine.org/peace-justice/dancing-the-world-into-being-a-conversation-with-idle-no-more-leanne-simpson.

80   Frances Van Zile (Mole Lake Sokaogon Chippewa Community), interview by author, Mole Lake, WI, 18 August 1999.

81   Grossman, *Unlikely Alliances,* 120–34.

82   Grossman, *Unlikely Alliances*, 183–84.

83   Lewis Kamb, "A Methane to their Madness: Tribes and Farmers Come Together—Over Cow Manure," *Seattle Post-Intelligencer*, 22 April 2003.

84   Nahal Ghoghaie, "Native/non-Native Watershed Management in an Era of Climate Change: Freshwater Storage in the Snohomish Basin," (master's thesis, The Evergreen State College, 2011).

85   Swinomish Climate Change Initiative, *Impact Assessment Technical Report*, October 2009, http://www.swinomish-nsn.gov/climate_change/Docs/SITC_CC_

ImpactAssessmentTechnicalReport_complete.pdf; Swinomish Climate Change Initiative, *Climate Adaptation Action Plan*, October 2010, http://www.swinomish-nsn. gov/climate_change/Docs/SITC_CC_AdaptationActionPlan_complete.pdf.

86   "City of Olympia and Nisqually Indian Tribe Announce Historic Regional Water Source Partnership," Press Release, 14 May 2008; Andy Hobbs, "Olympia's McAllister Springs site to return to Nisqually Tribe," *The Olympian*, 11 January 2017, http://www. theolympian.com/news/local/article125879539.html.

87   Zoltán Grossman and Alan Parker, *Asserting Native Resilience: Pacific Rim Indigenous Nations Face the Climate Crisis* (Corvalis: Oregon State University Press, 2012).

88   Audra Simpson, *Mohawk Interruptus: Political Life Across the Borders of Settler States* (Durham, NC: Duke University Press, 2014).

89   Paul Seamans (Dakota Rural Action), interview by author, Draper, SD, 3 April 2014.

90   Klein talk, 2014.

91   Harsha Walia, "Decolonizing Together," *Briarpatch*, 1 January 2012, http:// briarpatchmagazine.com/articles/view/decolonizing-together.

92   Cited in Zoltán Grossman, "Unlikely Alliances," *Counterpunch*, 12 June 2013, https:// www.counterpunch.org/2013/06/12/unlikely-alliances/.

Conserving Contested Ground: Sovereignty-Driven Stewardship by the White Mountain Apache Tribe and the Fort Apache Heritage Foundation

John R. Welch

This chapter links thinking and working in environmental conservation and historic site preservation to Indigenous sovereignty theory and practice.[1] Since 1992 I have worked for and with the White Mountain Apache Tribe ("the Tribe") at the Fort Apache and Theodore Roosevelt School National Historic Landmark in eastern Arizona. This experience reveals how stewardship for buildings and grounds that previously served as instruments for Western Apache colonization has converged with environmental protection while also advancing and actualizing conceptions of a Native nation's sovereignty. The quest to "save Fort Apache," while consistently well intentioned, initially adopted non-Apache ways of thinking and doing. The project's early focus on non-Apache sources of ideas, technical assistance, and heritage tourism markets implicitly imposed limits on engagements with and benefits to the local Apache community. The shift in the Fort Apache project's focus in the early 2010s, from externally driven research and preservation priorities to an internalist, sovereignty-driven approach, is opening still-unfolding possibilities for reclaiming and advancing White Mountain Apache rights to control their history, current affairs, land, and destiny. The project's emergent goal is to link Fort Apache's preservation and adaptive reuse as a "town centre" to the buttressing of five sovereignty constituents, or pillars—self-sufficiency, self-governance, self-determination, self-representation, and peer-recognition.[2] The case study also highlights three factors that foster success in community-focused collaborations among Indigenous nations, non-profit environmental organizations, and local citizens: partnership commitments to collective interests, values-based risk taking, and good management.

A brief review of how I came to be involved—personally as well as professionally—in the Fort Apache project provides the basis for my perspectives on how Fort Apache became the most important location in histories of White Mountain Apache colonization and decolonization. In my first year in graduate school I jumped at the chance to get to know White Mountain Apache lands and people. I subsequently took on projects elsewhere—Hawaii, Morocco, British Columbia, and Jemez Pueblo territory in New Mexico—but heartstrings tether my career to the Fort Apache Reservation. After several years of working as a contractor for the Tribe and the Bureau of Indian Affairs (BIA), I took a job as the local BIA archaeologist in 1992 and served as the Tribe's historic preservation officer from 1996 to 2005, when I vacated my post to enable the promotion of Mark Altaha, an Apache citizen. I get back to Apache lands every year to visit colleagues, to help out with the non-profit organization discussed in this chapter, and to otherwise volunteer my time to the places and people to whom I owe my career. I have written elsewhere about the family history and dynamics that impelled my entry into advocacy in general and my adoption of the Fort Apache project.[3] For this chapter, suffice it to say that Irish ancestry, a father who trained me to attend to whatever needed doing without a lot of guff, and a distinctive constellation of bosses, mentors, and colleagues left me destined to "save Fort Apache." The project has required teamwork, of course, but I was first drawn to it specifically because nobody else was willing to take it on. In this sense, the following case study of historic site preservation as environmentalism and of land and resource management activities as acts of sovereignty doubles as a reflexive review of the re-education of an academically trained archaeologist.[4]

This chapter's next section traces the history of the still-evolving place known as the Fort Apache and Theodore Roosevelt School National Historic Landmark (NHL) (Figure 3.1).[5] The site was the primary nexus for US government policies of Apache subjugation, assimilation, and control, a history that endowed the place with exceptional symbolic and practical potentials to contribute to sovereignty reclamation by the White Mountain Apache Tribe. Subsequent sections discuss contributions made through, and lessons learned by, the tribally chartered Fort Apache Heritage Foundation ("the Foundation"). The focus is on how the Foundation is replacing an initial set of operating principles, which used tourism-based economic development and "old-school" historic preservation, with community engagement and environmentalism grounded in place-based heritage stewardship.

The Fort Apache and Theodore Roosevelt School National Historic Landmark

Historical events and processes set in motion at and through Fort Apache made the Fort Apache Heritage Foundation both necessary and necessarily attentive to Apaches' needs and interests. Located in the eastern Arizona uplands, on the southwestern flanks of the White Mountains, the Fort Apache property was a US military facility from 1870 to 1922 (Figure 3.1). Established with the consent of local Apache leaders, the post played central strategic roles in the so-called Apache wars. After confining Western and Chiricahua Apache populations to reservations, the Army presence provided the coercive backstops for various colonial schemes that severed water, minerals, and timber from the reservations and otherwise excluded Apaches from their ancestral territories, economies, and spirituality. By 1922, when the Army finally acknowledged that the Western Apaches posed no threat to the United States and abandoned the post, the always-remote Fort Apache was the last US Army garrison made up only of infantry and cavalry (no mechanized or artillery units).[6]

Following the army's exit, the US government transferred the property to the Department of the Interior for use as an Indian school managed by the BIA. By mid-1923, children removed from their homes on Dine

FIGURE 3.1: White Mountain and San Carlos Apache reservations, including the location of the Fort Apache and Theodore Roosevelt School National Historic Landmark.

(Navajo) lands to the north occupied the soldiers' barracks and bunks.[7] By the later 1920s, as schools were built on Dine lands for Dine kids, Hopi, Pima, Yuma, and Apache children were transported to the erstwhile Fort Apache. The United States changed the place's name to Theodore Roosevelt School (T.R. School), replacing the soldiers and their guns with civilian bureaucrats and educators bearing almost equally dangerous policies.

Oblivious or indifferent to the socio-cultural and ecological damages accruing from its operations on Apache lands, the government's "3 C" mission (i.e., control, civilize, and commoditize Native Americans and their lands), pressed onward.[8] But the BIA made less headway with the 3 Rs (i.e., "reading, 'riting, and 'rithmetic"). Instead of academic schooling, the T.R. School curriculum emphasized vocational training. Boys learned Western ways to plant crops, hoe weeds, milk cows, tan hides, raise chickens, and fix small engines and vehicles. Girls learned how to clean non-Indian houses and to cook and do laundry using modern appliances. Ndee Biyati'i (Apache) and other Native languages were prohibited at T.R. School. Many students went on to jobs—and some to satisfying careers—as domestics, mechanics, equipment operators, and labourers. On the other hand, the preponderance of benefits from federal law and policy implementation went to non-Indian employers, government employees, loggers, miners, and cattlemen. The patent injustices assured that all T.R. School students learned at least one lesson: suspicion of non-Natives in general and BIA programs and personnel in particular.[9]

As subjugation and assimilation policies crumbled under the moral force of Native American demands for greater autonomy, the T.R. School lost value as a colonializing tool.[10] In 1960 the US Congress placed the Fort Apache buildings and about 400 acres of land in perpetual trust for the White Mountain Apache Tribe, "subject to the right of the Secretary of the Interior to use any part of the land and improvements for administrative or school purposes for as long as they are needed for the purpose."[11] This left the property underutilized. In 1969, the Tribe established the Apache Cultural Center and Museum in the oldest surviving log cabin at Fort Apache, among the first tribal museums in the United States. Fort Apache's land and army buildings were listed on the National Register of Historic Places in 1976. The museum moved to other historic buildings over the years, barely surviving a tragic 1985 fire that destroyed most of the collections. The museum was renamed Nohwike' Bágowa (House of Our Footprints) upon the opening of the new facility in 1997. Permanent exhibits installed since 2002 interpret Apache history and culture and provide educational opportunities for Apaches and for visitors from around the world (Table 3.1).[12]

As it became clear to most US policy makers that federal Indian policy would never enable good lives for people, the BIA lost moral, political, and

TABLE 3.1: Milestones in Preserving Fort Apache

1969	WMAT establishes first Tribal Cultural Center at Fort to rescue the historic site, perpetuate Apache cultural traditions, and reconcile past and present.
1976	National Park Service lists Fort Apache on the National Register of Historic Places. Tribe relocates Cultural Center into the surviving barracks at the Fort.
1993	WMAT adopts the *Master Plan for the Fort Apache Historic Park*, calling for property preservation for tourism-based economic development and interpretation.
1995	WMAT restores the last-remaining log cabin to serve as the WMAT Office of Tourism.
1996	WMAT stabilizes the last remaining stables; designates a tribal historic preservation officer (Welch); hires a professional museum director (Nancy Mahaney).
1997	WMAT dedicates the new Culture Center and Museum and the rehabilitated Elders Center at Fort Apache. The World Monuments Fund places Fort Apache on its 100 Most Endangered Sites list and provides $80,000 to WMAT to further preservation efforts.
1998	WMAT charters the Fort Apache Heritage Foundation; restores an endangered wood frame officer's quarters; initiates the *Fort Apache Survey and Assessment Report* to substantiate claims of BIA property mismanagement.
1999	WMAT files suit against the US in the Court of Claims to recover damages from the US for mismanagement of the Fort Apache property.
2000	With litigation ongoing, WMAT continues preservation work, including reconstruction of an imperiled wood frame officer's quarters, period fencing and outdoor lighting. FAFH host the first Great Fort Apache Heritage Reunion.
2003	Supreme Court finds in favor of Tribe and remands WMAT v. US to Claims Court; through stabilization efforts WMAT recognizes Kinishba Ruins National Historic Landmark as part of the Fort Apache Historic Park.
2004	President's Advisory Council on Historic Preservation recognizes WMAT as a Preserve America Community, the first tribe to receive the honor.
2005	FAHF completes NEH Challenge Grant legacy endowment campaign
2007	US Office of Special Trustee authorizes transfer of $12 million plus interest to an investment account dedicated to the perpetual preservation and maintenance of the Fort Apache property.
2012	Secretary of Interior Salazar designates Fort Apache and Theodore Roosevelt School as a National Historic Landmark; FAHF completes rehabilitation of the BIA Clubhouse to serve as offices for WMAT environmental programs

legal authority. Through the 1970s, 1980s, and 1990s, despite the Tribe's repeated affirmations of interests in preserving and using Fort Apache, BIA facilities managers repeatedly disregarded federal environmental and historic preservation laws by decimating the site's character and integrity. In a debate at a White Mountain Apache Tribal Council meeting I attended circa 1992, one council member opposed any effort to preserve Fort Apache. He suggested one way to deal with Fort Apache and its legacies: "bulldoze it." Other Apaches, including Council Chairman Ronnie Lupe, argued on practical grounds that Fort Apache held promise as part of the Tribe's tourism-focused economic development portfolio. Recognizing that Fort Apache's still-substantial value as a heritage tourism destination and interpretive site was being squandered, the council intervened. Joe Waters, one of the Tribe's planners, secured a grant from the Arizona Heritage Fund and, with matching support from the BIA's Fort Apache Agency, hired architect Stan Schuman to prepare a 1993 master plan to preserve and redevelop the property as the Fort Apache Historic Park.[13] Table 3.1 lists highlights from the long and ongoing campaign to repurpose Fort Apache for the benefit of the Ndee (Apache People) and White Mountain Apache Tribe.

The master plan envisioned rehabilitation of the historic buildings and surrounding lands for residential, recreational, educational, and commercial purposes. The plan was to be funded by anticipated revenues from outside visitors and investments by the Tribe and its partners to create offices and enterprises. But management capacities within the Tribe's Cultural Center and Planning Department were overtaxed, so I looked for ways to help. As the BIA's archaeologist, I worked initially to halt the BIA's destructive property use and to encourage the federal government's attention to the millions of dollars of deferred maintenance and repair needs. I gradually added master plan implementation to my duties as archaeologist and, beginning in 1996, the Tribe's historic preservation officer. My early efforts involved fundraising and project management for preservation treatments to Fort Apache's most endangered historic buildings.[14]

By 1998 it became clear that the Fort Apache project was too big for a lone archaeologist to do ad hoc. Even if a full-time specialist had been available, funding was tight. The most optimistic funding projections—via growth in local partnerships, external grants, tribal budget allocations, visitation, and associated museum revenues—would never provide the sustained financial backing needed for the preservation and adaptive reuse of the fort's historic buildings and grounds. The Tribe's response to this dilemma involved direct appeals for assistance to the US interior department secretary and former Arizona Governor Bruce Babbitt.

Efforts to persuade the federal government to do the right thing soon dead-ended. In 1999 the Tribe sued the United States for failing to fulfill its fiduciary obligations as the Fort Apache and T.R. School property manager and primary user.[15] The suit culminated in a 2003 victory before the US Supreme Court and a 2007 settlement that created a permanent fund to preserve the property and make it available for use in accord with the Tribe's needs and interests.[16] Three of the buildings would continue in use as a middle school for boarding and day students under the direction of a school board appointed by the White Mountain Apache Tribal Council. In separate interior department business, on 5 March 2012, Secretary of the Interior Ken Salazar officially recognized the site's national significance and designated it as a National Historic Landmark (Table 3.1).[17] The NHL designation provided full and final vindication for the Tribe's interests in taking proper care of Fort Apache as a nationally significant historic site and as a place uniquely qualified and equipped to assist the Tribe and the Apache people in the remediation of historical injuries and the persistent crippling effects of colonialism. As discussed in the next section, the tribally controlled Fort Apache Heritage Foundation non-profit emerged as the vehicle for advancing Apache interests in Fort Apache. Subsequent sections make the case that these interests are best understood and advanced in terms of sovereignty enactment.

The Fort Apache Heritage Foundation

As a further complement to legal action, in 1998 the White Mountain Apache Tribe chartered (and the US Internal Revenue Service recognized) the Fort Apache Heritage Foundation, Inc. to provide financial and technical support for further master plan implementation. When operations began in 1998, Foundation goals emphasized (1) preservation of the historic buildings and landscape features; (2) tourism-focused economic development and community betterment; and (3) promotion of the site as a place for intercultural reconciliation and the perpetuation of Apache heritage, both for the local Apache community and for all visitors. "We envision a future for the Fort Apache/T.R. School National Historic Landmark where tens of thousands of visitors will experience Arizona and the White Mountain Apache people's history each year and will leave with greater understanding and appreciation for this place, people and heritage."[18]

From 1999 to 2006, as the Tribe's lawsuit bumped through the courts, the cash-strapped Foundation struggled toward the creation at Fort Apache of a sort of "Decolonial Williamsburg of the West." During this period the Foundation tended to measure progress mainly in terms of creating tangible and experiential products for tourism markets. Indeed, as more buildings were rehabilitated, more exhibits added, and more publicity circulated, benefits accrued through modest growth in tourism and associated revenues. Registered visitation topped 15,000 annually in 2004, with guests from all over the world joining local and regional clientele.[19]

Big changes came in the wake of the Tribe's 2003 Supreme Court victory and the Tribe's recognition of the Foundation's steady performance and fiduciary potential. The 2007 settlement agreement that concluded the litigation named the Foundation as the BIA's successor to manage the Fort Apache and T.R. School property.[20] The agreement excluded BIA management from all but the three buildings (dormitory, classroom, cafeteria) essential to T.R. School operations, the landscaping associated with those school buildings, the BIA roads running through the property, and the former parade ground (i.e., current school playing field). The agreement also transferred $12 million plus interest into a permanent Fort Apache Property preservation fund (Table 3.1). The settlement agreement requires the Foundation to submit annual work plans and budget requests to the Tribal Council, and to retain at least half of the fund as a property maintenance endowment.[21]

Liberated for the first time from the burdens of project-by-project external fundraising, between 2007 and 2014 the Foundation completed preservation work on twenty-two of the twenty-seven historic buildings at Fort Apache and T.R. School. These projects included restoration of the 1892 Commanding Officer's Quarters; installation of a high-efficiency, solar-assisted central heating and cooling plant; and complete rehabilitation of the 1930 BIA Clubhouse as office space for the Tribe's hydrology, watershed, environmental planning, and historic preservation programs. By late 2014, the Foundation and its partners had addressed the most pressing preservation threats and initiated plans to rehabilitate the property's 400 acres of campus, pasture, farm, and river corridor. Through these actions and by boosting tenancy in the preserved buildings, the Foundation established practical, administrative, and financial competence as the facilities and lands manager. The Foundation expanded relationships with the Tribal Council, the T.R. School Board, the Tribe's Historic Preservation Office and Behavioral Health Program, the Arizona State Office of Tourism, the Johns Hopkins Center for American Indian Health, and other essential partners.

So What? Rethinking Foundation Clientele and Goals

In a speech made to acknowledge the successes listed in Table 3.1 and the National Historic Landmark designation, the Tribe's Council Chairman Ronnie Lupe graciously stated:

> Fort Apache has always been the main meeting ground between our Apache people and outsiders, the first place people have come when visiting our beautiful lands. We want this NHL designation to be a reminder that we have always welcomed government officials and private individuals into our territory. Some of these individuals and many of the federal policies they were there to implement caused harms to our people and our lands, but we are ready to move forward by adding to public knowledge about what happened at and through Fort Apache and T.R. School. Working with the Fort Apache Heritage Foundation and our other partners we will make Fort Apache a place of pride and prosperity. We will return it, respectfully, to active duty in service to education, commemoration and job creation.[22]

In a similar key, Ann Skidmore, who has served on Tribe's museum staff since 1981 and is currently the administrative manager at the Nohwike' Bágowa Museum, stated:

> Fort Apache is an important part of our history. I am very proud of the work that we have done here and of the lessons we can teach our children and our visitors from all over the world. We have been through difficult times, but we have also come very far in telling the stories of our people and of this place. Recognition of this place as a national historic landmark will help us continue to build Fort Apache as a centre for heritage tourism for the White Mountain Apache people.[23]

These remarks and the 2014 completion of a bundle of building preservation and property upgrades set the stage for Foundation Board reflections. The respite from two decades of frantic grant writing and preservation work to stem the tide of structural loss and degradation at Fort Apache prompted one Apache colleague to quip, "We won!" Indeed, as of 2018, the army troops and most BIA educators are gone, and with them the coercive underpinnings for repressive and extractive educational and administrative policies. Apaches, on the other hand, are unmistakably present and accounted for as a dynamic community. Not counting the roughly 9,000 Apache residents of the adjacent San Carlos Reservation, about 13,000 Apaches are living on ancestral homelands set aside as the Fort Apache Reservation.[24] Apaches continue making lives for themselves and their families, perpetuating long-standing traditions, creating new traditions, and pursuing futures distinct from the recent colonial past. The Tribe and the Apache people are the clear victors in the battle for Fort Apache.

Foundation satisfaction with saving Fort Apache and with the NHL designation runs generally parallel to that experienced by environmentalists responsible for including an imperilled ecosystem in a national park, monument, or wilderness area. On the ground, the success at Fort Apache means that during most business days more than two dozen Apache citizens are working and learning about the conservation and interpretation of watersheds, buildings, objects, and traditions—obvious progress since the dark period that prompted master planning in the early 1990s.[25] On the other hand, celebration of the 2012 NHL designation naturally prompted, "what's next?" questions. The many positive steps through 2012 swiftly emerged as points of departure rather than termini. Foundation Board discussions soon shifted away from primary concern with preservation and redevelopment efforts affecting twenty-seven buildings and 400 acres to the health and welfare of the surrounding Apache community.

The mandate to expand the positive impacts of the Fort Apache project beyond the property's boundaries is obvious in light of the local community profile. There can be little doubt that Apache people and their lands need whatever benefits can be mustered. White Mountain Apaches are among the loss leaders in the continental-scale struggle against the *Legacy of Conquest*.[26] Before Fort Apache's 1870 establishment, the Western Apaches were among the region's most potent, healthy, and land-rich people, respected by all. Today, the White Mountain Apaches and their San Carlos relatives and neighbours are some of North America's poorest, least educated, and least healthy subpopulations. There is no sugar-coating the reality that diabetes, substance abuse, and other social pathologies are all too prominent in community life around Fort Apache. In the search for an image to illustrate this point, I realized that virtually every photograph of Apache people since 1990 suffices. Figure 3.2 is a photograph at Fort Apache of four of the most powerful and successful Apache women in recent history—all members of the Tribal Council and recognized leaders. All have lost close family members to diabetes or substance abuse. The same is true for almost every Apache who works at Fort Apache and, tragically, anywhere on tribal lands.

Neither non-Apaches who work with the Tribe nor most Apaches think everything that has come by way of Fort Apache is bad and harmful. There are, nonetheless, many things that have been getting worse since the US Army established Fort Apache and asserted cultural superiority, and moral and governmental authorities led Apaches to believe the United States was their friend and ally and then proceeded to open their lands for mining, ranching, farming, logging, hunting, and other means of extracting wealth to benefit non-Indians. Research also belongs on this list of parasitic activities enabled and promoted by military and civilian authorities based at or supported by Fort Apache. Considering only

FIGURE 3.2: Four Tribal Councilwomen. Left to right: Mariddie Craig, Phoebe Nez, Margaret Walker and Judy Dehose—lead the procession for the first annual Ndee Ł'ade Fort Apache Heritage Reunion, Fort Apache, May 2000. Courtesy Nohwike' Bagowa Museum.

archaeological research, for example, White Mountain and San Carlos Apaches have boosted the careers of hundreds of archaeologists, including mine, by hosting University of Arizona archaeological field schools from 1931 through 2003. Yet archaeologists and curators have been slow to acknowledge the harmful effects experienced by our hosts from the excavations and collections or to respond in kind to the Apaches' generosity.[27]

The Foundation is trying to do better. Recognition of Fort Apache's historical, symbolic, and instrumental position in relation to the surrounding Apache community has, since 2012, become the essential context for deliberations on how the Fort Apache initiative can and must have truly consequential benefits. Still, the real work of reclaiming Fort Apache and T.R. School as an integral part of the Apache community and homeland has barely begun.

Sovereignty-Driven Heritage Conservation at Fort Apache

As of 2018, the reasons for the Foundation's incomplete success are fairly obvious: the campaign that began in 1992 to restore and redevelop the property was pursued primarily in accord with non-Apache principles and priorities. Despite excellent intentions, an understandable emphasis on addressing structural preservation issues, and the creation of many benefits to the Tribe and many of its citizens, Foundation efforts through 2012 sought, in the main, to engage, impress, and market to non-Apaches.

This initial focus was rational in terms of mandates to avoid the further loss of historic buildings and to create needed jobs, but it failed to escape the confines of colonialist mindsets and practices that subordinated local interests to quests for participation in external markets and partnerships. As the Foundation Board undertook revisions to the master plan, the need to systematically prioritize Apache values and interests became clear. In response, the Foundation has set a different course guided both by rigorous professionalism in management and by community engagement in all phases of Fort Apache planning and programming.

Foundation participation in more and better collaborations with the Tribe's citizens has also caused the Foundation to consider its roles and goals as a semi-autonomous subsidiary of the Tribe. How can the Foundation, a small non-profit organization, effectively identify and attend to the interests of the Tribe and its citizens as well as to its court-defined mission? The one-word answer also encapsulates what White Mountain Apaches want: *sovereignty*. Proposed here as the most concise means for describing the goals of all or most Indigenous communities, sovereignty stands in theory and practice as the effective opposite of colonialism. Although it is often conceptualized in grandiose terms, closer engagement with local Apache values and interests has led the Foundation to approach sovereignty, as Willow does, in terms of *doing*, as the veritable enactment of land and community stewardship.[28] Thought of in terms of stewardship at Fort Apache, and perhaps, elsewhere, sovereignty is inclusive, non-authoritarian, grounded in responsibilities to future generations, and exercised through five inter-braided "pillars" or pursuits:

1. Self-sufficiency—creation and maintenance of sustainable supplies of the food, water, shelter, and human relationships essential for people to survive and thrive;

2. Self-determination—policies and practices that foster and enable futures concordant with long-standing and emergent community values and interests;

3. Self-governance—internal capacities to pursue and sustain self-determination;

4. Self-representation—first-person portrayals of cultures, histories, and aspirations;

5. Peer Recognition—establishment of government-to-government and other peer relationships based on legitimate authority over territory, citizens, and resources.[29]

The five-pillar framework offers guidance on ways to serve and integrate the needs and interests of citizens, communities, and nation-scale institutions. Support for the exercise of White Mountain Apache Tribe sovereignty, at levels ranging from basic human needs to expansive intergovernmental relations, is guiding Fort Apache Foundation planning and programming for further decolonization of this emphatically colonial property. The Foundation Board now explicitly and consistently prioritizes local Apache preferences in planning future roles of the Fort Apache and T.R. School NHL in reservation and regional community development, in civic engagement, in citizen education, and in local economic stimulation.

The Foundation is engaging members of the Tribal Council, T.R. School Board, and other partners in ongoing discussions about Fort Apache's short- and long-term roles in building a White Mountain Apache future grounded in long-standing and emergent Apache values. Foundation experiments employing the NHL to effect sovereignty-enhancing policies, practices, and programming are obliging it to reach into the Tribe's civil society, up to the Tribal Council, and out to other partners. The Table 3.2

TABLE 3.2: Building Sovereignty's Five Pillars

	People	Place	Memory	Plans
SELF-SUFFICIENCY	Develop internal capacities to steward lands, water supplies, buildings, grounds, collections, and traditions	Rehabilitate the Fort Apache and T.R. School farm fields, orchards, and irrigation systems	Train Apache citizens to collect and conserve oral traditions, photographs, documents, and objects	Use Fort Apache as an enterprise zone for local commerce and reduce reliance on off-reservation businesses
SELF-DETERMINATION	Support T.R. School Board interests in creating an immersion school focused on instruction in Apache language and culture arts and traditions	Collaborate with the Johns Hopkins Center for American Indian Health in harnessing youth entrepreneurship to expand the Internet café in Building 103	Build existing collections into a world-class 'Apache National Archive' repository and center for research, and interpretation	Set aside the site's riparian corridors and other areas of high ecological integrity as Tribal preserves
SELF-GOVERNANCE	Host the Whiteriver Unified School District Junior Leadership Academy, serving middle schoolers in a four-week summer programs	Manage the Nohwike' Bágowa Museum Store to become the premier retail outlet for Apache artists and for raising funds to promote Apache arts	Use the Apache National Archives as the destination of tribal government records to boost administrative solvency	Transition the Foundation Board of Directors to (even) fuller control by White Mountain Apache citizens
SELF-REPRESENTATION	Assure the primacy of Apache voices in the interpretation of local and regional history and culture	Host each May the annual Ndee Ła' Ade (Gathering of the People) Fort Apache Heritage Celebration and Apache Song and Dance Competition	Maintain respectful separations between interpretations of Apache community history and status and interpretations of Fort Apache and T.R. School history	Privilege Apache values, knowledge and preferences in policies and daily practices (i.e., Board recruitment and decision making, aesthetic choices, menu planning, etc.).
PEER RECOGNITION	Provide staff and Board members as trainers for workshops on tribal museum and tribal historic preservation officer operations	Host the only Arizona Office of Tourism Local Visitor Information Center located on tribal lands	Initiate formal and informal intercultural reconciliation processes attended by representatives of groups with ties to Fort Apache and T.R. School history	Maintain and grow public- and private-sector partnerships; Attract federal, state, and private investments to support all of the above

summary of contributions to each of sovereignty's five pillars illustrates how the Foundation is creating synergistic connections among culture, landscape, architecture, local capacities and external audiences, markets, and clienteles.[30]

There are, of course, multiple overlaps and synergies among these five clusters of initiatives. Most projects and programs support and strengthen more than one of the pillars. The essential point illustrated in Table 3.2 and through work at Fort Apache is that sovereignty may be deconstructed and refocused to give meaning and direction to creative ways to harmonize varied interests in challenging contexts. With or without such conceptual deconstruction, sovereignty readily emerges as a practical guide for action directed toward community health, social vitality, and environmental rehabilitation. Fort Apache as an antidote to colonialism is all the more potent because of its early history as a hub for the imposition and enactment of non-Apache values and its recent history as the legal battleground between the Tribe and the United States. The Fort Apache project's ongoing transformation into a context and vehicle for experiments in sovereignty enactment provides the basis for a concluding discussion of factors affecting the initial success and longer-term sustainability of local conservation.

Tribal Sovereignty + Historical Preservation = Innovative Environmentalism

Embedded in the history, structure, and Apache community prioritization of the Fort Apache Heritage Foundation is the "seed" of a distinctive and potentially fruitful strategy for addressing sources and causes of ongoing harms to colonized peoples and rifts between Native and non-Native Americans and Canadians.[31] This strategy carries the promise of linking the Foundation's mandates to preserve Fort Apache with the White Mountain Apache Tribe's mandates to reclaim elements of sovereignty decimated by a century and a half of concerted colonial impositions and environmental damages.

The Foundation's rapidly accruing experience with community-engaged and sovereignty-driven conservation raises issues as well as hope. At least four sets of questions have emerged relating to Foundation efforts to facilitate enactments of Apache sovereignty. First, how will the Foundation and its partners incorporate and employ Apache ways of doing business? In other words, how can values, interests, preferences, and priorities originating within reservation borders be synchronized with external ("dominant society") goals and operating principles? Second, how readily can Fort Apache and the Foundation be altered and adapted to respond constructively to future changes in local community interests, preferences, and priorities? What might be done to be ready to shift Foundation plans and processes to accommodate community dynamics? Third, how is Fort Apache and FAHF changing the people it touches and those who touch the place and organization (staff, residents, partners, visitors, etc.)? Finally, what public goods (i.e., benefits free to all) are Fort Apache and FAHF producing? What informal social work, public security, aesthetic pleasures, remembering, recreation, and self- and collective care and organizing is happening at and because of Fort Apache? These questions deserve particular attention in a community characterized by underemployment, related social ills, and suspicions of organizations and authorities deeply grounded in historical experience.[32]

As of 2018, it remains uncertain when and how clear answers to these four cloudy questions will emerge, though emerge they must. Fort Apache remains something of an enclave, a place symbolizing a history of lost land, culture, and autonomy. Many Apaches remain suspicious of even the best-intentioned schemes, especially initiatives stemming from Fort Apache. Similar suspicions extend to individuals who seek positions of authority. Subtle and less subtle pressures that inhibit Apache participation in non-family organizations help explain why Apaches have yet to dominate the Foundation Board's membership.[33] A further complication is the fine line between serving the Tribe's interests as perceived by the Tribal Council and the community's interests as perceived by other Apache leaders and the Foundation Board. Respect for formal aspects of the Tribe's sovereignty require the Foundation to treat the eleven-member Tribal Council as the ultimate authority on the Fort Apache Indian Reservation.[34] On the other hand, the emerging vision for Fort Apache as a hub for community processes and civic activities means the Foundation must listen from the grassroots *up* as well as from the Tribal Council *down*. Apache citizens are teaching the Foundation how to better reach into elected and appointed leadership while increasing responsiveness to the rank and file of actual and possible property users and beneficiaries.

While firm answers to these four questions may be elusive for now, the Foundation's recent experience is bringing to the surface several criteria for taking sovereignty-driven conservation and research to the next level at Fort Apache. These criteria boil down to common sense reiterations of three emerging Foundation mandates: Apaches must be the exclusive or primary beneficiaries of Foundation activities; Apache citizens must continue to gain control over Fort Apache and Foundation governance; and lastly, as community engagement broadens and deepens, the Foundation must shift toward proactive support for community processes to bring to the fore local community views about the merits of the property and of Foundation management thereof.

A second set of criteria for advancing Tribe and Foundation goals derives from the science of sustainable resource conservation.[35] This literature identifies conditions under which communities and managers are likely to cooperate to the benefit of communities, environments, and resources. Research results indicate that cooperation is more likely when the resource being managed is culturally or economically important (or both), when it is adjacent to the community, and when it is managed in accord with community values, preferences, and needs. If these conditions are met, and if leaders emerge who are willing to take political risks to pursue collective benefits from restrictions on harmful environmental uses, then sustainable and community-engaged resource conservation becomes more likely.

All of these criteria are being met at Fort Apache. A growing number of White Mountain Apache citizens now view Fort Apache as a place of real opportunity. Its enclave status is being leveraged by reinventing the place as a sovereignty-driven incubator for creativity, professionalism, self-organizing, and entrepreneurship. The Nohwike' Bágowa museum, in particular, is regarded by most Apache citizens as a uniquely valuable educational and interpretive resource that represents and serves Apache values, preferences, and interests. Tribal leaders increasingly give priority attention to Fort Apache as the locus for new initiatives. Change is palpable and positive.

I close this chapter with an appeal for greater attention by scholars and advocates of all stripes to opportunities presented by the shared interests and goals of campaigns for historic preservation, local and Indigenous sovereignties, and environmental health and sustainability. The theory of progress manifest in Foundation activities and initial responses to the four sets of questions noted above is that community-engaged conservation of the primary locus of Apache subjugation and colonization will restore, enhance, and expand Apache sovereignty. Fort Apache is emerging as the hub for Apache reclamation of birthrights, cultural distinctiveness, territorial connectivity, political potency, and economic vitality. Much remains to be done, but Foundation responses thus far to the White Mountain Apache Tribe's struggles to address persistent social and environmental challenges have boosted opportunities for Apaches to safeguard and use the 400 acres, twenty-seven historic structures, and object and media collections under Foundation trusteeship. Self-sufficiency, self-governance, self-representation, self-determination, and peer recognition are being enhanced and expanded by and through the preservation and adaptive reuse of Fort Apache's buildings and landscapes.

Foundation activities are also revealing the interdependencies of biophysical and socio-cultural heritage conservation, including underappreciated connections among human-built and largely unmodified landscape elements. Indeed, historic preservation and environmentalism share core values, interests, and goals centred on fostering collective senses of place, honouring the complexity embedded in places and ecosystems, and passing on to future generations our ancestors' most significant, authentic, and valuable legacies. As Jane Jacobs observed a half-century ago—and as urban and regional planners continue to discover—people thrive in the complexity of multi-layered, multi-functional, "messy" spaces.[36] On a parallel and more materialist plane, historic preservation done properly, as it is being done at Fort Apache, results in reduced contributions of building demolition debris to landfills, lowered energy consumption and greenhouse gas emissions, perpetuation of skilled building trades, and reuse of already altered lands in lieu of new disturbance.[37] Preservation and conservation of historic buildings and sites *is* environmentalism.[38]

Re-Scaling Sovereignty to Boost Personal and Group Accountability and Sustainability

Even casual attention to environmental stories in major news suggests that the fate of our planet rests in the hands of elected and appointed officials in Washington, Ottawa, Beijing, and other national capitals. Major news outlets often features stories of heroes engaged in desperate quests to "stop this" or "save that." The dominant messages are that global-scale issues and concerns are what really matters and that those in positions of authority will take care of the problems. Contrary to the prevailing media focus on (inter)national law and policy, celebrity issues, and public relations campaigns, however, it is work by ordinary people and local institutions to spare specific places from drilling, logging, mining, and mismanagement that provides the essential determinants of environmental and community health and resilience.

The lessons emerging from Fort Apache and from the other stories related in this book offer another view. Few of us—perhaps only 1 percent of the 1 percent—actually live at global scales. Even so, each and all of us have the power to change our worlds. Regardless of how much money we make, we all dwell locally. We live in and take care of houses and apartments and neighbourhoods and towns and cities. We work in businesses and schools and bureaucracies. We make decisions—dozens and even hundreds of them every day—about what to eat, how to move about, who and what to care for, and who and what to ignore for now or later. These decisions, whether made on the basis of our own personal values and preferences or because of duties imposed by circumstances, aggregate into social processes and patterns that define and animate our institutions and societies. Individual acts are the undeniable building blocks of society and history.

Amidst media blitzes relating to global-scale changes in climates, oceans, and supplies of fresh water and farmland, it is easy to forget that one of the most important levels and scales of environmentalism is local, personal, and even attitudinal. Of equal importance to parliamentary debates or United Nations resolutions are the intrinsically individual commitments to save the world or at least a treasured bit of it. It is seldom, if ever, easy to find unity, much less harmony, amidst the cacophony of individual interests and preferences. But the history of effective conservation in general, and that of the Fort Apache Heritage Foundation and some of the other organizations showcased in these pages, proves that it is possible and worth trying to pull off.

As nations within nations, tribes and First Nations may seem natural contexts for experiments in sovereignty-driven conservation, but the approach can also guide any place- and culture-based community interested in perpetuating definitive or distinctive relations with their lands and traditions. The decolonizing policies and practices described above provide concrete steps for collaborations among Native and non-Native environmentalists, advocates, managers, and researchers committed to the stewardship of places, objects, and traditions.

Notes

1   For an apt review of essential tensions between sovereignty enactment and policy, see Anna J. Willow, "Doing Sovereignty in Native North America: Anishinaabe Counter-Mapping and the Struggle for Land-Based Self-Determination," *Human Ecology* 41 (2013): 871–84. See also chapters in this volume by Willow and Grossman.

2   John R. Welch, "The Last Archaeologist to (Almost) Abandon Grasshopper," *Arizona Anthropologist* (Centennial Edition) (2015): 107–19, https://journals.uair.arizona.edu/index.php/arizanthro/article/download/18856/18499.

3   John R. Welch and Neal Ferris, "'We have Met the Enemy and It is Us': Improving Archaeology through Application of Sustainable Design Principles," in *Transforming Archaeology: Activist Practices and Prospects*, ed. Sonya Atalay, Lee Rains Clauss, Randall H. McGuire, and John R. Welch (Walnut Creek, CA: Left Coast Press, 2014), 91–93; George P. Nicholas, John R. Welch, and Eldon C. Yellowhorn, "Collaborative Encounters," in *Archaeological Practice: Engaging Descendant Communities*, ed. Chip Colwell-Chanthaphonh and T. J. Ferguson (Walnut Creek, CA: AltaMira Press, 2008), 288–90.

4   Sonya Atalay, *Community-Based Archaeology: Research with, by, and for Indigenous and Local Communities* (Berkeley: University of California Press, 2012).

5   NHL designation is the highest recognition the federal government bestows on properties in the United States that are not managed directly by the National Park Service as national monuments or national historic sites.

6   Lori Davisson, "Fort Apache, Arizona Territory: 1870–1922," *The Smoke Signal* 78 (Tucson, AZ: Tucson Corral of Westerners, 2004); Lori Davisson, with Edgar Perry and the Original Staff of the White Mountain Apache Cultural Center, *Dispatches from the Fort Apache Scout: White Mountain and Cibecue Apache History Through 1881*, ed.

John R. Welch (Tucson: University of Arizona Press, 2016); John R. Welch, "National Historic Landmark Nomination for Fort Apache and Theodore Roosevelt School" (Washington, DC: National Park Service, 2011).

7   Welch, "National Historic Landmark Nomination."

8   Welch, "National Historic Landmark Nomination."

9   John R. Welch and Ramon Riley, "Reclaiming Land and Spirit in the Western Apache Homeland," *American Indian Quarterly* 25, no. 1 (2001): 5–12; John R. Welch, "Reconstructing the Ndee Sense of Place," in *The Archaeology of Meaningful Places*, ed. Brenda Bowser and M. Nieves Zedeño (Salt Lake City: University of Utah Press, 2009); John R. Welch, "Places, Displacements, Histories and Memories at a Frontier Icon in Indian Country," in *Monuments, Landscapes, and Cultural Memory*, ed. Patricia E. Rubertone (Walnut Creek, CA: World Archaeological Congress and Left Coast Press, 2008).

10   Welch, "National Historic Landmark Nomination."

11   John R. Welch and Robert C. Brauchli, "'Subject to the Right of the Secretary of the Interior': The White Mountain Apache Reclamation of the Fort Apache and Theodore Roosevelt School Historic District," *Wicazo Sa Review* 25, no. 1 (2010): 47–73.

12   Welch and Brauchli, "Subject to the Right."

13   Stan P. Schuman, "Master Plan for the Fort Apache Historic Park," prepared for the White Mountain Apache Tribe and the US Bureau of Indian Affairs (Tucson, AZ: CGD Architects, 1993).

14   John R. Welch, "The White Mountain Apache Tribe Heritage Program: Origins, Operations, and Challenges," in *Working Together: Native Americans and Archaeologists*, ed. Kurt E. Dongoske, Mark Aldenderfer, and Karen Doehner (Washington, DC: Society for American Archaeology, 2000), 67–83, http://www.saa.org/Portals/0/SAA/publications/SAAbulletin/16-1/SAA9.html. In 2005, Karl Hoerig, the Tribe's museum director, took over the escalating responsibilities for master plan implementation and revisions.

15   Welch and Brauchli, "Subject to the Right."

16   Welch and Brauchli, "Subject to the Right," 67–69.

17   White Mountain Apache Tribe and Fort Apache Heritage Foundation, last updated 2018, http://www.fortapachearizona.org.

18   Fort Apache Heritage Foundation, Award nomination submitted to the Arizona Office of Tourism, Phoenix (2012).

19   John R. Welch, Karl A. Hoerig, and Raymond Endfield, Jr., "Enhancing Cultural Heritage Management and Research through Tourism on White Mountain Apache Tribe Trust Lands," *The SAA Archaeological Record* 5, no. 3 (2005): 15–19; Mark Nelson and Will Pittz, "Building the Fort Apache Heritage Foundation: Developing an Organizational System, Management Plan, and Strategic Vision," Report prepared for the White Mountain Apache Tribe and the Fort Apache Heritage Foundation, Harvard Project on American Indian Economic Development, http://fngovernance.org/resources_docs/Fort_Apache_Strategic_Vision_Case_Study.pdf.

20   Welch and Brauchli, "Subject to the Right."

21   Welch and Brauchli, "Subject to the Right," 67–68.

22   Ronnie Lupe, "Fort Apache Pasts and Presents" (speech delivered at the ceremony designating the Fort Apache and Theodore Roosevelt School National Historic Landmark, Fort Apache, Arizona, 12 May 2012).

23   Ann Q. Skidmore, personal communication to Karl Hoerig, Fort Apache, Arizona, 17 August 2012.

24   Ohio Valley University, American Indian Population by Reservations and Statistical Areas, "American Indian Reservations and Alaska Native Village Statistical Areas With Largest American Indian and Alaska Native Populations: 2010," http://www.ovc.edu/missions/indians/indresju.htm.

25   This group of collaborators includes Foundation personnel and the staffs of the Tribe's Museum, Historic Preservation Office, Hydrology and Watershed Protection Program, and Environmental Planning Office: see, for example, Jonathan W. Long, Delbin Endfield, Candy S. Lupe, and Mae Burnette, "Battle at the Bridge: Using Participatory Approaches to Develop Community Researchers in Ecological Management," *Natural Resources and Environmental Issues*, vol. 12, art. 10 (2004), 19–44, http://digitalcommons.usu.edu/nrei/vol12/iss1/10.

26   Patricia N. Limerick, *Legacy of Conquest: The Unbroken Past of the American West* (New York: W. W. Norton, 1987). For a consideration of the links among colonialism, loss of sovereignty, and community health, see Thurman L. Hester, *Political Principles and Indian Sovereignty* (New York: Routledge, 2001).

27   John McClelland, "Repatriation and Collaboration: Opening Our Doors to Indigenous Communities," http://www.statemuseum.arizona.edu/blog/repatriation-and-collaboration-opening-our-doors-to-indigenous-communities/, posted 4 January 2013; Welch, "The Last Archaeologist to (Almost) Abandon Grasshopper"; John R. Welch and T. J. Ferguson, "Putting Patria into Repatriation: Cultural Affiliations of White Mountain Apache Tribe Lands," *Journal of Social Archaeology* 7 (2007): 171–98; Welch and Riley, "Reclaiming."

28   Willow, "Doing Sovereignty."

29   It is, of course, important for community leaders to assess and critique the sovereignty framework offered here, taking what seems useful and offering appropriate amendments. See John R. Welch, "Sovereignty-Driven Scholarship," in *Giving Back: Research and Reciprocity in Indigenous Settings*, ed. R. D. K. Herman (Corvalis: Oregon State University Press, 2018), 307–29; and John R. Welch, Mark Altaha, Doreen Gatewood, Karl Hoerig, and Ramon Riley, "Archaeology, Stewardship, and Sovereignty," *The SAA Archaeological Record* 6, no. 4 (2006): 17–20.

30   Karl A. Hoerig et al., "Expanding Toolkits for Heritage Perpetuation: The Western Apache Ethnography and Geographic Information Science Research Experience for Undergraduates," *International Journal of Applied Geospatial Research* 6 (2015): 60–77.

31   Grossman (this volume); Willow (this volume). See Justin B. Richland, "Beyond Listening: Lessons for Native/American Collaborations from the Creation of the Nakwatsvewat Institute," *American Indian Culture and Research Journal* 35 (2011): 105–9.

32 The questions draw upon James C. Scott, *Two Cheers for Anarchism* (Princeton, NJ: Princeton University Press, 2013).

33 Another reason for the lack of an Apache majority on the Foundation Board is a prevailing expectation for financial compensation for service on the Tribe's boards and committees. Foundation bylaws embrace the organization's de facto status as the trustee for Fort Apache by prohibiting payments to board members, except reimbursement for travel expenses, and by otherwise excluding all incentives for self-interested participation. Because Foundation decision making is determined more by strength of ideas and consensus, Apache citizens on the board have disproportionate influence.

34 "Constitution of the White Mountain Apache Tribe of the Fort Apache Indian Reservation Arizona," 18 June 1934, as amended, http://wmat.us/Legal/Constitution. html.

35 Arun Agrawal, "Common Resources and Institutional Sustainability," in *The Drama of the Commons*, ed. Elinor Ostrom et al. (Washington, DC: National Research Council, 2002), 41–86; Evelyn W. Pinkerton, "Coastal Marine Systems: Conserving Fish and Sustaining Community Livelihoods with Co-Management," in *Principles of Ecosystem Stewardship: Resilience-Based Natural Resource Management in a Changing World*, ed. F. Stuart Chapin, III, Gary P. Kofinas, and Carl Folke (New York: Springer-Verlag, 2009), 241–58; Evelyn W. Pinkerton and Leonard John, "Creating Local Management Legitimacy: Building a Local System of Clam Management in a Northwest Coast Community," *Marine Policy* 32, no. 4 (2008): 680–91; John R. Welch et al., "Treasure Bearers: Personal Foundations for Effective Leadership in Northern Coast Salish Heritage Stewardship," *Heritage and Society* 4, no. 1 (2011): 83–114.

36 Jane Jacobs, *The Death and Life of Great American Cities* (New York: Random House, 1961); Mathias Wendt, "The Importance of *Death and Life of Great American Cities* (1961) by Jane Jacobs to the Profession of Urban Planning," *New Visions for Public Affairs* 1 (Spring 2009): 1–24.

37 On saving energy through historic preservation, see a case study in the application of the US Department of Energy's Federal Energy Management Program at https://www. energy.gov/eere/femp/downloads/aspinall-courthouse-gsa-s-historic-preservation-and-net-zero-renovation; on using historic site conservation as a context for community engagement and empowerment, see Chris Landorf, "A Framework for Sustainable Heritage Management: A Study of UK Industrial Heritage Sites," *International Journal of Heritage Studies* 15, no. 6 (2009): 494–510.

38 Patrice Frey, "Making the Case: Historic Preservation as Sustainable Development," (Washington, DC: National Trust for Historic Preservation, 2007); Kathryn Rogers Merlin, "Report on Historic Preservation and Sustainability," http://www.dahp. wa.gov/sites/default/files/sustainability_SummaryReport.pdf (Seattle: Washington State Department of Archeology and Historic Preservation, 2011). For a discussion of decolonization from within to address biophysical environmental health, see Elizabeth Hoover et al., "Indigenous Peoples of North America: Environmental Exposures and Reproductive Justice," *Environmental Health Perspectives* 120, no. 12 (2012): 1645–49, https://ehp.niehs.nih.gov/1205422/. As is true for historic preservation, advances in community health foster and feed upon improvements in environmental health.

From Southern Alberta to Northern Brazil: Indigenous Conservation and the Preservation of Cultural Resources

Sterling Evans

"Native National Park!" screamed the headlines of the *New York Times* on 23 June 2013. The article that followed described how the US National Park Service (NPS) and the Oglala Lakota (Sioux) Nation were working to move from a joint management agreement for Badlands National Park in South Dakota to developing a tribal national park. The proposal, underway at various stages since 1976, awaits full Congressional approval; signs at the park borders as of fall 2015, however, do say "Entering Badlands National Park, in Cooperation with Oglala Sioux Tribe." The initiative sets aside the South Unit of the park, 53,320 hectares, to be operated by the Oglala, creating the first tribal national park in the United States.[1]

Perhaps it takes a front-page *New York Times* article to remind us about the relationship between Native peoples and national parks in the United States and elsewhere.[2] But the evolving nature of this relationship and how it has been studied is not exactly new, especially as there are works that have explored Native conflicts and solutions with park development across the world.[3] Specifically for the United States, there have been several studies that provide historical analysis of removal of Natives from national parks, most of which are very critical of US policy that first used Aboriginals as tourist features in park settings and then removed them from park boundaries altogether.[4]

These studies logically cannot cover every dimension or geographical area of Native peoples–national park relationships and tend to neglect state and provincial parks (a broader theme that DeWitt addresses in this volume). Oddly, few of the works on the Global South mention the Costa Rican experience with parks and Native people, despite that country's impressive conservation record. While many of the works deal extensively with Brazil's more famous national parks that include Indigenous lifeways in the Amazon, none mentions the significance of Sete Cidades and Serra da Capivara national parks in the northern Brazilian state of Piauí, which work to preserve prehistoric cultural resources. By bringing these examples into view alongside examples from Canada and the United States, this chapter deepens our comparative understanding of the relationship between Native peoples and conservation efforts in the preservation of cultural resources.[5] As governments continue to understand the need for reconciliation with Native peoples for past and present injustices, we can see how conservation continues to play a vital role in the process. This chapter thus illustrates a changing relationship between the state and nature, especially with focus on historical Indigenous rights that are reflected in acknowledging a Native sense of place and the importance of access to land across the Western hemisphere. "Conservation" and protected areas, as well as environmentalism, can no longer be seen as merely for the purpose of ecological preservation, and this broader understanding has implications beyond Native-park relationships.

With those thoughts in mind, this chapter contributes to the goals of *Environmental Activism on the Ground*, especially in terms of how Indigenous people have worked as small-scale conservationists to promote the development and management of protected areas in their home regions. Indeed, as the book's editors have alluded to in their introduction, Indigenous people have made a measurable "splash" on the local environmental scene in many parts of the Americas. And as such, the scope of this chapter, from southern Alberta to northern Brazil, offers a comparative, transnational approach to a wide array of Native natural and cultural conservation initiatives.

The chapter is divided into three parts. The first offers a historiographical background and comparative analysis of conservation units in the Americas that aid in our understanding of Native-park relations. It hopes to show that the case studies discussed in the next two sections are not isolated examples but representative of a broader trend. Part II explores and compares two different zones of ancient Native cultural preservation: Writing-on-Stone Provincial Park, Alberta, and Sete Cidades National Park, Brazil. Both are characterized by badlands, rock formations caused by extensive erosion over time, and ancient petroglyphs. Finally, Part III examines three case studies of Indigenous conservation areas, including Badlands National Park, South Dakota; Death Valley National Park, California; and Indigenous reserves in Costa Rica.

I: Comparisons of Indigenous Conservation across the Americas

The examples of Indigenous and other local resident–national park relationships that are at the heart of this chapter are part of a larger, historic, community-based conservation (CBC) system of park planning that emerged in the 1980s.[6] CBC is a much-needed trend in national park development, one nearly absent for most of the worldwide history of conservation. Yet by the end of the twentieth century its time had come. Mexican ecologist Arturo Gómez-Pompa made this clear: "We can no longer earmark an area as a 'Nature Reserve: Keep Out' and have it policed, while multitudes of starving peasants in the vicinity are looking for a suitable spot to plant next season's crops."[7] Park planners across the Global South have come to realize this. James Nations, an ecological anthropologist who has done extensive field work in the Lacandón Rainforest of Chiapas, Mexico, has argued that "national parks and reserves must go beyond the goals of protecting species and preserving habitat. . . . [They] must take into account the needs of local people."[8] The Lacandón, North America's largest montane rainforest, is an example of a place where that did not immediately occur when UNESCO, with the Mexican government's blessing, created the Montes Azules Biosphere Reserve in 1978. The local backlash, especially from Indigenous peoples of the region, was swift and fierce. They insisted there be an "Indian Farmers' Preserve" instead, and urged local residents to seize parts of the "unoccupied jungle."[9]

This scenario could have been avoided if UNESCO and Mexico had incorporated a community-based system. In their seminal volume on CBC, Western and Wright defined the strategy as that which includes "the coexistence of people and nature, as distinct from protectionism and the segregation of people from nature." They explore how CBC can take on many different forms, and is dependent on factors such as culture and funding, but "if nothing else . . . can help buffer areas from ecological impoverishment"—especially as the world's 8,000 national parks and protected areas that cover 4 percent of the earth's surface suffer from ecological degradation, habitat fragmentation, edge effects, and species extinction. This concept illustrates well the importance of the Costa Rican Indigenous reserve system described below in which Native lands adjoin national parks and help provide biological connectivity and ecological corridors. As Western and Wright suggest, the end sum is vital: "At stake is nothing less than the fate of the natural world and its resources."[10]

There are problems that accompany CBC. Stan Stevens has warned that because too often the initiatives are based on funding sources far from a park "they can fall short of real community-based conservation," and leaders of sponsoring NGOs or foundations "may have different ideas from Indigenous communities about what community-based conservation is." But the values of linking Indigenous rights with conservation are worth the efforts. Native peoples' contributions include an "intimate knowledge of local geography and ecology," knowing "sacred places and species," and being "skilled and concerned observers" of changing land uses.[11] Indigenous groups gain in the process, too, especially with attaining greater recognition as distinct nations with their own communal lands, and by gaining benefits that involve local economic development and control over tourism.

Comparatively, there are places in the Western Hemisphere that in many ways adhere to CBC, and have for decades, but perhaps without labelling their strategies as such. For example, in Mexico, the government of Lázaro Cárdenas (1934–1940) established national parks more as community parks for access to local populations and ecological restoration than as tourist destinations. Most of those were rather small, but designed to be near where Mexicans would use them for day outings, and to protect watersheds for sustaining local forests and water sources.[12] And while these parks do not exactly advance the CBC model, they can be viewed as alternatives to park systems in First World countries, especially as the Mexicans established them for local use, without confiscating large sections of land that had been used for agriculture, grazing, and forestry for generations. More similar in Mexico to the CBC strategy is the country's system of community forests. Not a part of the national parks, Mexico's vast network of community forests, managed at local levels by *campesino* and Indigenous groups, represent conservation based on local input. And while important ecological benefits are accrued in the process, the community forests are primarily for economic uses of the land (logging and forest products), but with a more sustainable focus than that of industrial forestry. They should not be lumped in with how other countries are incorporating parks into CBC but are worthy of comparative mention here.[13]

Farther south in Honduras. there have been successes to move away from "fortress conservation" to Indigenous CBC models, especially at UNESCO's Río Plátano Biosphere Reserve in coastal Miskitia. While some human activity is prohibited there for purposes of environmental conservation, local Miskito Indians maintain access to lands within the reserve for subsistence agriculture, especially as they understand and maintain a highly gendered commitment to land tenure and farming. Still, some of UNESCO's plans for "sustainable systems" are more on paper than in reality, as according to Sharlene Mollett, "paradigms for national development and notions of national progress continuously devalue Indigenous tenure arrangements and land-use systems."[14]

In Panama there have been notable successes in Indigenous conservation initiatives via parks. In the 1980s the Kuna Indians on Panama's Caribbean coastal islands established what anthropologist Jason Clay has called "the world's first internationally recognized forest park created by an indigenous group." The park creates revenues for the Kuna from ecotourists eager to learn about the tropical rainforest, and from their sale of "research rights" to scientists who come to the region for tropical research projects. The Kuna control all access to the park and require reports from the scientists before they leave. They require the research teams to hire Kuna assistants to accompany them throughout the forest. As Clay suggests, the

Kuna have "established a precedent for other indigenous groups, and even countries, regarding research undertaken on their land."[15]

Similarly, in Colombia, in a successful attempt to restore Indigenous lands that mining companies and large-scale ranches had nearly destroyed, in 1984 a group of fifty-six Indian communities banded together to form a cooperative to replant, restore, and protect their forests along with their cultures and human rights. Working with nurseries run by local communities in southern Colombia, the Indians planted thousands of native-species trees. The renewed forests help protect watersheds, provide fruits and nuts for local consumption and sale, and produce sustainable stands for firewood. Thus, the forests are essential to the long-standing welfare of these Native groups.[16] The Colombian government enshrined these concepts into law in 1994, creating Zonas de Reserva Campesina (Rural Workers Reserves) recognizing that Indigenous groups are allied in the effort to conserve protected areas and allowing them more rights in them than for squatters who move in. Thus, as a part of the Colombian national park system, these reserves help conceive a newer notion of conservation, one that blends rural Indigenous groups and working peoples within the concept of nature.[17]

Perhaps these types of community-based initiatives are reflective of what famed Amazonianist anthropologist Darrell Posey has called "the conscience of conservation." Using the model of Brazil's national park development, which includes Kayapó Indigenous forest uses in remote parts of the Amazon, he has advocated for a bridge between natural, social, and folk sciences. Posey's research on Kayapó understandings of the environment shows how even their language reveals nuanced ways to understand different species of plants, their botanical and medicinal uses, and their role in local economies. Likewise, the Indians' methods of extracting resources from the plants and knowledge of how and when to harvest them and how to conserve them over time are valuable by-products of the ways in which conservation can be a bridge between Brazil's national park system and its agency for Indigenous affairs, and between environmentalist agendas for forest protection and human rights organizations' agendas for survival of Indigenous groups. Due to this conservation strategy, the Kayapó and other groups continue surviving on their own well-established understandings of the rainforest and the foods, pharmacopeia, and economic resources it provides.[18]

II: Preserving Native Cultural Resources

Southern Alberta: "A Magical Landscape"

Writing-on-Stone Provincial Park, also called the Áísínai' pi National Historic Site of Canada, in the Milk River Valley of southern Alberta represents one of the greatest collections of prehistoric petroglyphs (rock carvings) and pictographs (rock drawings) in the Western Hemisphere. In fact, *Áísínai' pi* is Blackfoot for "where the drawings are." The valley is characterized by an arid landscape spotted with eroded sandstone gullies and coulees, or badlands, and rock formations typical of this part of the Northwestern Plains. At Writing-on-Stone, the coulees are deep, forming large cliff walls and an amazing array of capstone, mushroom-shaped rocks known as hoodoos created by thousands of years of erosion from brutal winds, blowing sand, harsh rain, and continuous cycles of freezing and thawing ice. Geologists estimate that approximately 15,000 to 20,000 years ago the receding and melting glaciers of the last Ice Age sent great quantities of water through this area, helping to shape the valley's unique formations. In promotional literature, the government of Alberta has declared that these processes "created fantastic shapes and a magical landscape."[19]

On the cliffs that form the backdrop of this park are the petroglyphs that tell stories of early peoples in the area, what they hunted, the conflicts that they had with other groups, and the arrival and use of horses (by the eighteenth century), and include depictions of relations with European newcomers as time moved into the nineteenth century. There are an incredible 50,000-odd drawings, extending from the prehistoric period to the 1920s.[20] This is the historical region of the Southern Piegan (part of the Blackfoot Nation, or in the United States, the Blackfeet), whose ancient descendants may have been the artists of the petroglyphs and who today maintain a very real presence and management role for Writing-on-Stone

Provincial Park. The Cree Nation also considers this a sacred place from its past.

According to Blackfoot beliefs, it was Old Man, or Napi the supernatural trickster, who created the world, and formed the badlands from his travels in the region. He taught the people how to survive in this country, and the land remains today much as he created it then. The cliff walls provided shelter from the Chinook winds (warming winds from the Pacific Ocean that cross the Rockies and descend into interior regions, causing higher temperatures and snow to melt) that characterize southern Alberta—shelter that attracted the Blackfoot and Cree to hunt, gather firewood and food, and make encampments there as early as 3,000 years ago. While the Blackfoot are the First Nation most affiliated with the park, other Native peoples like the Gros Ventre, Blood or Piegan, Assiniboine, Crow, Kootenay, and Shoshone frequented the area and likely contributed to the petroglyphs. Some groups occasionally wintered here, again making use of the natural shelters and abundant wood and game. The dry valleys made for useful travel routes and places where hunting and war parties could conceal themselves from bison and other game and from enemy peoples. Due to the hoodoos and ancient drawings, the area became a sacred space for Aboriginals, a place to revere and fear the spirit world, to seek spiritual guidance by practising rituals and vision quests. To them the hoodoos were actually giant men turned to stone by the Great Spirit as punishment for evil deeds. The area also became an important burial ground for deceased elders of the Blackfoot and other peoples who placed the corpses in crevices and caves abundant in the sandstone formations, allowing "the spirits of the dead easy access to the afterworld."[21]

The petroglyphs represent a wide variety of cultural recording. Native artists used charcoal and red ochre to paint the figures, and much of the artwork was biographical, commemorating events like battles and hunts. We learn that the people here hunted bison, deer, bear, elk, and bighorn sheep, and in battles they used bows, shields, spears, hatchets, and, much later, guns. We see evidence of tipis and travois, and the dogs that helped move them. There are also likely depictions of dreams, visions, and spiritual rituals.[22]

That the government of Alberta established Writing-on-Stone Provincial Park in 1957 helped in a major way to preserve the First Nations' cultural resources and to end the looting, vandalism, and graffiti that threatened to destroy the artwork in the nineteenth and twentieth centuries.[23] It also signalled how the park could serve as a place for cultural and environmental education and as a boon to the local economy as it draws tourists visiting Dinosaur Provincial Park just north of Writing-on-Stone and the Canadian Rockies to the west.[24] Access to the petroglyphs is limited at Writing-on-Stone; tour guides, usually Native, must lead visitors on guided hikes that require advance ticketing as a way to protect against vandalism and to ensure that visitors get Native perspectives. That the Blackfoot are so integral to the park, serve as its trail guides, and continue to use the area for sacred ceremonies, as do other First Nations, speaks well for Writing-on-Stone being a prime example of Indigenous park conservation and the protection of cultural resources. In many ways all of this represents a decolonizing process, in that the Blackfoot are maintaining their own power to control the narrative of their past, whereas Indigenous voices or presence are virtually absent in many North American national parks. Both the Blackfoot and the Alberta government worked with the United Nations Educational, Scientific, and Cultural Organization (UNESCO) to declare the park a world heritage site.

Writing-on-Stone is the northernmost site of these ancient Indigenous petroglyphs. It is among many such sites that include similarly preserved Native artwork, including Columbia Hills and Pictograph Cave state parks in Montana; Medicine Lodge State Archaeological Site, Castle Gardens, Legend Rock, and White Mountain Petroglyphs in Wyoming; Nine Mile Canyon (supposedly the "world's longest art gallery") and Dry Fork Petroglyphs in Utah; Tumamoc Hill and Deer Valley Petroglyph Preserve in Arizona; Inscription Rock at El Morro and Petroglyph national monuments in New Mexico; and Serranía de Chiribiquete National Natural Park in Colombia.[25] One of the southernmost sites is Sete Cidades National Park in Brazil.

Northern Brazil: Sete Cidades National Park

The state of Piauí in northern Brazil is home to some of the world's most numerous prehistoric Indigenous petroglyphs and pictographs, and according to some archaeologists, the very earliest ones in the Americas.

They are divided between Serra da Capivara National Park in southeastern Piauí (the park that is home to what are considered the oldest petroglyphs in the Western Hemisphere) and Sete Cidades National Park in the northern part of the state.

Brazil's second national park, proclaimed by President Jânio Quadros in 1961, Sete Cidades protects one of the country's (and perhaps all of South America's) most extensive array of prehistoric Indigenous petroglyphs and pictographs. Meaning the "seven cities" in Portuguese, Sete Cidades is home to seven different groupings of rock outcrops and formations, all resembling little "cities" that are characterized by Indigenous artwork recording many facets of prehistoric lifeways and spirituality, and which provide clues regarding the wildlife of the region in past times. The national park consists of 6,304 hectares and is located within the Brazilian Northeast's *cerrado* ecosystem, a bioregion comprised of a xeric and thorny scrubforest. The *cerrado* here abuts the *caatinga*—another ecosystem unique to the Brazilian Northeast that is characterized by dry, deciduous forest and desert-like savanna. The two overlapping ecosystems create a high level of biodiversity and endemism that the park helps to protect. Most of the park, in fact, is kept provisionally closed to visitors as a means to protect the fragile environment. As at Writing-on-Stone, the dry climate of the *cerrado* has helped preserve the artwork at Sete Cidades over time. Remarkably, the petroglyphs at Sete Cidades resemble very closely those in the North American West.

The biggest difference with Sete Cidades, however, is that there are very few Indigenous peoples in Piauí or the surrounding area who descend from the prehistoric peoples who created this artwork. The region at one time was inhabited or visited by the now extinct Poti and Quirridi peoples, and possibly by ancestors of the Tabajara tribe. Radio-carbon testing has estimated that many of the petroglyphs were created as long as 10,000 years ago, although some could be as recent as from the nineteenth century.[26] After centuries of being enslaved and slaughtered by colonists in northeast Brazil and dying from European diseases, only a few communities of Tabajara remain in remote parts of southern Ceará (bordering Piauí to the east). But the national park protects this site that was frequented by ancient peoples. As a sign at the park entrance states (translated from

Portuguese), "The mark of prehistoric man should make us remember the constant respect for our ancestors, our heritage, and above all else, nature."

Likewise, the national park protects an amazing array of badlands formations that date back to their possible creation 190 million years ago. The sandstone outcroppings and formations are from the Devonian strata of the Parnaiba sedimentary basin that formed during the Palaeozoic era. As at Writing-on-Stone, it was wind and pluvial water that created the formations on which the petroglyphs were drawn.[27] In the seven different "cities" are drawings of deer, hunting rituals, spiritual deities (especially the sun god), and many examples of human hands (one with six fingers). Some scholars believe the hands could be from the Tabajara people from 6,000 years ago.[28]

Thus, like its North American counterparts, Sete Cidades combines conservation of cultural and natural resources. It preserves prehistoric images while protecting the flora and fauna of the fragile and threatened *cerrado* ecosystem. There is little to no interpretative literature available at the park, and there are no Tabajara who work there. Likewise there are very few publications about the park, especially books (and none in English). Thus, the opportunity is ripe for more research, especially that of comparative analysis with similar areas across the Americas. Such analysis would have to include discussion on how and why a Native voice is more absent in these parks, and how the state, while indeed working to conserve Indigenous cultural resources against vandalism or excessive commercialism, has manipulated such archaeological treasures to its advantage (for tourism, economic development, etc.). In such areas with few extant Indigenous communities, it seems easy to relegate Native history to prehistoric times, when a robust opportunity also presents itself at such parks to have more interpretation and presentation on the results of a larger colonization project and Indigenous demographic decline, as well as on the rights of remaining Native peoples.

III: Indigenous–National Park Relations

Western South Dakota: Badlands National Park

As mentioned above, the Southern Unit of Badlands National Park is set to become the first Native national park in the United States. The land in question was originally part of the Pine Ridge Reservation, including Sheep Mountain Table, which the Oglala consider sacred, but which the US government excised from the reservation during the Second World War to be used as the Pine Ridge Aerial Gunnery Range. In 1968, as the gunnery range ceased to be in operation, the government transferred the land to Badlands National Park, which it abuts, but without seeking input from the tribe. Hence, the Oglala (a band of the Lakota Sioux) logically wanted it back. In 1976, the NPS entered into a joint management agreement with the Oglala for the South Unit, with most of the employees being Native who are responsible for the day-to-day operations of the unit. The plan to form a new park expands on that initiative, could employ up to 200 Oglala park managers and workers, and is being viewed by most Oglala as a way to regain their rights. The tribal park will also include a Lakota Heritage and Education Center and an archaeological research centre that would be set aside to catalogue artifacts from the area. According to an NPS document, the heritage centre would be the "primary visitor contact area for the park." Part of the restructuring includes a name change for the South Unit, tentatively to be called Crazy Horse Tribal National Park (after the famed Oglala leader whom a force of US Cavalry murdered in 1877 in western Nebraska).[29]

According to the NPS, the new park will work to restore "the health and vibrancy of the prairie," will expand the bison herd, and will allow visitors "to experience the natural grandeur of the South Unit and the heritage of the Oglala Sioux people." The Lakota term for "bad lands" (or more literally, "no good soil") is *mako sika*, and inside the visitors' centre at this park is a banner explaining, "For the Lakota, the White River Badlands is a part of home. Its harsh splendor reflects the people's journey through time, as nomads, as residents, as citizens of two nations." The Oglala have already started running an 800-head herd of bison on the national park land, with hopes of increasing it to 1200.[30] This is in addition to previous grazing rights that the US government restored to them earlier, as Badlands is one of the only national parks to allow livestock grazing and haying operations within park boundaries, although some tribal members wonder if these rights will be taken away with the newer park designation. Likewise, the NPS had already established that certain parts of the unit were off limits to non-Native tourists to respect Oglala ceremonial sites.[31]

Thus has begun the historic transfer within Badlands National Park. It is new ground for the NPS, admitted park superintendent Eric Brunnemann: "We don't know what a Tribal National Park is." Officials from both sides have been working to define it since 2013, but there are various layers of approval, especially that of Congress, which are needed before it can officially be created (as of October 2015 there had not been much administrative change).[32] The NPS will work with the Oglala to increase citizen involvement for park management and law enforcement. While the park will be tribal, federal funding will still be assured while the Oglala implement their own entrance fees to be used for park operations. Likewise, for the duration of the transition, current NPS employees will assist in the on-the-job training for managing the park, with Oglala members filling administrative and other posts and assuming all park responsibilities when ready. Finally, policy changes will allow tribal members to hunt in the national park, part of the plan "to preserve cultural and historic resources and values."[33]

Southeastern California: Death Valley National Park

The name itself conjures up images of barrenness and evil like other badlands areas of the North American West (think Hell's Half Acre, Wyoming; Valley of Fire, Nevada; Devil's Kitchen and Goblin Valley, Utah; El Malpais [Spanish for "the bad country"], New Mexico; Craters of the Moon, Idaho; and the list goes on). Death Valley, mainly in southeastern California but with a triangular corner crossing into Nevada, is centred squarely in the Mojave Desert, where summers are brutally hot (with temperatures regularly in the 40s Centigrade), and where one can visit the lowest point in North America (63 metres below sea level). But it is uniquely beautiful, with rock formations and sweeping desert valleys, and it has been home for generations to the Western Shoshone Indians, who have more recently named themselves the Timbisha Shoshone Band.[34]

The Timbisha's relationship with Death Valley can be traced to long before Euro-Americans invaded the region and is imbued with a sacred connectedness to place. Their creation story recalls how the people began at Ubehebe Crater, where Coyote carried them in. Later they crawled out of his basket and dispersed to live around Death Valley, and have now been there "since time immemorial." Anthropologists relate how the Timbisha descended from prehistoric peoples who spent summers in the park's Panamint Mountains and wintered on Death Valley's floor. Such an arrangement led to survival in the harsh terrain, as the different ecological zones produced different types of plants and animals on which the Shoshone depended. Especially important was their harvesting piñon nuts and mesquite pods, and hunting deer, desert bighorn sheep, and rabbits.[35] In the modern era, the relationship they have had with the NPS has (to put it mildly) not been good since the park came into existence, first as Death Valley National Monument in 1933.[36] When its status changed to Death Valley National Park in 1994, relations between the NPS and the Timbisha began to improve, but only after decades of fighting by the Timbisha for their land.

The Shoshones' story is quite different from that of the Oglala in South Dakota. The Indigenous population of Death Valley is small and there has been no move for co-management or to create a separate park. Instead, the Shoshones have fought and won to have their own reservation within the park—the only US national park to have that distinction. The road to 1994, when that finally became a reality, however, was pockmarked with racist policy, resentment of local mining companies and ranchers in the region toward Native Americans, and a lack of understanding of American Indian rights.

That scenario started like so many other national park cases of Native dispossession around the United States, with the NPS creating parks devoid of people. It is also a typical story of interagency squabbling and different interpretations of policy, as both the Bureau of Indian Affairs (BIA) and NPS had roles in governing the Western Shoshone. Native land claims, the Dawes Act allotment, policy changes during the 1930s when

BIA director John Collier brought more enlightened values to the agency, the termination era (the Western Shoshone did not have official government recognition until 1983), and many policies since affected the Timbisha. Other Native groups living near national parks around the United States were affected by NPS policies, but the difference here is that the Shoshone lived *within* the park and refused to leave, even when bauxite mining operators put pressure on the government to have them ousted in the 1930s. But after going around and around on the issue for seven decades, Congress finally passed the California Desert Protection Act of 1994. Among other things, the Act changed Death Valley from a national monument to a national park, and in a roundabout way led to the Timbisha Homeland Act, which President Bill Clinton signed into law in 2000. The Timbisha Shoshone finally got their reservation, smaller than originally hoped for at 3,030 hectares, but they viewed the act as a triumph. Apart from this landmark success, as one study reported, it also represented how the NPS "attained a new sensitivity to Native concerns."[37]

Southern Costa Rica: Indigenous Reserves

The final case study here is that of the Costa Rican experience. Overall, it is quite different from Native conservation initiatives in other countries, but because it is less known, and because it involves national policies instead of park-by-park ones, it can serve as a fitting comparative to this study on hemispheric Native conservation. Costa Rica is a small nation in Central America (51,100 square kilometres, just smaller than West Virginia) and has a percentage of Native peoples much smaller than countries such as Guatemala or Honduras. This is primarily due to the fact that there was only a small Indigenous population in the region at the time of the European invasion, as Costa Rica was never part of a large Native empire like that of the Maya further to the north or the Inca in the Andes. But like Indigenous peoples everywhere, pre-Columbian Natives here adapted culturally to local tropical environments and thrived, although not in densely populated urban areas.[38] Likewise, after their invasion Spaniards quickly took over the areas that were most conducive to European-style agriculture and ranching, such as the Central Valley, which could sustain grain production and grazing, and Guanacaste in the Northwest, which, unlike the tropical rainforest that covers much of Costa Rica, is characterized by dry deciduous forest that was also excellent for grains, cotton, and cattle. Alfred Crosby has referred to such areas as "neo-Europes" in a process for Costa Rica that Carolyn Hall has called "ecological colonialism."[39] But Native peoples did not disappear, and have sustained their cultures and communities over time. At a population of around 36,500, they primarily live in twenty-two Indigenous reserves (representing twenty-two distinct tribes), the vast majority of which are located in the southern end of the country and adjacent to national parks.[40]

This proximity gives the Indigenous communities a special relationship to the protected areas, and in some ways their reserves are protected like the parks themselves. For example, Costa Rica's *Ley Indígena* (Indigenous Law) of 1977 established important legal parameters, including the stipulation that no non-Indians could own land on the reserves. The law is enforced by the National Commission on Indigenous Affairs (CONAI), an autonomous agency that is the government's link to Costa Rican Indigenous people. CONAI has worked with various tribes to consolidate their lands, and with various Indigenous cooperatives that have formed to protect lifeways, sustainable agriculture, and the local environment on reserves that surround national parks. Some groups have affiliated with international movements for financial support for cultural and environmental conservation.[41]

The environmental problems that the Costa Rican Indigenous groups face are grave. The Térraba people have been especially concerned with illegal logging that occurs in and around their reserve. Other groups have struggled economically and are now raising local products organically for international markets. The Bribri grow organic cacao on their reserve for a US market and are diversifying into organic nutmeg, ginger, cinnamon, and bananas for European consumers. They and other groups are getting broad international support for the initiatives, which are being tied to environmental protection of the region that includes linking the Indigenous reserves with national parks. Since the mid-1990s, the private organization The Nature Conservancy has worked with a local Indigenous association in southern Costa Rica on its Parks in Peril project, which seeks to connect La Amistad National Park and its surroundings (including Native reserves) into a biological corridor stretching to the Caribbean. As one

CONAI official put it, "many of the national parks were created near indigenous communities in the South because of their [the Indians'] good maintenance of the environment. . . . The Indians kept the land well."[42]

Finally, on the southern Caribbean coast is Cahuita National Park—a paradise-like setting with pristine beaches, tropical forest, abundant wildlife, and an endangered reef. When the government established the park in the 1970s, it was based on wise environmental foresight to protect a beautiful, fragile area threatened by commercial development.[43] But there was no local input, and residents resented the plan. As one study related, at the time there was "little direct experience in responding to the large majority of rural peasant cultures living in and around Costa Rican national parks." The government confiscated land via eminent domain and relocated people out of the parks—actions that have been costly and disruptive even though the larger results were for national conservation objectives.[44]

But the end of the story is better than the beginning. Management objectives began to change in the 1980s to include residential use of park resources. Consideration of local lifestyle would have "important implications" for how park managers could achieve "conservation objectives for the park in its sociocultural context." This was tricky, as for generations many local residents lived off hunting and marketing sea turtles that lay their eggs on Cahuita's beaches. But as sea turtles were severely endangered, park officials needed to work with local residents, instituting environmental education measures and allowing other areas for resource uses, and opening more tourist-based employment opportunities for local residents. In the end, the plan was to work with residents (in this region, a blended mix of Indigenous and non-Indigenous peoples) and cooperate with surrounding landowners, so that park managers could slow down or prevent clearcutting of the forests in and around Cahuita and promote ecological restoration on affected lands.[45]

Conclusion: Reasons For Hope

The case studies presented here provide good reason to believe that relations between Native peoples and state-enacted protected areas are indeed improving across the Western Hemisphere. As the editors for this volume proclaimed at the end of their Introduction, an important goal of the workshop that we contributors attended, and for the book, was to illustrate how hope and optimism are "a more accurate reflection of the recent history of small-scale, local, and Indigenous environmental activism than a book that measured their failures." For the United States, in addition to the studies offered here from South Dakota and California, there now is a history of improved relations between Native groups and American parks. Starting in 1931 the Navajo Tribal Council and the NPS formed an agreement to manage Canyon de Chelly National Monument (which protects Anasazi cliff dwellings) in northeastern Arizona as a joint venture, since the park is entirely on Navajo Reservation lands.[46] Since 1975, the Havasupai people of Arizona and the NPS reached a landmark decision that created the Havasupai Use Lands within Grand Canyon National Park, an arrangement that provided legal rights to the Indians to carry out traditional land uses, including livestock grazing, within the park—the first such Indigenous land use agreement in any US national park. The Ute Nation established its own Ute Mountain Tribal Park in southwestern Colorado that is run entirely on their terms and with rigidly enforced visitation policies. The Navajo created and manage Monument Valley Tribal Park in northeastern Arizona and southeastern Utah, taking advantage of an important US highway that runs through the region with millions of tourists a year eager to see the unforgettable buttes and rock formations and to frequent the Native gift shops. They also run the park and tourist centre at the Four Corners monument. The Gwich'in people of Alaska have attained recognition of their lands within the Alaska National Wildlife Refuge, and have gained stricter protection of the calving grounds for the Porcupine caribou herd. And in all Alaskan national parks Native peoples are now permitted to hunt, fish, and trap.[47] This is especially important for the Tlingit, who regularly collect seabird eggs as part of their cultural lifeway and food production in Glacier Bay National Park. These improved relations are reflected in the Sitka language at the Historical Park and Indigenous Culture Center.[48] All of these practices of Native hunting and fishing provoke questions about what happens when there are endangered and threatened species at stake, and at times this has caused significant issues between Indigenous groups and environmental organizations. Yet Native peoples should have the right to hunt and fish according to their traditions, and often they do ensure conservation measures.[49]

Other success stories abound from around the United States, especially after the NPS released a document entitled "Native American Relationship Management Policy" in 1987. The policy spelled out the NPS's responsibility for confronting issues between American Indians and the national parks and, for the first time, provided park personnel with a directive to recognize and consult Native Americans with connections to national park lands. The document also called for recognizing the right of Indigenous peoples to use national park lands for harvesting of plants and animals for traditional, subsistence, and religious activities.[50] Examples of improved relations since that policy was enacted include Hopi Indians being allowed into Mesa Verde National Park in southwestern Colorado to perform traditional ceremonies to honour their ancestors, the Anasazi, whose cliff dwellings are preserved there. In northern Montana, the Blackfeet Indians no longer have to pay entrance fees at Glacier National Park, have access to places there that they consider sacred, and have the right to gather wild plants by permit.[51] In northern California, the Yurok Indians and the NPS have come to agreements on various levels of co-management of some sectors of Redwoods National Park. In Montana, the Kootenay-Salish have worked with the US National Forest Service and the Department of Highways to ensure that elk and wolves have conduits for their annual transmigrations and roaming.[52] As John Welch (this volume) has shown, Native conservation and resource management need not be centred solely within national, state, or provincial parks, but indeed, as the case of the White Mountain Apache Tribe in Arizona attests, there can be "sovereignty-driven" heritage conservation.

Likewise, there are examples of the concept of Native conservation being applied in venues outside of national park settings via environmental organizations. The National Wildlife Federation has entered into "conservation partnerships" with a variety of tribes across the country to learn from and work with them on wildlife protection programs. Those include the Cocopah Nation of Arizona and a project to conserve the lower Colorado River ecosystem as an important migratory point for neotropical and other wetlands birds while at the same time working to restore and protect the river for the Tribe's own economic and cultural resources; a partnership with the Intertribal Bison Cooperative on the Northern Plains to protect Yellowstone bison and develop buffalo herds for return to tribal lands;

an initiative to work with the Natives of the Campo Kumeyaay Reservation in southern California who are establishing a wind turbine farm on their lands to generate cleaner electricity for the reservation and to sell to local power companies; a program to work with the Red Lake Chippewa of Minnesota to restore and protect lakes and wetlands on their lands that generates an increase in the walleye fishery so vital to the Chippewa's culture and economy; and a program with the Northern Cheyenne of Montana and a "coalition of uncommon allies" made up of hunters, anglers, ranchers, environmentalists, and Indians "to protect the environmental and cultural landscape" of the Powder River Basin.[53]

Canada has made significant steps in recognizing Indigenous rights within national parks, only after first following a US colonialist conservation model by excluding Native peoples from some of the first national parks.[54] Beginning in the 1970s, Minister of Indian Affairs Jean Chrétien vowed that newly created Kluane, Auyuittuq, and Nahanni national parks in the Yukon and the Northwest Territories would not interfere with the traditional lifeways and wildlife resources of Canada's northern Native peoples. Parks Canada officially endorsed the policy in 1979 for parks in the territories, and later in 1994 for elsewhere in the country. The federal agency also provided language about involvement of Aboriginal peoples and integrated co-management into the structure of park operations. With these policies in mind, as Brad Martin relates in *A Century of Parks Canada*, the Inuvialuit peoples took a very active role in the creation of Ivvavik National Park in Yukon Territory.[55] And as we see here in this volume (Willow), Native rights for resource management in western Ontario are not only strategies for survival but also serve as a case study of First Nations environmentalism.

This record, however, as historian John Sandlos has described it, is not without problems, especially ones related to co-management objectives, "bureaucratic approaches" rather than Indigenous understandings of conservation, and ones that arise when First Nations people serve only "of an advisory nature." Such a colonial mentality allows the federal government of Canada to "claim that it has adopted a participatory approach without requiring the surrender of its political authority in the region," whereas a more appropriate approach would be "to include restoring Native management regimes that existed prior to the advent of state management."[56]

There has been more success in combatting such colonialism in British Columbia, perhaps, with the development of Indigenous tribal parks. As Emery Hartley has shown, 2014 marked the thirtieth anniversary of the Meares Island Tribal Park Declaration (renewed in ceremony in 2014) of the Tla-o-qui-aht First Nation and with the support of the NGO Friends of Clayoquot Sound. The declaration originated to oppose industrial logging operations on the island that would have destroyed a Tla-o-qui-aht sacred space and significantly altered the island's old-growth temperate rainforest environment. It was in 1984 that Chief Moses Martin initiated a blockade against corporate giant MacMillan Bloedel, leading the standoff with the now famous words, "You are welcome to visit our garden, but leave your chainsaws in the boat"—words that inspired what Hartley describes as a significant "paradigm shift" not only for BC but for "other nations, building global networks for the conservation of place and culture."[57]

In Latin America there have been similar success stories but with taints of colonialism still apparent. Brazil was the first country to recognize Indigenous lifeways back in 1961 when the government established Xingu National Park in the Amazon. A principal goal of the park was to ensure that resident Xingu Indians had a place to maintain their way of life and culture without fear of encroachment by non-Indigenous peoples or industries vying to extract minerals. Peru's Huascarán National Park, created in 1975 to protect the nation's highest peak, provides for Indigenous grazing rights in the lower elevations of the park. Panama's Darién National Park (another UNESCO biosphere reserve and World Heritage Site), established in 1980, includes and protects inhabited Indigenous lands. So do Peru's Manu National Park and Biosphere Reserve (home to several Amazonian Indigenous peoples), Ecuador's Yasuní National Park and Biosphere Reserve, Venezuela's Canaima National Park (home to the Pemon Indians), and Colombia's Cahuinarí National Park and Sierra Nevada de Santa Marta National Park and Biosphere Reserve, which were established in the late 1970s and 1980s. At Sierra Nevada de Santa Marta, 70 percent of the park is an Indigenous reserve for the Kogi Indians, with exclusive subsistence rights. Such efforts got a significant boost when the International Union for the Conservation of Nature instituted new guidelines in 1984 on how national parks and nature preserves must be more sensitive to Indigenous peoples and their rights and uses to lands within parks.[58]

But similar to Canada, in Latin America conservation initiatives are often coupled with colonial mentality and state control. In Guatemala, for example, the Los Altos de San Miguel Regional Municipal Park encompasses Mayan communities and protects communal grazing, forestry, and water management. The park is helping to shed concepts of "fortress conservation," but challenges yet exist in ensuring that the initiatives reinforce local management goals and that livelihood from forest resources continues for the regional Native population. Pressures exist on the system from outside land-grabbing ventures, exploration for biofuels, and international organizations wanting to create ecological preserves—initiatives that often have official state support for national economic development.[59] In Peru's Asháninka Communal Reserve of the Peruvian Amazon, as Emily Caruso has shown, the "comanagement of communal resources" has been more a "state tool for discipline of a marginal space" and for "bringing Indigenous peoples into the bureaucratic fold." While Native peoples hold the view that they are in control of their land enclosed within Asháninka Reserve, the state actually maintains a large presence; the reserve is "imagined, narrated, and produced as a material place requiring state intervention."[60]

All the examples here, including the more specific case studies from Alberta, South Dakota, California, Costa Rica, and Brazil, discuss different levels of Native-park relations, and admittedly there is nothing typical about their comparative experiences.[61] Case studies and models do not have to be equal in scope to point out valuable lessons. But each speaks to different qualitative ways to measure success. Each suggests that while significant problems remain, Native-park relations are improving across the Americas, providing hope that conservation can continue to play a vital role in the process of improving relations between state powers and Indigenous peoples. After all, a common theme expressed in all but the Sete Cidades experiences here is the Native quest for control of their own lands. Changes and advances in the structure of conservation in national, provincial, state, and tribal parks, and on other public lands to include Native understandings, voices, ceremonial practices, and management, are welcome as appropriate first steps in that direction. Legal changes, like those in Death Valley National Park for the Timbisha Shoshone, of Crazy Horse National Tribal Park for the Oglala Lakota, and in Costa Rica for a variety of different Indigenous groups, will hopefully follow around the hemisphere. Finally, lessons learned from across the Americas, from southern Alberta to northern Brazil, should be compared and evaluated as the hemisphere and the world continue to shrink in size in terms of communication and transnational connections but not in the growing recognition of Native survival that is so dependent on land and on natural and cultural resources.

Notes

I thank research assistant Courtney Kennedy for her help on this chapter; in Brazil, Antonio Carlos Alves da Silva and Edilson Rodrigues for field research at Sete Cidades National Park; workshop participants Anna Willow, Liza Piper, and Jon Clapperton for their useful suggestions on revisions; and the University of Calgary Press's peer reviewers for compelling thoughts and wise suggestions. Funding for the research of this chapter in Canada and Brazil was gratefully supported by the Louise Welsh Chair in History at the University of Oklahoma.

1   "Native National Park," *New York Times*, 23 June 2013, 1. As of September 2016 there has not been much change to the status, as the Lakota people are still waiting complete congressional approval.

2   The terms "Native" and "Indigenous" people will be used interchangeably in this chapter, respecting preferred terms of peoples being discussed. Above the 49th parallel I will use "First Nations," as that is the standard convention in Canada, whereas in the United States most Native peoples still prefer the term "American Indian."

3   Stan Stevens, ed., *Indigenous Peoples, National Parks, and Protected Areas* (Tucson: University of Arizona Press, 2014); Patrick C. West and Steven R. Brechin, eds., *Resident Peoples and National Parks: Social Dilemmas and Strategies in International Conservation* (Tucson: University of Arizona Press, 1991); Stan Stevens, *Conservation through Cultural Survival: Indigenous Peoples and Protected Areas* (Washington, DC: Island Press, 1997); Jim Igoe, *Conservation and Globalization: A Study of National Parks and Indigenous Communities from East Africa to South Dakota* (Belmont, CA: Thompson and Wadsworth, 2004); Mark Dowie, *Conservation Refugees: The Hundred-Year Conflict between Global Conservation and Native Peoples* (Cambridge, MA: MIT Press, 2009); P. G. Veit and C. Benson, *When Parks and People Collide*, Carnegie Council for Ethics in International Affairs (16 October 2009); Ezra D. Rashkow, "Idealizing Inhabited Wilderness: A Revision to the History of Indigenous Peoples and National Parks," *History Compass* 12 (2014): 818–32; Dennis Martinez, "Protected Areas, Indigenous Peoples, and the Western Idea of Nature," in *People, Places, and Parks: Proceedings of the 2005 George Wright Society Conference on Parks, Protected Areas, and Cultural Sites*, ed. David Harmon (Hancock, MI: The George Wright Society, 2006); and M. Colchester, "Conservation Policy and Indigenous Peoples,"

Environmental Science and Politics 7, no. 3 (2004): 145–53. Specifically for agriculture and conservation, see Bruce Campbell and Silvia López Ortíz, eds., *Integrating Agriculture, Conservation, and Ecotourism: Societal Influences* (New York: Springer, 2012).

4   Mark Spence, *Dispossessing the Wilderness: Indian Removal and the Making of National Parks* (New York: Oxford University Press, 1999); Karl Jacoby, *Crimes against Nature: Squatters, Poachers, and the Hidden History of American Conservation* (Berkeley: University of California Press, 2001); Robert H. Keller, Jr., and Michael F. Turek, *American Indians and National Parks* (Tucson: University of Arizona Press, 1998); Phillip Burnham, *Indian Country, God's Country: Native Americans and the National Parks* (Washington, DC: Island Press, 2000).

5   For newer analysis on this topic for the United States, see Jeanette Wolfley, "Reclaiming a Presence in Ancestral Lands: The Return of Native People to the National Parks," *Natural Resources Journal* 56 (Winter 2016): 55–80.

6   Standard works are David Western, ed., *Natural Connections: Perspectives on Community-Based Conservation* (Washington, DC: Island Press, 1994); Gary Meffe et al., eds., *Ecosystem Management: Adaption, Community-Based Conservation* (Washington, DC: Island Press, 2002); and J. Peter Brosius et al., eds., *Communities and Conservation: Histories and Politics of Community-Based Natural Resource Management* (Lanham, MD: AltaMira Books, 2005).

7   Quoted in James Nations, "Protected Areas in Tropical Rainforests," in *Lessons of the Rainforest*, ed. Suzanne Head and Robert Heinzman (San Francisco: Sierra Club Books, 1990), 214.

8   Ibid., 213.

9   Craig Urquhart, "In the Jungle, Civilization Approaches," *Toronto Star*, 1 October 2009, 15. Much of the opposition was spearheaded by the Zapatista Army for National Liberation, which came onto the scene in 1994 to protest the North American Free Trade Agreement (NAFTA).

10   David Western and R. Michael Wright, "The Background of Community-Based Conservation," in Western, *Natural Connections*, 8–9.

11   Stan Stevens, "Lessons and Directions," in Stevens, *Conservation through Cultural Survival*, 287, 266–67.

12   See Emily Wakild, *Revolutionary Parks: Conservation, Social Justice, and Mexico's National Parks, 1910–1940* (Tucson: University of Arizona Press, 2011).

13   See David Barton Bray et al., eds., *The Community Forests of Mexico: Managing for Sustainable Landscapes* (Austin: University of Texas Press, 2005). See also Martin Hébert and Michael Gabriel Rosen, "Community Forestry and the Paradoxes of Citizenship in Mexico: The Cases of Oaxaca and Guerrero," *Canadian Journal of Latin American and Caribbean Studies* 32, no. 63 (2007): 9–44.

14   Sharlene Mollett, "'Bargaining with Patriarchy': Miskito Struggles over Family Land in the Honduran Río Plátano Biosphere Reserve," in Stevens, *Indigenous Peoples*, 206, 209, quotation at 212. See also Peter Herlihy, "Indigenous Peoples and Biosphere

Conservation in the Mosquitia Rain Forest Corridor, Honduras," in Stevens, *Conservation through Cultural Survival*, 99–129.

15   Jason Clay, "Indigenous Peoples: The Miner's Canary for the Twentieth Century," in Head and Heinzman, *Lessons of the Rainforest*, 115. For more on the Kuna, see Stan Stevens, "New Alliances for Conservation," in Stevens, *Conservation through Cultural Survival*, 52.

16   Clay, "Indigenous Peoples," 116.

17   Claudia Leal, "¿Estado Natural? Historia de las áreas protegidas en Colombia," in progress, paper in author's possession, 3–4. For more on Colombia, see Stephen Amend and Thora Amend, eds., *¿Espacios sin habitantes? Parques nacionales de América del Sur* (Caracas: Editorial Nueva Sociedad, 1992); Astrid Ulloa, *La construcción del nativo ecológico: Complejidades, paradojas, y dilemas de la relación entre los movimientos indígenas y el ambientalismo en Colombia* (Bogotá: Instituto Colombiano de Antropología e Historia-Colciencias, 2004); and Julia Premauer, "Rights, Conservation, and Governance: Indigenous Peoples-National Parks Collaboration in Makuira, Colombia" (PhD diss., University of Manitoba, 2013). For another perspective on community involvement in parks, see Claudia Leal, "Conservation Memories: Vicissitudes of a Biodiversity Conservation Project in the Rainforests of Colombia, 1992–1998," *Environmental History* 20, no. 3 (2015): 368–95.

18   Darrell A. Posey, "Diachronic Ecotones and Anthropogenic Landscapes in Amazonia," in William Balée, ed., *Advances in Historical Ecology* (New York: Columbia University Press, 1998), 104–18, quotations at 104.

19   "Writing-on-Stone Provincial Park, Áísínai' pi National Historic Site" (Edmonton: Government of Alberta, 2009), 3; Neil L. Jennings, *In Plain Sight: Exploring the Wonders of Southern Alberta* (Surrey, BC: Rocky Mountain Books, 2010), 83–85.

20   From a conversation with Writing-on-Stone park guide Juanita Tallman (Blood, Blackfoot), 18 July 2012.

21   Government of Alberta, "Writing-on-Stone Provincial Park," 4–13, quotation at 12; Jennings, *In Plain Sight*, 84, 87–89, 92.

22   Personal observations; Jennings, *In Plain Sight*, 89, 92–93.

23   Significant evidence of vandalism and destruction is present in the archival material on the park's creation, especially eliciting calls for its development in the mid-1930s. Mutilation and "willful destruction" from rifle shootings and other vandalism became a central concern. See letters to Parks Department Alberta and to the provincial Ministry of Lands and Mines in files 83.498, 663, box 17, Provincial Archives of Alberta.

24   On Dinosaur Provincial Park, see Sterling Evans, "Badlands and Bones: Towards a Conservation and Social History of Dinosaur Provincial Park, Alberta," in *Place and Replace: Essays on Western Canada*, ed. Adele Perry, Esyllt W. Jones, and Leah Morton (Winnipeg: University of Manitoba Press, 2012), 250–70.

25   For important works on Native American pictographs, see Polly Schaafsma, *Indian Rock Art of the Southwest* (Albuquerque: University of New Mexico Press, 1986);

James D. Keyser and Michael A. Klassen, *Plains Indian Rock Art* (Seattle: University of Washington Press, 2001); Richard A. Rogers, *Native American Rock Art in the Contemporary Cultural Landscape* (Salt Lake City: University of Utah Press, 2018); and Paul Goldsmith, *Talking Stone: Rock Art of the Casos* (Salt Lake City: University of Utah Press, 2017). Specifically for Nine Mile Canyon in Utah, important works include Jerry Spangler, *Nine Mile Canyon: The Archaeological History of an American Treasure* (Salt Lake City: University of Utah Press, 2013); Jerry Spangler and Donna Kemp Spangler, *Last Chance Byway: The History of Nine Mile Canyon* (Salt Lake City: University of Utah Press, 2016); and Jerry Spangler and Donna Kemp Spangler, *Horned Snakes and Axle Grease: A Roadside Guide to the Archaeology, History, and Rock Art of Nine Mile Canyon* (Salt Lake City: Uinta Publishing, 2003).

26   Edilson Rodrigues, guide at Sete Cidades National Park, personal communication, 6 January 2014.

27   Jorge della Favera, "Sete Cidades National Park, Piauí State," Geological and Paleontological Sites of Brazil-025 (7 December 1999), 1–2, www.sigep.cprm.gov.br/sitio02english.htm (accessed 30 November 2013, site discontinued). See also F. Fortes, *Geologia de Sete Cidades* (Teresina, PI: Fundação Cultural Monsenhor Chaves, 1996).

28   della Favara, "Sete Cidades," 5.

29   "Native National Park," 1; Brandon Ecoffy, "Park Planners Respond to Critics," *Native Sun News*, 1 July 2013, 1–3, www.indianz.com/News/2013/012056.asp; United States National Park Service and Oglala Sioux Tribe Parks and Recreational Authority, "South Unit, Badlands National Park: Final General Management Plan and Environmental Impact Statement," US Department of the Interior, National Park Service (April 2012), v.

30   See also Jim Kent, "Managing Bison in the Badlands South Unit," *Classical* 24 (South Dakota Public Broadcasting, 16 May 2014), http://listen.sdpb.org/post/managing-bison-badlands-south-unit.

31   Igoe, *Conservation and Globalization*, 137.

32   Kent, "Managing Bison in the Badlands South Unit," 2.

33   United States National Park Service and Oglala Sioux Tribe Parks and Recreation Authority, "South Unit, Badlands National Park," vi. For Lakota environmentalism, see Bornali Halder, "Ecocide and Genocide: Explorations of Environmental Justice in Lakota Sioux Country," in *Ethnographies of Conservation: Environmentalism and the Distribution of Privilege*, ed. David Anderson and Eva Berglund (New York: Bergham Books, 2003), 101–18.

34   For a general history of the Shoshone Nation, see Steven J. Crum, *The Road on Which we Came: A History of the Western Shoshone* (Salt Lake City: University of Utah Press, 1994).

35   Hal K. Rothman and Char Miller, *Death Valley National Park: A History* (Reno: University of Nevada Press, 2013), 71–72.

36   National monuments are managed by the NPS. Presidential decrees establish national monuments (as per the Antiquities Act of 1906), whereas Congress creates national

parks. For more on the differences, see Hal Rothman, *America's National Monuments: The Politics of Preservation* (Lawrence: University Press of Kansas, 1994).

37   Ibid., 96. For a different take on California Indians, see Dowie, *Conservation Refugees*, chap, 1 "Miwok."

38   See Leonardo Merino, "Zonas de influencia cultural en la Costa Rica indígena y sus relaciones con el medio ambiente," *Ilé: Anuario Ecológico, Cultura y Sociedad* 5, no. 5 (2005): 143–53.

39   Alfred Crosby, *Ecological Imperialism: The Biological Expansion of Europe, 900–1900* (Cambridge: Cambridge University Press, 1986), 134; Carolyn Hall, *Costa Rica: A Geographical Interpretation in Historical Review* (Boulder, CO: Westview Press, 1985), 83.

40   Sterling Evans, *The Green Republic: A Conservation History of Costa Rica* (Austin: University of Texas Press, 1999), 210–14, 266–67.

41   Evans, *Green Republic*, 210–11.

42   "Talamanca's Sweet Success," *Nature Conservancy* 47, no. 1 (1997): 14–15; Mario Alvarado (CONAI) interview, in Evans, *Green Republic*, 212.

43   See Evans, *Green Republic*, 79–80.

44   Kurt Kutay, "Cahuita National Park, Costa Rica: A Case Study in Living Cultures and National Park Management," in West and Brechin, *Resident Peoples and National Parks*, 117–18.

45   Kutay, "Cahuita National Park," 126, 124. See also Richard Donovan, "Boscosa: Forest Conservation and Management through Local Institutions (Costa Rica)," in *Natural Connections: Perspectives on Community-Based Conservation*, ed. David Western (Washington, DC: Island Press, 1994), 215–33.

46   Steven R. Brechin et al., "Resident Peoples and Protected Areas: A Framework for Inquiry," in West and Brechin, *Resident Peoples and National Parks*, 28n7.

47   Examples are from Stevens, "New Alliances for Conservation," 48, 6; Igoe, *Conservation and Globalization*, 135, 161–62; Brechin et al., "Resident Peoples and Protected Areas," 28n7. For further discussion on the Havasupai, see John Hough, "The Grand Canyon National Park and the Havasupai People: Cooperation and Conflict," in West and Brechin, *Resident Peoples and National Parks*, 215–30.

48   See Thomas F. Thornton, "A Tale of Three Parks: Tlingit Conservation, Representation, and Repatriation in Southeast Alaska's National Parks," in Stevens, *Indigenous Peoples*, 121–24.

49   For more on this topic, and specifically on whaling, see Joshua L. Reid, *The Sea is My Country: The Maritime World of the Makahs* (New Haven, CT: Yale University Press, 2018).

50   For further information, see Jacilee Wray et al., "Creating Policy for the National Park Service: Addressing Native Americans and Other Traditionally Associated Peoples," *The George Wright Forum* 26, no. 3 (2009): 43–50; and Igoe, *Conservation and Globalization*, 135–36.

51   Igoe, *Conservation and Globalization*, 136, 137.

52   Sterling Evans, "Conclusion," in Evans, ed., *American Indians in American History, 1870–2001: A Companion Reader* (Greenport, CT: Praeger Press, 2001), 196.

53   Garrit Voggesser, "When History Matters: The National Wildlife Federation's Conservation Partnership with Tribes," *Western Historical Quarterly* 40, no. 3 (Autumn 2009): 349–57, quotation at 356.

54   See Theodore Binnema and Melanie Niemi, "'Let the Line be Drawn Now': Wilderness, Conservation, and the Exclusion of Aboriginal People from Banff National Park in Canada," *Environmental History* 11, no. 4 (2006): 724–50.

55   Stevens, "New Alliances for Conservation," 48–49; Brad Martin, "Negotiating a Partnership of Interests: Inuvialuit Land Claims and the Establishment of Northern Yukon (Ivvavik) National Park," in *A Century of Parks Canada, 1911–2011*, ed. Claire Campbell (Calgary: University of Calgary Press, 2011).

56   John Sandlos, "National Parks in the Canadian North: Comanagement or Colonialism Revisited?" in Stevens, *Indigenous Peoples*, 146–47.

57   Emery Hartley, "Tribal Parks: Thirty Years and Counting," *Friends of Clayoquot Sound* (Summer 2014), 1–2. For further information on Indigenous peoples and national parks in the bi-national Pacific Northwest, see Jonathan Clapperton, "Stewards of the Earth? Aboriginal Peoples, Environmentalists and Historical Representation," (PhD diss., University of Saskatchewan, 2012).

58   Stevens, "New Alliances for Conservation," 48, 53, 54, 47, 43–44.

59   See Brian W. Conz, "Conservation and Maya Autonomy in Guatemala's Western Highlands: The Case of Totonicapán," in Stevens, *Indigenous Peoples*, 241–59.

60   Emily Caruso, "State Governmentality or Indigenous Sovereignty? Protected Area Comanagement in the Ashininka Communal Reserve in Peru," in Stevens, *Indigenous Peoples*, 151.

61   For further analysis, see Patrick C. West and Steven R. Brechin, "National Parks, Protected Areas, and Resident Peoples: A Comparative Assessment and Integration," in West and Brechin, *Resident Peoples and National Parks*, 364–99.

5

Parks For and *By* the People: Acknowledging Ordinary People in the Formation, Protection, and Use of State and Provincial Parks

Jessica M. DeWitt

Provincial and state park history is still underdeveloped in the larger field of environmental history. National parks garner the most celebratory and analytical attention within scholarship and from society at large. The provincial and state park histories that go beyond surface-level treatment lean toward political and institutional histories or "great men" narratives, both of which focus on those in elite positions in society. The voices and unique experiences of the citizens for whom the parks were supposedly created are often pushed to the background, glossed over, or ignored completely. A refocus on more ordinary people—whether tourists, business owners, volunteers, or others—in park historiography enables historians to examine the ways in which economic and cultural practices interact with and change the environment at ground level by taking park landscapes, their people, and their flora and fauna out of the abstract and placing them at the forefront of park histories. This in turn requires that studies of small-scale conservation or environmental organizations expand to include individuals and groups that do not readily fall into conventional perceptions of environmental activism, but whose actions, be they recreational or work-based, have tangible effects on the creation and management of state and provincial parks.

The neglect of non-elite narratives reflects the difficulties in writing a park history that focuses on the viewpoints and experiences of ordinary people. The sources, if they exist at all, are challenging to find. In contrast, official park service documents and the personal papers of conservationists and politicians abound. Another reason for this neglect is the general disconnect between environmental and social history, as described by Stephen Mosley in "Common Ground: Integrating Social and Environmental History."[1] The very nature of the field of social history rests on its focus on "ordinary people, rather than the elite."[2] Further, it claims that these ordinary people have complex pasts that shaped greater historical processes and deserve the same kind of serious analytical attention given to political and intellectual figures.[3] The absence of social history's capacity for illuminating the common person's experience is one of environmental history's failings, despite the fact that both fields "seek the structures lurking behind the more conspicuous but short-term events" and are typically grounded in "present-mindedness."[4] In his article "Modes of Prophecy and Production: Placing Nature in History," William Cronon argues that the greatest weakness of environmental history is its failure to look at individual stories and "[tease] apart the diverse material roles and perceptual experiences of different people in the holistic 'system.'"[5] Mosley explicates on this issue further, stating that in environmental history "ordinary people, with their different interests, desires, and experiences, can disappear from view."[6]

Park historiography is a microcosm of this larger divide between social and environmental history. One reason is that environmental history that does succeed in a "from-below" approach tends to have what Karl Jacoby calls a "lopsided understanding of the past"[7] that focuses primarily on the urban working and middle class and ignores rural residents and working- and /middle-class experiences gained outside the urban landscape. Another reason is park history's obsession with origin stories. Park histories that focus on the battle to preserve a piece of land under park legislation usually end at park conception, leading to stories that are heavy on policy and political manoeuvring but do little to illuminate the way in which park creation affects those on the ground before, during, and after the park is created. To gloss over or ignore the experiences and opinions of those individuals for whom the parks were meant is a common oversight of park historians. Individuals within the general populace tend to be lumped into vague groups—"the public supporters," "the people," "park users," "environmentalists," "conservationists"—enabling their inclusion in the narrative without a clear understanding of who they are and what motives may be driving them.[8]

The role of ordinary people in provincial and state park history is arguably just as vital, if not more so, than their role in national park history.[9] Although they are often treated as a less important after-effect of national park creation, it is important to acknowledge that provincial and state parks have their own unique history that deserves individual investigation. Inclusion of ordinary people is important to both national and urban park history as well, but this chapter will focus on provincial and state parks. Provincial and state parks were created as part of wider attempts to democratize recreation in Canada and the United States. Yet they typically have not been as prominent in the tug-of-war between recreation and preservation as have national parks. Accessible recreation and its resulting revenues have almost always been the main objective of provincial and state parks.[10] As Ney C. Landrum points out, "state [and provincial] parks occupy a central position in the overall gamut of public outdoor recreation, bridging the critical gap . . . between the largely playground types of recreation provided by America's cities and towns and the contrasting backcountry recreational experiences available in the vast national parks."[11] The rallying cry of the original National Conference on [State] Parks (1921), "a state park every hundred miles," highlights the importance of public accessibility as a goal in the creation of state and provincial parks.[12]

Recent developments in state and provincial park historiography have begun to include more ordinary voices and experiences. In their introduction to a special issue of *Environment and History*, Keith Thor Carlson and Jonathan Clapperton point out the general neglect of non-national parks in historical literature despite their debatably greater impact on the lives of the general populace. National parks have received more attention by historians, they argue, largely because the homogeneity of the national parks' "central structure . . . makes it easier to create interpretive metanarratives."[13] Carlson and Clapperton highlight the opportunity for non-national park histories to illuminate the role that parks play in local processes of community-building ideology, along with the prospect of unearthing and focusing upon subaltern perspectives. One of these underdeveloped perspectives in provincial and state park history, to which Carlson and Clapperton pay especial attention, is that of Indigenous peoples. They argue that too often Indigenous voices are lost in the sea of vagueness that characterizes historical treatments of adjacent park citizenry, failing to acknowledge the unique set of experiences and concerns that separate Indigenous groups from the dominant society.[14] Evans' chapter (this volume) offers some insights in this regard as he compares a provincial park and Indigenous reserves with national parks across the Americas.[15]

To create a more complete history of provincial and state parks, historians must also turn their attentions to the peripheries of the parks, for the effects of park formation and management are more far reaching than park boundaries suggest. In order for this to happen, historians need to broaden their scope when looking at park histories. Mosley offers three main frameworks under which environmental and social history can begin to grow together: environments and identities, environmental justice, and environment and consumption.[16] These frameworks are helpful for thinking about how park historians can better acknowledge the experiences of a broader spectrum of people, and also make connections between local histories from across Canada and the United States. In park history, stories of identity and stories of consumption and the environment tend to blur together. For example, the consumption of the environment at children's summer camps in and around Algonquin Provincial Park, as shown in Sharon Wall's *The Nurture of Nature*, facilitated the development of a modern Ontario identity anchored in performative anti-modernism.[17] Additionally, research that addresses the development of tourism in state and provincial parks, as discussed later in this chapter, demonstrates the way in which the selling and purchasing of outdoor experiences contribute to the identity-formation of both business owners and tourists. Issues of environmental justice stand to enrich park historiography significantly. Recent efforts to integrate such issues have been made most notably in William E. O'Brien's *Landscapes of Exclusion*. O'Brien traces the way in which Jim Crow laws affected the development of the American South's state park systems and African American access to outdoor recreation.[18] Inspired by the work of the above scholars, this chapter explores the methods, approaches, and opportunities that will enable historians to better understand the role of ordinary people in provincial and state park history. I have chosen to focus on Ontario and Pennsylvania because their park systems represent two of my dissertation case studies and they effectively illuminate cross-border similarities in park creation and management. Specifically, I examine several thematic approaches that offer important insights, including broadening our understanding of the character of environmentalism; looking beyond park boundaries to explore connections between tourism and park history in particular; and examining the important place of work and voluntarism in shaping state and provincial parks. The chapter closes with a consideration of some important source materials for studying this kind of small green environmentalism.

Expedient Environmentalism

In an interview about *Black Faces, White Spaces*, Carolyn Finney states, "We don't hear about them [African Americans] because nobody calls [their actions] 'conservation.' They don't fit into the way we talk about environmentalism in the mainstream."[19] This assertion can also be applied generally to non-elite voices in provincial and state park history. The word "environmentalism" typically fosters images of impassioned protest. Furthermore, it often assumes a level of education and understanding of ecological processes on the part of the environmental activist that automatically eliminates a large proportion of the population from inclusion in the term "environmentalist." One cause of non-elite neglect in provincial and state park historiography is that these parks tend not to lend themselves to titillating stories of flashy environmental protest. Although these kinds of stories do exist, more often than not provincial and state parks' histories are shaped by more subtle societal movements and individual actions. To better flesh out these subtleties, it is helpful to expand one's definition of environmentalism to consider instances of both unintentional and expedient environmentalism. Unintentional (or accidental) environmentalism refers to the actions of an individual or group that are undertaken for non-environmental reasons but that have an unintended positive effect on the environment. Expedient environmentalism is characterized by environmentally positive actions that are undertaken for a desired outcome other than environmentalism, such as economic gain or positive publicity.[20] Chad Montrie introduces this concept in his article on Appalachian coal mining and the United Mine Workers of America (UMW). He demonstrates that with regard to surface mining, the UMW believed that "promotion of limited regulation seemed likely to stave off stricter regulation or abolition that would cut into strip mine employment."[21] The UMW supported mining regulation not because of environmental concerns but rather because it represented the most likely avenue by which to ensure the continued, long-term employment of its members. The concept of "unintentional environmentalism" is linked to the idea of "environmentalism of the poor," which is more commonly used in studies outside North America and Europe, although Leeming (this volume), among others, has connected it to the Canadian context.[22]

Cook Forest State Park in Cooksburg, Pennsylvania, offers an effective case study for examining the way in which broadening one's definition of environmentalism can augment the stories of ordinary people in park history. Cook Forest is on land originally owned by the Cook lumber dynasty. It is ecologically significant because the park contains the largest stand of old-growth forest in the United States east of the Mississippi River. Despite this significant fact, this parcel of old-growth timber was not easy to save. It took eighteen years, numerous personal and political battles, and a national campaign to get the Pennsylvanian government to purchase the land for the purpose of a state park; in the end the state only pledged $450,000 of the $650,000 needed to buy the tract of land, while the other $200,000 had to be raised by public donations.

The eighteen-year campaign to preserve the forest as a park can be divided into two distinct phases.[23] The first phase, from 1910 to 1923, was defined by its leader, M. I. McCreight—a banker, philanthropist, and good friend of the Cook family patriarch, A. W. Cook—who attempted to unite his elite friends and the Pennsylvanian government around the Cook Forest State Park idea under a rallying call for "practical" conservation. McCreight's efforts largely fell on deaf ears because what he advocated for, namely preservation for preservation's sake, was not, at that time, viewed by either the public or the government as a viable reason for saving a piece of land.[24] The second phase of the Cook Forest campaign began in 1924 when Pittsburgh industrialist and conservationist Thomas Liggett took over the cause and founded the Cook Forest Association, the membership of which was made up of local industrialists and politicians. Liggett successfully ended the campaign with a victory in 1928 by cleverly inviting non-elites into the cause and adopting utilitarian-based, recreation-based, and economically based rhetoric. Although it can be argued that without the participation of non-elites in the last stages of the campaign the state would not have created Cook Forest State Park, the story of the park's creation, as told by historians to date, remains focused on McCreight, Liggett, Cook, and other elite players in the campaign, including national conservation figures Gifford Pinchot and J. Horace McFarland.

One way to more effectively extrapolate the role of ordinary citizens in the Cook Forest campaign saga is to further investigate the demographics, identities, and motivations of the local residents who contributed money to the campaign. The Cook Forest Association assigned specific donation goals to the surrounding counties and towns. Venango County, for instance, was expected to raise $125,000 toward the purchase of the old-growth tract and surrounding land.[25] To assist in this endeavour, Cook Forest Association hosted "County Days" to both reward and enlist donors.[26] The association emphasized that no donation was too small and publicized every donation of $1 or more; the average donation by local residents was $75.[27] A list of all donors once existed at the park but has since been lost.

Surviving historical sources indicate that much of the local populace supported the Cook Forest State Park campaign for reasons other than preservation. For instance, residents of Pleasantville, located thirty miles northwest of Cook Forest, supported the Cook Forest campaign because it was an opportunity to push their regional agenda and to attract attention and state money to their often-neglected, rural portion of the state. "Pleasantville residents see the forest," an article in the *Titusville Herald* read, "not only as an opportunity to preserve the last available tract of virgin timber but an incentive to auto traffic that will help in the local appeal for more paved highways in the district."[28] Cook Forest was also supported by local residents because of the opportunity to benefit from tourism revenue in an otherwise financially challenged region. Nearby towns competed for the title "Gateway to Cook Forest." Liggett and other Cook Forest Association members promised local residents that their towns would see upward of $500,000 in revenue each year from park tourism. One local newspaper article read that Cook Forest "is a proposition which every man and woman in this section should get behind and boost, if not for sentimental reasons, from a purely business standpoint."[29] Cook Forest and its stand of virgin timber was saved not because of its ecological value but rather because of its potential direct and indirect use and existence values. Glenn C. Blomquist and John C. Whitehead define existence value, also known as off-site value or passive use value, as "the maximum willingness to pay for preserving the natural resource even though the individual does not visit the site."[30] It was more advantageous for local residents and the Pennsylvanian government to help save the timber than it was to let it fall to the axe. Examples of this kind of expedient environmentalism are numerous in state and provincial park history.

Beyond Park Borders

Further progress can be made to unearth the voices of common people in Cook Forest's past by expanding the park's history beyond park borders— to see the park as a regional instrument of environmental restoration and economic activity, not just as an island of preservation. When one looks beyond the artificial boundaries of the park, one finds that it is part of a much larger, complex, and neglected story. Cook Forest's relationship to the Clarion River, which runs through the park, is an example of why park history needs to expand its reach. The Clarion River runs from Johnsonburg, Pennsylvania, to just south of Emlenton, Pennsylvania, where it meets the Allegheny River. Throughout the nineteenth and into the early twentieth century, the Clarion served as a corridor of timber, tanning, paper, and wood chemical industries. Millions of gallons of waste and chemicals were dumped into the river daily.[31] Declared ecologically dead in 1909 and described as "unfit for life" and "black like ink,"[32] the Clarion River has since come back. A portion of it is now labelled a National and Wild Scenic River, and it serves as a recreational focal point for visitors to western Pennsylvania.[33]

The accounts of how this ecological revivification occurred follow a typical trajectory. Deforestation caused the timber industry to decline, subsequently leading to the decline of the tanning and wood chemical plants along the river, with the last plants closing in 1963 and 1948 respectively.[34] The major paper mill in Johnsonburg slowly cleaned up its act by modernizing its facility. The Clarion was initially identified as a study river by the Wild and Scenic Rivers Act, but it was considered too polluted for inclusion in the National Wild and Scenic Rivers System until 1996, when 17.1 miles of the river were declared "scenic" and 34.6 miles of the river were labelled "recreational."[35] This restoration was credited largely to the decline of the area's industry and to state and federal legislation, and was also vaguely attributed to increased public interest in the river. The "Clarion River and Mill Creek Wild and Scenic Eligibility River Report," for instance, states that "these changed conditions were brought about, in part, by renewed public interest for long-term protection of this river and improved industrial conditions affecting the river."[36]

The problem with this explanation of the Clarion River's rebound is threefold. Firstly, it does not consider the role of reforestation. Secondly, it does not delve deeply into why there was renewed public interest in the health of the river beginning in the 1960s. Thirdly, it does not take into account the creation of the Allegheny National Forest (1923), Clear Creek State Park (1922), or Cook Forest State Park (1928) along its banks. The oversight that draws these three issues together is the omission of any consideration of the parallel development of the area's tourism industry and the restoration of the river. Vacation cabin rental businesses popped up on the outskirts of Cook Forest in the late 1920s. After the park's creation, the area became one of the chief vacation destinations for middle- and working-class families from nearby cities, namely Pittsburgh and Cleveland. By 1956, the Cook Forest Vacation Bureau's brochure listed over twenty places to stay in the area immediately surrounding the park.[37] The prevalence of privately owned accommodations and recreational attractions, like horseback riding and canoeing, increased exponentially through the early 1990s. In this time, as described by several current and former business owners, park usage patterns changed.[38] When the park was initially created, visitors flocked to the Forest Cathedral—the stand of the tallest old-growth pine in the park. However, as the years passed the recreational focus of the park gradually moved to the river. Today, during the summer, the river is lined with cars, and hundreds of individuals swim, canoe, and float down the river each day. The rise in the popularity of canoeing also denotes a move from state-sponsored recreation within the park to recreation provided by private businesses.

There is no record—at least that has been found to date—of any organized protest or support for the cleanup of the river on the part of the business owners. Instead, the parallel stories are connected by a quiet and utilitarian approach to environmentalism on the part of these individuals. They supported the restoration of the river and reforestation because these measures were good for business, and this business, in turn, helped lead to the restoration of the river. As Scott Moranda argues, when tourism enters a post-extraction landscape, like that of western Pennsylvania, the "tourism industry transform[s] the built and natural environments to better serve consumers. Tourists and locals . . . develop . . . expectations (sometimes conflicting) for the appearance of that landscape based on their local needs, leisure preferences, or larger national traditions."[39] Expedient environmentalism connects what goes on inside parks with what goes on outside. When it is overlooked, as in the basic narrative of the Clarion's restoration, the role of locals is overshadowed by governmental actors and policies, and larger environmental groups.

The Clarion River/Cook Forest link serves as an example of the important connections between private tourism and provincial and state parks, which warrant greater attention in environmental historiography. As Moranda observes in a historiographical essay, "in many ways, historians of tourism have always written about the environment,"[40] but it is not until relatively recently that historians have purposely and successfully meshed the fields together. Aaron Shapiro's *The Lure of the North Woods: Cultivating Tourism in the Upper Midwest* draws from the "Minnesota Resort Industry Oral History Project" and other collections to create a more complex understanding of the interconnection between the environment, tourism, and personal experience.[41] Shapiro demonstrates that "like earlier lumbermen, [tourist business owners] also saw profit in nature . . . they relied on the regenerative forces to provide a new cash crop, a forested and lake-dotted countryside offering outdoor recreation for the masses."[42] In the case of Cook Forest, the area surrounding the park developed into a working and middle-class vacationland operated by small business owners who were a mix of locals looking for economic opportunity and outsiders looking for more serene, rural settings in which to make a living. The presence of these businesses and their owners affected the way in which the park and its surrounding area developed during the twentieth century. Shapiro's study is only partly about state parks; most of his analysis is directed toward the larger region in which the parks were situated. The role of privately owned tourism operations outside and inside provincial and state parks accentuates the importance of looking at developments both inside the parks and along the park peripheries.

Work, Voluntarism, And Parks

In her article "Laboring the Earth: Transnational Reflections on the Environmental History of Work," Stefania Barca argues that the intersection of work and nature is underrepresented in environmental history literature. She suggests "three arenas where the connections between work and environment can be investigated. The first presents the landscape as reflective of past human labor. The second examines the workplace and its relationship with the local community. The third focuses on working-class and labor environmental activism."[43] The place of labour within parks is part of the larger integration of work and environmental history and acts as another avenue by which ordinary people can be repositioned inside parks history.

From Ontario, in *Algonquin: The Park and Its People*, Liz Lundell and photographer Donald Standfield focus, by way of interviews and photographs, on the stories of individuals who have made their living in a park setting.[44] By studying parks and their peripheries as a kind of workplace, historians can better understand the role of labour in shaping the process of "emparkment."[45] When it comes to voluntarism, the opportunities for historical research are readily apparent. In both Canada and the United States, many national, provincial, and state parks enjoy an allied connection to "Friends of . . . " and other similar cooperating, philanthropic associations. Most "friends" groups rely on a mixture of private and corporate donations, special event proceeds, and grants.[46] Such organizations exemplify one form of small-scale environmentalism directly tied to the history of parks. Historically, although the size and success of these groups varied, most friends groups associated with provincial and state parks were managed by local citizens and were relatively small. A handful, like Ontario's The Friends of Algonquin Park (FOAP), were large enough to support paid staff. The FOAP originated in 1983 when the Ontario Ministry of Natural Resources approached private citizens about their willingness to work with a cooperating association if one were to be founded. The FOAP was the first provincial park cooperating association in Ontario. These original citizens, according to the FOAP, were motivated by a mutual passion for the park.[47] Under the original agreement between the Ontario Ministry of Natural Resources and the FOAP, the FOAP took over the financing of park publications, using the profits for mutually agreed-upon educational and interpretive programs within the park.[48] Before the creation of the FOAP, the Ontario government had handled the publication of all Ontario parks material. This revenue was shared between all parks, and that led to a shortage of printed material at more popular parks like Algonquin. With its creation, the FOAP took over "responsibility for selling and reprinting official [Algonquin] Park publications using the revenue generated from their sale. This sales revenue would no longer return to the Ontario Government, but rather stay in the [p]ark to enhance educational publication offerings and more."[49] Between 1983 and 1988, the gross revenue of the FOAP increased from $34,869 to $316,277.[50] By 2007, the organization had 3,069 members.[51] Today Algonquin Provincial Park and the FOAP are entirely interdependent. The FOAP runs the gift shops, organizes workshops and activities, pays many of the employees associated with the park, supports research of park history and a park archive, publishes the park publications, and even raised millions to build the park's visitor centre and logging museum.[52] Without the presence of this charitable organization, Algonquin Provincial Park would only be a shadow of what it is today.

Pinery Provincial Park, also in Ontario, has its own group, founded in 1989. The Friends of Pinery Park (FPP), although smaller than the FOAP, began under similar circumstances—a desire by concerned local residents to educate park visitors and the general public about the park's environment. The FPP describes itself as "a charitable organization dedicated to the education, promotion, preservation and support of Pinery Provincial Park."[53] Like the FOAP, the FPP, since its inception, has relied on the sale of park-related publications, products, and memberships to fund their park programs. FPP park programs such as poster contests and Father's Day canoe hikes are all aimed at fostering a balance between increased park visitation and public knowledge of the park's delicate environment.[54]

Charitable organizations like the FPP and the FOAP ride the line between non-elite and elite status. Some, like the FOAP, raise enough money to carry serious clout in the conservation realm, but they do not have any legislative powers. They are also often run by private citizens with high levels of education and relative influence in their communities. However, they are fundamentally organizations run by the "people," funded by small donations that typically amount to less than $100 and fuelled by volunteer participation. These "friends" groups deserve closer scrutiny in the histories of provincial and state parks because their rise in the 1970s, 1980s, and 1990s coincided with cuts in funding to provincial and state park systems. The upsurge in these organizations represents a takeover of basic park functions by volunteers. Who were (and are) these people? The records of the FOAP show that board members have included teachers, insurance agents, filmmakers, and attorneys.[55] What motivated them? What changes occurred in the park systems to necessitate the development of these cooperative organizations? What effect did the presence of these organizations have on recreational and preservationist aspects of provincial and state parks? What would provincial and state parks look like today if these volunteer organizations had not stepped in to help? These are questions that deserve fuller attention in provincial and state park historiography, and they are questions that will lead to a more complete understanding of the role of non-elites in the management of parks.

New Sources, New Stories

To find non-elites in state and provincial park histories, historians must both expand and fine-tune their research to include lesser-known and non-manuscript items. Source materials to watch for, which can sometimes be found within the governing files of individual provincial parks, are public surveys and petitions. Jenny Clayton demonstrated how to use such sources in her article "'Human Beings Need Places Unchanged by Themselves': Defining and Debating Wilderness in the West Kootenays,

1969–74," in which she opens with several quotes from letters and petitions written by local Kootenay residents.[56] The use of public surveys in park planning and management by provincial and state governments grew exponentially during the 1970s. In Canada, this growth coincided with the near-urban park movement; originating in Ontario and spreading across the country to other provincial park systems, this movement aimed to increase accessibility to outdoor recreation.[57] This spirit of public inclusion in the 1970s also infiltrated the park-planning processes of new and established rural parks, an example of which is Rondeau Provincial Park.

Created in 1894, Rondeau is Ontario's second oldest provincial park and one of the few parks in the system that still supports the leasing of park land to cottage owners. Today, the cottages in Rondeau are protected as a heritage conservation district.[58] However, the cottage community is not uncontroversial, as many individuals still believe that cottage communities have no place in provincial parks and threaten the ecological integrity of the parks.[59] This conflict has deep-seated roots dating as far back as the 1920s.[60] The James Gordon Nelson fonds at the Laurier Archives at Wilfrid Laurier University contain a wealth of documents relating to the 1970s manifestation of the cottager-versus-preservation battle.

Hidden within the collection are two folders that contain hundreds of letters and completed surveys written by local residents of Ontario's Rondeau Provincial Park in response to proposed changes to the parks management plan in the 1970s.[61] In May 1974, the Rondeau Provincial Park Advisory Committee was created to gather expert opinions on the future of the park as well as to solicit "the views of the public . . . in the form of letters or briefs from individuals and groups with an interest in the planning of the park."[62] Local residents were sent a "comment sheet" that provided "topics for consideration" such as "What are your views about the character and image of the park? Why?" and "Which activities and/or facilities should be included and encouraged in the park?"[63] The response rate was high. Residents were particularly vocal in the files about proposed removal of the private cottages in the park and the authorization/prohibition of hunting in the park. From these letters and surveys there are several discernible themes.

First, residents viewed the removal of the cottages to be an unnecessary action that trampled on their rights, illustrating a conflict between public and private land uses. One concerned citizen wrote, "If the ministry wishes to buy my cottage now, at full value, not 10% per year decrease, then rent it back to me for a reasonable amount. . . . I am prepared to consider this step . . . in the democratic process, people do have certain rights. One of these is to be treated in a *fair* and *equal* matter—especially by government."[64] Second, the letters demonstrate that the public's expectations for the park often clashed with Ontario Ministry of Natural Resources strategies and environmental programs. Many residents saw no conflict between increased development in the park and the park's ecology. One individual suggests that the park would benefit from the addition of a zoo, a "beautiful restaurant," and a boardwalk along the beach of at least six feet in width.[65] Third, the letters illustrate a belief that local knowledge of the park trumped that of so-called experts. One long-time cottage goer commenting on individuals who grew up summering at the park stated, "These same young people have walked the several miles of Beach, searched the woods for wild flowers and wild life and probably understood the Balance of Nature better in that Park than some of our experts who have not been brought up near Rondeau Park."[66] The records show that the advisory committee found it difficult to tabulate and summarize the variety of responses given, not to mention using them to implement changes.[67]

Additionally, the letters illuminate class tensions between different types of park users—tensions that do not come to light when park users are lumped together as one homogenous group. Some of the letters state that campers, day-users, and cottage owners have coexisted harmoniously.[68] However, other letters suggest that the white, Christian, middle-class cottage owners were the "right" kind of park user; that they, unlike the tent camper and day-use visitor, were invested in the long-term health of the park and were essentially on-site caretakers. One letter writer speaks to racial tensions in the park, stating that removal of "white cottagers" might lead park use to become "oriented to the Shrewsbury and North End black communities."[69] Examination of these kinds of sources often demonstrate the disconnect between policies that supported the democratization of outdoor recreation and how these policies played out on the ground, nuances that are often not brought to the forefront in policy-driven park histories.

These letters bring to light a set of voices all too often ignored or brushed over in provincial and state park historiography and reveal the thoughts, opinions, and emotions of ordinary people toward these parks. Aside from these kinds of manuscript sources, provincial and state parks can benefit from the fact that much of their history has occurred in the relatively recent past, opening the way for the utilization of non-manuscript sources, such as oral history and photographs. Ben Bradley has explored the use of photography that juxtaposed high and low elevations by the British Columbia Parks Division.[70] There exists enormous potential for comparable photographic essays of family photos from provincial and state parks to be conducted, for it was with photography that many individuals captured what was most important to them. Uncovering these photos and other sources that better illuminate the role of common people in provincial and state park history will require closer relationships between historians and the public.

Oral history is an invaluable resource for enriching documentary resources, like photographs, and for unearthing the stories of underrepresented individuals who have not left or are unlikely to leave a documentary trail behind. It also has the potential to broaden park historiography by exposing activities like vacationing and working inside parks that rarely leave a paper trail and highlighting the significance of individual experiences that may otherwise be deemed unimportant.[71] As Barbara Allen Bogart states, "the very act of asking people about their experiences can give . . . narrators a new awareness of the significance of those experiences."[72] The history of Indigenous peoples and the effect of park making on their communities stands to gain the most from more targeted, oral history–driven, provincial and state park historical investigations. Speaking in relation to the history of work in Northern Californian Native American communities, William Bauer comments that oral history "helps us avoid the frustration stemming from the pithy and often biased documents historians find in archives. With assiduous use, oral histories help provide an Indigenous-centred history and reveal the manner in which Indigenous peoples of North America remember and interpret historical changes in their lives."[73]

Lastly, one promising new means of uncovering the stories of park visitors and other non-elites associated with state and provincial parks lies in social media and crowdsourcing initiatives.[74] One example of this kind of initiative is run by the Yosemite Conservancy, which on its "Your Yosemite, Your Story" page asks, "What does Yosemite mean to you?" "We are all part of the Yosemite family," the web page states, "we've hiked and biked and camped. We've shared a picnic lunch in a shady grove or on a vista gazing into the Valley."[75] The conservancy then invites people to share their story. Another example can be found in New York on the Letchworth State Park Facebook page. In preparation for the opening of the park's new Nature Center, the park invites people to "be part of the story" by submitting their own Letchworth memories. The stories vary in length and subject matter, but they all contain a charming personal touch. One example connects the state park to the exuberance of young love:

> It was a few years after graduation when I came back to visit my baby. Our eyes met at the Kenwood and it was go time all over again. We stayed up all night parking in our favorite spot in the rock quarry. We made plans to go for a bike ride the next day in my favorite place Letchworth State Park. My heart was racing as he hauled ass there. But once we passed the front gate, he slowed down and covered every inch of that park. Stopping on the side of the road to make out and tease each other. He brought a blanket for us to lounge on in the bright autumn sun. We walked the tracks overhead to get the best view possible of the gorgeous gourge [sic] below. He held my hand the whole time being so protective over me. Once again promised things that you could not deliver. But I liked listening to your dreaming stories of how our life would pan out. I will love you forever is no joke.[76]

These are the kind of stories that are missing from the vast majority of park histories. The stories that reflect the essence of humanity interwoven into each park's history, the personal connections that make the parks relevant in the day-to-day life of the average person. Historians need to use the full range of resources available to better represent these stories in academic scholarship.

Finding viable sources is the greatest challenge facing the movement of park historians toward the acknowledgement of ordinary people in the formation, protection, and use of state and provincial parks. However, in order to find these sources, historians must also step away from narratives that focus on park legislation defined by elite actions and government leaders and accounts that are limited by park boundaries. Historians need to look to the peripheries of parks, to the communities of individuals pushed out of the parkland by park legislation or drawn to the parks by promises of opportunity. Historians should aim to broaden their definition of environmentalism to include actions not conventionally categorized under the term. Lastly, park and environmental historians need to continue to make further linkages to research conducted in social history and tourism history. The long-term desire of Canadian and American citizens for places of outdoor recreation and tourism revenue has had lasting effects on the North American environment and society that go far beyond drawing park boundaries on a map.

Notes

I am thankful to the Department of History at the University of Saskatchewan for providing the funding that made this research possible, as well as the Laurier Archives and their Joan Mitchell Travel Award, which enabled me to access the James Gordon Nelson fonds used in this chapter.

1   Stephen Mosley, "Integrating Social and Environmental History," *Journal of Social History* 39, no. 3 (2006): 915–33.

2   Peter R. Stearns, "The New Social History: An Overview," in *Ordinary People and Everyday Life: Perspectives on the New Social History*, ed. James B. Gardner and George Rollie Adams (Nashville, TN: American Association for State and Local History, 1983), 4.

3   Stearns, "The New Social History," 4.

4   First quotation from Alan Taylor, "Unnatural Inequalities: Social and Environmental Histories," *Environmental History* 1, no. 4 (1996): 8; second quotation from Donald M. MacRaild and Avram Taylor, *Social Theory and Social History* (New York: Palgrave Macmillan, 2004), 6.

5   William Cronon, "Modes of Prophecy and Production: Placing Nature in History," *Journal of American History* 76, no. 4 (1990): 1129.

6   Mosley, "Integrating," 920.

7   Karl Jacoby, *Crimes Against Nature: Squatters, Poachers, Thieves, and the Hidden History of American Conservation* (Berkeley: University of California Press, 2001), xvi.

8   For further reading on state and provincial park history and examples of the historical approaches noted above, see: Ney C. Landrum, *The State Park Movement in America: A Critical Review* (Columbia: University of Missouri Press, 2004); Thomas R. Cox, *The Park Builders: A History of State Parks in the Pacific Northwest* (Seattle: University of Washington Press, 1988); Gerald Killan, *Protected Places: A History of Ontario's Provincial Parks System* (Toronto: Dundurn Press, 1993); Rebecca Conard, *Places of Quiet Beauty: Parks, Preserves, and Environmentalism* (Iowa City: University of Iowa Press, 1997); George Warecki, *Protecting Ontario's Wilderness: A History of Changing Concepts and Preservation Politics, 1927–1973* (New York: Peter Lang, 2000); John C. Lehr, "The Origins and Development of Manitoba's Provincial Park System," *Prairie Forum* 26, no. 2 (2001): 241–55; Roy W. Meyer, *Everyone's Country Estate: A History of Minnesota's State Parks* (St. Paul: Minnesota Historical Society Press, 1991).

9   Suggested reading on North American national parks includes: Claire Elizabeth Campbell, *A Century of Parks Canada: 1911–2011* (Calgary: University of Calgary Press, 2011); Carolyn Finney, *Black Faces, White Spaces: Reimaging the Relationship of African Americans to the Great Outdoors* (Chapel Hill: University of North Carolina Press, 2014); John Sandlos, *Hunters at the Margin: Native People and Wildlife Conservation in the Northwest Territories* (Vancouver: UBC Press, 2007); Ted Binnema and Melanie Niemi, "'Let the Line be Drawn Now': Wilderness, Conservation, and the Exclusion of Aboriginal People from Banff National Park in Canada," *Environmental History* 11, no. 4 (2006): 724–50; Alan MacEachern, *Natural Selections: National Parks in Atlantic Canada, 1935–1970* (Montreal: McGill-Queen's University Press, 2001); Bill Waiser, *Park Prisoners: The Untold Story of Western Canada's National Parks, 1915–1945* (Calgary: Fifth House, 1995); Leslie Bella, *Parks for Profit* (Montreal: Harvest House, 1987); Paul Kopas, *Taking the Air: Ideas and Change in Canada's National Parks* (Vancouver: UBC Press, 2007); William R. Lowry, *The Capacity for Wonder: Preserving National Parks* (Washington, DC: Brookings Institution, 1994); Chris Armstrong and H. V. Nelles, *Wilderness and Waterpower: How Banff National Park Became a Hydroelectric Storage Reservoir* (Calgary: University of Calgary Press, 2013); Alfred Runte, *National Parks: The American Experience* (Lincoln: University of Nebraska Press, 1979).

10   For further discussion of the argument, see Keith Carlson and Jonathan Clapperton, "Introduction: Special Places and Protected Spaces: Historical and Global Perspectives on Non-National Parks in Canada and Abroad," *Environment and History* 18, no. 4 (2012): 481–83.

11   Ney C. Landrum, *The State Park Movement in American: A Critical Review* (Columbia: University of Missouri Press, 2004), xi.

12   See Landrum, *State Park Movement*, 74–110.

13   Carlson and Clapperton, "Introduction," 481.

14   For examples of Indigenous experience integration into park historiography, see: Jonathan Clapperton, "Desolate Viewscapes: Sliammon First Nation, Desolation Sound Marine Park and Environmental Narratives," *Environment and History* 18, no. 4 (2012): 529–59; Roger Spielmann and Marina Unger, "Towards a Model of Co-Management of Provincial Parks in Ontario," *Canadian Journal of Native Studies* 20, no. 2 (2000): 455–86; Bruce W. Hodgins and Kerry A. Cannon, "The Aboriginal Presence in Ontario Parks and Other Protected Places," in *Changing Parks: The History, Future and Cultural Context of Parks and Heritage Landscapes*, ed. John S. Marsh and Bruce W. Hodgins (Toronto: Natural Heritage/Natural History, 1998), 50–76.

15   The 2011 special issue of *BC Studies* focused on "Provincial Parks and Protected Areas" also included several articles that addressed the general public's involvement in provincial park history. See Ben Bradley, "Manning Park and the Aesthetics of Automobile Accessibility in 1950s British Columbia," *BC Studies* 170 (Summer 2011): 41–65; Jenny Clayton, "'Human Beings Need Places Unchanged by Themselves': Defining and Debating Wilderness in the West Kootenays, 1969–74," *BC Studies* 170 (Summer 2011): 93–118; Philip Van Huizen, "'Panic Park': Environmental Protest and the Politics of Parks in British Columbia's Skagit Valley," *BC Studies* 170 (Summer 2011): 67–92; Bradley's recent research focuses upon the history of "bad" behaviour in provincial parks, illuminating not the way in which common people's behaviour benefits parks but rather how their behaviour often clashes with park rules and broader social norms. "Wild Behaviour in Wild Spaces: Provincial Parks as Habitat of the Canadian 'Yahoo,' from Hippies to Headbangers" (paper presented at Annual Meeting of the Canadian Historical Association, St. Catharines, ON, 26 May 2014).

16   Mosley, "Integrating," 924–28.

17   Sharon Wall, *The Nurture of Nature: Childhood, Antimodernism, and Ontario Summer Camps, 1920–55* (Vancouver: UBC Press, 2009).

18   William E. O'Brien, *Landscapes of Exclusion: State Parks and Jim Crow in the American South* (Amherst: University of Massachusetts Press, 2015).

19   Francie Latour, "Hiking While Black: The Untold Story," *Boston Globe*, 20 June 2014.

20   Of course the "positive" aspect of an environmentally positive action is subjective. The same action may be considered positive or negative by different individuals and groups.

21   Chad Montrie, "Expedient Environmentalism: Opposition to Coal Surface Mining in Appalachia and the United Mine Workers of America, 1945–1975," *Environmental History* 5, no. 1 (2000): 76–77.

22   For a discussion of this kind of environmentalism, see Ramachandra Guha and Juan Martinez-Alier, *Varieties of Environmentalism: Essays North and South* (London: Earthscan, 2006), 3–21.

23   Jessica DeWitt, "A Convergence of Recreational and Conservation Ideals: The Cook Forest State Park Campaign, 1910–1928" (master's thesis, University of Rochester, 2011).

24   DeWitt, "A Convergence of Recreational and Conservation Ideals," 28–48.

25   "To Form 10 Groups of Volunteers to Work for Cook Forest Funds," *Franklin News-Herald*, 16 August 1926.

26 See "Indian Braves," *Brookville Republican*, 5 August 1926; "Seneca Indians Will Feature Big Picnic Saturday," *Brookville Republican*, 5 August 1926; "Elsie Baker, Indians and Liggett Entertain, Thrill Throngs in Cook Forest," *Brookville American*, 12 August 1926; "Cook's Forest," *Clarion Republican*, 12 August 1926; "To Organize Workers to Save Forest," *Oil City Blizzard*, 16 August 1926; "Cook Forest," *Oil City Blizzard*, 16 August 1926; "Slocum Counts the Cars," n.d., *Cook Forest Scrapbook*, Archive, Jefferson County Historical Society, Brookville, Pennsylvania.

27 "To Open Cook Forest Drive This Morning," n.d., *Cook Forest Scrapbook*, Archive, Jefferson County Historical Society, Brookville, PA.

28 "Organize to Raise $5,000 in Titusville," *Titusville Herald*, 16 September 1926.

29 "Community Has Vital Financial Interest in Preservation of Cook Forest, Says Thos. Liggett at Meeting," *Brookville Republican*, 15 July 1926.

30 Glenn C. Blomquist and John C. Whitehead, "Existence Value, Contingent Valuation, and Natural Resources Damages Assessment," *Growth and Change* 26, no. 4 (1995): 576. Mariano Torras writes that "indirect use value is associated with benefits that individuals experience indirectly, or as a consequence of the primary function of a given resource . . . option values refer to all use values (both direct and indirect) that can be realized at some point in the future." "The Total Economic Value of Amazonian Deforestation, 1978–1993," *Ecological Economics* 33, no. 2 (2000): 286.

31 Charles E. Williams, "Tanneries Wood Chemicals, and Paper Pulp: Early Industrial History and Environment along Pennsylvania's Clarion River" (presentation before North Fork Chapter, Society for Pennsylvania Archaeology, Brookville, PA, 15 November 2013); Pennsylvania Department of Health, "Industrial Waste Survey of the Clarion River Basin," in *Tenth Annual Report of the Commissioner of Health of the Commonwealth of Pennsylvania*, 1915, 1279–1316.

32 A. E. Ortmann, "The Destruction of the Fresh-Water Fauna in Western Pennsylvania," *Proceedings of the American Philosophical Society* 48, no. 191 (1909): 106.

33 "Clarion River, Pennsylvania," National Wild and Scenic Rivers System, last updated 2018, http://www.rivers.gov/rivers/clarion.php.

34 Williams, "Tanneries."

35 "Clarion River, Pennsylvania."

36 National Wild and Scenic Rivers System, "Clarion River and Mill Creek Wild and Scenic River Eligibility Report," March 1996, 10.

37 The area's primary business association. It is still in operation.

38 In 2007, I interviewed twenty-three current and former business owners in the Cook Forest area. Jessica DeWitt, "A Lifestyle Off the Beaten Path: Cook Forest State Park and the Men and Women of Its Tourism Industry" (senior thesis, Bethany College, 2008). Names withheld for privacy. These interviews can be accessed at the Jefferson County History Center in Brookville, PA.

39 Scott Moranda, "The Emergence of an Environmental History of Tourism," *Journal of Tourism History* 7, no. 3 (2015): 269.

40   Moranda, "The Emergence," 270.

41   To access these interviews, visit "Minnesota Resort Industry Oral History Project, 1991–2000," *Minnesota Historical Society*, http://collections.mnhs.org/voicesofmn/index.php/10002530.

42   Aaron Shapiro, *The Lure of the North Woods: Cultivating Tourism in the Upper Midwest* (Minneapolis: University of Minnesota Press, 2013), xiii.

43   *Environmental History* 19, no. 1 (2014): 3–4. Nevertheless, there is some good literature on the topic: see Neil M. Maher, *Nature's New Deal: The Civilian Conservation Corps and the Roots of American Environmental Movement* (Oxford: Oxford University Press, 2008); Joseph M. Speakman, *At Work in Penn's Woods: The Civilian Conservation Corps in Pennsylvania* (University Park: Pennsylvania State University Press, 2006); Kay Rippelmeyer, *Giant City State Park and the Civilian Conservation Corps: A History in Words and Pictures* (Carbondale: Southern Illinois University Press, 2010).

44   Liz Lundell, *Algonquin: The Park and Its People* (Toronto: McClelland & Stewart, 1993).

45   In *Regulating Eden: The Nature of Order in North American Parks* (Toronto: University of Toronto Press, 2002), Joe Hermer (at p. 4) coined the term "emparkment" to describe the process by which a landscape becomes a park, which is generally the result of a landscape being "enclosed under the protection of legislation and managed within a detailed juridical framework."

46   Jacqueline Vaughan and Hanna J. Cortner, *Philanthropy and the National Park Service* (New York: Palgrave Macmillan, 2013), 97.

47   "History of the Friends of Algonquin Park," Algonquin Provincial Park: Official Website of the Friends of Algonquin Park, last updated 2018, http://www.algonquinpark.on.ca/foap/history/index.php.

48   The Friends of Algonquin Park, "Members Newsletter No. 1," 22 April 1985, *The Friends of Algonquin Park: 1985–1989 Newsletters*, Archive, Algonquin Provincial Park.

49   "History of the Friends of Algonquin Park."

50   The Friends of Algonquin Park, "Members Newsletter No. 5," April 1989, *The Friends of Algonquin Park: 1985–1989 Newsletters*, Archive, Algonquin Provincial Park.

51   The Friends of Algonquin Park, "Members Newsletter No. 23," 2007, *The Friends of Algonquin Park: 2004–2007 Newsletters*, Archive, Algonquin Provincial Park.

52   "Purpose of The Friends of Algonquin Park," *Algonquin Provincial Park: Official Website of The Friends of Algonquin Park*, last updated 2018, http://www.algonquinpark.on.ca/foap/purpose/index.php.

53   Friends of Pinery Park, last updated 2018, http://pinerypark.on.ca/who-we-are/.

54   "Friends of Pinery Poster Contest, 1991," and "An Invitation to The Friends of Pinery Park's: Father's Day Canoe Hike, Sunday June 16, 1991," both in Gerald Killan fonds, box 11, folder 6.20, Cardinal Carter Library, King's University College, London, ON.

55   The Friends of Algonquin Park, "Members Newsletter No. 1," 22 April 1985, *The Friends of Algonquin Park: 1985–1989 Newsletters*, Archive, Algonquin Provincial Park.

56   Clayton, "Human Beings Need Places Unchanged," 93.

57   For more on the "Near-Urban Park Movement" see Killan, *Protected Places*, 207–9, 212–13, 220–23, 244–45; and Walter H. Kehm, "Near-Urban Parks: What Are They?" *Park News: Journal of the National and Provincial Park Association of Canada* 13, no. 1 (1977): 8–16.

58   MacNaughton Hermsen Britton Clarkson Planning Limited (MHBC), *Municipality of Chatham-Kent: Rondeau Heritage Conservation District Study* (Kitchener, ON: MHBC, 2015), http://portal.chatham-kent.ca/Council/CouncilMeetings/2015/Documents/July/Jul-13-15b.pdf.

59   Trevor Terfloth, "CK council approves cottage heritage district," *Chatham Daily News*, 25 October 2016, http://www.chathamdailynews.ca/2015/10/26/ck-council-approves-cottage-heritage-district.

60   Killan, *Protected Places*, 53–54.

61   Rondeau Provincial Park Files, James Gordon Nelson fonds, 1.5.7.1.26.3.1, 1.5.7.1.26 (1), and 1.5.7.1.26 (2), Laurier Archives, Waterloo, ON [hereafter LA].

62   "Public Information Package: Rondeau Provincial Park Master Plan," June 1974, James Gordon Nelson fonds, 1.5.7.26.3.1, LA.

63   Emphasis in original. "Comment Sheet," June 1974, James Gordon Nelson fonds, 1.5.7.26.3.1, LA.

64   Emphasis in original. Names of letter writers omitted for privacy. Letter to Rondeau Provincial Park Advisory Committee, 15 July 1974, James Gordon Nelson fonds, 1.5.7.1.26 (1), LA.

65   Letter to Rondeau Provincial Park Planning Committee, 23 July 1974, James Gordon Nelson fonds, 1.5.7.1.26.1 (1), LA.

66   Letter to Rondeau Provincial Park Planning Committee #1, Undated (circa 1974), James Gordon Nelson fonds, 1.5.7.1.26.1 (1), LA.

67   Art Holbrook, Memo to Members of Rondeau Park Advisory Committee, "A Summary of Briefs Presented to the Rondeau Provincial Park Advisory Committee," 18 December 1974, James Gordon Nelson fonds, 1.5.7.26.3.1, LA.

68   Letter to Rondeau Provincial Park Planning Committee, 17 July 1974, James Gordon Nelson fonds, 1.5.7.1.26.1 (1), LA.

69   Letter to Rondeau Provincial Park Planning Committee #2, Undated (circa 1974), James Gordon Nelson fonds, 1.5.7.1.26.1 (1), LA.

70   Ben Bradley, "Photographing the High and Low in British Columbia's Provincial Parks: A Photo Essay," *BC Studies* 170 (Summer 2011): 153–69.

71   For discussion of the history of oral history as methodology, see Ronald J. Grele, "Oral History as Evidence," in *History of Oral History: Foundations and Methodology*, ed. Thomas L. Charlton, Lois E. Myers, and Rebecca Sharpless (Toronto: AltaMira Press, 2007), 37–38; Lynn Abrams discusses the potentiality of oral history to empower individuals and groups in "Power and Empowerment," in *Oral History Theory* (New York: Routledge, 2010), 153–74.

72   Barbara Allen Bogart, "A Two-Way Street: Explaining and Creating Community through Oral History," in *Oral History, Community, and Work in the American West*, ed. Jessie L. Embry (Tucson: University of Arizona Press, 2013), 39.

73   William Bauer, "'Everybody Worked Back Then': Oral History, Memory, and Indian Economies in Northern California," in Embry, *Oral History, Community, and Work*, 78.

74   Enrique Estellés-Arolas and Fernando González-Ladrón-de-Guevara, "Towards an Integrated Crowdsourcing Definition," *Journal of Information Science* 38, no. 2 (2012): 197.

75   "Your Yosemite, Your Story," Yosemite Conservancy, accessed November 2014, http://secure.yosemiteconservancy.org/share/; the material gathered in this initial effort is now displayed at "Your Yosemite Moments," last updated December 2017, https://www.yosemiteconservancy.org/blog/your-yosemite-moments.

76   Letchworth State Park, "Be Part of the Story," Facebook page, November 2014, https://www.facebook.com/LetchworthStatePark/app_632512050174886.

PART 2

HISTORIES

Alternatives: Environmental and Indigenous Activism in the 1970s

Liza Piper

Alternatives (also known as *Alternatives Journal* or *A/J*) was founded in 1971 as a "journal/magazine hybrid that would transform scholarly research into tangible ideas for community activism."[1] Initially based at Trent University in Peterborough, Ontario, *Alternatives* grew out of the Peterborough affiliate of the Toronto-based activist organization Pollution Probe.[2] Notwithstanding its scholarly apparatus (in the early 1980s, *Alternatives* would move to the University of Waterloo and adopt peer review, and in 1995 it became the official journal of the Environmental Studies Association of Canada), the quarterly periodical has always served to bridge academic and activist communities and offers an important window into Canada's environmental movement as it has evolved from the 1970s to the present.

    Alternatives aimed to connect intellectuals, activists, and consultants to private enterprise and government, politicians, and others from across the broad spectrum of research areas that were relevant to the burgeoning environmental movement of the day. *Alternatives* was by no means the only environmentalist publication in Canada launched in this period: Energy Probe, another offshoot of Pollution Probe founded in 1969, published *The Probe Post* from 1978 until 1991, as a means to keep members and the wider community informed; the Science Council of Canada, in its aim to promote the transition from Canada as a consumer to a conserver society, published the *Conserver Society Notes* beginning in October 1975.[3] As a stand-alone publication the *Notes* were short-lived, lasting only until June 1977. They were then picked up and incorporated into *Alternatives* beginning in the summer of 1979. For several issues, the *Notes* were printed on different paper and set apart in appearance and form from the main publication. Beginning in the Fall 1984 issue, the *Notes* were incorporated physically into the rest of the journal but still distinguished by a separate heading. The *Notes* endured thus until appearing for the last time in volume 15, issue 1, published in January 1988.[4]

To fully assess *Alternatives*' role in and relationship with small green activism in Canada would require a closer consideration of its audience, reach, subscription base, and evolution over time. Such an analysis would offer important insights but is beyond the scope of this present short chapter. Rather, what is presented here draws on 231 contributor biographies printed in *Alternatives* in its first decade of publication (from the summer issue in 1971 through the spring/summer issue in 1981) in combination with consideration of the kinds of topics they covered in 253 separate articles for the journal, to better understand the relationships between environmental and Indigenous activism in Canada in the 1970s. Beyond an analysis of who participated in the discussions and on what topics, as published in *Alternatives* in its first decade in print, this piece aims to contextualize the reprinted article that follows (Chapter 7), which was authored by Tobasonakwut Peter Kinew and appeared in *Alternatives* in 1978. Kinew's article stands in its own right as an important expression of Indigenous politics in this period; he elucidates the connection between the Treaty 3 chiefs' struggle against a new coal-fired generating station and the larger context of Indigenous activism against resource development in northern Ontario, and demonstrates the often complicated relationships between Indigenous and environmental activists—a theme developed elsewhere in this collection by Willow, Grossman, and Clapperton in particular. The question I wish to address is: Where does Kinew's piece stand in relationship to other articles published in *Alternatives* in this first decade and what can Kinew's contribution to *Alternatives* tell us about Indigenous-environmentalist activist relationships in Ontario and Canada in the 1970s?

Alternatives in this period reflected the wide umbrella that 1970s environmentalism extended over many other affiliated areas of activism, with articles and special issues on topics including population growth, pollution, nuclear power, the limits to growth, soft energy paths, artistic and literary responses to environmental crisis, militarism, solar power, and the Conserver Society. Each issue typically included several feature articles of varying length (as short as one page but rarely as long as ten pages) as well as book reviews of both scholarly and popular works. In the earliest issues, there were "eco-tactics" that appeared throughout and spoke to readers about everything from airtight shelters in Inverhuron Provincial Park to be used in case of hydrogen sulphide releases (#24), to calling for greater controls on snowmobiles (#18).[5] Occasional bibliographies surveyed topics that included Canadian Conservation History, Transportation and Ecology, Fossil & Nuclear Fuels, Water Diversions, Environment and Design, and Food Production from Farm to Table. *Alternatives* also advertised how to purchase reprints of popular articles and copies of their full selection of bibliographies.[6] *Alternatives* was not exclusively a venue for small green activist writing but included contributions that ranged from the highly local (for example, a series of articles about the construction of Inco's high stack in Sudbury in 1973, or a photographic essay of rocks on Manitoulin's south shore), to national (for example, calling for a national energy policy), to much broader in scope (for example, articles about public health and the environment, or on the "Relevance of Classical Political Theory for Economy, Technology, and Ecology").[7]

Where *Alternatives* was at its most local and small scale it served as a forum for environmentalists and allies in central Ontario. Indeed, Trent University professors and students frequently supplied content to the journal in its first decade and were among the most common repeat authors.[8] This local connection was further evidenced in the way the journal was used to advertise Camp Wanapitei, an "ecology wilderness camp in Northern Ontario."[9] Bruce Hodgins, a repeat *Alternatives* contributor, helped to direct the camp; Wanapitei was also used as a base for an "experiential wilderness conference on labour and the environment" held in 1974, organized by the journal and which brought union members together with environmentalists from government, universities, and volunteer groups.[10] This conference in itself spoke to the breadth of *Alternatives*' mandate and its strong connections to labour and working-class issues in central Ontario. From the very first issue, published in the summer of 1971, *Alternatives* also featured international contributions. In its first decade, 41 of the 231 unique contributors (17.7 percent) gave their affiliation as outside of Canada. The vast majority of these (33 contributors, or 14.3 percent) were from the United States, and included such notable figures of the environmental movement as Barry Commoner. After the United States, a handful of contributions came from authors based in the United Kingdom, Scandinavia, Japan, and Germany.

When it came to who these contributors were, whether based in the US or Canada, the majority were academics. Almost all the contributors supplied a short biography to the journal, and from these it was possible to distinguish four categories: academic, environmentalist, politician (including civil servants), and professionals (including, for instance, consultants, journalists, lawyers). Some of these categories overlapped: Robin Harger, for instance, who co-authored an article in the autumn 1971 issue, was both an assistant professor of Zoology at the University of British Columbia and a former president of the Society for Pollution and Environmental Control (SPEC) (it is in this latter capacity that Harger appears in Chapter 10, this volume). Harger was therefore categorized as both an "academic" and an "environmentalist," as I did not attempt to fix each contributor into only one category.[11] Those with an academic affiliation were most numerous: 64.2 percent, or 129 of 201 unique contributors (30 contributors either did not given an affiliation or were categorized as "other"), although 33 of these 129 also identified another affiliation as well.[12] There were 53 environmentalists (26.4 percent), 39 professionals (19.4 percent), and 28 politicians (13.9 percent). Among the politicians and civil servants from Canada, most either worked for Environment Canada or the Science Council of Canada, or were involved in the nuclear power industry.

Unsurprisingly, given the number of academics writing for the journal, many of the articles featured in the first decade were conference papers, versions of lectures, or drawn from other published works. Commoner's contribution, for instance, was a revised version of an address he gave in Ottawa in 1978 to the Conference on Jobs and Environment, an event sponsored by the Canadian Labour Congress. Work by professionals likewise often drew on work they had produced in reports for government or public distribution. Representation of different perspectives was un-evenly distributed across each issue of *Alternatives*. Special issues, in par-ticular, might draw on only one particular type of expertise. Two striking instances of this were the autumn 1973 issue on "Decentralization, En-vironment, and Community," which was put together by the Ottawa and Toronto–based Institute for the Study of Cultural Evolution (ISCE)—a group that aimed to build an "intentional community" that would func-tion with "a minimum interference with nature's renewing cycles and with a minimum use of non-renewable resources."[13] The small green activists behind this initiative used the issue to detail the project and its many tech-nical aspects. By contrast, in the spring 1979 issue on "Behaviour in the 'Crunch,'" every article but one was authored by an academic, most of whom were psychologists or sociologists (the so-called "crunch" was an anticipated rapid shift across many different aspects of society and econ-omy in response to intensifying environmental and economic pressures, foregrounded by the energy crises of the 1970s).

Indigenous issues, if less so voices, had an important place in *Alter-natives* pages from early on. There were 253 articles published in *Alter-natives* in its first decade. The difference between the number of articles (253) and the number of unique contributors (231) signals the frequency with which some authors published multiple times in the journal. The category of "articles" was determined by those pieces that were identified with unique titles in the table of contents for each issue. This category does not normally include the "eco-tactics," reviews, editorials, letters to the editor, or bibliographies, which also appeared in *Alternatives* with varying frequency and regularity in the period studied. In identifying Indigenous content, the count tallied all references to Indigenous peoples in Canada or elsewhere in the pages of *Alternatives* where they were variously re-ferred to as specific nations (for example, "Mohawks") or using broader categories (for example, "Native people" or "Indians"). Those articles with Indigenous content ranged significantly from detailed discussion or whole articles examining Indigenous activism, issues, or communities, for in-stance, to more general references to Indigenous peoples, representations, or lifeways. The former (detailed discussion of Indigenous issues, cultures, or activism) amounted to thirty-one articles, or 12.3 percent of the arti-cles in this period that had significant Indigenous content. This can be compared to fifty-five articles that addressed energy (21.7 percent), nineteen focused on pollution (7.5 percent), and twelve focused on population control (4.7 percent), and keeping in mind that some of these categories overlapped. An additional eleven articles, or 4.3 percent, mentioned Indigenous people or issues in passing. Among the pieces that made passing reference to Indigenous issues or peoples were those that addressed ecological issues in the context of the longer scale of human history, including pre-industrial relations with the environment; others that made use of "Ecological Indian" stereotypes—such as the ISCE special issue that noted they had named their intentional community Bakavi, the Hopi word for reeds, as the Hopi "have for thousands of years lived in harmony with their surroundings."[14] As well, toward the end of the decade, and in the wake of the Mackenzie Valley Pipeline Inquiry, articles that addressed the impacts of resource development often acknowledged potential impacts on northern Indigenous peoples and livelihoods but did not necessarily engage with them in detail.[15]

Development, resources, energy, and the North were the topics where Indigenous peoples and issues figured most prominently.[16] There is no better example of this than the first article in *Alternatives* that gave significant attention to Indigenous peoples, a "Position Paper on the James Bay Project" that appeared in the summer 1972 issue. This article detailed the project at that moment in time, its anticipated consequences, and specifically the impacts on the Indigenous inhabitants of James Bay and the ways in which they had been excluded from decision making to that point. The article was authored by the James Bay Committee, which included two Indigenous groups (the Indians of Quebec Association and the Quebec Metis and non-Status Indians Association), as well as several small green organizations (including the Société pour Vaincre la Pollution, the Voice of Women, and the Montreal Field Naturalist Club).

Energy projects and their impacts on Indigenous livelihoods came up repeatedly in the pages of *Alternatives*, whether in reference to James Bay, the Alberta oil sands, or the Mackenzie Valley Pipeline (or Berger) Inquiry. Articles that dealt with Canadian resource development (forestry and mining, as well as oil and gas projects), more often than not gave significant attention to Indigenous communities.[17] There was significant overlap in *Alternatives*' meaningful coverage of the North (whether

Ontario's provincial north or Canada's territorial north) and its attention to Indigenous people. Indeed, Kinew's article, reprinted here as Chapter 7, was part of a special issue on the North, published in 1978.[18] That said, not all northern coverage included Indigenous people. Two articles on "The Arctic in Perspective" that appeared in 1973 and 1974 gave virtually no attention to Arctic inhabitants, except for a dismissive note that "a distinctive feature of the Canadian Far North is that a majority of the tiny population is native."[19] Likewise, articles addressing resource-related pollution did not necessarily consider impacts on Indigenous people, or any people at all, for that matter; some of these pieces exclusively focused on environmental impacts.[20] However, some of the key moments of environmental injustice with disproportionate impacts on Indigenous people from this period—mercury poisoning at Grassy Narrows, tailings from uranium mining in the Serpent River, arsenic exposure in Yellowknife, and contamination from the Saint Lawrence Seaway project—all featured in articles in *Alternatives* in the decade under review.[21]

What is missing topically from *Alternatives*' coverage of environmental issues and activism in the 1970s is any significant consideration of the ways that Aboriginal rights, as they would come to be defined by the courts and through the process of constitutional renewal that was underway in this period, would reshape the possibilities for environmental activism in the ways that we see at work in the twenty-first century (Grossman and Willow, this volume).[22] Several articles in this period addressed how the law could be used to engage with environmental issues, in both Canada and the United States, and lawyers contributed regularly to the journal.[23] One article, for example, by Geoff Mains, published in the spring 1980 issue, looked specifically at "Some Environmental Aspects of a Canadian Constitution."[24] In Kinew's article we see Treaty 3 chiefs putting great emphasis on legal tools, from the newly passed Ontario Environmental Assessment Act to the possibility of a reference to the International Joint Commission (IJC), to ensure the protection of lands and people. However, none of the articles reviewed from this period made reference to possibilities for using treaty, or what would be termed Aboriginal rights in the context of constitutional debates in the 1980s, as pathways to achieve environmentalist goals. This serves as an indispensable reminder that while many of the key decisions that enabled Indigenous-environmentalist coalitions in the 1990s and beyond came about in the 1970s or shortly thereafter—including the Calder case (1973), the James Bay and Northern Quebec Agreement (1975), the Mackenzie Valley Pipeline Inquiry (1974–77), and the inclusion of Aboriginal rights in the new Constitution Act (1982)—it took time for the opportunities created by these decisions to be realized. While there were long-standing philosophical connections between environmental and Indigenous activists, and concern for resource development in Canada especially brought Indigenous issues to the forefront of the environmentalist agenda (even if, as Kinew's article reminds us, this did not always result in effective collaboration), practical possibilities for strategic alliances rooted in Aboriginal rights were contingent on the shifting political discourses of the 1980s and 1990s. This history, which Clapperton addresses in his chapter on Clayoquot Sound, is a subject that warrants closer attention, as it is informed not only by the example of "the War in the Woods" but also the earlier mobilization of southerners around northern energy projects, and later episodes such as the Piikani Nation's Lone Fighters' opposition to the Oldman Dam in southern Alberta in the late 1980s and early 1990s.[25]

Almost all of those who wrote on Indigenous issues and peoples for *Alternatives* did not identify themselves in their biographies as Indigenous. Of the thirty-one articles with significant Indigenous content only three had Indigenous authors, and only one of these, the article by Tobasonakwut Peter Kinew, originally published under the name Peter Kelley, had unambiguous and solo Indigenous authorship.[26] The other two included the article authored by the James Bay Committee mentioned above; this committee included two Indigenous organizations, although it appears that Dorothy Rosenberg, a southern activist, was the one responsible for much of the group's writing.[27] Lastly, in the winter 1978 issue, Lloyd Tataryn authored "Notes from the Territories: Arsenic Poisoning," which detailed and contextualized the concerns that had arisen in Yellowknife around arsenic contamination from the Giant Mine. With the author's biography was a note that the article was "based on a presentation delivered by Noel Starblanket, President of the National Indian Brotherhood, to the Canadian Public Health Association Task Force on Arsenic, March 1977."[28] This was not necessarily an instance of wholesale appropriation, however, as Tataryn himself was identified as "a journalist and consultant on environmental issues to the National Indian Brotherhood."[29]

Tataryn's role here speaks to the other distinguishing feature of some of the work published in *Alternatives* by non-Indigenous authors on Indigenous topics in this period: among these authors were people who worked as staff or consultants for Indigenous communities and organizations. This includes not just Tataryn but also Peter Usher ("a geographer and Consultant to the Inuit Tapirisat of Canada"), Melville Watkins ("a Professor of Political Economy at the University of Toronto and Economic Consultant to the Indian Brotherhood of the Northwest Territories"), Henry Lickers ("Acting Director of the St. Regis Akwesasne Environmental Division"), and Ted Jackson ("a researcher for the Canadian Association in Support of Native People [CASNP], in Ottawa, Ontario"). These authors certainly foregrounded these affiliations in order to lend credibility to their ability to speak to Indigenous issues, and they remained, nevertheless, a minority of those writing on Indigenous topics in *Alternatives*. However, their contributions help to explain why the substance of the pieces published in *Alternatives*, while rarely espousing an Indigenous perspective, were at times more grounded in Indigenous realities than preoccupied with constructions of the Indigenous "other," as was often the case in environmentalist writings from this era.

"Marmion Lake Generating Station," 1978

What follows as Chapter 7 was the article published in *Alternatives* and written by chief of the Sabaskong or Onigaming First Nation, Tobasonakwut Peter Kinew, describing Anishinaabe opposition to a planned coal-fired generating station to be built on Treaty 3 lands, west of Thunder Bay on Highway 11, and close to the First Nations communities of Asubpeeschoseewagong (Grassy Narrows) and Wabaseemoong (Whitedog). In the fall of 1977, Ontario Hydro announced that construction of a coal-fired generating station outside Atikokan, a settler community based on mining, logging, and transportation, was to begin within three months. The project was exempted from Ontario's Environmental Assessment Act (1975) on the grounds that planning for the generating station was well advanced when the Act was proclaimed.[30]

Kinew details the character of Anishinaabe opposition to the project, framed in three ways. First, he maintained that Ontario Hydro had failed to properly consult with people living in the area whose livelihoods stood to be affected by the proposed development. Anishinaabeg from Seine River and Lac La Croix wanted to know how "trapping, hunting, fishing, logging, wild rice picking, and the tourist camps" would be affected.[31] Second, their concerns about the effects on the land and wildlife were not in a vacuum but shaped by their experiences with the impacts of mining, pulp and paper, and logging operations in the area, specifically the devastating health and ecological impacts of mercury contamination at Grassy Narrows.[32] The former concern meant that First Nations had lived experience with the extinction of sturgeon as a result of pollution and the effects of raised water levels on fishing and trapping. The Treaty 3 Chiefs Council also drew on the expertise of a McMaster University biologist, J. R. Kramer, who was concerned with the buffering capacity of local waters. Kramer asserted that "emissions from the proposed development must be considered as adding to the background which is at present marginal for most susceptible lakes."[33] Combined, these concerns demonstrate critical awareness of what would only later come to be recognized as cumulative effects: that the ecological impacts of resource and energy projects needed to be considered not only in isolation but in historical and regional context.[34] Third, and lastly, the effects of pollution at Grassy Narrows not only led to heightened concern about mercury contamination from resource projects like the proposed Atikokan generating station but also ensured that the concerns of the Treaty 3 Chiefs Council as representing local Anishinaabe views were heard nationally and internationally. The *Globe and Mail*, *Toronto Star*, and *Ottawa Citizen* carried articles and opinion pieces about the proposed Marmion Lake development and local opposition.

The Treaty 3 Chiefs Council brought their concerns to the hearings of the Ontario Royal Commission on the Northern Environment (Hartt Commission), as it gathered testimony in Dryden, Ontario. The commission was prompted by public concerns over proposed new pulp and paper developments in northern Ontario and the growing awareness of the devastating impacts at Grassy Narrows.[35] Kinew, the main public spokesperson in media reports at the time, emphasized that the commission's response to Treaty 3 concerns about the development at Marmion Lake was a measure of its willingness to act on the issues surrounding resource exploitation and First Nations in northern Ontario.[36] While commissioner Hartt convened a meeting between representatives of Treaty 3 and Ontario Hydro in early 1978, the conversation between the different parties had no consequential impact on the outcome of the project, and thereafter Hartt refused to focus on Marmion Lake and the Atikokan generating station.

The Treaty 3 chiefs had more success when it came to international pressure. Kinew notes in his piece in *Alternatives* that the proposed generating station would fall within Canada's and Ontario's SO_2 guidelines (sulphur emissions were directly linked to acid rain, a major environmental issue of the day) but not within the stricter emissions standards south of the border.[37] Kinew and the Treaty 3 Chiefs Council specifically called for scrubbers to be installed to mitigate sulphur dioxide emissions. These were what Ontario Hydro deemed too expensive in their 1978 meeting. However, as boundary waters in a protected wilderness area were among those that stood to be affected by the proposed generating station, not only was Kinew able to ensure media attention in the United States but US representatives formally requested that the Atikokan power project be referred to the IJC for review, a request that Canada denied.[38] That Ontario, with the federal government's support, was so invested in the Atikokan project and unmoved by First Nations' concerns about its environmental impacts reflected not only the unyielding power inequities of the late twentieth-century colonial state but also, as part of this, the desire to ensure ongoing "development" in northern Ontario. Advocates for the Atikokan generating station emphasized the potential for new jobs, particularly in light of the anticipated closure of the local iron mine.[39] As well, in the mid-1970s, Ontario Hydro greatly overestimated the future electricity needs of the province.[40] Anticipated growth in demand led Ontario Hydro to commit to several new power plants, including the one at Marmion Lake. It was not until later in the decade and into the 1980s that the plans for new power developments would be scaled back.

Notwithstanding the environmental concerns highlighted by Kinew, the project received the green light. But construction of the Atikokan generation station was first delayed in 1979 and then only partially realized, as only one of the two planned 200-megawatt (MW) generating units was built. The generating station opened in December 1984 and operated into the twenty-first century, when greater public awareness of the role of coal-fired power plants in greenhouse gas emissions led Ontario to close or repurpose its thermal generating stations.[41] And so, between 2012 and 2014, Atikokan generating station became the site of the Atikokan biomass conversion project, using wood pellets sourced from Ontario forests to continue to produce 200 MW at full capacity.[42] The Pembina Institute, an NGO focused on clean energy issues, produced a report on behalf of Ontario Power Generation (a successor to Ontario Hydro) on the sustainability of such biomass projects in April 2011 that included among its socio-economic criteria that "Aboriginal peoples should have the authority to control biomass operations on their lands" and that full and meaningful consultation with Indigenous residents was key.[43] Nevertheless, local First Nations, including Treaty 3 residents and a former chief of the Seine River First Nation, "were the least supportive" of the Atikokan biomass project, highlighting a range of ecological and economic concerns, as well as their enduring opposition to the limited control that Treaty 3 First Nations could exert over this and other resource projects in the area.[44]

In closing his 1978 article in *Alternatives*, Kinew raised four essential questions about the proposed generating station at Marmion Lake: Was this power source necessary? How could damaging ecological effects be prevented or mitigated? How can Indigenous people be "truly involved" in public consultations? And lastly, "Where were the environmental interest groups when we needed them?"[45] Each of these questions resonates through the small green struggles examined throughout this volume, in particular, the critical intersection between Indigenous sovereignty and environmental activism explored by Welch, Grossman, and Evans. However, it is the last question that is perhaps most revealing about the character of 1970s environmental activism as represented in *Alternatives*. Kinew calls out environmentalists for their failure to effectively join forces with Indigenous opponents to the proposed power project. In the next issue of *Alternatives*, Jan Marmorek with Energy Probe replied to these concerns, claiming that Kinew had misunderstood Energy Probe's role.[46] But it was Marmorek who missed the forest for the trees. Kinew's closing comments emphasized the need for ongoing, close, cross-cultural communication between Indigenous peoples and environmental groups in order to build a "strong alliance." Kinew was calling for relationships to be built, predicated on shared concerns. Marmorek suggested that better communication could be achieved through Energy Probe's new publication, *The Probe Post*. But if this analysis of *Alternatives* is any indication, small green activist publications were not a meaningful forum where Indigenous and non-Indigenous voices alike could hold equal sway. So Kinew asked, "Were environmental groups founded only to work with the white middle class?" Here Kinew takes Richard White's well-known provocation, "Are you an environmentalist or do you work for a living?" and resituates it in a colonial context.[47] Who did 1970s environmentalists work for? The white middle class? Or for the land and the people, fundamentally interconnected in Kinew's perspective? That his remained the only prominent Indigenous voice published in *Alternatives* in its first decade was ultimately the most powerful evidence of the limits to engagement between small green and Indigenous activists in this early history of Canada's modern environmentalist movement.

Notes

1   For a short history of the journal, see "The Alternatives Journal Story," last updated 2018, http://www.alternativesjournal.ca/about/history.

2   Ryan O'Connor, *The First Green Wave: Pollution Probe and the Origins of Environmental Activism in Ontario* (Vancouver: UBC Press, 2014), 66.

3   For more on the Conserver Society, see McLaughlin, this volume; Henry Trim, "Planning the Future: The Conserver Society and Canadian Sustainability," NiCHE: Network in Canadian History and Environment, 8 October 2015, http://niche-canada.org/2015/10/08/planning-the-future-the-conserver-society-and-canadian-sustainability/.

4   The *Notes* are not included in the analysis of *Alternatives*' contributors presented here.

5   "Eco-tactic no. 18," *Alternatives* 1, no. 4 (1972): 19; "Eco-tactic no. 24," *Alternatives* 2, no. 4 (1973): 10. For more on the hydrogen sulphide releases at Inverhuron, see Joy Parr, "Smells Like? Sources of Uncertainty in the History of the Great Lakes Environment," *Environmental History* 11, no. 2 (2006): 269–99.

6   An example of these advertisements appeared in *Alternatives* 3, no. 2 (1974): 12.

7   See, respectively, multiple articles in *Alternatives* 2, no. 3 (1973): 6–37; James Hodgins, "Manitoulin South Shore," *Alternatives* 8, no. 1 (1978): 11–14; Sanford Osler, "For a National Energy Policy," *Alternatives* 2, no. 4 (1973): 18–19; Trevor Hancock,

"Ecological Sanity and Social Justice: Public Health in the Age of Osiris," *Alternatives*, 9, no. 4 (1981): 11–18; Mulford Q. Sibley, "The Relevance of Classical Political Theory for Economy, Technology, and Ecology," *Alternatives* 2, no. 2 (1973): 14–35.

8   John Marsh, professor of Geography at Trent, authored seven separate articles in this period, and Jamie Benidickson, "a Peterborough resident" and researcher, five, making them the two most frequent contributors aside from the editor (Robert Paehlke, who authored three articles and many editorials) and David Brooks with Energy Probe, who also authored five articles.

9   Jamie Benidickson, "The Meaning of the North in Canada," *Alternatives* 2, no. 3 (1973): 4.

10   Ted Schrecker, "Labour and Environment: *Alternatives* Conference Report," *Alternatives* 4, no. 2 (1975): 34–43.

11   That said, unless a contributor specified an environmentalist affiliation or described themselves explicitly as such, I did not assume that every contributor was an "environmentalist," although perhaps an argument could be made that, given the venue, I should have.

12   I made no attempt to judge which affiliation was more important, for example, whether for Harger, his status as an assistant professor was more or less meaningful than his work with SPEC.

13   Quotations from editorial authored by Robert C. Paehkle, "Decentralization, Environment & Community," *Alternatives* 3, no. 1 (1973): 2.

14   For examples of the first type, see R. K. Vastokas, "A Hint from the Past," *Alternatives* 1, no. 1 (1971): 10–11; Gary Moffatt, "Evolving into Freedom," *Alternatives* 3, no. 1 (1973): 34; n.a., "ISCE," *Alternatives*, 3, no. 1 (1973): 5. The one example from this decade of a sustained examination of Indigenous people that was highly romanticized was Allison Mitcham, "The Wild Creatures, The Native People, and Us: Canadian Literary-Ecological Relationships," *Alternatives* 7, no. 2 (1978): 20–23.

15   See, for example, A. R. Lucas and Sandra K. McCallum, "Looking At Environmental Impact Assessment," 5, no. 2 (1976): 30. Articles that addressed Indigenous peoples in detail in the context of resource development are counted among those with "significant" Indigenous content.

16   And not just in Canada: see, for example, Hanna J. Cortner, "Development, Environment, Indians and the Southwest Power Controversy," *Alternatives* 4, no. 1 (1974): 14–20.

17   See, for example, Ted Jackson, "Clearcutting Canada's Forests," *Alternatives* 6, no. 2 (1977): 28–31; and Glen Scobie, "The Proposed Hat Creek Valley Coal Development: A Report," *Alternatives* 9, no. 2 (1980): 2–4.

18   Bruce Hodgins and Shelagh Grant (both from Trent) would go on to co-author a 1986 review in *Acadiensis* (a history journal) that discussed how the Berger inquiry and environmentalist concern had reshaped northern historiography—they did so even as both contributed directly to this trend as authors in *Alternatives* (Hodgins, in particular, as he co-edited the 1978 special issue on the North). Bruce W. Hodgins and

Shelagh D. Grant, "The Canadian North: Trends in Recent Historiography," *Acadiensis* 16, no. 1 (1986): 173–88.

19   W. P. Adams and J. R. Glew, "'The Arctic' In Perspective," *Alternatives* 3, no. 2 (1974): 37.

20   For instance, J. R. Kramer, "Atmospheric Composition & Precipitation of the Sudbury Region," *Alternatives* 2, no. 3 (1973): 18–25.

21   See n.a., "Minamata: Canada," *Alternatives* 5, no. 1 (1975): 36–39; Jim Harding, "Nuclear Power and Public Health: The Eldorado Refinery Proposal," *Alternatives* 9, no. 4 (1981): 37–41; Lloyd Tataryn [and Noel Starblanket], "Notes from the Territories: Arsenic Poisoning," *Alternatives* 7, no. 2 (1978): 12–15; Henry Lickers, "Saint Regis, the Shrouded Nation," *Alternatives* 8, no. 1 (1978): 33–36. There were other articles on social justice and racism, including one by Wilson Head, "The Canadian Case," addressing historical racism in Canada, in *Alternatives* 8, no. 2 (1979): 18–20; Janet McClain, "Energy Savings at Home – A Reasonable Place to Begin?" *Alternatives* 9, no. 3 (1980): 23–25, which addressed briefly housing inequity on reserves; and Jim Harding, "Development, Underdevelopment and Alcohol Disabilities in Northern Saskatchewan," *Alternatives* 7, no. 4 (1978): 30–33, which addressed social and health issues facing northern Indigenous people in Saskatchewan.

22   I use "Aboriginal rights" rather than "Indigenous rights" here and elsewhere in this chapter to specifically identify the rights under discussion in the constitutional debates of the 1970s and 1980s, as this was the language employed at the time.

23   See, for instance, David Estrin, "Legal Weapons for Environmental Quality," *Alternatives* 2, no. 1 (1972): 4–9.

24   Geoff Mains, "Some Environmental Aspects of a Canadian Constitution," *Alternatives* 9, no. 2 (1980): 14–17.

25   For more on the Oldman Dam, see David Boyd, *Unnatural Law: Rethinking Canadian Environmental Law and Policy* (Vancouver: UBC Press, 2003), 46, 159, 222.

26   There is no evidence that any of the 222 articles without significant Indigenous content had Indigenous authors.

27   Dorothy Rosenberg was a prominent peace and environmental activist later profiled in *Peace Magazine*, February–March 1986, 10, http://peacemagazine.org/archive/v02n1p10.htm.

28   Tataryn and Starblanket, "Notes from the Territories: Arsenic Poisoning," 12.

29   Ibid., 12

30   The Environmental Assessment Act, 1975, SO 1975, c. 69. The Atikokan generating station was not the only energy project exempt at this time; so too was the Darlington Nuclear Generating Station: see Hugh Winsor, "Could Public be Right?" *Globe and Mail*, 2 March 1979, 7; and John Swaigen, "Environmental Law 1975–1980," *Ottawa Law Review* 12 (1980): 452. For a broader history of environmental assessment legislation in Ontario, see Mark S. Winfield, *Blue-Green Province: The Environment and the Political Economy of Ontario* (Vancouver: UBC Press, 2012).

31 Peter Kelley [Tobasonakwut Peter Kinew], "Marmion Lake Generating Station: Another Northern Scandal?" *Alternatives* 7, no. 4 (1978): 14.

32 High levels of mercury in water and fish downriver from the Dryden Chemical pulp and paper plant were discovered in 1969–70, and by 1977 the Grassy Narrows and Wabaseemoong First Nations had initiated legal action against the company responsible. For a timeline, see Delores Broten and Claire Gilmore, "The Story of Grassy Narrows," *Watershed Sentinel*, 19 January 2017, https://watershedsentinel.ca/articles/story-grassy-narrows/.

33 Kinew, "Marmion Lake," 14.

34 A brief overview of the recent history of recognizing the importance of cumulative effects in one of Canada's most intensively developed industrial regions—the Athabasca oil sands—is described in Steven A. Kennett, *Closing the Performance Gap: The Challenge for Cumulative Effects Management in Alberta's Athabasca Oil Sands Region* (CIRL Occasional Paper #18, May 2007), vii.

35 See Roger Suffling and Gregory Michalenko, "The Reed Affair: A Canadian Logging and Pollution Controversy," *Biological Conservation* 17 (1980): 5–23; Michael Coyle, "Addressing Aboriginal Land Rights in Ontario: An Analysis of Past Policies and Options for the Future – Part II," *Queen's Law Journal* 31 (2006): 796–845; Ontario, Royal Commission on the Northern Environment, *Final Report and Recommendations of the Royal Commission on the Northern Environment* (Toronto: Ontario Ministry of the Attorney General, 1985). One opinion piece on the Hartt Commission noted that it had been modelled on the Mackenzie Valley Pipeline Inquiry: see Jonathan Manthorpe, "Time Hartt Started Talking Tough," *Toronto Star*, 19 January 1978, A10.

36 See, for instance, Michael Moore, "Credibility has Dipped, Hartt is told," *Globe and Mail*, 18 January 1978, 8. Kinew is variously referred to as John or Peter Kelly or Kelley in news reports and other media from the time.

37 Dimitry Anastakis has examined the reasons behind and consequences of these different emissions standards in "A 'War on Pollution'? Canadian Responses to the Automotive Emissions Problem, 1970–80," *Canadian Historical Review* 90, no. 1 (2009): 99–136.

38 There is an important history of environmental impacts along the US-Canada border in forcing industrial change and mitigation in Canada: see, for instance, J. D. Wirth, "The Trail Smelter Dispute: Canadians and Americans Confront Transboundary Pollution, 1927–41," *Environmental History* 1, no. 2 (1996): 34–51; Daniel Macfarlane, *Negotiating a River: Canada, the US, and the Creation of the St. Lawrence Seaway* (Vancouver: UBC Press, 2014).

For the specifics on the IJC reference in 1978, see "No IJC Inquiry on Coal Plant at Atikokan," *Globe and Mail*, 23 March 1978, 8; Victor Malarek, "Acid Rain Report Called Grossly Inaccurate: Ontario Attacks U.S. Agency," *Globe and Mail*, 12 May 1979, 1. For the longer history of the IJC's role in regulating the ecological health of Ontario boundary waters, see Jennifer Read, "'A Sort of Destiny': The Multi-Jurisdictional Response to Sewage Pollution in the Great Lakes, 1900–1930," *Scientia Canadensis* 22–23 (1998–99): 103–29.

39 Michael Moore, "Hydro Denies all Responsibility for Damage in Indian Graveyard," *Globe and Mail*, 30 November 1977, 10; "Massive Hydro Project Renewing Faith in Economic Future of Atikokan Area," *Globe and Mail*, 12 October 1977, 10.

40 Thomas Claridge, "Ontario Hydro Has Large Power Glut," *Globe and Mail*, 25 February1983, 17.

41 See, for example, Keith Leslie, "Ontario to Close Four Coal-Fired Generating Units," *Globe and Mail*, 4 September 2009, A6; Winfield, *Blue-Green Province*, 136–39.

42 Ontario Power Generation, "Atikokan Biomass Conversion," last updated 2018, https://www.opg.com/generating-power/thermal/stations/atikokan-station/pages/atikokan-station-biomass-conversion-project.aspx.

43 Pembina Institute, "Biomass Sustainability Analysis: Summary Report," April 2011, 7.

44 Cassia Sanzida Baten, "Woody Biomass-Based Bioenergy Development at the Atikokan Power Generating Station: Local Perceptions and Public Opinions," (PhD diss., Lakehead University, 2014), 120, 130.

45 Kinew, "Marmion Lake," 15–16.

46 "Letters," *Alternatives*, 8, no. 1 (1978): 44.

47 Richard White, "'Are You an Environmentalist or Do You Work for a Living?': Work and Nature," in *Uncommon Ground: Rethinking the Human Place in Nature*, ed. W. Cronon (New York: W. W. Norton, 1996), 121–85.

7

Marmion Lake Generating Station: Another Northern Scandal?

Tobasonakwut Peter Kinew [1]

Twenty miles west of Atikokan, in northwestern Ontario, lies the Ojibway reserve of Seine River, a community of about 500 people who have traditionally made their livelihood hunting, trapping and fishing. More recently, logging and tourist guiding have been introduced. Although they live within commuting distance of the iron ore mines of Atikokan, Seine River people have not benefited from this development.

About 80 air miles southwest of Seine River is another Ojibway village of about 150 people. Lac La Croix is situated on the northwest edge of the wilderness of Quetico Provincial Park, and is accessible only by air and water. There, the people continue to live the traditional way, supplementing their income only by seasonal construction work and some guiding.

Last fall, both these communities became aware of the coal-fired generating station Ontario Hydro proposes to build at Marmion Lake, seven miles outside the town of Atikokan. The first phase of the 800-megawatt plant is scheduled to begin operation in September, 1983 and the plant should be fully operational in fall, 1984.

Ontario Hydro asserts that the corporation undertook a public participation program to involve fully the people of the area. No one in Seine River or Lac La Croix heard of the project until the fall of 1977—three months before construction was to begin, three months after the Ontario government had given the project final approval and one year after the government had exempted the project from any review under the 1975 Ontario Environmental Assessment Act.

The Grand Council Treaty No. 3, an organization of Chiefs of the 25 reserves in the Treaty No. 3 part of northwestern Ontario, met with the two communities to discuss the project and the effects of the plant's effluent on the land and on wildlife. How would trapping, hunting, fishing, logging, wild rice picking, and the tourist camps be affected? Through the years the people had witnessed the effects of other developments. Sturgeon had become extinct because of the wood fibre pollution from log drives along the river. Other fishing and trapping had been spoiled by raised water levels from dams erected to assist iron ore mining. And the people had shared the suffering of neighbouring communities affected by development, notably Grassy Narrows, Whitedog and Lac Seul.

As a starting point from which to address the Ontario government, Treaty No. 3 Chiefs Council chose to bring the issue to the Ontario Royal Commission on the Northern Environment (the Hartt Commission) at its hearings in northern Ontario. On the third day of the hearings in Dryden, Ontario, Treaty No. 3 presented its argument:

> While the proposed power plant will meet the sulphur dioxide standards of Canada and Ontario, the project will violate the U.S. and Minnesota standards. . . . If the Ontario government has its way, there will be no careful examination of the serious potential environmental consequences of their power plant. . . . The sulphur dioxide emissions will snuff out the life of many of our lakes. . . .
>
> Your duty is to make the government of Ontario abide by its own law—namely the Environmental Assessment Act. Your credibility will be greatly enhanced if you can convince the government that it is eminently reasonable . . . to have the International Joint Commission hear evidence on Ontario Hydro's Atikokan project.[2]

Prof. J. R. Kramer, a biologist at McMaster University and consultant to the International Joint Commission, appeared before the Hartt inquiry to state his concern about the buffering capacity of the lakes in northwestern Ontario. Pollutant levels, said Kramer, "will probably double by the year 2000 without any SO_2 emission scrubbing and will probably stay the same with the state of the art of technological abatement. . . . Emissions from proposed development must be considered as adding to the background which is at present marginal for most susceptible lakes. Therefore, any additions to this background must be carefully considered."[3]

Justice Hartt requested that Ontario Hydro respond to Treaty No. 3 at a later hearing. Three weeks later, in Nakina, Ontario, Hydro related that the projected was conceived after the government decided in 1973 that further generation facilities were needed in Ontario Hydro West System. Atikokan was the chosen site and, following some environmental studies undertaken by Hydro, Acres Consulting, and Proctor-Redfern, the site was acquired and Cabinet exempted Ontario Hydro from the provisions of the Environmental Assessment Act because of its "advanced stage of planning prior to the proclamations of the Act."[4] Hydro did not respond directly to the concerns of Treaty No. 3, and the Native group again called on Hartt to intervene by calling a direct meeting between Hydro and representatives of Treaty No. 3.

On December 8, 1977, Justice Hartt convened a meeting between three representatives of Treaty No. 3 and three representatives of Hydro, including the corporation's chairman, Robert Taylor. Hydro reiterated its stand that all laws had been complied with, all environmental standards would be met, and that the cost of installing scrubbers (capital costs $60 million; annual operating cost, $8–10 million) would be unjustified and financially irresponsible. Treaty No. 3 would have to address itself directly to Cabinet, said Hydro.

At this point, Treaty No. 3 went to the press. Both the *Toronto Star* and the *Ottawa Citizen* ran stories about the concern over acid rain fallout as a result of SO_2 emissions, and about the possibility of mercury releases into lakes in the affected area. An NBC-TV news program followed up by coming to the Treaty No. 3 area, filming the people of Lac La Croix at work on the land, and talking with them about the possible effects of the plant. The story was broadcast in the United States on March 4, 1978, but by then other developments were in the offing.

The United States have been making representations to both the Ontario and federal governments since 1976 about the possibility that SO$_2$ emissions would exceed state and federal pollution levels for the wilderness area on the border south of Quetico Park, the Boundary Waters Canoe Area, classified as Class I, or "pristine." American officials were pressing Ontario Hydro to include scrubbers (flue gas desulphurization equipment) in the design of the plant. Hydro had consistently refused, arguing that its own precautions were enough—incorporation of a 650-foot stack, precipitators claimed to be 99.5% efficient, and the use of low-sulphur coal from Alberta.

These very same precautions were used by the Saskatchewan Power Corporation in the design of its Poplar Hill Plant. The International Joint Commission has judged them not adequate to protect the environment.

On January 17, 1978, Treaty No. 3 again appeared before Justice Hartt, asking him to restore some sanity to the deliberations and to recommend a public inquiry with strong Native input into the planning of the generating station at Marmion Lake. Further evidence of the need for scrubbers was presented.

> Let us now consider the arguments put forward by Ontario Hydro. Ontario Hydro has stated that it will cost too much to install the scrubbers at Marmion Lake, but now we have a formula available to assess how much it will cost *not* to install scrubbers. A federal government study was recently released of the costs the public must bear for the decision to allow the Sudbury Nickel operations to dump 4½ thousand tons of sulphur dioxide a day into the Sudbury air. The cost to the public in terms of health and environmental damage, was almost four hundred and fifty million dollars a year.
>
> Let us now apply the same formula to the Marmion Lake project. The sulphur content of western sub-bituminous coal is 0.53%. The potential sulphur dioxide emissions from this coal would be about 1%, by weight, of the coal burnt. At Marmion Lake, Hydro expects to burn an average of 2.5 million tons of coal a year, or about 68,500 tons of coal a day. This means that Ontario Hydro will be pump-

ing about 685 tons of SO_2 into the Northwestern Ontario and Minnesota environment each and every day. If we now apply the formula used in the assessment of SO_2 damages in the Sudbury area to Marmion Lake, we find that the cost to the public will be over 60 million dollars per year. Consider the fact that it will cost Ontario Hydro 70 million dollars to install the special equipment needed to scrub their fumes clean. I would suggest that Ontario Hydro would have the cost of their scrubbers paid off in less than two years if they are only willing to take into account the social, environmental and health costs the people of Northwestern Ontario will be forced to pay.

One other point, in Scandinavia, fish biologists were puzzled by the unexpectedly high mercury levels in fish in a lake where no mercury had been dumped. The natural mercury in the environment was no greater in this lake than in the lakes of Scandinavia without a mercury problem. The Scandinavian scientist concluded that acid rain had fallen on the high mercury lake. The acid rain had caused an unusual amount of mercury to escape into the atmosphere and be absorbed by the fish. As you know, we have far too much mercury in our river systems already. We do not need any more.[5]

Atikokan residents appeared before a subcommittee of the International Joint Commission—the Upper Great Lakes Reference Group—at a December meeting in Thunder Bay to express their concern regarding the pollution from the plant. Meanwhile, Hydro hit the Thunder Bay papers with threats of power outages in northwestern Ontario until Marmion Lake generating station, and an extension of a Thunder Bay station, were completed. Support for the Treaty No. 3 position, and for that of northern environmentalists, came at that time from the President of the Kenora District Camp-owners Association. He expressed fears that the pronouncements of Hydro and the Ontario Government "smelled like another mercury decision. . . . if there is no problem as we are led to believe, we must ask why the Vice-President of the United States is going to Ottawa to discuss this issue with the Prime Minister."[6]

In January, the United States, Minnesota, Canada and Ontario held their second meeting as planned in August 1977 to discuss the studies they had made on the Marmion Lake plant with the information they had shared. The US continued to press for the installation of scrubbers, a proposal which Hydro rejected. Both sides discussed plans for monitoring of the plant for both air and water pollution, and the fact that Hydro would be willing to take corrective action if needed—and would be obliged to do so under the Ontario Environmental Protection Act of 1971. Although a joint statement was issued indicating some agreement, the US asked Canada to consider referring the project to the IJC for study. The importance of this request—and the immense amount of political pressure being drummed up in the US for this review—was emphasized by the fact that Vice-President Mondale had discussed this issue with Prime Minister Trudeau during an Ottawa visit the week before.

Ontario Hydro came out publicly against any further delay, and construction began on schedule in January 1978. The Ontario Ministry of Energy withdrew provincial support for any further talks with the Americans. The *Toronto Star* reported that "the ministry's tough stance may influence a series of other trans-boundary pollution disputes from coast to coast."[7] And an IJC recommendation on the Poplar River generating station in Saskatchewan prompted speculation that "the IJC appeal to halt construction on the Saskatchewan project may only harden Ontario's resolve to shun the acknowledged avenues of cross-border difficulties."[8] Although Saskatchewan still held out hope for an agreement on the western project, the outlook for Ontario was not good: "In future, similar projects may have to wait for a complete environmental study before construction can begin."[9]

Near the end of March, the federal government announced that it was rejecting the notion of an IJC review of the Marmion Lake project. At the beginning of April the Hartt Commission tabled its interim report to the Ontario Legislature. The report did not recommend an environmental assessment of the project—only that "the government of Ontario should immediately provide comprehensive information on the planned Atikokan Generating Station, and in consultation with local affected people and communities, ensure public discussion of this information to promote understanding of the project and its possible environmental effects."[10]

The people of Seine River and Lac La Croix appeared to be losing the battle.

On April 6 it was learned—again through the press—that "Canadian officials were astonished to learn that the U.S. Environmental Protection Agency is doing a study on the possible environmental effects of Atikokan (GS [generating station]) without Canada having been informed."[11] It seemed Minnesota congressmen had convinced Secretary of State Cyrus Vance that the study had to be done as a basis for a firmer negotiating position with Canada. Treaty No. 3 felt it ironic that its interests were being protected by a foreign government better than by Canada's.

Some very basic questions about Atikokan remain unanswered.

1. *Is this power source necessary?*

Ontario Hydro claims that the station is required to meet the needs of the 1980's. Yet existing possibilities and trends in the area of alternative sources of energy in the north have been ignored. More and more pulp and paper operations—by far the largest consumers of power in northwestern Ontario—are turning to wood wastes as fuel. Conservation is becoming part of our national consciousness. Many northerners are trying wood fuel, solar energy and wind power. And two energy-eaters—the iron ore mines at Atikokan—are scheduled to close down three years before the Marmion Lake station opens. And a new Manitoba government may be more willing to consider continuation of Ontario's present power purchase agreements with that province.

2. *How can the effects of sulphur dioxide on vegetation and people be offset? How can the process of mercury releases from rocks due to sulphur dioxide emissions be stopped?*

The only answer seems to be scrubbers. They would effectively remove almost all sulphur dioxide from the plant's emissions. Indian people have seen the devastation that mercury has wrought in the communities of Whitedog and Grassy Narrows. In the words of a Whitedog leader, Tony Henry, "[Indian people] wish to ensure that any future industrial development must only be considered once all voices have been heard and evaluated. . . . Anything destructive or potentially life-endangering must not be carried out."

3. *How can Native people be truly involved in a public participation program?*

Ontario Hydro's public participation process is a sham. The first step in the Marmion Lake case was to have a committee of "representative" people from the Thunder Bay area review six sites for a coal generating station. As Thunder Bay residents wanted no part of the attendant pollution, all six were rejected. Under political pressure to save Atikokan from economic extinction when the iron mines close (in 1979 or 1980), the Marmion Lake site was chosen. It was not on Hydro's list of six sites.

The only meetings held in the town took place after the project site had been purchased and the project exempted from the Environmental Assessment Act. No attempt was ever made to contact nearby Indian reserves. The environmental impact statements prepared by consulting firms considered only the town of Atikokan, not any of the effects on health and livelihood of nearby communities, either white or Indian.

4. *Where were the environmental interest groups when we needed them?*

When the native communities found out about the Marmion Lake generating station, it was almost too late to act. It was an uphill battle with government and Hydro, and even interesting the media in the issue at such a late stage was difficult.

Yet it was later learned that representatives of the Environment North group in Thunder Bay were on the original review committee which decided against the six sites and allowed the Marmion Lake site to be chosen. Representatives of Energy Probe in Toronto attended at least one public participation meeting of Hydro's in Atikokan about five months before Cabinet gave final approval to the project. Yet no one from these groups contacted the nearby reserves or the Treaty No. 3 organization.

There was, and is, a potential for a strong alliance between environmental and native groups—but only if information is shared and

Tobasonakwut Peter Kinew

continuous contact established. It may take more effort and time to work with people from another culture. But were environmental groups founded only to work with the white, middle class? Or is the real object to protect the land and the people—all the people?

Notes

1 "Marmion Lake Generating Station" is reprinted with permission of the family of the late Tobasonakwut Peter Kinew and AlternativesJournal.ca (A/J). The author's name appeared in *Alternatives* 7, no. 4 [1978] as Peter Kelley. Indian Affairs gave his family the surname Kelly, but he returned to his traditional name in the 1990s. The author's original biography included with the article read: "Peter Kelley is Chief of the Sabaskong Reserve, situated on Lake of the Woods halfway between Kenora and Fort Frances and the Area Tribal Chief for the Grand Council Treaty No. 3."

   As this article has been reprinted, we chose to preserve the original formatting and content in its entirety and without revision.

2 Submission of Grand Council Treaty No. 3 to Royal Commission on the Northern Environment (RCNE), Dryden, November 1977.

3 Kramer to RCNE, Dryden, November 1977.

4 Ontario Hydro, "Supplementary statement to RCNE," Nakina, November 28, 1977.

5 Grand Council Treaty No. 3 submission to RCNE, Kenora, January 17, 1978.

6 "Plant concerns KDAC President," *Kenora Miner and News,* January 31, 1978.

7 "Angry Ontario cuts pollution talks with US," *Toronto Star,* January 22, 1978.

8 "Poplar River development may harden Ontario opposition to an IJC study of Atikokan," *Eco/Log Week*, February 10, 1978.

9 "Environmental factors may block SPC plant," *Globe and Mail*, March 9, 1978.

10 Interim Report of RCNE, April 1978, p. 15.

11 "US is told of Canada's concern over proposals for dam project," *Globe and Mail*, April 6, 1978. [This is a paraphrase rather than a direct quotation from the article authored by John Picton – eds.].

Environmental Activism as Anti-Conquest: The Nuu-chah-nulth and Environmentalists in the Contact Zone of Clayoquot Sound

Jonathan Clapperton

Clayoquot Sound, on the western edge of Vancouver Island, British Columbia, is a renowned ecotourist paradise replete with temperate rainforests, sandy beaches, and, increasingly, luxury resorts. Additionally, for environmentalists, Clayoquot Sound stands out as one of the legendary sites of the Canadian environmental movement's coming-of-age victories. Beginning in the summer of 1993, thousands of environmental activists, representing myriad local/small-scale and major international organizations, from the Friends of Clayoquot Sound to Greenpeace respectively, journeyed to a hastily constructed "Peace Camp" in opposition to the provincial government's decision to permit the powerful forestry corporation MacMillan Bloedel (in which the province owned a majority of shares) to conduct extensive clearcut logging throughout the area. Environmentalists would eventually claim at least partial victory after the government and industry bowed to public pressure to change forest-management standards and limit clearcuts. While environmentalists fought for an end to this logging practice, much of their campaign hinged on recognition of the local Nuu-chah-nulth First Nations' Aboriginal rights to their traditional territories.

Throughout the campaign and afterward, the former patted themselves on the back for what they considered staunch advocacy on behalf of the area's Indigenous peoples. It is the nature of Aboriginal-environmentalist relationships in Clayoquot Sound that I explore here.

Environmentalists from all organizations involved in Clayoquot Sound throughout the 1980s and 1990s depicted their relationships with the Nuu-chah-nulth as two marginalized groups uniting for a common cause—the liberation of both Aboriginal peoples and environmentalist ideology.[1] But, as geographer Bruce Braun observes, "That few Natives [actually] joined the protestors on the blockades is a topic that has still not received the attention it deserves."[2] Case in point: Margaret Horsfield and Ian Kennedy's recent, voluminous *Tofino and Clayoquot Sound: A History* largely writes First Nations out of the narrative when discussing the 1993–94 protests, smooths out the differences between the two groups and instead highlights only the joint First Nations–environmentalist efforts to protect Meares Island in the mid-1980s.[3] Braun goes on to say that environmentalist support for First Nations was actually ambivalent and sought to erase Indigenous peoples' presence from the land because of the former's focus on virgin, untouched spaces; environmentalism depends upon colonialism because its ultimate goal is to remove permanent settlement from "wild" spaces.[4] Niamh Moore contends that Braun pays too little attention to environmentalists' strategies and the role of the media in framing events.[5] The chapter presented here overcomes these shortcomings. It focuses specifically on environmentalist, as well as Indigenous, strategies and tactics, and relies heavily as well on discourse analysis of environmentalist-authored publications, over which they would have had full control, in order to provide balance to what may have been biased and/or sensationalist media coverage.

Other scholars, whether focusing on Clayoquot Sound specifically or similar cases elsewhere, have echoed Braun's position. Drawing attention to what is sometimes referred to as "green" or "eco-" imperialism, they have largely appraised environmentalist-Aboriginal relationships in the same light: environmentalists are prone to authoritarian thought; their focus on their own culturally specific conception of environmentalism above everyone else's often erases Indigenous peoples (among others) from supposedly "natural" spaces; and even though environmentalists have criticized colonialism, they still question the ability of Indigenous peoples to manage natural resources and reserve the right to criticize them when they act in ways contrary to environmentalist ideology.[6] Indeed, Greenpeace's Tzeporah Berman, one of the key environmentalist organizers during the 1993–94 protests, recognized in her recent autobiography that environmentalists made many missteps in their relationship with the Nuu-chah-nulth, but she still contends that environmentalists have a moral authority to criticize the practices of First Nations writ large.[7]

While both images of environmentalists as benevolent heroes or as neo-colonialists have some basis, the former problematically represents Aboriginal peoples as little more than environmentalist sidekicks, while the latter portrays them as victims overwhelmed by the structurally entrenched forces of colonial elites. In either situation, environmentalists remain at the centre of history and Aboriginal peoples are denied any significant measure of agency. Using Indigenous and environmentalist activism at Clayoquot Sound from the early 1980s through the 1990s as a case study demonstrates that post-colonial critiques of environmentalists' strategies are justified. But it also reveals that the Nuu-chah-nulth capitalized on both the presence of environmentalist organizations and the protest events to create new political, economic, and discursive spaces for themselves within numerous colonial structures. They then employed these spaces to assert control over their traditional territories and the natural resources therein. In other words, the Nuu-chah-nulth, far from being caught between and injured by the competition for dominance between various colonial forces, managed to use these competitions to their advantage and sometimes even orchestrated them.

The Nuu-chah-nulth (formerly referred to as Nootka) consist of fourteen First Nations, divided into three regions. Those who would be most involved in the Clayoquot Sound protests were from the Central Region, which includes the Ahousaht, Hesquiaht, Tla-o-qui-aht, Toquaht, and Ucluelet. The Nuu-chah-nulth—as with all Indigenous peoples—far from living in a "pristine wilderness," have inhabited, inherited, managed, and enhanced an environment ample in marine and forest resources since time immemorial. They were highly proficient whalers, and relied, and continue to depend on, both marine and terrestrial resources such as salmon, shellfish, forest animals, and plants. Equally as important for the

Nuu-chah-nulth, "the forests and waters of Clayoquot Sound were and still are the source of food, medicine, and history; they provide sustenance, education and a connection to the spiritual world."[8] The same giant cedar and Sitka spruce forests that environmentalists sought to protect, and many came to worship with religious fervour, were central to the Nuu-chah-nulth world.[9]

While non-Aboriginal newcomers and the Nuu-chah-nulth have long encountered one another—the Nuu-chah-nulth were, after all, some of the earliest Indigenous peoples in the Pacific Northwest to interact with Europeans, beginning in the 1770s—their exchange with environmentalists since the 1980s would mark episodic revivals of what Mary Louise Pratt terms the contact zone: the space of colonial encounters where peoples once separated establish ongoing relations, "usually involving conditions of coercion, racial inequality, and intractable conflict."[10] A wide range of scholars have utilized the "contact zone" to frame analyses of places where white Westerners, as agents of colonialism—whether conscious of their position or not—occupied the space of colonial encounter between Aboriginal peoples and newcomers, although I am unaware of any that apply the concept to environmentalists or spaces of environmentalist activism.

The "contact zone" was established between some of the Nuu-chah-nulth First Nations and local environmental activists in the early 1980s in response to logging interests. In 1980, MacMillan Bloedel announced it would log much of Meares Island (*Wah nah jus/Hilth hoo is*)—on which Opitsaht, the main community of the Tla-o-qui-aht, sits—after obtaining a timber licence to a portion of it. As with the majority of land in British Columbia, neither the provincial nor federal governments had negotiated a treaty with the local Indigenous population to acquire it; Meares Island was unceded Indigenous territory. Unsurprisingly, the Nuu-chah-nulth immediately opposed the plan. The same year, the Nuu-chah-nulth Tribal Council presented a land claim to their traditional territory, including Meares Island, to Canada's federal government. Non-Aboriginal residents in Tofino, which has a view of Meares Island, were also concerned, given that logging the island posed a threat to Tofino's only source of domestic water, as well as the area's lucrative tourism, fish, and mariculture (the cultivation of marine organisms for food and other products) industries.

Three years later, the federal government accepted the Nuu-chah-nulth's claim for negotiation and the provincial government approved MacMillan Bloedel's logging application, though it stipulated that the part of the island visible from the resort town of Tofino was off limits for twenty years.[11] In response, both the Tla-o-qui-aht and Ahousaht nations then asserted their jurisdiction over the whole of the island. Utilizing the settler-colonial rhetoric of conservation and park creation as a benevolent means of laying claim to territory, the Tla'o'qui'aht Band Council and hereditary chiefs drew on the discourse of environmental conservation and declared Meares Island a tribal park on 21 April 1984. Such action was especially poignant given that Canada's Pacific Rim National Park, established in 1971, was located within unceded Nuu-chah-nulth territory and went around reserve lands, thus denying those First Nations access to resources therein. The Tla'o'qui'aht distinguished a tribal park from other such settler-colonial spaces, however, in that the Nuu-chah-nulth could continue to use and manage the environment as they saw fit. It also provided the opportunity for joint use with non-Aboriginal people, though noting in no uncertain terms that the Nuu-chah-nulth controlled Meares Island. As the proclamation stated, "native people are prepared to share Meares Island with non-natives" dependent on a number of conditions, including adhering to "the laws of our forefathers," as well as outsider recognition of Nuu-chah-nulth land claims.[12]

Both the Friends of Clayoquot Sound (FOCS) and the Western Canadian Wilderness Committee (WCWC) threw their full support behind the designation. The FOCS was formed in Tofino in 1979, largely in response to the threat of logging Meares Island, while the WCWC was founded in Victoria in 1980—after getting assistance from Greenpeace at its headquarters in Vancouver—with a broader mandate to protect and preserve wilderness.[13] When loggers employed by MacMillan Bloedel headed toward the island in 1984 to begin cutting, they were preceded by a number of Tla'o-qui'aht and non-Aboriginal environmentalists, mostly those from Tofino belonging to the FOCS, who prevented the crews from landing by occupying strategic areas of the island. The Tla'o-qui'aht invited the MacMillan employees to visit the island provided they left their chainsaws behind.[14] Thereafter, the FOCS helped to maintain a "forest protectors' camp," established by the Tla-o-qui-aht at Heelboom (*C'is-aquis*) Bay (the proposed logging site).[15]

A local, non-Aboriginal, environmental activist campaign, again led in large part by the FOCS—then around sixty members[16]—and the WCWC intensified, with environmentalists sometimes working on their own, and at other times with the Nuu-chah-nulth. Among other activities, environmentalists handed out protest leaflets,[17] produced and distributed newsletters regarding the area's importance for those living in and beyond Tofino, and published their unequivocal support for the Nuu-chah-nulth.[18] Tofino resident William Tielemen—a MacMillan Bloedel shareholder— even presented a motion at the company's annual meeting to request that logging on Meares Island not proceed.[19] Local activists convinced the Tofino Village Council to formally oppose the logging decision.[20] Some activists spiked trees.[21] The Tla'o-qui-aht and FOCS constructed a trail on Meares Island so visitors—notably journalists—could access some of the oldest and largest trees.[22] Perhaps the most visible example of joint Nuu-chah-nulth and non-Aboriginal activism was the protest held on 20 October 1984, outside the provincial legislature in Victoria, British Columbia's capital, where the 23-foot-high welcome figure *Haa-hoo-ilth-quin* ("Cedar Man") carving (the image on the cover of this volume), by Nuu-chah-nulth artist Joe David, was on display.[23]

The issue ultimately went to the courts, beginning in 1984, for a lengthy, expensive legal battle, which successfully quieted the chainsaws in a quagmire of litigation that dragged on for years. As legal scholar Douglas Harris explains, "the case came before the courts in the form of requests for injunctions, one from MacMillan Bloedel to stop the protest-ors from blocking its access to the island, another from the Clayoquot and Ahousaht . . . to stop the company from logging pending the resolution of the claim to Aboriginal title."[24] Even though the activists at Meares Island amounted to a relatively small number of people, estimated around fifty or sixty for both Nuu-chah-nulth and non-Aboriginal,[25] the resistance, along with its eventual movement of the "contact zone" to also encom-pass the courts, was nonetheless profound. It allowed the Nuu-chah-nulth a highly visible public forum—both in the courts and in the media the cases generated—to express their claim to their traditional territory and its multi-faceted importance to them. In short, the range of the contact zone expanded to both encompass the physical space of the courts and extend into peoples' homes via the news media.

Defeat in the courts for the First Nations seemed likely at first. The chambers judge held that "the claim of the Clayoquot and Ahousaht to Aboriginal title had no prospect of success at trial. . . . [It] had been too long in coming" and that the injunction against logging would, if granted, have "'potentially disastrous consequences' for the provincial economy given the extent of unresolved claims to Aboriginal title and the possibility that the grant of an injunction in this case would set a precedent that would spread across the province."[26] However, the British Columbia Court of Appeals disagreed.[27] Recognizing the island's importance from a Nuu-chah-nulth point of view, Justice Seaton, in justifying the Court of Appeal's order for MacMillan Bloedel to stop logging pending the outcome of the Nuu-chah-nulth's claim to Aboriginal title, wrote, "It appears that the area to be logged will be wholly logged. The forest that the Indians know and use will be permanently destroyed. The tree from which the bark was partially stripped in 1642 may be cut down, middens may be destroyed, fish traps damaged and canoe runs despoiled. Finally, the island's symbolic value will be gone."[28]

Some accounts have criticized environmentalists for essentially abandoning the Nuu-chah-nulth after the injunction and turning their attention to battles elsewhere; such a generalization is not entirely accurate and requires a more nuanced explanation.[29] Local environmental organizations continued to work to prevent the island's logging and coordinated with the Nuu-chah-nulth. For instance, the WCWC built a network of trails on Meares Island in order "to attract hikers and others to the area and gain public support for its campaign to halt logging."[30] Such trails were, according to former Tla-o-qui-aht band chief Moses Martin, fully supported by the Nuu-chah-nulth. The WCWC also undertook a seven-month project with the Ahousaht to train twenty First Nations and non-Aboriginal youth in ecotourism.[31] Local environmental activists who supported the Tla-o-qui-aht and Ahousaht legal action also established the Meares Island Legal Fund to help offset expensive litigation costs; nonetheless, the brunt of these were born by the First Nations themselves. At times the Nuu-chah-nulth Tribal Council even came close to withdrawing from their legal battle due to lack of funds.[32] Claim costs for the Tla-o-qui-aht and Ahousaht bands, as of 1991 when the case returned to the courtroom in the hopes of making the injunction permanent, were reportedly $1.5 million, and they were preparing to spend another $1 million.[33] Moreover, once the injunction successfully halted logging and Meares Island was considered safe for Tofino residents, it appears that many in the community discarded their impromptu alliance. For instance, Tofino's Village Council opposed a 1988 Nuu-chah-nulth proposal to redesignate former residential school land on a small beach near Tofino as an Indian Reserve because non-Aboriginal residents felt a reserve near the town would scare tourists away. The Nuu-chah-nulth, in turn, organized a boycott of Tofino businesses.[34] Many in the Nuu-chah-nulth community, feeling betrayed, were thus wary of local non-Aboriginal interests and well aware of the possible limits of their support, and of environmentalist organizations' limitations, well in advance of the major protest events of 1993–1994.

As British Columbia's "war in the woods" became more caustic through the rest of the 1980s, then Premier William Vander Zalm, expressing shock at clearcut scars, set up a task force with representatives from industry, environmentalist organizations, government agencies, First Nations, and unions in 1989 to come to some sort of compromise. The task force proved ineffective, meeting for the last time in 1990 when it failed to come to an agreement, and fell apart in 1992. In April 1993, with newly elected Premier Mike Harcourt in power, the provincial government released its now infamous "Land Use Decision," without consulting First Nations, which put forward a plan to allow substantial clearcut logging in Clayoquot Sound. Thereafter, Clayoquot Sound would once again become a space of colonial encounters where thousands of environmental activists, representing myriad environmental organizations, converged to (re)establish relations with the local Indigenous population. Environmentalists knew that they needed to develop a plan that would legitimize their cause and to separate themselves from other colonial, non-local entities seeking to exploit this hinterland for their own purposes, as well as—for at least those familiar with the regional context—to escape years of animosity generated between the local settler-colonial population and the Nuu-chah-nulth. While environmentalist organizations are, of course, varied, in 1993 the organizations present at the protest ended up, to borrow from Pratt again, practising a form of "anti-conquest" whereby they represented themselves as innocent witnesses of human and environmental injustices at the same time as they asserted their hegemonic view of how people should, and, equally importantly, should not, interact with the environment.

Part of this feigned innocence included environmental groups claiming to act on behalf of, and thus speak for, many others. Among these others were Aboriginal peoples writ large who were denied title to their traditional territories and politically and economically marginalized by industry and the state. Simultaneously, as during the 1980s, the WCWC and the FOCS, as well as other environmentalist organizations such as Greenpeace, strategically sought to link the resolution of their goals with those of First Nations; if their goals were the same, then environmentalists could speak and act on their behalf. Both these aspects are evident in a book of essays titled *Clayoquot & Dissent*. In its introduction, Berman, then an organizer for Greenpeace, wrote, "The first protests were the beginning of a growing relationship between First Nations and the environmental community. . . . We are at a point of consensus between the environmental and native communities—that clearcutting irreparably damages our ecological, social and cultural landscapes."[35] In another essay provocatively titled, "Clayoquot: Recovering from Cultural Rape," Loys Maignon argued that "environmentalists comprise a distinct group with cultural similarities to First Nations," and, after pointing to some similarities in ideology and history which "ha[ve] led to common positions regarding environmental issues," asserted, "These similarities also leave environmentalists open to the same system of societal abuses."[36] Elsewhere, Robert Kennedy Jr., of the American-run Natural Resources Defence Council, proclaimed, "In Clayoquot Sound the fight to save 1000 year old cedars and hemlocks intertwined with the Aboriginal peoples' struggle to control traditional lands and their economic destiny." The Clayoquot protestors' greatest inspiration, he continued, "was the dissolution of ancient boundaries as the First Nations of Clayoquot Sound made partnerships with local and international environmentalists to defend age-old forests. . . . The power of their partnerships will not subside until the clear-cutting stops and the Native land rights are permanently ensured."[37]

In order to further establish themselves as allies fighting for a common cause, environmentalists regularly emphasized Nuu-chah-nulth title over the Clayoquot area even as they also claimed possession of Clayoquot Sound for non-Aboriginal peoples. Environmentalist organizations, from the small-scale, including the FOCS and WCWC, to the larger, international ones, such as Greenpeace and the Sierra Club, proclaimed Clayoquot Sound as a national—not just a local—treasure that all Canadians needed to protect and control. The Sierra Club and Greenpeace went even further, arguing that Clayoquot Sound, due to its ecological importance and aesthetic beauty, actually belonged to the world. Vicky Husband, representing the Sierra Club of Western Canada, stated that "Clayoquot Sound does not just belong to the Alberni and Clayoquot district anymore. It belongs to the world."[38] As such, non-locals had a stake in what happened to *their* land and were thus entitled to determine how the land was used; environmentalists, conveniently, proclaimed themselves as the representatives of this national and international voice. Instead of being logged, they argued, Clayoquot Sound should become a protected area that relied on ecotourism for its economy. This would be best, they believed, for everybody involved, including the First Nations. Husband paternalistically remarked that only "limited logging by native bands" in the area was acceptable.[39] Along similar lines, Gordon Brent Ingram acknowledged that while environmentalists needed to provide "unconditional support" to the Nuu-chah-nulth, he wrote in the context of doing so to "counter the pressures and enticements of the logging companies" and to support the Nuu-chah-nulth's environmental conservation activities.[40]

Many of the assumptions of environmentalists regarding Nuu-chah-nulth political and cultural desires came from the former's often uncritical belief in, and reproduction of, the stereotype of the "Ecological Indian." Environmentalist-authored literature, produced throughout the 1980s and into the 1990s, equated Natives with nature, referring to both as "prehistoric" or "ancient" and in need of saving from extinction. An excellent example of such rhetoric is a WCWC publication titled *Clayoquot on the Wild Side*, written by Cameron Young, a journalist and environmental activist, and full of lavish, full-colour photographs taken by Adrian Dorst, a resident of Tofino. When venturing on the ocean, one section of the book romantically explains, one is "never alone. Paddling *like the wind* beside

[you] are the spirits of the Nuu-chah-nulth whalers, slim and sinewy men fired by a long-lost passion, powering their way through the unforgiving waters in exquisite canoes crafted from the trunks of centuries-old western red cedars."[41] The book reproduces colonial stereotypes of the "vanishing Indian" through its depiction of traditional—pristine, even—Aboriginal culture as being in its twilight, if not faded completely. When exploring an abandoned village, Young writes tragically,

> The light is fading on this long summer day, and during that slow ebb into darkness, Adrian can faintly imagine the sounds of cedar canoes being hauled up on the beach, the chatter of fishermen unloading their halibut, and the strong smell of smoking salmon in the air. For a brief moment Adrian is able to conjure up these ghostly images, and the beach seems to come alive. But out at Pachena Point, evening sports fishermen have tired of riding the ocean swells and are racing back to Bamfield. The roar of their outboards drives the ghosts back into hiding.[42]

For Young, the Nuu-chah-nulth ghosts are literally fleeing modernity, fleeing contact, and, in essence, erased from the present. Out of sight, however, is the fact that such events as described above still occurred among the Nuu-chah-nulth, or that, until the collapse of the west coast fishery in the 1980s, Aboriginal peoples including the Nuu-chah-nulth were heavily engaged in the industry and often owned their own commercial fishing fleets. In a twisted, though certainly not intentional bit of irony, the only good Indigenous person, in this section of the book where the author seeks to resurrect pre-contact life, is a dead one. Not only did such rhetoric reproduce colonial categories of Indigeneity, but it also effectively created a *terra nullius* in Clayoquot Sound where environmentalists could stake their claims.[43]

In arguing these positions, environmentalists alerted the Nuu-chah-nulth to their intentions, and the latter perceived the limits of their supposedly solid support for First Nations land rights, sovereignty, and decolonization. Indeed, even Premier Mike Harcourt's April 1993 Land Use Decision—the very decision that sparked the wide-scale protests—included many concessions for environmentalists, such as protected areas, but few for First Nations. Chief Richard Lucas of Hesquiaht First Nation responded to the Land Use Decision by saying that environmentalists and loggers, though both unhappy with it, at least received some concessions, but for the Nuu-chah-nulth, "after parks, wilderness and logging areas had been designated, there was little of our traditional homeland [remaining]."[44] Two years later, George Watts continued his opposition to such park creation, arguing it was merely another land grab by the provincial government to keep such spaces off the table for treaty negotiations.[45] Meanwhile, environmentalists were upset only with the small amount and poor quality of land to be preserved.[46] Additionally, the WCWC was simultaneously pressing the provincial government to preserve 30 to 40 percent of the land in British Columbia, including areas in Clayoquot Sound, in the form of parks and wilderness spaces at the same time that Nuu-chah-nulth council members were condemning state park creation as neocolonialism.[47] An environmentalist group called the UVic Temperate Rainforest Action Group criticized (in vain) Greenpeace, the FOCS, the WCWC, and the Sierra Club for ignoring the mistreatment of Aboriginal peoples when calling for the establishment of a park in Clayoquot Sound that would be run largely by, and for, non-Aboriginals.[48] Though one cannot forget that environmentalists established many long-term friendships and partnerships with the Nuu-chah-nulth, and that the environmental movement did not express a unified voice, all sides were working to meet their own agendas.[49]

The Nuu-chah-nulth, in turn, had plans of their own. While environmentalists argued that they supported Aboriginal rights without question but in reality sought an end to clearcut logging by any means, the Nuu-chah-nulth made it abundantly clear that they wanted control over their traditional territories and that part of this control included plans for industrial-scale logging. The Nuu-chah-nulth did not, however, reject environmentalist support out of hand. Aware of their allies' economic and popular influence, the Nuu-chah-nulth were able to capitalize on environmentalist protests and presence to access, change, and even take control of some existing colonial structures, including those of the government, the logging industry, and environmentalist organizations.

Throughout the protests in 1993, Harcourt's New Democratic Party (NDP) government was reeling in response to the sustained and completely unexpected size and strength of the environmentalist campaign. While within British Columbia communities and individuals were divided over the issue, across Canada and abroad popular opinion tended to side with the environmentalists. Furthermore, the international community increasingly criticized British Columbia for its colonialist policies, and a number of European importers cancelled millions of dollars' worth of contracts for Clayoquot Sound wood products. The NDP leadership knew they had to act fast in order to quell the protests and, more importantly, halt the economic damage being done. Outright force using police to break up the protest—its first tactic—had failed despite the arrest of more than 800 activists, and protests were ongoing.[50] The government then turned to negotiation, and the Nuu-chah-nulth saw their opening. While they certainly appreciated environmentalist declarations of support for Aboriginal title and had worked with environmentalists on a number of projects such as trail building and ecotourism, the Nuu-chah-nulth also recognized the key position they held in sitting between warring parties. They were willing to negotiate with the government toward a middle ground, whereas environmentalists were far more uncompromising in their demands.

In October 1993, with environmentalist blockades still in place, the government's first concession came when it established the Scientific Panel for Sustainable Forest Practices in Clayoquot Sound. The panel, which excluded government, industry, and environmentalist members, was mandated to combine First Nations' traditional knowledge with Western scientific practices in establishing "world class logging standards."[51] So while the Nuu-chah-nulth had benefited from their own and environmentalist pressure for the government to include Indigenous people in the ecological management of their traditional territories, it was the environmentalists who were subsequently excluded from the Nuu-chah-nulth's gain. While the Nuu-chah-nulth perceived this gain as a fracture in colonial control, environmentalists dismissed the panel's creation as a stalling tactic designed to "divide and conquer" supposedly staunch allies.

In some ways, environmentalists had a valid point. Logging in Clayoquot Sound was ongoing at this time, and the Scientific Panel had only an advisory capacity. However, the Nuu-chah-nulth did not trust the government either and had over a century of experience dealing with a provincial government that continually broke its promises to First Nations, so they continued to maintain their strong links to the environmentalist movement. They also threatened to launch a court injunction that would halt logging in the region entirely if the government did not agree to more substantive measures. The NDP thus had little choice but to sign an Interim Measures Agreement (IMA) in December 1993, after more than a month of negotiations with the Nuu-chah-nulth, that secured the Nuu-chah-nulth a greater grip on both government and logging activity in the area until the Scientific Panel could complete its work. Among other measures, the IMA recognized Nuu-chah-nulth traditional governance structures and a government-to-government relationship between the Nuu-chah-nulth and the province. Most significantly, the agreement provided the Nuu-chah-nulth with, according to Tla-o-qui-aht Chief Francis Frank, a veto on logging operations, and logging was to continue at a reduced capacity and according to Nuu-chah-nulth standards.[52] When Premier Harcourt was quoted saying that the IMA merely provided the Nuu-chah-nulth with an advisory role, Frank threatened to call in his environmental allies, in particular Robert Kennedy Jr., for support.[53]

Threatened with significant opposition and more blockades, Harcourt was forced to bend. He agreed to support a Nuu-chah-nulth logging veto and then provided them with additional funding for both tourism and logging development. Prominent Nuu-chah-nulth council member Clifford Atleo hailed the agreement as "the beginning of change in terms of the management of resources in that it's going to provide an opportunity for First Nations to have a say—something that we've aspired to for over 125 years."[54] Based on extensive fieldwork in 1997 conducting interviews with Nuu-chah-nulth co-managers, leaders and community members, Tara C. Goetze found that the IMA was well received among the community, and she argued that the IMA gave the Nuu-chah-nulth "determinative authority *to make decisions* about resource use in Clayoquot Sound."[55] Nonetheless, most environmentalists were less than enthusiastic about the agreement and recognized that they were being pushed aside. The IMA provided for no input from any environmentalist organizations, though the Nuu-chah-nulth offered them a token advisory role on the management board, with no decision-making power.[56] Environmentalists had, as one reporter wrote on the Agreement, "throughout the entire Clayoquot controversy . . . claimed to have the Natives on their side. [Natives] meanwhile, maintained they were on nobody's side but their own."[57] Some environmentalists decried the IMA as merely a stalling tactic while logging continued, and Ingram referred to it as a "pact of semi-colonization."[58] All these criticisms effectively implied the Nuu-chah-nulth were merely being beguiled by a more politically savvy opponent and delegitimized the Nuu-chah-nulth's decision to act on their own. Yet, the IMA symbolized much more than that; it was one of many steps the Nuu-chah-nulth would take to further entrench their authority within the province's bureaucratic and legal structure. Additionally, it was more proof that the Nuu-chah-nulth would not be controlled by anyone else's agenda or romantic stereotypes regarding how they should act.

Nowhere was this independence more apparent than when former Nuu-chah-nulth Tribal Council chairperson George Watts travelled to Europe with Premier Harcourt on a promotional tour for British Columbia's logging industry and the Nuu-chah-nulth's economic ties to it.[59] Though met by Greenpeace opponents at every stopping place on the ten-day tour, Watts, it was reported,

> moved an audience of environmentalists and academics with an emotional speech, saying a boycott would cripple the already anaemic economies in Native communities. [Watts] told a packed university in Hamburg: "Most of our people get up in the morning and think about how they are going to be fed and clothed. They don't have the luxury of sitting in some bloody office dreaming about what the environment should look like."[60]

Watt's defence of the government, the reporter continued, "appeared to sideswipe the environmentalists, who have traditionally viewed aboriginals as allies in their fight."[61] Indeed, while apparently most of the Nuu-chah-nulth never opposed logging outright, only their exclusion from it along with the practice of clearcutting, and Nuu-chah-nulth activists had avoided using uncomplicated assertions of being "Ecological Indians" throughout the campaign, environmentalists continued to be surprised by this stance. At a Clayoquot benefit hosted by the Sierra Club at the University of Victoria, some Aboriginal leaders reportedly stunned many of the 800 people in attendance. Clifford Atleo, spokesman for Ahousaht, told the crowd, "We are not opposed to logging and we are not opposed to jobs." He continued that "Natives become annoyed when non-native environmental leaders make public statements such as 'not another tree will fall' in Clayoquot Sound."[62]

It does need to be recognized that the Nuu-chah-nulth, as with the environmentalist community, was not wholly united, and non-Aboriginal environmentalists no doubt appraised Nuu-chah-nulth culture and politics in the context of many Nuu-chah-nulth who simultaneously identified as environmentalists and campaigned alongside non-Aboriginal environmentalist organizations. Joe Martin (Tla-o-qui-aht) undertook a six-week tour of Europe with environmentalists to call for a boycott of logging products from Clayoquot Sound.[63] Annie George, a Kwagiulth artist who married into an Ahousaht chiefly family, had to defend her active support of the environmentalists against other Nuu-chah-nulth who wanted group cohesion.[64] Willie Sport, a seventy-year-old Ohiat Band member and activist, was recorded telling environmentalists, "I am proud of you, proud of what you are doing. I look at what you are doing compared to members of my tribe and other tribes who are so afraid to speak out because they fear it will affect their native land claims. . . . The protest movement has had an effect. . . . The land claims are keeping many of my people from speaking out about forest practices. It's sad, but true."[65] While Sport's observation may have been correct and many Nuu-chah-nulth were cognizant of ongoing litigation and land claim negotiations, the Nuu-chah-nulth's strategic positioning did lead to political gain.

In addition to moving into government circles, the Nuu-chah-nulth also entered into other structures from which they had been largely excluded. For example, the BC Federation of Labour, largely composed of loggers and positioned against both First Nations and environmentalists, saw the opening for a working relationship with the Nuu-chah-nulth and for economic stability in the region. They pledged support for the Clayoquot First Nations' treaty process and promised to integrate them into the logging economy.[66] Soon thereafter, various bands within the Nuu-chah-nulth Tribal Council began negotiating with logging companies themselves. The Ahousaht, for example, created a joint-venture company with MacMillan Bloedel called Isaak Forest Resources Ltd. on terms that the Ahousaht felt were favourable to them: they owned 51 percent of the company and received a timber sale licence as well as infrastructural and institutional assistance for entering into the logging business.[67] Environmentalists, mostly unaware of these negotiations until they were released to the press, were angered that their "allies" were working with the "enemy," but they really could not do anything to prevent these kinds of negotiations taking place.[68] While most environmental organizations endorsed the deal, the FOCS refused to endorse anything that allowed for old-growth forests to be logged.[69]

Nonetheless, First Nations of the Nuu-chah-nulth Tribal Council realized that they could, even acting independently of environmentalists and often counter to their goals, still threaten the government with environmentalist support. Having forged an alliance with the influential Natural Resources Defence Council and Robert Kennedy Jr., for example, the Nuu-chah-nulth continued to use its and his influence. They frequently invited Kennedy Jr. to visit Clayoquot Sound—something that he and the Nuu-chah-nulth knew kept the pressure on Harcourt because of Kennedy's vocal criticism of British Columbia's logging practices along with the legal advice his association provided to the Nuu-chah-nulth in their land and treaty claims.[70] In another instance, Larry Baird of the Ucluelet band threatened the government that should anything happen to derail the treaty negotiation process, "We will go to the markets of the world and tell them what you are doing. We are well connected . . . and we will use these relationships to harm this province if you are going to harm us. . . . I have some influential friends who would dearly love to tackle you head on."[71] The Huu-ay-aht First Nation at Bamfield threatened to create another "Clayoquot Sound" unless the provincial government and the forest industry negotiated terms with them.[72] This strategy kept both the government and environmentalists in check. The Nuu-chah-nulth used these groups' respective structural constraints—for the government, its legally binding agreements and its dependence on a stable political situation within the forest industry from which it received a significant portion of its operating budget and, for environmentalists, their position of

FIGURE 8.1: Adrian Raeside's editorial cartoons, here and in Figure 8.2, highlight the hypocrisy of environmental activists proclaiming support for First Nations while simultaneously attempting to control their actions with respect to resource use. Victoria *Times Colonist*, September 10, 2006.

anti-conquest via pledges to support Aboriginal rights and land management while decrying colonialism—to their advantage.

All groups in Clayoquot Sound were involved in competing strategies of self-representation for political manoeuvring. For environmentalists, this meant that they had to come up with a strategy that would give them the authority to stop clearcut logging, but to do so without recolonizing the Nuu-chah-nulth's space. In some ways, they were quite successful. Environmentalists helped to bring issues of colonial injustice to the forefront of the public's attention in British Columbia, in Canada, and internationally; the Nuu-chah-nulth's plight was suddenly thrust onto the world stage and logging operations did decline. The Nuu-chah-nulth, who have always proclaimed their hereditary right to manage the resources

Jonathan Clapperton

FIGURE 8.2: Adrian Raeside's editorial cartoon. Victoria *Times Colonist*, February 3, 2010.

in their traditional territory, seized the opportunity to draw power from the environmentalist organizations' support while distancing themselves enough from environmentalists that the provincial government and the logging industry considered the Nuu-chah-nulth as the only respite from the environmentalists' pressure. The Nuu-chah-nulth were thus able to break, in significant ways, into government and industry structures that had for so long kept them out.

Environmentalists, in turn, received much widespread support, but they also severely restricted themselves in the extent to which they could interfere with Nuu-chah-nulth decisions without appearing as hypocrites. In fact, the Nuu-chah-nulth even determined the direction of environmentalist actions in many ways. For example, the WCWC only conducted activities that were pre-approved by the local Tla-o-qui-aht. The Nuu-chah-nulth had also publicly denounced Paul Watson, former Greenpeace member and founder of the confrontational conservation organization the Sea Shepherd Conservation Society, for advocating a tree-spiking strategy.[73] They banned Greenpeace from their territory and shut down a Greenpeace and FOCS blockade that had been erected without Nuu-chah-nulth permission.[74] Overall, Berman would later recount of the protests that environmentalists were continually caught off guard by Nuu-chah-nulth actions that defied the former's expectations of the latter.[75] Consequently, environmentalist groups who attempted any actions on their own without consulting with, and getting approval from, the Nuu-cha-nulth were quickly forced to withdraw when the Nuu-chah-nulth complained or be seen as hypocrites and no different than other colonial actors. Indeed, when the FOCS, among other environmentalists, opposed Nuu-chah-nulth logging in 1996, 2006, and 2010, they faced just such criticism.[76] (See Figures 8.1 and 8.2.)

Environmentalists, striving to be the principal authority on human-nature interactions and who had largely directed the momentum of the protest campaign during the summer of 1993, arguably ended up being furthest away from the levers of power. Though they always had popular support, they ended up losing control where they wanted it the most: official government policy and legal decision-making circles, spaces the Nuu-cha-nulth increasingly occupied. Environmentalists could only, if they wanted to be effective and considered legitimate, offer support to the Nuu-cha-nulth and take what advisory roles the Nuu-chah-nulth offered them. Ultimately, this case study provides an important instance of Indigenous peoples using all the tools at their disposal, including the support of small green organizations with whom they are often in regular contact, to direct their own history as well as that of settler-colonists.

Notes

1   Tzeporah Berman et al., *Clayoquot and Dissent* (Vancouver: Ronsdale Press, 1994); Ronald MacIsaac and Anne Champagne, *Clayoquot Mass Trials: Defending the Rainforest* (Gabriola Island, BC: New Society Publishers, 1994); Paul George, *Big Trees Not Big Stumps: 25 Years of Campaigning to Save Wilderness with the Wilderness Committee* (Vancouver: Western Canadian Wilderness Committee, 2006); Marnie Anderson, *Women of the West Coast: Stories of Clayoquot Sound Then and Now* (Sidney, BC: Sand Dollar Press, 2004), 123, 219.

2   Bruce Braun, *The Intemperate Rainforest: Nature, Culture, and Power on Canada's West Coast* (Minneapolis: University of Minnesota Press, 2002), 8.

3   Margaret Horsfield and Ian Kennedy, *Tofino and Clayoquot Sound: A History* (Madeira Park, BC: Harbour Publishing, 2014).

4   Braun, *The Intemperate Rainforest*, 6–8, 27, 81, 107.

5   Niamh Moore in *The Changing Nature of Eco/Feminism: Telling Stories from Clayoquot Sound* (Vancouver: UBC Press, 2015), 18–19.

6   See, for examples: Roger Hayter, "'The War in the Woods': Post-Fordist Restructuring, Globalization, and the Contested Remapping of British Columbia's Forest Economy," *Annals of the Association of American Geographers* 93, no. 3 (2003): 711–12; Karena Shaw, "Encountering Clayoquot, Reading the Political," in *A Political Space: Reading the Global through Clayoquot Sound*, ed. Warren Magnusson and Karena Shaw (Minneapolis: University of Minnesota Press, 2003), 25–66; Alx Dark, "Public Sphere Politics and Community Conflict over the Environment and Native Land Rights in Clayoquot Sound, British Columbia," (PhD diss., New York University, 1998), 137; Paul Drissen, *Eco-Imperialism: Green Power, Black Death* (Bellevue, WA: Free Enterprise Press, 2003); Ariffin Yohan, "On the Scope and Limits of Green Imperialism," *Peace Review: A Journal of Social Justice* 22, no. 4 (2010): 373–81; and Mark Dowie, *Conservation Refugees: The Hundred-Year Conflict between Global Conservation and Native Peoples* (Cambridge, MA: MIT Press, 2009).

7   Tzeporah Berman, *This Crazy Time: Living Our Environmental Challenge* (Toronto: Alfred A. Knopf Canada, 2011), 94. Much work remains to be done examining the ongoing, often conflictual history of relationships between Greenpeace and First Nations, Métis, and Inuit. This chapter only scratches the surface, and it is beyond the scope of Zelko's chapter (this volume). For further reading see: Frank Zelko, "Scaling Greenpeace: From Local Activism to Global Goverance," *Historical Social Research* 42, no. 2 (2017): 318–42; David Rossiter, "The Nature of Protest: Constructing the Spaces of British Columbia's Rainforests," *Cultural Geographies* 11 (2004): 139–64; John-Henry Harter, "Environmental Justice for Whom? Class, New Social Movements, and the Environment: A Case Study of Greenpeace Canada, 1971–2000," *Labour / Le Travail* 53 (2004): 83–119; Aaju Peter et al, "The Seal: An Integral Part of Our Culture," *Études/Inuit/Studies* 26, no. 1 (2002): 167–74; George Wentzel, "'I Was Once Independent': The Southern Seal Protest and Inuit," *Anthropologica* 29, no. 2 (1987): 195–201.

8   Tara C. Goetze, "Empowered Co-Management: Towards Power-Sharing and Indigenous Rights in Clayoquot Sound, BC," *Anthropologica* 47, no. 2 (2005): 250.

9   Umeek (E. Richard Atleo) provides a detailed explanation of Nuu-chah-nulth culture and history in *Tsawalk: A Nuu-chah-nulth Worldview* (Vancouver: UBC Press, 2004).

10 Mary Louise Pratt, *Imperial Eyes: Travel Writing and Transculturation* (New York: Routledge, 1992), 6.

11 Claudia Noezke, *Aboriginal Peoples and Natural Resources in Canada* (Concord, ON: Captus Press, 1994), 98.

12 Noezke, *Aboriginal Peoples and Natural Resources in Canada*, 249.

13 George, *Big Trees Not Big Stumps*, 1, 19.

14 Dimitri Portier, "The Meares Island Case: Nuu-chah-nulth vs. the Logging Industry," *Native American Studies* 14, no. 1 (2000): 31.

15 Paul George, Western Canadian Wilderness Committee letter to editor, *Sunshine Coast News*, 7 July 1985, 15.

16 "Community fights plans for logging on B.C. island," *Globe and Mail*, 21 November 1984, N4.

17 Ian Mulgrew, "A Nice Place to Visit—and Hard to Leave," *Globe and Mail*, 5 May 1982, 8.

18 Western Canadian Wilderness Committee, *Meares Island News*, Summer 1985.

19 "Workers' Appeal on Plywood Plant Fails," *Globe and Mail*, 26 April 1984, BC1.

20 Ian Mulgrew, "A Long Battle to Avoid Scars," *Globe and Mail*, 8 August 1984, 11.

21 "Logging Firm Gets Injunction Against Meares Protesters," *Globe and Mail*, 4 December 1984, 3. Tree spiking refers to the act of inserting a metal rod, nail, or similar material into a tree trunk, where it is difficult to see, rendering the tree potentially dangerous to cut or process. For sources on Meares Island tree spiking, see, for example, Mike Roselle, "Meares Island: Canada's Old Growth Struggle," *Earth First! Journal* 5, no. 3 (2 February 1985). Paul Watson claims to have invented tree spiking; though this is not possible, he certainly claims to have spiked the trees on Meares. For more reliable sources, see Rik Scarce, *Eco-Warriors: Understanding the Radical Environmental Movement* (Walnut Creek, CA: Left Coast Press, 2006), 75; and Dave Foreman, *Confessions of an Eco-Warrior* (New York: Crown Trade Paperbacks, 1991), 33, 133. For a good definition of tree spiking, see Dave Foreman and Bill Haywood, eds., *Ecodefense: A Field Guide to Monkeywrenching*, 3rd ed. (Chico, CA: Abbzug Press, 2002).

22 Horsfield and Kennedy, *Tofino and Clayoquot Sound*, 503.

23 Jeanette C. Mills describes the work of Joe David and other Nuu-chah-nulth artists who supported the Meares Island campaign in "The Meares Island Controversy and Joe David: Art in Support of a Cause," *American Indian Art Magazine* 14, no. 4 (1989): 60–69.

24 Douglas C. Harris, "A Court Between: Aboriginal and Treaty Rights in the British Columbia Court of Appeal," *BC Studies* 162 (Summer 2009): 148. See also Portier, "The Meares Island Case," 31–37.

25 "Judge Won't Ban Activists from Island Logging Site," *Globe and Mail*, 18 December 1984, 5.

26 Harris, "A Court Between," 148.

27 "Appeal Court Prohibits Meares Island Logging," *Globe and Mail*, 28 March 1985, 1–2.

28 Justice Seaton, cited in Harris, "A Court Between," 149.

29 Claudia Noezke identifies, and repeats, these accounts in *Aboriginal Peoples and Natural Resources in Canada*, 101.

30 Mark Hume, "MB Tries to Block Meares Trails," *Vancouver Sun*, 5 July 1988, A1.

31 Lorna Stefanick, "Baby Stumpy and the War in the Woods: Competing Frames of British Columbia Forests," *BC Studies* 130 (Summer 2001): 59.

32 "Legal Costs Imperil Meares Island Case," *Globe and Mail*, 11 February 1986, 5. See also Shaw, "Encountering Clayoquot, Reading the Political," 32; and Horsfield and Kennedy, *Tofino and Clayoquot Sound: A History*, 502–5.

33 "Natives Spending Millions to Defend Meares Island Claim," *Vancouver Sun*, 15 August 1991, A13; and Marc Edge, "Fight for Meares Trees Resumes," *Vancouver Province*, 1 October 1991, A12.

34 Shaw, "Encountering Clayoquot, Reading the Political," 30; and Horsfield and Kennedy, *Tofino and Clayoquot Sound*, 512.

35 Berman, "Takin' it Back," in Berman et al., *Clayoquot and Dissent*, 3.

36 Loys Maignon, "Clayoquot: Recovering from Cultural Rape," in Berman et al., *Clayoquot and Dissent*, 164–65.

37 Robert Kennedy Jr., "Foreword," in MacIsaac and Champagne, *Clayoquot Mass Trials*, ix.

38 John Hogbin and Richard Watts, "Persistent Furor Over Tree-Cutting in Clayoquot Surprises All Sides," *Victoria Times Colonist*, 4 October 1993.

39 Hogbin and Watts, "Persistent Furor."

40 Gordon Brent Ingram, "The Ecology of a Conflict," in Berman et al., *Clayoquot and Dissent*, 58–59.

41 Adrian Dorst and Cameron Young, *Clayoquot: On the Wild Side* (Vancouver: Western Canadian Wilderness Committee, 1990), 20.

42 Dorst and Young, *Clayoquot*, 42.

43 This discursive trope was certainly not unique to the WCWC publication, nor to others produced surrounding Clayoquot Sound. For instance, David A. Rossiter describes how, in environmentalist publications meant to protect nature on Haida Gwaii in the early 1990s, "the dominant representation throughout the book of a pristine natural environment under threat has the effect of marginalizing the importance of Haida land claims; within the cultural politics of nature, the Haida voice was being pushed aside by the loud and clear discourse of ecology and romantic appeals to a pristine, non-human natural world." See Rossiter, "The Nature of a Blockade: Environmental Politics and the Haida Action on Lyell Island, British Columbia," in *Blockades or Breakthroughs:*

Aboriginal Peoples Confront the Canadian State, ed. Yale D. Belanger and Whitney Lackenbauer (Montreal: McGill-Queen's University Press, 2014), 77.

44   Gerard Young, "Natives Won't be Used for Display at Games, says Clayoquot Leader," *Victoria Times Colonist*, 24 September 1993.

45   Dirk Meissner, "Parks a Ploy, Natives Say—Govt Rushing to Grab what is Left," *Victoria Times Colonist*, 28 April 1995.

46   Young, "Natives Won't be Used for Display at Games."

47   Malcolm Curtis, "Environmentalists Want 40% of Land Preserved," *Victoria Times Colonist*, 25 November 1995; Richard Watts, "Activists: Native Rights a Priority," *Victoria Times Colonist*, 2 February 1994; and Meissner, "Parks a Ploy."

48   Watts, "Activists: Native Rights a Priority."

49   This is true with the Nuu-chah-nulth who self-identified as environmentalists as well, some of whom even criticized their bands for inaction.

50   Richard Watts, "Logging Battle Legacy: Clayoquot Protests 10 Years Ago Signalled Start of Dramatic Change," *Victoria Times Colonist* 8 August 2003.

51   Clayoquot Sound Scientific Panel, *Report on Scientific Panel for Sustainable Forest Practices in Clayoquot Sound*, 31 January 1994.

52   Richard Watts, "Wood Boycott Continues Despite Deal," *Victoria Times Colonist*, 11 December 1993.

53   Hogbin and Watts, "Persistent Furor;" Les Leyne, "Bands Get Limited Control of Logging," *Victoria Times Colonist*, 11 December 1993; and Richard Watts, "Natives May Continue Lumber Boycott if Role in Clayoquot Deal Not Clarified," *Victoria Times Colonist*, 14 December 1993.

54   Stewart Bell, "Natives Get Voice in Logging: Harcourt Signs Consensus Pact," *Vancouver Sun*, 21 March 1994, A3.

55   Goetze, "Empowered Co-Management," 253.

56   Les Leyne, "Native Leader Lauds Forest Deal Anew," *Victoria Times Colonist*, 15 December 1993.

57   Watts, "Wood Boycott Continues Despite Deal."

58   Ingram, "The Ecology of a Conflict," 59.

59   Braun, *Intemperate Rainforest*, 107.

60   Brian Kennedy, "Harcourt Survives European Tour with Full Honours," *Victoria Times Colonist*, 6 February 1994.

61   Kennedy, "Harcourt."

62   Adrian Chamberlain, "Native's Pro-logging Stance Startles some in UVic Crowd," *Victoria Times Colonist*, 5 November 1993.

63   Dark, "Public Sphere Politics," 158.

64   Dark, "Public Sphere Politics," 17, 233.

65   Bill Smith, "Ohiat Native Supports Protestors," *Victoria Times Colonist*, 6 August 1994.

66   Gerald Young, "Natives Hail Clayoquot Backing," *Victoria Times Colonist*, 2 December 1993.

67   Chamberlain, "Native's Pro-logging Stance Startles some in UVic Crowd."

68   Braun, *Intemperate Rainforest*, 105–7; and Dark, "Public Sphere Politics," 174–75.

69   Richard Watts, "Former Foes Seek Compromise on Clayoquot Logging," *Victoria Times Colonist*, 10 December 1993.

70   Richard Watts, "Kennedy, Island Natives Keep Ties," *Victoria Times Colonist*, 16 December 1993.

71   Hayter, "'The War in the Woods,'" 722.

72   John Hogbin, "The Next Clayoquot? The Natives Next Door are Poised to Protest," *Victoria Times Colonist*, 17 September 1996.

73   Hayter, "'The War in the Woods,'" 722.

74   Geoffrey Castle, "Greenpeace Suspends Blockades—Native Leaders Upset They Were Never Told About Logging Protest," *Victoria Times Colonist*, 23 June 1996.

75   Berman, *This Crazy Time*, 82–105.

76   Tensions between environmentalists and the Nuu-chah-nulth, including environmentalist blockades of Nuu-chah-nulth logging in 1996, are briefly discussed in Jeremy Wilson, *Talk and Log: Wilderness Politics in British Columbia, 1965–96* (Vancouver: UBC Press, 1998), 58.

9

Local Economic Independence as Environmentalism: Nova Scotia in the 1970s

Mark Leeming

Environmentalism in Nova Scotia during the formative years of the 1970s and 1980s was very much a concern of the province's rural population, whose environmental activism strongly resembled the ecological distribution conflicts characteristic of Juan Martinez-Alier's "environmentalism of the poor."[1] The centrality of these groups to Nova Scotian activism, to its successes and its organizational transformation, suggests that the privileged "post-materialist" activist was more the exception than the rule in early Canadian environmentalism, and that a clear look at activist cultures in the industrialized world might reveal much more such diversity than is often acknowledged. After a short historiographical examination of the meaning of "environmentalism," the following pages will trace the thread of local economic independence as environmentalism through several Nova Scotian controversies from the late 1960s to the early 1980s. First isolated local harbour-protection activists, then alliances of local anti-nuclear and anti-uranium activists, will demonstrate the centrality of the local level and an implicit understanding of local environment and economy as a functioning whole.

* * *

Historians are indeed known by the causes they select for emphasis, but the history of environmentalism and environmental movements has been marked since its beginning by a difference of interpretation over both causes and the effects they are meant to explain. One set of researchers has long favoured an exclusive definition, insisting for more than three decades that the "lifestyle" environmentalism of the affluent world in the 1960s—characterized by the pursuit of clean air, clean water, and outdoor recreation—is a qualitatively new development in the social history of the Western world, uniquely deserving of the label "environmentalism," a product of demographic and economic changes following the Second World War, and a social movement set apart from contemporary and antecedent movements. Others favour instead a more inclusive definition, ranking such lifestyle environmentalism alongside prior anti-industrial movements and contemporary environment-themed activism in the less wealthy world, all of them motivated by reactions against modernity, specifically against the undesirable effects of industry, capitalism, and the dominance of scientific thinking.

The roots of the former (exclusive) view lie with one of the earliest and best-known theories of the origin of 1960s environmentalism, put forward by the sociologist Ronald Inglehart in 1977 in a book called *The Silent Revolution*. Inglehart insisted on the newness of environmental concern above all. According to his theory, unprecedented postwar North American affluence freed a generation from exclusive fixation on "material well-being and physical security" and allowed it to pursue "belonging, self-expression, and quality of life," defined as racial, sexual, and generational equality, participatory democracy, clean air and water, and opportunities for recreation in nature.[2] These "post-material" values were not ideals but "amenities," objects of consumption distinguished from consumer items only by their immaterial nature and their appeal to those whose material needs were already satisfied. In other words, "the environment" was a luxury commodity invented in the wealthy West. The theory of post-materialism offered an easily understood explanation for the social movements of the 1960s, and it has proven enormously popular among sociologists and historians of environmentalism, who since the 1970s have often preferred to focus their energies on quantifying or recording the conditions under which new movements emerge and flourish rather than complicating the explanation of why they emerge. Using measures of resource mobilization, social network integration, and political opportunity, they have pursued the how of environmentalism, frequently to the exclusion of the why.[3]

The historian best known for leaning on the post-materialist thesis is Samuel Hays. Already well known for his 1959 history of American conservation politics, in later works he insisted that conservation "gave way to environment after World War II amid a rising interest in the quality of life beyond efficiency in production," and that the two distinct movements "often came into conflict as resources long thought of as important for their material commodities came to be prized for their aesthetic and amenity uses."[4] His *Beauty, Health, and Permanence* is an excellent history of environmental politics in the United States, but the only variation it acknowledged in the nature of the popular movement was limited to the pace of change in one region or another and the different nature of the issues encountered by, say, rural and urban environmentalists.[5] Hays did not dwell on the possibility of different reasons for action, because the reason was provided by the post-materialist definition of environmentalism. Recent Canadian research on environmentalist history is more nuanced than Hays', but often carries on the (sometimes unspoken) assumption that environmentalism as a phenomenon has largely been the leisure activity of an urban economic and social elite.[6]

The common element among Hays and those who share his view is the assumption that environmentalism as a social movement is exclusive to the affluent global North. That much is to be expected from a group so steeped in post-materialist theory. Turning to the more inclusive analyses, it is appropriate therefore that the major challengers to the post-materialist group come from the fields of global and post-colonial history, and doubly so that they are led by the same man who challenged Hays' careful separation of nineteenth-century conservation and the twentieth-century environmental movement. Ramachandra Guha's work with the Spanish environmental economist and historian Juan Martinez-Alier has revealed a world full of different environmentalisms: reactions to industrialism based on the defence of traditional economies, home places, and non-economic values. Martinez-Alier's best-known book, *The Environmentalism of the Poor*, traced such activist movements in Peru, Ecuador, Indonesia,

India, and beyond. At the heart of their analysis is a return to genuinely environmental explanations for historical change: diverse environmental values are a given, and activism arises when environmental degradation results from industrial development and inequality of power. As Guha wrote in 2006:

> Wherever there is autocracy there are dissenters asking for democratic rights. Where there is capitalism, socialists will rise to oppose it. Where there is patriarchy, there will be women who resist it. The form, shape, and intensity of these protests varies; the oppositional impulse remains constant. So, one might say, wherever there is industrialization, there is environmentalism.[7]

This alternative approach owes a great deal to European social movement theorists, especially Jürgen Habermas, who focused on the role of new social movements as a step beyond the Marxist fixation on distribution struggle as the central conflict of society, and into a more complex set of values and grievances triggered by the rise of modernity. Accordingly, the varieties of environmentalism studied by Guha and Martinez-Alier find their origins in the nature of the relevant power relationships. In the United States, for example, it may take the form of a race-based environmental justice movement, fighting the disproportionate exposure of poor Black and Native communities to environmental hazards, while in India it manifests as agrarian villagers bodily intervening between their village forests and loggers sent by the Indian Forest Department. Nor is there any restriction in this analysis to the post-1945 era; Indian resistance to the Forest Department, for example, was just as fierce when the department's name was prefaced by the word "British." In response to the post-materialists, Martinez-Alier has pointed out that while "the hierarchy of needs among poor people is such that livelihood is given priority over marketed goods . . . livelihood depends on clean air, available soil, clean water." Moving on to his analysis of noneconomic values, he argued that many third-world environmental conflicts are "ecological distribution conflicts" provoked by the imposition of an unfavourable monetary "discount rate" on the sacred sites, home places, and other economically incommensurable values held by poorer people.[8] Unfortunately, much of the international history remains trapped in the post-colonialists' jaundiced view of the global North: with the exception of the environmental struggles of a racial underclass, post-materialist notions of privileged "amenity" or "full-stomach" environmentalism dominate the view of activists in Europe and North America. Research into environmental justice movements in the industrialized world often focuses on racially framed conflicts rather than on ecological distribution conflicts generally.[9]

As the remainder of this chapter will argue, via the story of one Canadian province, ecological distribution conflicts are a part of the story of environmentalism in much more than only the poorer countries of the world, and post-materialism is a poor explanatory framework upon which to model a complex social movement. Environmental activism on the ground is difficult or impossible to understand without acknowledgement of the multiple ecological distribution conflicts at play in environmentalist alliances, as ably demonstrated by Zoltán Grossman's analysis of Northwest North American anti–fossil energy activism in this volume. Scholarship on developed-world environmentalism would benefit from a broad application of Guha's and Martinez-Alier's ideas in the investigation of activism among all social and economic classes, including environmentalism from below.

* * *

Environmentalism in North America is typically characterized as an urban phenomenon, but the strength of rural activism in Nova Scotia in the 1960s demonstrates the centrality of rural protest groups to the establishment of a provincial movement. Building on the tradition of resource conservation, and augmented by back-to-the-land immigrants comfortable with social movement politics, activists in Nova Scotia reacted to the personal experience of industrial developmentalism by drawing on a global rhetoric of environment, social justice, and democracy. The change from relatively conservative and elite activism in the 1950s to a scientifically populist style in the late 1960s, with the promise of sustained future opposition to government development plans, alarmed the government in Halifax, much as 1960s radicalism alarmed governments everywhere. There was tremendous variety within environmental activism in Nova

Scotia in the 1960s, and attempts by government to control and channel the energy of public opinion with targeted funding produced yet more, leading to the creation of less politically contentious groups in the city, such as the Ecology Action Centre (EAC). Yet the defence of local and traditional economies from the negative effects of state-directed industrial modernity remained central to environmentalist argument everywhere in the province.[10]

Most environmental activism in Nova Scotia in the 1960s and 1970s was isolated, the work of local groups, typically limited to one town and its hinterland (or a group of nearby towns and theirs), with minimal links to other local groups. Almost never did these local groups comprise members from more than a single county, and those that did, such as the South Shore Environmental Protection Association (SSEPA), based their organization on an established economic association within the area (the South West Nova Scotia Lobster Fishermen's Association, for SSEPA). There were common elements, however. Threats to bodies of water, for example, signalled the beginning of a new age in environmental concern at the end of the 1960s. In this, as in so much else, Nova Scotia's experience reflected and amplified the pattern in the rest of North America and the world. The provincial government's quest for economic development during the prior decade had literally changed the face of the province, often for the worse, and the change was not evenly distributed. New industrial projects tended to cluster around harbours for a number of reasons, including ease of access, available workers, clean water supplies, and the availability of the ocean as a sink for industrial waste. By natural extension, the new activism of the era centred on the same locations, the majority of them rural, as local residents fearing for their traditional lifestyles and livelihoods under new land use and water use regimes found the traditional politics of dissent ineffective against polluters working hand-in-hand with government. Fed by direct observation of environmental ills and mistrust of government, as well as by a rising global environmental consciousness, new ideas and patterns of activist behaviour spread across the province from their estuarine enclaves. Environmentalists made increasing use of scientific research, not to convince politicians of their claims as their conservationist forebears had done, but to draw ever greater popular support to their campaigns of political pressure. And with the new style of environmental politics came

Mark Leeming

a new and lasting pattern of participation, with a much greater presence of women, young people, Mi'kmaq, and working-class Nova Scotians.

An efflorescence of environmental activism at the end of the 1960s built, piecemeal, the conditions for a sustained movement, beginning mostly around polluted harbours such as Boat Harbour in Pictou County and Chedabucto Bay in Guysborough and Richmond counties, and moving from there to other areas and issues.[11] The first instance of populist and non-modern environmental activism as a defence of local economy came at Boat Harbour, where in 1965 the provincial government finally enticed the Scott Paper Company to build its newest, state-of-the-art kraft pulp mill at Abercrombie Point, with an unusual provision in the agreement that had the province rather than the pulp company operating the mill's effluent treatment facility. Seizing on the natural lagoon of nearby Boat Harbour as a cheaper alternative to a purpose-built treatment plant, the Nova Scotia Water Resources Commission put up dams in the lagoon to divide settling and aeration ponds, walled it off from the sea, and constructed a pipeline underneath the East River of Pictou to carry 25 million gallons each day of effluent water, dissolved and suspended bits of wood pulp, and various toxic leftovers from the kraft bleaching process to the new facility. Economically, at least, it was a success story; the Scott mill prospered. Boat Harbour, on the contrary, died. Once a popular site for swimming, boating, and fishing, its waters promptly turned black after the mill opened, as the oxygen demands of decomposing wood pulp left nothing to support life.[12]

Particularly keen to celebrate their sense of belonging to a particular place and particularly ill-treated during the creation of the facility, the Mi'kmaq of Pictou Landing were among the first to react to the environmental downside of developmentalism, though even at Pictou Landing they were not alone.[13] From the perspective of the band's negotiators, the destruction of the harbour was not even supposed to have happened. They had been dispatched to meet with federal and provincial officials early in the province's talks with Scott, after the band indicated that they would not accept the conversion of their reserve's beautiful natural harbour into an industrial facility. In 1966, they were taken to a pulp mill in Saint John, New Brunswick, where water issued clear and clean from the outflow pipe, and were reassured that the same conditions would prevail in Pictou.

With an offer of $60,000 compensation for fishing rights on the table and, according to Pictou delegate Louis Francis, a generous supply of alcohol as well, the band's team agreed to the government's terms.[14] When effluent began flowing into Boat Harbour, they realized their mistake. The Saint John lagoons they had been shown were not even receiving effluent at the time of their visit, and $60,000 was a pittance next to the millions it would cost to build a truly state-of-the-art facility, for example, $4 million for the most modest improvements at Boat Harbour proposed by the optimistic and quite conservative Rust report in 1970.[15]

Members of the Pictou Landing Band had good reason to feel helpless in 1970. "I guess we're beaten," was Chief Raymond Francis's assessment, but they would not give up, and in their fight they had allies as well, willing as never before to challenge the authority of the state.[16] Though environmentalist coalition across the province was not yet common, local solidarity was, and non-Native residents of Pictou Landing felt nearly as deceived as the band. Since 1965 they too had been demanding answers from the Water Resources Commission, and had received similar assurances that no pollution of water or air would result from the project. As the progressive degeneration of the harbour and its surroundings confirmed their fears, however, more and more residents turned to a local citizens' committee (eventually named the Northumberland Strait Pollution Control Committee—NSPCC) to press for answers. Municipal councillor and NSPCC member Henry Ferguson wrote for the people of Pictou Landing in 1970:

> With the winds down the harbour we get air pollution from Scott Paper, then with the winds east we again get pollution, this time from Boat Harbour. The fumes are really terrible, almost unbearable. Then we get water pollution coming down the East River from leaks in the pipe across from the Scott Paper Co. to Pictou Landing. Then water pollution from Boat Harbour when the tide is coming up and runs along Lighthouse Beach and into Pictou Harbour.

To that, he added swarms of mosquitoes and gnats, expropriation through flooding of harbour-side land without notice and with minimal compensation, and threats to the Northumberland Strait lobster fishery.[17] The last was particularly worrying in communities along the shore, where the Maritime Packers Division of National Sea Products reported a 26.7 percent drop in lobster landings in 1968 and a 42.2 percent drop in 1969.[18] In fact, the threat to the fishery became the major rallying point for activists.

Official response to public outrage at Pictou Landing was muted at best. Accustomed to working without heed to local opinion, E.L.L. Rowe, the chairman of the Water Resources Commission and a former chemical industry employee who had designed the leaking sub-river pipeline and had promised minimal disruption to life around Boat Harbour, doubled down on his defence of the facility. He insisted that he personally found the smell of the rotting lagoon and the "rotten egg" hydrogen sulfide fumes from Scott's stacks inoffensive, and that the province could not make funds available for the solution of merely aesthetic problems. He also made it clear that mercury contamination of the mill effluent from the associated Canso Chemicals plant would have to be tolerated, as the development of the plant had "gone too far" and cost too much to be altered.[19] Other officials and politicians holding similar views attracted attention from time to time, including the agriculture minister, Harvey Veniot, who dismissed the affected locals with the oddly poetic epithet "calamity howlers," or the fisheries experts at the Department of Fisheries in Ottawa, who would only repeat that Boat Harbour's effluent had been tested and proven non-toxic to lobster larvae.[20]

Local activists refused to be put off the issue. Unable to secure a hearing and unable to sue the province for nuisance without permission from the government, they turned fully to public opinion as a source of influence. And as a tool for generating public support, they turned to science, with a strong focus on the impact of the facility on the lobster fishery. The NSPCC commissioned a report from Delaney and Associates that followed the brown film of Boat Harbour effluent twenty kilometres down the shore and calculated that about 185 tons of organic solids spilled into the sea from the harbour each day.[21] D. C. MacLellan at the Marine Studies Centre at McGill University found the effluent resulting in an unusually great mortality among the plankton at the base of the Northumberland Strait food chain, and Dr. J. G. Ogden at Dalhousie University answered the federal fisheries experts by reminding them that, toxic or not, dark brown effluent that blocked sunlight from reaching the sea floor would deprive lobster of both food and sheltering seaweeds. "A sheet of opaque glass put over the lawn is not toxic," he said, "but it will kill the grass. The effluent from Boat Harbour is as effective as a sheet of black plastic."[22] So armed with expert authority of their own, the NSPCC members pursued their environmental justice arguments in the press on behalf of the Mi'kmaq and Northumberland Strait fishermen deceived or ignored by the federal agencies designated to safeguard their interests. Nor were their aims narrowly or selfishly defined; one fisherman-activist told reporter Tom Murphy that compensation for losses might not be welcome, if it allowed the condition of the strait to continue deteriorating. "We want our environment cleaned up, rather than subsidies for a dirty environment," he said.[23]

Boat Harbour represents the most bitterly fought of the late 1960s battles, but it was far from the only one. At the same time as Pictou County was discovering the need for citizen activism, other groups were forming in the province after their own personal experiences with the dark side of developmentalism. Some focused on local economies almost exclusively, for instance those resident on the shores of Chedabucto Bay in 1970, when the *Arrow* oil spill drove home the threat posed by the Canso Strait industrial complex to the fisheries. But none became more than a local cause, until 1972.[24]

The triggering event that brought the province's scattered environmental activists together in a lasting way was a surprise to almost everyone. The first indication to the public that the new Regan provincial government might be considering a nuclear project came in June 1972 from the Halifax *Chronicle Herald*. Claiming to have information from a source inside government, the newspaper reported that the premier had met personally and in secret with representatives of a US company, Crossley Enterprises Ltd., that wished to build a nuclear plant on tiny Stoddard Island, near the southwest tip of the province.[25] Details remain scarce, because the project never moved past the informal proposal stage; however, the plan, as it emerged from further leaks and admissions over the rest of the summer and the following winter, was to build ten US-style light water reactors (LWRs) on Stoddard Island and transmit the electricity generated there directly to New England via undersea cable. Had it been built, the complex would have been the largest generating station in the world, at 12,000 megawatts, though some immediately doubted that the plan could even work.[26] But the details, or indeed the feasibility of the plan, were not at issue in the summer of 1972, for the simple reason that the details were not available. Members of the Regan government and the publicly owned Nova Scotia Power Corporation (NSPC) initially refused to comment on the leak for several days, and when the premier did eventually speak, he offered only equivocal denials that any earnest negotiations were afoot, which did nothing to quiet speculation.[27] By then, it was too late. The opposition Progressive Conservatives (PCs) had discovered the issue and happily forced Premier Gerald Regan into fresh and ever less credible denials as more information came to light, repeatedly highlighting the government's reluctance to volunteer any facts on new developments.[28] If any issue can be said to have initially united those opposed to the Stoddard Island proposal, it was the secrecy around the project. For every declaration of disinterest by the federal energy minister ("unless," he said, Canadian CANDU reactors could be used instead of American LWRs), there was a countervailing shock, as when Crossley Enterprises' Canadian holding company was revealed to have purchased Stoddard Island in 1971, or when the man who handled the acquisition, Halifax lawyer Ian MacKeigan, was appointed Nova Scotia's new chief justice in 1973.[29] Through a year of uncertainty, suspicion of the government's intentions was the link that bound environmentalists together.

Unsurprisingly, the earliest reactions from existing ENGOs (environmental non-governmental organizations) focused on the issues of government secrecy and public participation. But local fishermen were not content to let established agencies—governmental or activist—monopolize the issue, when one of the key unknowns about the project was the potential impact on ocean ecosystems of a large reactor complex in the middle of the richest lobster fishing area in the province. Thermal pollution and entrainment were well-known concepts among interested fishermen.[30] Organized over the winter of 1973, the new South Shore Environmental Protection Association (SSEPA) would go on to hold a central role in the province's environmental movement for a decade. For now, it targeted all three levels of government in an attempt to defeat the Stoddard Island proposal politically, rather than merely request public participation or work at public education. Following the lead of the Southwestern Nova Scotia Lobster Fishermen's Association (and sharing members with it—essentially a joint organization), SSEPA won unequivocal support from Barrington and Yarmouth municipal councils, PC offshore resources critic and MP for South Shore Lloyd Crouse, and Liberal Social Services Minister and Shelburne County MLA Harold Huskilson, by impressing upon them that, in the words of fishermen's association president Glen Devine, "this whole area [and its voters] depends entirely on fish."[31] Under the leadership of author and activist Hattie Perry, SSEPA found its greatest success in October 1973, when Premier Regan attended a public meeting in the tiny village of Barrington Passage, about ten kilometres from Stoddard Island, and found waiting for him hundreds of nearby residents who wanted only one thing. He gave it to them: a clear promise for public consultation on any proposed nuclear plant in Shelburne County, and another that no project would be approved that might harm the fishery.[32]

Political pressure won a victory for SSEPA. The assurances given at Barrington Passage, combined with the failure of the proponent to quickly address the federal Atomic Energy Control Board's (AECB) suggestion of CANDU reactors, seemed to spell the end of the Stoddard Island proposal by 1974. There was, however, no corresponding revival of trust in government and no dissolution of the groups that led the fight. If anything, the continued commitment of the Regan government to two badly functioning heavy water plants built to supply the Canadian nuclear industry in the late 1960s at Glace Bay and Port Hawkesbury suggested a continued interest in nuclear technology.[33] SSEPA continued enthusiastically to lead opposition to any and all nuclear development schemes, leaning on other groups' research and adding their own on alternative energy sources and the health effects of radiation. This research and activism drew on an international discussion of nuclear dangers but always returned to the threat posed to the local fishing economy and the lack of appreciable local benefit.[34] SSEPA led Nova Scotian opposition to New Brunswick's Point Lepreau reactor project, on account of the shared Bay of Fundy ecosystem. SSEPA also showed its continuing concern over the threat of government secrecy at an Environmental Control Council public hearing in Yarmouth a month after the Barrington Passage meeting, where according to the ECC, "the people present cited the example of the apparent lack of an environmental assessment study for the Strait of Canso [refinery and shipping complex] as evidence that these kinds of projects and developments can and will go forward without public approval."[35]

Environmentalism in Nova Scotia did not remain such a congeries of independently operating parts after the Stoddard Island episode. Success bred further cooperation, first against New Brunswick's reactor project, then against the Nova Scotia government's encouragement of chemical forestry. Regional cooperation in the mid-1970s also developed very much like the budding intra-provincial cooperation in Nova Scotia. Phone trees, frequent correspondence, and infrequent meetings linked small groups from the Chaleur Environmental Protection Association in northern New Brunswick to SSEPA in southwest Nova Scotia, mostly around the issue of New Brunswick's proposed reactor but particularly within the context of a proposed single regional electrical utility (the Maritime Energy Corporation). Political cooperation at the regional level begat activist cooperation at the same. New Brunswick's reactor project, however, unlike Nova Scotia's, enjoyed the strong support of both the provincial government in Fredericton and the federal atomic energy agency. As a result, Nova Scotia's established activist network protested impotently from the sidelines of a provincial debate in New Brunswick dominated by pro-nuclear positions. In the end, New Brunswick's anti-nuclear moment did not arrive until 1979, in the aftermath of the Three Mile Island disaster in the United States, and Nova Scotia activists could achieve no more than the withdrawal of their own government (along with Prince Edward Island) from the regional utility, incidentally removing the main motivation to pursue regional activist cooperation.[36]

The defence of local economies remained a feature of Nova Scotian environmental conflicts, large and small, throughout the 1970s and early 1980s, but no episode so effectively gave a voice to those defenders as the battle over uranium mining in 1982 and 1983. The province's initial venture into uranium mining during the 1970s had little to do with energy policy and much to do with the continued quest for regional economic development. With the encouragement and assistance of the federal government, provincial governments in Atlantic Canada in the middle years of the decade set about attracting capital investment in the form of geological exploration and active mining.[37] Just like oil and gas extraction, also on the province's development agenda, mining rarely makes for stable or lasting economic blessings, but from the perspective of a growth-hungry polity, potentially mineable deposits of zinc, lead, silver, copper, iron, tin, and uranium were too tempting to resist. The first hint that uranium might be found in commercially attractive quantities sent geologists rushing into the sandstone region of the province's north shore and Fundy shore in 1976, and from there into the Cobequid Highlands and the vast South Mountain Batholith, stretching from Halifax to Yarmouth.[38] As a favoured development project, uranium mining was promoted by the province as an engine of economic growth, but it also threatened the security of existing industries, especially agriculture in the heavily explored Annapolis Valley area.

The first new citizen action against uranium exploration in Nova Scotia came from an apparently unexpected source: the Women's Institutes. Nova Scotia's Women's Institutes began existence early in the twentieth century as service clubs for rural women, promoting education, civic engagement, and cultural activities. By the 1970s, however, they were often dismissed as conservative assemblies of older women still in the "citizen-apprentice" mode, and rapidly being left behind by the more progressive and politically savvy "citizen-activist" organizations like the Voice of Women for Peace and its even more recent peer organizations.[39] Yet the institutes were far from moribund or unresponsive to changing times, and in fact had much in common with the feminist peace groups that joined the earliest anti-nuclear activism in Halifax. The pesticide debates of the late 1970s drew a great deal of attention in agricultural communities and among institute members who considered the health of farm families a traditional women's issue. Some institutes also enjoyed a reinvigorated membership with the arrival of back-to-the-land families including women with experience in peace and social justice activism. Early in 1980, several Women's Institutes received information and assistance from the Department of Environment toward setting up Environmental Awareness Committees, and within months institutes in Hants and Kings counties were already at work gathering information on uranium mining.[40] By November, the Women's Institutes of Hants County moved from gathering information into building support for an anti-uranium movement, via presentations at the Farm Women's Conference in Truro and preparations

for a very leading questionnaire to be printed in the local paper, supposedly to determine the extent of popular concern about the health and economic effects of uranium mining.[41]

In early 1981, a rare Maritime-wide anti-nuclear gathering under the
banner of the fast-fading Maritime Energy Coalition served to unite interested parties in demanding a moratorium and inquiry into uranium
mining, but a common set of demands alone made for neither a full-scale
movement nor a strategy for organizing one.[42] What remained to be found
was a triggering event, something personal.

The winter of 1981 provided one, as news spread that one of the companies with claims in the Vaughan/New Ross area southwest of Windsor
was no longer looking for uranium so much as looking at a mineable de-
posit of it. If any single factor turned uranium from the obscure preoccu-
pation of a relatively small number of peace activists, anti-nuclear groups,
and Women's Institute members into a major environmental controversy,
it was the prospect of an actual uranium mine operating within a few
years at a known site in close proximity to the most productive agricultural region in the province. With the encouragement of Women's Institute
members who had spent most of the previous year studying the issue, statements of support for a moratorium on uranium mining and prospecting
came from the Hants and Digby counties' Federations of Agriculture, and
from the provincial NDP leader Alexa McDonough. Most worrying of all
from the industry's perspective, the West Hants Municipal Council's vote
to request a provincial moratorium was the direct result of the work of the
Women's Institutes.[43]

Making the public aware meant appealing to people's personal identification with their home place and their economic interests in the same.
Publishing a map of the province's combined uranium claims did that,
offering visual proof of the extent of uranium prospecting in the watersheds of populous coastal settlements. So too did constant reminders of
the incompatibility of uranium mining and agriculture, an echo of the
economic justice arguments made by south shore fishermen during the
Stoddard Island nuclear debate. In the aftermath of the 1982 provincial
election, which saw uranium mining become a major campaign issue,
activists redoubled their efforts to reach the public and persuade Nova
Scotians of the danger and foolishness of uranium mining. The Annapolis

URANIUM CLAIMS MAP

(after N.S. Dept. Mines & Energy

DETAILED MAP FOR HANTS, KINGS & LUNENBURG COUNTIES SHOWN ON REVERSE PAGE. COMPLETE DETAILS ON CLAIMS AVAILABLE FROM N.S. DEPT. MINES & ENERGY, JOSEPH HOWE BLDG HOLLIS STREET, HALIFAX

WHAT IF URANIUM COMPANIES' COME KNOCKING ON YOUR DOOR?

They must seek your permission before prospecting on your lands. If you choose to refuse permission, the company may apply to the Minister of Mines & Energy, Hon. Ron Barkhouse, for a special licence. It would be a good idea for you to express your concerns to the minister. His phone number in Halifax is 424-6657. Even if you don't call him, the minister will ask for your concerns before judging whether terms and conditions justify a special licence. BUT CALL HIM.

WHAT IF YOU FIND THEIR SURVEY MARKS ON YOUR LAND WITHOUT PERMISSION?

Again, call the minister right away: 424-6657

FOR MORE INFORMATION,
PHONE C.A.P.E. 757-3220
       or 757-3352
OR C.O.P.E.
   389-2410

WHAT CAN YOU DO
TO HELP STOP
URANIUM EXPLORATION/MINING
UNTIL IT IS PROVEN SAFE?

Write the Premier with your concerns.

and Phone the Minister of Mines & Energy

and Speak to your MLA

and Join one of the citizens' action groups.

URANIUM EXPLORATION CLAIMS
JULY 1981

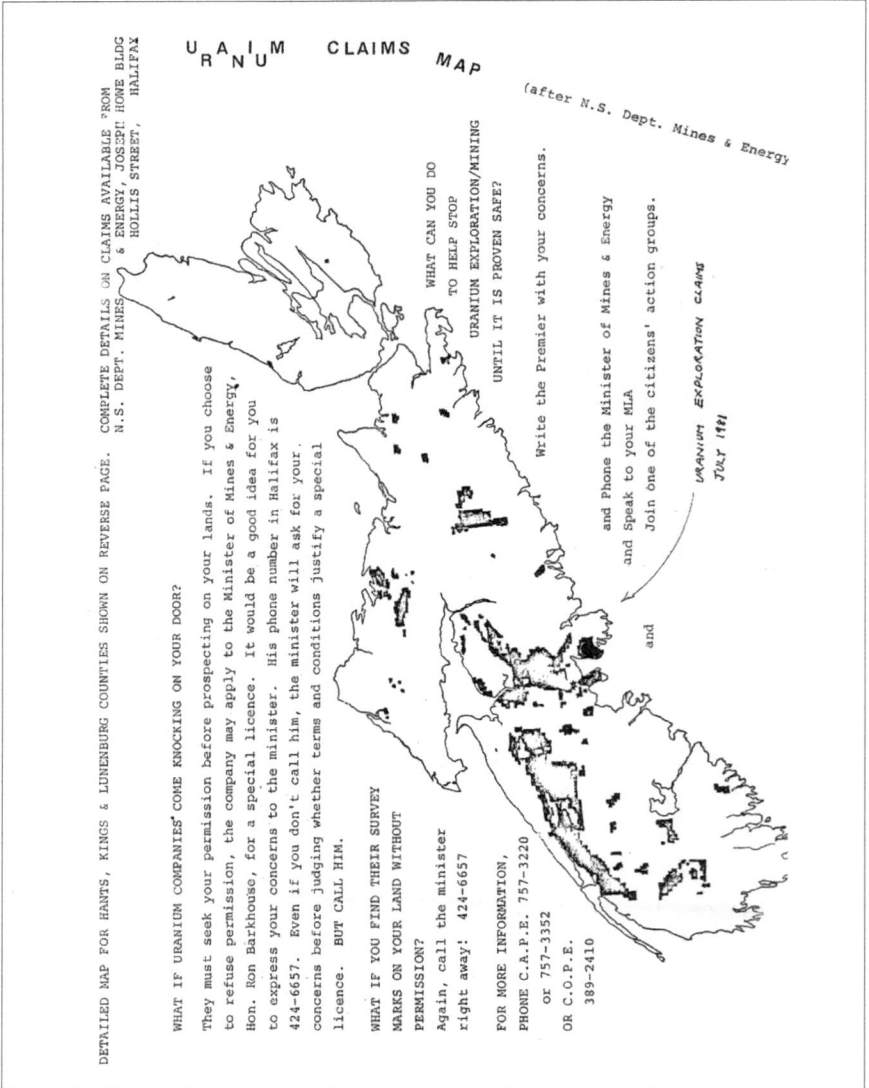

FIGURE 9.1: Uranium Claims Map. Courtesy of the Ecology Action Centre Fonds (MS-11-13), Dalhousie University Archives, Halifax, Nova Scotia.

Mark Leeming

Valley Branch of the Nova Scotia Medical Society resolved in November of the same year to join the call for a full moratorium, followed two weeks later by the General Council of the provincial Medical Society.[44] Agricultural groups continued to lend their names to the effort as well: the Cream Producers Association, the Kings County Federation of Agriculture, and more.[45] And new local anti-uranium groups sprang up like spring grass. Rather than expand geographically, members of the first single-issue anti-uranium group, Citizen Action to Protect the Environment (CAPE), helped local activists start their own groups in Kings County (Kings Association to Save the Environment [KASE]), in Vaughan (Residents Enlisted to Save Communities from Uranium Exploration [RESCUE]), in New Ross (Communities Organized to Protect the Environment [COPE]), and in Chester (Citizens Against Uranium Mining [CAUM]). In Cumberland County and in Colchester County, established anti-nuclear activists launched into anti-uranium campaigns as well, all of them, like the South Mountain groups, arguing that uranium mining held the potential for ruin in agricultural communities.[46] As ever in Nova Scotia, the diverse economic character of local communities, along with the difficulty and expense of communication and assembly for working people in scattered towns and villages, made local organization natural and much more attractive to activists with no pressing reason to form unitary provincial groups.

The uranium controversy in Nova Scotia was relatively short-lived, on account of the successful transformation of the provincial Royal Commission on Uranium Mining (declared shortly after the election) from an apolitical sideshow to a major source of political embarrassment for Premier John Buchanan's Progressive Conservative government, which had come into power in 1978 determined to avoid engaging with the environmental controversies that had dogged the previous Liberal government under Gerald Regan. While it lasted, the inquiry gave advocates of local economic autonomy and traditional industries a venue in which to air their views, which they did with enthusiasm. From the very first hearing, in New Ross, Lunenburg County, where Michael Keddy warned the audience that "it is only after exploration has taken place that the Landowner sees the folly of putting his trust in someone whose interests lay not in the land but in the provincial deficit,"[47] presenters returned again and again to a claim of authority based on a close relationship with the land and a warning against economic developmentalism that favoured industries profitable to governments and metropolitan populations at the expense of locals. The connection with fishing industries was clear, and at least one presenter, the celebrated pollution-fighter Robert Whiting, promised to pursue court action under the federal Fisheries Act if uranium mining went ahead.[48] Agricultural communities provided more numerous commentators, however, like Ron Leitold of New Germany, who derided transnational mining companies' inability to make "a personal commitment—concern, devotion, loyalty, love (call it what you will) for a particular area and its way of life," or Jacqueline Sanford of Avonmouth Farms in Summerville, who explicitly warned about the impact of uranium mining on farmers, and against trading "three hundred years of land settlement at great cost, in patient work . . . for a dozen or so years of doubtful gain and two thousand years of filthy radiation."[49]

Though it is sometimes common to attempt a distinction between environmental defence of a home place and economic defence of the same, it is clear from the testimony of those who made claims of authority based on affinity with the land that the idea of pristine nature and the division between human and environment held little sway over their minds. The most articulate statement of their indivisibility came when Muriel Maybe and the Lunenburg County Women's Group drew upon Aldo Leopold's land ethic to describe how "we are obligated to respect and cooperate with the land if we hope to ensure our continued existence . . . we are, in fact, members of a community of interdependent parts. We need the soil, the water, the plants, the animals."[50] Maybe was by no means alone, however, and others, like SSEPA's Hattie Perry, still speaking in defence of the local fishing economy, made equally explicit reference to the fact that "one cannot separate man from the environment, for what affects one affects the other."[51]

The more explicitly political presentations to the inquiry frequently included localist themes and environmental justice arguments. In fact, the discontents of metropolitanism formed a shared language of environmental activism across Canada. In British Columbia's uranium inquiry, and especially in Saskatchewan's, anti-uranium activists had vigorously challenged the imposition of environmental risks on western Canadian hinterland areas in order to produce benefits that would accrue mainly to urban centres and to the national capital.[52] It had not escaped notice in Nova Scotia that since the withdrawal of the Vaughan/New Ross claim-holder from Nova Scotia the project had been pursued by the federal Canada Development Corporation, with the support and encouragement of Atomic Energy of Canada Ltd.[53] "They are here in Nova Scotia," argued CAUM's Brian McVeigh, "because this province acts as a hinterland for exploiting cheap resources to feed the manufacturing mecca of the central region of Canada, where one in three light bulbs are powered by nuclear power."[54] Worse yet, for several of the rural presenters, was the compounded imperial pressure from the provincial capital; as an angry Robert Finck complained to Inquiry Commissioner Robert McCleave in Bridgewater, "it's just another example of second-class citizens getting the dirt while the Halifax gentry get the gravy."[55]

* * *

These brief vignettes of Nova Scotian environmentalism serve to illustrate the simple proposition that environmental activism in the province was not always, or even often, concerned with "the environment" in abstract, nor with world-spanning issues of universal impact (though there was much connection of local and global issues). Fishermen, farmers, and foresters in Nova Scotia's 1970s and 1980s were environmentalists involved in ecological distribution conflicts, well aware of the interdependence of ecological systems and local economies, and keen to defend that unified human environment against industrial development that discounted the values of people in place. As C. J. Byrne complained at a hearing of the Royal Commission on Uranium Mining, governments pursuing economic growth in simple numerical terms were too ready to listen to "some bloody economist or systems analyst talking about costs as if he or she were talking about buying jellybeans down at the corner store or Woolies [when] they never talk about the other and more serious cost, the heartache and sorrow brought about because people have to leave an area they have learned to live with and love."[56] Few of these activists would have recognized themselves in Ronald Inglehart's description of the "post-materialist" environmentalist, or in the narrowly racial definition of an environmental justice advocate.

Notes

1   Juan Martinez-Alier, *The Environmentalism of the Poor: A Study of Ecological Conflicts and Valuation* (Northampton, UK: Edward Elgar, 2002).

2   Ronald Inglehart and Jacques Rene-Rabier, "Political Realignment in Advanced Industrial Society: From Class-based Politics to Quality-of-Life Politics," *Government and Opposition* 21, no. 4 (1986): 456–79.

3   Ronald Inglehart, *The Silent Revolution: Changing Values and Political Styles Among Western Publics* (Princeton, NJ: Princeton University Press, 1977). This is not actually a very new idea of environmentalism, especially if one adheres to a broad definition including the Romantic movement; it echoes what Aldous Huxley wrote in the essay "Wordsworth in the Tropics," in *Do What You Will* (London: Chatto and Windus, 1956 [1929]). For the sociologists of environmentalism, see J. Craig Jenkins, "Resource Mobilization Theory and the Study of Social Movements," *Annual Review of Sociology* 9 (1983): 527–53; David Snow, Louis Zurcher, and Sheldon Ekland-Olson, "Social Networks and Social Movements," *American Sociological Review* 45, no. 5 (1980): 787–801; Peter Eisinger, "The Conditions of Protest in American Cities," *American Political Science Review* 67, no. 1 (1973): 11–28.

4   Samuel Hays, *Beauty, Health, and Permanence: Environmental Politics in the United States, 1955–1985* (Cambridge: Cambridge University Press, 1987), 3.

5   Ibid.

6   For example: Ryan O'Connor, *The First Green Wave: Pollution Probe and the Origins of Environmental Activism in Ontario* (Vancouver: UBC Press, 2015); Jennifer Read, "'Let Us Heed the Voice of Youth': Laundry Detergents, Phosphates, and the Emergence of the Environmental Movement in Ontario," *Journal of the Canadian Historical Association* 7, no. 1 (1996): 227–50; Mark MacLaughlin, "Green Shoots: Aerial Insecticide Spraying and the Growth of Environmental Consciousness in New Brunswick, 1952–1973," *Acadiensis* 40, no. 1 (2011): 3–23.

7   Ramachandra Guha, *How Much Should a Person Consume? Environmentalism in India and the United States* (Los Angeles: University of California Press, 2006), 8. Guha credits the definition to G. M. Trevelyan in the 1931 Rickman Godlee Lecture, titled "The Calls and Claims of Natural Beauty." Similar ideas appear in Mahesh Rangarajan, *Fencing the Forest: Conservation and Ecological Change in India's Central Provinces 1860–1914* (Delhi: Oxford University Press, 1996); and E. P. Thompson, *Customs in Common* (London: Merlin Press, 1991).

8   Ramachandra Guha, *The Unquiet Woods: Ecological Change and Peasant Resistance in the Himalaya,* 2nd ed. (Oxford: Oxford University Press, 1989); Juan Martinez-Alier, *Ecological Economics: Energy, Environment, and Society* (Oxford: Basil Blackwell, 1990); Martinez-Alier, *The Environmentalism of the Poor;* R. Guha and J. Martinez-Alier, *Varieties of Environmentalism: Essays North and South* (London: Earthscan, 2006); Jurgen Habermas, "New Social Movements," *Telos* 49 (1981): 33–37. Also, with Habermas, Nick Crossley, *Making Sense of Social Movements* (Buckingham, UK: Open U Press, 2002).

9   For example, Ramachandra Guha, "Radical American Environmentalism and Wilderness Preservation: A Third World Critique," *Environmental Ethics* 11, no. 1 (1989): 71–83; Carl Zimring, *Clean and White: A History of Environmental Racism in the United States* (New York: New York University Press, 2015); Eileen McGurty, *Transforming Environmentalism: Warren County, PCBs, and the Origins of Environmental Justice* (New Brunswick, NJ: Rutgers University Press, 2007); Andil Gosine, *Environmental Justice and Racism in Canada: An Introduction* (Toronto: Emond Montgomery, 2008).

10 Mark Leeming, *In Defence of Home Places: Environmental Activism in Nova Scotia* (Vancouver: UBC Press, 2017).

11 Other areas on the list of hosts of estuarine environmental movements include Shelburne Harbour, Mahone Bay, Bedford Basin, and Purcell's Cove. Ibid., 16–24.

12 Rust Associates, *A Review of the Boat Harbour Waste Treatment Facilities for Nova Scotia Water Resources Commission* (Montreal: Rust Associates, 1970).

13 The Mi'kmaq are the Indigenous inhabitants of Nova Scotia, and Pictou Landing is home to one of many small territories reserved to their ownership.

14 "Special Report: The Death of Boat Harbour," *Mysterious East*, September 1970, 21.

15 "The Death of Boat Harbour," 23.

16 "The Death of Boat Harbour," 22. The Pictou Landing Band did eventually win in court a recognition of the deception perpetrated in part by the federal government, and a settlement in 1993 that paid $35 million: Settlement agreement, 20 July 1993, http://boatharbour.kingsjournalism.com/wordpress/wpcontent/ uploads/ pdfs/15.199335millionagreement.pdf (accessed March 2013, site discontinued).

17 Henry Ferguson to Rust Associates, 24 March 1970, http://boatharbour. kingsjournalism.com/wordpress/documents/ (accessed March 2013, site discontinued).

18 "The Death of Boat Harbour," 22.

19 "The Death of Boat Harbour," 26. Reverend D. Glass, Sharon–Saint John United Church Stellarton, to Premier G. I. Smith, 16 August 1970, http://boatharbour.kingsjournalism. com/wordpress/wpcontent/ uploads/pdfs/09.1970smithfromchurch.pdf (accessed March 2013, site discontinued). Dr. J. B. MacDonald to Rust Associates Consulting Engineers, 22 March 1970, http://boatharbour.kingsjournalism.com/wordpress/ wpcontent/ uploads/pdfs/07.1970macDonaldLetterComplete.pdf (accessed March 2013, site discontinued).

20 "Special Report: The Death of Boat Harbour," *Mysterious East*, September 1970, 23. Reverend D. Glass, Sharon–Saint John United Church Stellarton, to Premier G. I. Smith, 16 August 1970, http://boatharbour.kingsjournalism.com/wordpress/ wpcontent/ uploads/pdfs/09.1970smithfromchurch.pdf (accessed March 2013, site discontinued).

21 "Report by J. A. Delaney and Associates on Pollution in Boat Harbour," box 116.6, Dalhousie University Institute of Public Affairs/Henson College fonds, UA-26, Dalhousie University Archives and Special Collections (hereafter DUA-SC).

22 "The Death of Boat Harbour," 22, 26.

23 "The Death of Boat Harbour," 22.

24 Silver Donald Cameron, interview by author, 1 November 2011. Others of the type included the Cole Harbour Environment Committee and the opponents of the Anil Hardboard Plant in Lunenburg County. See Leeming, *In Defence of Home Places*, 30–39.

25 "Air of Secrecy Surrounds Talks," *Chronicle Herald*, 6 June 1972, 1.

26 Alan Ruffman, interview by author, 21 February 2012. "Information Packet No. 1 on the Proposed Stoddard Island Nuclear Power Plant," March 1973, vol. 2, no. 2, Ecology Action Centre fonds, Public Archives of Nova Scotia (hereafter PANS-EAC).

27 "Regan Denies Talks," *Chronicle Herald*, 8 August 1972, 3.

28 "Nuclear Danger Feared," *Chronicle Herald*, 13 June 1972, 17.

29 "Federal Assistance for Proposed Nuclear Plant 'not likely unless . . . '," *Chronicle Herald*, 10 June 1972, 2; Ralph Surette, *Montreal Star*, 22 September 1973, clipping file, vol. 2, no. 2, Ecology Action Centre fonds, PANS-EAC.

30 A complex of the proposed size, operating at full capacity, would have used 10 million gallons of water each minute, and released it back into the ocean 20 degrees warmer than taken. And regardless of temperature, the volume of water would have included a great many living creatures, few of which would survive their passage through the cooling system.

31 "Lobster Fishermen Would Fight Plant," *Chronicle Herald*, 17 June 1972, 4; "Some Facts on the Problems and Dangers of Atomic Energy," December 1972, vol. 3421, no. 20, PANS-EAC; "Necessary to Get All the Facts, says Regan," *Chronicle Herald*, 25 October 1973, 10; "Participate in Energy Policy," EAC application to O.F.Y., 1973, box 39.6, Ecology Action Centre fonds, Dalhousie University Archives and Special Collections (hereafter DAL-EAC).

32 "Necessary to Get All the Facts, says Regan," 10.

33 Bruce Little, "Glace Bay Plant: Trying to Fix Costly Blunder," *Montreal Gazette*, 16 May 1973, 33; AECL, *Canada Enters the Nuclear Age* (Montreal: McGill-Queen's University Press, 1997), 337; Robert Campbell, "Heavy Water: Jewel to Millstone," *Mysterious East*, August 1970, 11–13. The Glace Bay plant was officially opened in 1967 but did not function until 1975, while the Port Hawkesbury plant began operations in 1970 but operated at far less than full capacity until refurbished in 1974.

34 The risks posed by low-level radiation exposure were (and still are) a well-known and bitterly contested point of debate among activists, nuclear scientists, and medical researchers in much of the world, as they had been since the famous Russell-Einstein Manifesto on radioactive fallout in 1955. See, for example, Roger Clarke, "Control of Low-Level Radiation Exposure: Time for a Change?" *Journal of Radiological Protection* 19, no. 2 (1999): 107–15.

35 ECC meeting report, 26 November 1973, box 41.20, DAL-EAC.

36 For more on regional anti-nuclear and other environmental activist cooperation, and on the New Brunswick and PEI movements, see Adrian Egbers, "Going Nuclear: The Origins of New Brunswick's Nuclear Industry, 1950–1983," (master's thesis, Dalhousie University, 2008); McLaughlin, "Green Shoots," 3–23; Mark Leeming, "The Creation of

Radicalism: Anti-Nuclear Activism in Nova Scotia, c.1972–1979," *Canadian Historical Review* 95, no. 2 (2014): 217–41; Alan MacEachern, *The Institute of Man and Resources: An Environmental Fable* (Charlottetown: Island Studies Press, 2003).

37 Province of Nova Scotia, Department of Mines and Energy, *Uranium in Nova Scotia: A Background Summary for the Uranium Inquiry – Nova Scotia, Report 82-7* (Halifax: Government of Nova Scotia, 1982), 3–9.

38 Bruce Little, "Shades of the Klondike in Atlantic Canada," *Atlantic Insight* 1, no. 2 (1979): 25; Province of Nova Scotia, Department of Mines and Energy, *Uranium in Nova Scotia*, 3–9. Companies exploring for uranium in the province included Lacana, Gulf, and Noranda on the north shore, and Esso, Aquitaine, Shell, Eldorado, Norcen, and Saarberg on the southern mainland.

39 Frances Early, "'A Grandly Subversive Time': The Halifax Branch of the Voice of Women in the 1960s," in *Mothers of the Municipality: Women, Work, and Social Policy in post-1945 Halifax*, ed. Judith Fingard and Janet Guildford (Toronto: University of Toronto Press, 2005), 28, 36.

40 Jocelyn Rhodenizer, South Berwick Women's Institute, to EAC, 17 September 1980, box 43.2, DAL-EAC; Document on NS Women's Institutes, 21 January 1980, vol. 3433, no. 38, PANS-EAC.

41 "Farm Women's Conference," *Rural Delivery* 5, no. 8 (1981); Burlington and Summerville Women's Institutes, *The Hants Journal,* 25 February 1981, 5.

42 "Conference on Health Effects of Radiation, Moncton," 20–22 February 1981, box 30.10, DAL-EAC.

43 Al Kingsbury, "Uranium Moratorium Urged," *Mail-Star* (Halifax), 13 March 1981, 52; "Aquitaine Mines a Rich Vein of Controversy," *Atlantic Insight* 3, no. 8 (1981): 16; EAC Board of Directors Meeting minutes, 28 January 1981, vol. 3420, no. 25, PANS-EAC; Burlington Women's Institute, "Brief Presented to the West Hants Municipal Council on the Subject of Uranium Mining," 12 March 1981, vol. 206, no. 28, Royal Commission on Uranium Mining fonds, PANS (hereafter RCU).

44 *Chronicle Herald,* 6 November 1981, Clipping File, vol. 206, no. 28, RCU; "Medical Society of Nova Scotia General Council, Community Health Committee Report," 20–21 November 1981, vol. 201, no. 10, RCU.

45 *Chronicle Herald,* 26 October 1981, Clipping File, vol. 206, no. 28, RCU, vol. 206, no. 28.

46 Donna Smyth, "The Public Debate Begins," *Rural Delivery* 6, no. 7 (1981).

47 Michael Keddy, transcripts of New Ross hearing, hearing #1, 2 April 1982, vol. 195, no. 12, RCU.

48 Whiting was well known for his leadership of a campaign of public pressure to clean up the Anil Hardboard plant in Lunenburg County in the early 1970s. Robert Whiting, transcript of Chester hearing, hearing #21, 7 July 1982, vol. 198, no. 3, RCU.

49 Ron Leitold, transcript of Bridgewater hearing, hearing #3, 20 April 1982, vol. 195, no. 16, RCU; Jacqueline Sanford, transcript of Vaughan's hearing, hearing #19, 25 June 1982, vol. 197, no. 12, RCU.

50 Muriel Maybe, Lunenburg County Women's Group, transcripts of Bridgewater hearing, hearing #3, 20 April 1982, vol. 195, no. 16, RCU. Other good examples include Ron Leitold, New Germany, transcripts of Bridgewater hearing, hearing #3, 20 April 1982, vol. 195, no. 16, RCU; and Norma Flynn, RESCUE, transcripts of Vaughan hearing, hearing #19, 25 June 1982, vol. 197, no. 12, RCU.

51 Hattie Perry, transcripts of Barrington hearing, hearing #14, 8 June 1982, vol. 197, no. 2, RCU.

52 Ralph Torrie, "BC's Inquiry and Moratorium," *CCNR's Transitions* 3, no. 1 (1980); Jim Harding, *Canada's Deadly Secret: Saskatchewan Uranium and the Global Nuclear System* (Halifax: Fernwood, 2007).

53 Ernest Forbes, *The Maritime Rights Movement 1919–1927: A Study in Canadian Regionalism* (Montreal: McGill-Queen's University Press, 1979); Margaret Conrad, "The Atlantic Revolution of the 1950s," in *Beyond Anger and Longing: Community and Development in Atlantic Canada*, ed. Berkeley Fleming (Fredericton: Acadiensis, 1988), 55–98; Jennifer Smith, "Intergovernmental Relations, Legitimacy, and the Atlantic Accords," *Constitutional Forum* 17, no. 3 (2008): 81–98.

54 Brian McVeigh, transcripts of Chester hearing, hearing #5, 30 April 1982, vol. 195, no. 21, RCU. Michael Marshall pointed out that mining companies accustomed to operating in the Canadian North, where they felt few constraints on their activities, failed to see the difference between Nova Scotia and Canada: transcripts of Halifax hearing, hearing #10, 21 May 1982, vol. 196, no. 6, RCU.

55 Robert Finck, transcripts of Bridgewater hearing, hearing #3, 20 April 1982, vol. 195, no. 16, RCU.

56 Dr. C. J. Byrne, transcripts of Halifax hearing, hearing #10, 21 May 1982, vol. 196, no. 6, RCU.

"Not an Easy Thing to Implement": The Conservation Council of New Brunswick and Environmental Organization in a Resource-Dependent Province, 1969–1983

Mark J. McLaughlin

In the 1960s and 1970s, the formative years of modern environmentalism, nascent environmental groups had to grapple with decisions about how to effect real and lasting change. As the following exchange indicates, this was not an easy task, as various social, economic, and political barriers stood in the way.

Brian Harvey, an employee with the Conservation Council of New Brunswick (CCNB), wrote to Fredericton's *Daily Gleaner* on 23 April 1980 in response to a letter to the editor by a woman named Marilee Little.[1] Little's "Open Letter to the Doomsday People" had appeared in the previous day's issue of the newspaper, and in it she explained that she had bought into the "theory" that the Earth's resources were limited but could not "begin to tell you the anguish all the recycling and reusing has caused me!" The list of anguish was long: her compost pile was "stinky," did not biodegrade below temperatures of zero degrees Celsius, and had seeped into a neighbour's yard during a rainstorm; firefighters had had a hard time finding the furnace during a routine check because of all of the recyclable bottles and containers that had accumulated in her basement; and her family complained bitterly about the meals of "bulgur wheat and soy grits" as she tried to wean them off meat. Little concluded, "So, my doomsday friends, I have tried, I am trying, and I will continue to try. But, I wish I was still ignorant. The guilt you have imposed on me is almost unbearable. Every time I drive my gas guzzler to a fast-food joint, bite into a quarter-pounder and imbibe my milk shake through a plastic straw in a plastic container, I think of you and it just doesn't taste as good as it once did."[2] In his response, Harvey first expressed to Little that she had his "admiration and respect for at least attempting to practice some of the basic principles of a Conserver Society." He then proceeded to advise her in ways to deal with all the sources of her anguish, including how to compost "properly," the locations of recycling sites around the city, and how to gradually introduce vegetarian meals to "a family that has been raised on meat and potatoes." Harvey also stated that he was not surprised that Little had been "skeptical from the start," because a "Conserver Society is not an easy thing to implement in a culture that has evolved to consume and waste resources to the extent our society has." In conclusion, he urged her not to give up, provided the CCNB's telephone number in case she had more questions, and closed with a simple sentence: "Welcome to the Conserver Society."[3]

Faced with such barriers, the Holy Grail for many environmentalists in terms of trying to make change happen was effective engagement with government officials, but the latter were not always receptive. In much of Canada during this period, state-sponsored resource development, often in the form of megaprojects, was a key mechanism employed by policy makers as part of programs designed to modernize regions that were considered economically, and sometimes socially, backward. Consequently, government officials were keen to mitigate any forms of resistance, including from environmental groups, that might impede resource development and the realization of their political and economic objectives.[4] Environmental organizations thus came up with a variety of novel approaches and strategies to try to convey their concerns as effectively as possible to governments that were very determined to exploit natural resources on a grand scale.

The formative years of the CCNB, New Brunswick's first and main environmental group, serve as a good case study of what many small Canadian groups went through in their search for effective environmental organizing, and offer insight into at least two of the broader themes addressed by this edited collection. The first theme is scale. During its first several years in existence, the CCNB focused a lot of organizational time and energy on a small, decentralized network of regional chapters. The chapters were mostly based in the southern half of the province, were run by volunteers, and to a great extent dealt with environmental issues of local concern. This was followed by a period of lost momentum in the mid-1970s, one experienced by numerous Canadian environmental groups and characterized by decreases in membership and funding. The road to revitalization was paved with the concept Harvey described in his response to Little's letter to the editor, that of the "conserver society." It was devised by the Science Council of Canada in the aftermath of the 1973–1974 oil crisis as a loosely outlined vision of how the country could transition away from the economic model of indiscriminate growth. The CCNB was one of the environmental groups that used national interest in the conserver society as an opportunity for self-revitalization. In the late 1970s and early 1980s, under the dynamic leadership of Dana Silk, the group moved away from its decentralized, volunteer roots, and developed a centralized and professional institutional foundation. Many small Canadian environmental organizations undertook this transition in scale, from the more local to the provincial and beyond, and so an examination of the CCNB example has the potential to reveal much about modern Canadian environmentalism in general.

Of course, any mention of the term "scale" necessitates a discussion of its application. I contend that throughout the period covered by this chapter, from 1969 to 1983, the CCNB remained a small-scale environmental organization. It may have been New Brunswick's first and main environmental group, and as a result also the largest, but its membership hovered around 200 to 250 for most of the 1970s, and then only reached about 350 during the institutionalization process in the late 1970s and early 1980s.[5] Combined with the facts that the CCNB never employed more than a few modestly paid staff and limited most of its operations to New Brunswick, the country's third smallest province in both population and total land area, at no time did the organization ever come close to the scale of Canada's larger environmental groups, such as Pollution Probe or Greenpeace.

The second theme, deeply intertwined with that of scale, is the notion of efficacy. The CCNB adopted two different styles of government engagement in the 1970s. Earlier in the decade, the decentralized, volunteer organization embraced a collaborative approach based on personal relationships and face-to-face lobbying. Some environmental regulatory infrastructure and frameworks were established, but largely because doing so did not impede or threaten the New Brunswick government's economic agenda. It was only after the CCNB's transition of organizational time and energy from the local to the provincial scale that political barriers became really impenetrable. As part of the transition within the organization, Silk and his contemporaries adopted a confrontational approach to government engagement, seemingly becoming even more of a threat to the provincial state's resource development schemes, and thereby provoking backlash and even some retrenchment. The limited success of the CCNB's engagement with government officials, despite its adoption of two different lobbying styles in the 1970s, raises questions about how we have measured the effectiveness of the modern environmental movement in Canada. There were distinct reasons why Marilee Little had such a hard time changing hers and her family's wasteful ways, but they had less to do with the so-called ineffectiveness of environmental organizations and more to do with the obstructionism of the state.

In New Brunswick, environmental awareness emerged as the provincial government promoted forestry as being central to the successful implementation of social and economic modernization in the 1950s and 1960s. Forest exploitation had been the most important component of the New Brunswick economy since the early nineteenth century, and so it is not surprising that the trend toward environmentalism was rooted in residents' concerns about certain forestry practices. The two main issues that fuelled public reaction and citizen mobilization were the spruce budworm spraying program and water pollution from pulp and paper mills, which were both associated with large-scale industrial forestry. In each case, the New Brunswick government adopted a different regulatory approach, neither of which was all that successful by the late 1960s. In the wake of what was generally perceived as government inaction, and by some as pandering to the forestry companies, the CCNB was founded in 1969.[6]

The CCNB was originally conceived as an educational, advocacy, and lobbying organization focused mainly, but not exclusively, on scientifically informed conservation and "wise use" of natural resources. In April 1969, members of the New Brunswick Institute of Agrology hosted a meeting of individuals who were concerned about the conservation of the province's natural resources. Those at the meeting decided to form an umbrella organization to coordinate the activities of the numerous conservation-oriented groups in New Brunswick—a so-called council of conservation. Kenneth Langmaid, a soil scientist at the University of New Brunswick, was named provisional chairman of the new organization, and a "number of prominent citizens" were invited to form the council's directorate.[7] The CCNB's founding board of directors consisted primarily of resource scientists, from both the public and private sectors, but it also included professionals, retirees, a former politician, and a well-known author. The organization's official founding meeting, one that was accessible to the broader public, was held in Fredericton on 18 October 1969. At the meeting, Langmaid, now the CCNB's president, read aloud the group's terms of reference, as they were understood at that time:

> The pollution of land, air, and water, the destruction of wildlife, the unwise use of our forests, the indiscriminate employment of chemicals in agriculture, these are but some of the ways that man is ruining the world in which he lives, in which it is his duty to serve. They are in many ways related and must be fought with a common purpose. It will thus be a prime task of the Conservation Council to coordinate and to foster research and to take remedial action wherever it is needed. This will entail a closest cooperation with other conservation bodies in the province. To this end, committees of experts will be set up to investigate conservation problems. The council will assemble, collate, and disseminate information about conservation matters. It is vitally necessary that the grave dangers which face mankind and the natural world should be brought home by all possible

means to the public at large and that every school pupil and every adult should become concerned with conservation. The Conservation Council will speak with a strong and factual voice, [and] will have no partisan connection.[8]

The objectives of education, advocacy, and lobbying were still central when Langmaid and others filed to incorporate the CCNB in 1970, although the catch-all term of "pollution," commonly used during this period to denote a variety of conservation and environmental issues, featured prominently in four out of the five points listed under "purpose."[9] Within the formal constitution, the language changed again; the organization placed more emphasis on phrases such as "understanding of the human environment," "awareness of the relationship between man and the environment," and "environmentally sound policies and programs."[10] Nonetheless, the CCNB's basic guiding principles remained the same.

In terms of structure, the CCNB's founders designed it to be a decentralized, volunteer organization. There were seven classes of membership available at varying prices, and the "geographical organization of members of the CCNB" was in "regional groups, to be known as Chapters." Each chapter dealt with specific issues of local concern, while the provincial body handled matters that were considered to be of broader interest but had particular resonance within New Brunswick. At both the provincial and chapter levels, officers, such as president, vice-president, and secretary-treasurer, were elected at annual general meetings, and the provincial officers and the presidents of the regional chapters were all members of the CCNB's board of directors.[11] All of the leadership positions were occupied by volunteers, and the organization had no paid staff. Indeed, there were seldom provincial or chapter headquarters, so incoming correspondence was usually addressed to the presidents' homes or places of work.[12]

The main strategy adopted by the CCNB to engage government officials in the early 1970s was a collaborative style of lobbying that relied in large part on personal relationships and face-to-face interactions. Langmaid once explained in an April 1972 letter to Donald J. Blackburn, a member of the Department of Extension Education at the University of Guelph, that "we have had no great confrontations here but we have met with Provincial Cabinet Ministers and their Deputies from time to

Mark J. McLaughlin

time, trying to get legislation adopted and enforced." He further noted that "we have had a very low key co-operative approach to the matter of conservation. I prefer to consider the whole thing as conservation rather than anti-pollution etc. I believe it is a more positive approach."[13] In general, the CCNB's founders were well-educated, middle-class, Anglophone men, resource scientists and the like, and in a small provincial capital such as Fredericton in the late 1960s and early 1970s, the conservationists and environmentalists were often acquaintances and sometimes good friends with government officials.[14] This dynamic of similar levels of education and established relationships likely provided members of the CCNB with more direct access to individuals with political power than they would have been able to gain otherwise. It also proved beneficial that the "co-operative," "positive," and non-radical approach advocated by the CCNB during this period was not seen as a major threat to economic growth by the New Brunswick government. Langmaid's statement that he preferred "to consider the whole thing as conservation rather than anti-pollution" was reference to the CCNB's belief in the wise use of natural resources, a stance that the state would have deemed as far less hostile than demands for strict curtailment of resource development. Despite this establishment of good rapport with government officials, the CCNB's intimate lobbying style had its critics. According to Langmaid in late 1970, "the major criticism of the organization has been that it has not been militant enough."[15]

The CCNB's main accomplishment of the early 1970s was successfully lobbying for the creation and implementation of environmental regulatory infrastructure and frameworks within the provincial bureaucracy. Langmaid laid the groundwork for this outcome in October 1970, when he wrote to the leaders of New Brunswick's three main political parties, asking each of them to take "a clear stand" on such issues as the spruce budworm spraying program, "special privileges" accorded to the pulp and paper industry, and environmental degradation associated with "uneconomical" industries, "so that voters may choose wisely" in that month's election. Of all the party leaders, Progressive Conservative Richard Hatfield was the most receptive to Langmaid's missive, stating in a letter that, if elected, his party would "implement a comprehensive pollution control program including controls, incentives, research, education and enforcement. Projects for eradication of existing pollution will be undertaken."[16]

As it happened, voters chose the Progressive Conservatives to form the next government on October 26, and Hatfield, sensing a shift in the political winds, became the first New Brunswick premier to actively engage with environmental issues. Under his leadership, and partly in response to Langmaid's letter and other CCNB lobbying efforts, an environmental division was set up within the Department of Fisheries in 1971, and then a separate Department of the Environment was established in 1975.[17] Furthermore, within six weeks of its founding meeting in October 1969, the CCNB announced that it was going to conduct a study of the types, amounts, and applications of pesticides in the province, making it the organization's first major endeavour as an environmental group and "the first detailed report on the problem of its kind" in New Brunswick.[18] The CCNB's pesticide committee, chaired by Dr. George Gerald Shaw, delivered its final report in the summer of 1970, and its biggest criticism was the unregulated and unchecked way that pesticides were utilized in the province. The pesticide report and the CCNB's subsequent lobbying on the issue, as well as the end of federal support for the spruce budworm spraying program, were the primary motivators behind the Hatfield government's enactment of the Pesticides Control Act in early 1973. The Act provided, for the first time, a regulatory and licensing framework within the Department of Agriculture for the use and sale of pesticides in the province.[19] In addition, the CCNB effectively lobbied for the passage of the Clean Environment Act, which allowed for government regulation of a broadly defined list of "contaminants," in 1971. The Act also authorized the appointment of an environmental council of five members, who were not elected representatives or government employees, to conduct studies at the behest of the minister of the environment and to receive submissions "from any person concerning any matter coming within this Act."[20]

Each regional chapter of the CCNB also made at least some minimal gains on the issues with which they were most concerned. There were four main chapters in the province, Woodstock, Saint John, Moncton, and Fredericton, all founded in 1970, and all generally located in the more affluent, Anglophone urban centres of southern New Brunswick, although there were CCNB chapters in Musquash-Lepreau and the Miramichi region for at least a short period of time.[21] Local officers and members had common environmental interests, from educational initiatives to anti-litter campaigns, but each chapter also dealt with specific issues of concern.

The major issues for the chapter in Woodstock were agricultural pesticides and pollution in the Saint John River. Many of the Woodstock members had been involved with the Association for the Preservation and Development of the Saint John River in Its Natural State, formed in 1964 over concerns about the planned construction of a massive hydroelectric dam in the Mactaquac region.[22] In Saint John, the province's industrial centre and deepwater seaport, the local chapter focused on contaminants from manufacturing plants, general pollution in the harbour, and air quality.[23] The Moncton chapter, an affiliate of Pollution Probe, was a general environmental group, strongly anti-pollution, and it was one of the founding members of the Maritime Energy Coalition, an amalgam of organizations dedicated to stopping nuclear power development, in the early 1970s.[24] The chapter in Fredericton was the most active, and this was in large part because of the intense dedication of its president, Richard Tarn, a plant scientist. It was mainly interested in air and water pollution from the Nackawic pulp and paper mill, land use planning in and around Fredericton, and collaboration with student groups on issues of common concern.[25]

However, the CCNB often regarded the environmental gains it was able to extract from the New Brunswick government as being insufficient or incomplete. The group had several immediate criticisms of the Clean Environment Act, including the fact that it did not override other provincial legislation in areas of potential conflict, such as resource development.[26] As for the Pesticides Control Act, the CCNB later testified before the New Brunswick Pesticide Advisory Board, a key consultative component of the Act derived from the group's 1970 pesticide report but not fully realized until the late 1970s, that the board itself had numerous flaws, including that it did not evaluate "risk to the public" when considering permit applications.[27]

This supposed insufficiency or incompleteness of legislation was actually part of the Hatfield government's strategy to mitigate environmental resistance. As I have argued elsewhere, the state used such measures as the creation of environmental divisions and departments within government bureaucracies in the 1960s and 1970s to legitimate its presumed function as the manager or steward of natural resources and ecosystems within its territorial borders, with the intention of appeasing enough environmental concerns so as to maintain largely uninterrupted economic growth.[28]

The passage of environmental legislation in New Brunswick adhered to this trend. The provincial government was solidly committed to a program of social and economic modernization through resource development during this period.[29] Even with the establishment of good rapport with government officials, the CCNB was unable to convince the state to implement more than a minimal set of environmental regulations in the early 1970s. It also did not help that many of the group's leading members were civil servants, potentially limiting how aggressively they could pursue environmental matters even if they so desired.

By the mid-1970s, the CCNB was having difficulty maintaining organizational momentum. The regional chapters recorded significant drops in membership from 1971 to 1974: both Fredericton and Saint John went from around one hundred members to eighty-four and fifty-four respectively, Woodstock from thirty to twelve, and Moncton from approximately twenty to twelve. The situation continued to get worse in 1975. The chapters described in their formal reports to the CCNB's board of directors, now sometimes nothing more than a couple of paragraphs, even further decreases in enrolment and an ebbing sense of direction and effectiveness. It was finally reported in mid-1976 that, with regard to the Fredericton, Woodstock, and Saint John chapters, no meetings had been held or executives elected for several months. Moreover, Pollution Probe–Moncton was no longer considered one of the CCNB's regional chapters, since most of its attention was being devoted to the Maritime Energy Coalition and the issue of nuclear power.[30]

The CCNB's loss of momentum can be best explained as the result of a combination of factors. First, it was part of a national pattern of environmental groups that made gains on localized issues in the late 1960s and early 1970s (what has been referred to as the first wave of the Canadian

Mark J. McLaughlin

environmental movement) but then arguably struggled to make the successful transition to larger, more abstract concerns in the mid-1970s. It was easier to make headway and demonstrate results to members when both access to those with power to make change and the impacts from gains on issues were immediate and tangible rather than distant and esoteric. This aforementioned transition in scale, from the more local to the provincial and beyond, resulted in widespread drops in membership and funding.[31] Another factor was that many of the CCNB's original members left the organization for personal reasons. Harold Hatheway, one of the founders, noted in a December 1977 letter that he had not been involved with the CCNB for three years because he "got too involved with working for a living with the provincial government."[32] Kenneth Marsh, who replaced Richard Tarn in 1972, explained in his presidential report to the 1974 annual general meeting of the Fredericton chapter that eleven members had moved away in the previous year, or close to 14 percent of 1973's membership.[33] In a university town like Fredericton, a number of those involved with the organization would have been students, so some of the decline can probably be attributed to them leaving town after completing their studies. It is also highly likely that certain CCNB members left due to fatigue, as the demands of a volunteer organization can be great, especially one advocating conservation and environmental values in a resource-dependent province. The final factor was the organization's decentralized structure. In letters exchanged in the fall of 1970, Richard Tarn and William Mackenzie, president of the Saint John chapter, discussed how "the present lack of a clear policy on membership dues, and the relationship between our Chapter and the Council over membership are making many problems," as was "the rather obvious policy of keeping control of the organization in the hands of certain people," and "the President's failure to back up his Branches when they take a position in any matter."[34] Many of the "worst kinks" with the membership and fee structures had been worked out by 1973 with amendments to the CCNB's constitution and bylaws, but problems of trust and communication remained, leading to the sense of aimlessness and ineffectiveness expressed in the 1975 chapter reports.[35] As research by Ryan O'Connor on Pollution Probe in Toronto and Jonathan Clapperton (this volume) on the Society for Pollution and Environmental Control in Vancouver demonstrate, this process of internal fracturing was not unique to the CCNB but rather a common growing pain experienced by Canadian environmental organizations during this period.[36]

The decline of the regional chapters sparked a debate within the CCNB's board of directors about the future of the organization. In essence, the debate revolved around whether an attempted revitalization of the CCNB should be concentrated at the level of the provincial body or the chapters. At a meeting of the directors in May 1976, Dana Silk, a master's student in the forestry faculty at the University of New Brunswick, was the voice for narrowing efforts to the provincial body, while Richard Tarn, who had succeeded Kenneth Langmaid as the CCNB's president in 1972, "asked all directors to commit themselves to revitalizing the Chapters." The final consensus, after much discussion, was "that a major rebuilding job is necessary and that it should begin at the Chapter level."[37]

From 1976 to 1978, the CCNB tried to revive the regional chapters and increase its membership and funding. The Fredericton, Saint John, and Woodstock chapters held occasional meetings and conducted some activities, such as presenting to the town council or setting up a booth at the local fair, but momentum and interest had largely dissipated by mid-1977.[38] The CCNB also launched a membership drive by printing 5,000 copies of a bilingual brochure and running radio advertisements to promote the organization. All members were expected to seek out new sign-ups, and CCNB directors were even once encouraged to "make an effort to obtain 5 new members before the next board meeting. A prize will be provided." In the end, membership numbers and associated funding through fees went up only slightly.[39]

As the CCNB struggled to revitalize, other environmental groups, policy makers, academics, and assorted commentators were engaged in an international discussion about alternatives to the economic model of indiscriminate growth. Modern environmentalism had been concerned with human impacts on ecologies of all types since its inception, but the publication of the books *The Population Bomb* (1968) and *The Limits to Growth* (1972) focused attention on the possible dangers of exponential human and economic growth to the survival of the planet.[40] Then, in 1973 and 1974, the shock stemming from the embargo instituted by oil-producing nations in the Middle East and North Africa led concerns about the social, economic, political, and environmental costs of cheap energy and the finiteness of natural resources to become mainstream across North America and Europe.[41] Coupled with the publication of the book *Small is Beautiful* (1973) by E. F. Schumacher, which contained ideas about "human scale," decentralization, and "appropriate technologies," the oil crisis of 1973–74 prompted a broader dialogue about alternative ways to structure societies and economies that crossed political party lines and national borders.[42] It has been pointed out that the 1973–74 oil shock was one of the factors that helped end the "first wave" of the Canadian environmental movement.[43] While this is accurate, the aftermath of the crisis presented environmental groups with opportunities for revitalization.

In Canada, much of the national conversation about alternatives to indiscriminate growth was driven by the Science Council of Canada and the concept of the "conserver society." Composed of scientists and senior civil servants, the Science Council was founded as a federal advisory board in 1966, then underwent the transition to a Crown corporation in 1968. It researched and published on a range of topics related to science and technology, and what were eventually referred to as "conserver principles" permeated its reports in the late 1960s and early 1970s.[44] The first time the full term "conserver society" appeared in print was in the council's nineteenth report, published in January 1973. It was recommended that "Canadians as individuals, and their governments, institutions and industries, begin the transition from a consumer society preoccupied with resource exploitation to a conserver society engaged in more constructive endeavours. Ideally, Canada could provide the leadership necessary to work toward more equitable distribution of the benefits of natural resources to all mankind."[45] The Science Council adopted a proposal at its June 1973 meeting to create a committee to explore "The Implications of a Conserver Society," but the start of the study was delayed until March 1975 because of the untimely death of the original chairperson, W. J. Cheesman. The work of the four-person committee, now chaired by Ursula Franklin, a member of the Department of Metallurgy and Materials Science at the University of Toronto, received widespread coverage in news media, and it maintained a public exchange of ideas through a quarterly journal called *Conserver Society Notes*, distributed to a mailing list of over 1,500 "interested respondents." In February 1976, the Franklin committee released an interim "statement of concern," declaring that "Canadians are entering an era of transition, in the course of which many features of the way we do things will change. Indiscriminate growth for growth's sake will have to give way to a more selective growth."[46] The interim statement was re-published in *Science Forum*, *Québec Science*, and *Canadian Consumer* in June 1976, and was read into the US Congressional Record in March 1977. The committee delivered its final report, *Canada as a Conserver Society*, in September 1977, and "the basic ideas set out in the Report continued to grow, appearing in articles, books, university curricula and even in new political movements."[47] Pollution Probe's Lawrence Solomon, for example, further developed many of the ideas put forward by the Franklin committee in his book *The Conserver Solution* (1978).[48]

The Franklin committee's report on the concept of the conserver society was a loosely outlined, made-in-Canada, technocratic vision of how to combine limits-influenced environmentalism and decentralized responsibility and innovation with the liberal market economy.[49] As the report explained:

> It is important to emphasize that we [the Franklin committee] are not attempting to set out a complete blueprint for a new society, nor to specify the exact modes of transition or how long they may take. The Report should be seen as our view of some new directions related to science and technology that the conserver principles imply, and some actions in those directions that agencies at all levels—government, business, labour, and private citizens—can take.[50]

There were five "Principal Policy Thrusts of a Conserver Society" described in the report. The first was "Concern for the Future," or a heightened awareness that the short-term policies and actions of the past must be replaced with long-term goals and thinking, including "responsible" stewardship of knowledge and natural resources, taking advantage of new opportunities in science and technology, and conserving "to keep options open" and avoid "one supply crisis after another." The next one was "Economy of Design," that is, a societal shift from "bigger is better" to "do more with less," with particular attention to "*total* social efficiency and best use of resources" and recycling becoming "part of the fabric of all production activities—not an afterthought." "Diversity, Flexibility and Responsibility" was the third policy thrust, denoting that greater diversity in all areas of society, from transportation to electrical generation to consumer products, increased "flexibility, adaptability, and resiliency" and allowed for "decentralization of responsibility, and optimal performance from local resources." Fourth, "Recognition of Total Costs" meant addition of the full and "true" environmental costs into the production process and price of products, which would lead to "innovation using the conserver approach" and "eventual improvement in the quality of life for everyone." The final one was "Respect for the Regenerative Capacity of the Biosphere," or promotion of "techno-socio-economic processes that are in principle sustainable."[51] The report also discussed at length how the five policy thrusts could be applied in four general areas: energy efficiency and conservation, renewable energy, materials, and new business and employment opportunities, and provided specific recommendations regarding "Things to Do Immediately" and "Things to Think About."[52]

The conserver society–infused national conversation about alternatives to indiscriminate growth provided environmental groups across the country with opportunities for revitalization in the late 1970s and early 1980s. Numerous groups "adopted the conserver society as both a principle to organize around and an alternative method of development through which to analyze government policy" as part of efforts to regain some of the organizational momentum lost in the mid-1970s. Furthermore, much of the bureaucratic attention of Environment Canada and the federal Department of Energy, Mines, and Resources was fixated on the realization of conserver principles by the late 1970s. This included the creation of various programs and grants, often in conjunction with the provinces, designed to implement and to educate the wider public about some of the Franklin committee's recommendations. Environmental groups frequently accessed these programs and grants and shrewdly used them for their own particular purposes, such as revitalization, all the while operating within funding parameters.[53]

One of the groups that took advantage of the opportunities to revitalize was the CCNB, and the agent for this change was the aforementioned Dana Silk. Born in London, Ontario, Silk spent his childhood and formative years in London, England, and Summerside, Prince Edward Island, and received a Bachelor of Design in environmental planning from the Nova Scotia College of Art and Design in 1973 and a Master of Forestry from the University of New Brunswick in 1975. His "real introduction to environmental issues" was through land use planning, and he became involved with the CCNB during his master's degree, often attending meetings in the basement of the Tarn household, and later joined the Maritime Energy Coalition and the nuclear power debate. Silk was a member of the CCNB provincial executive in the mid to late 1970s, but his chance to effect serious change within the organization arrived when he replaced Richard Tarn as president in late 1978.[54]

In many ways, Silk was precisely the sort of leader that the CCNB needed at that time. Silk astutely recognized the emergence of indiscriminate growth as an important matter of environmental concern, and he and other members worked to ensure that the CCNB was involved in this pan-Canadian conversation by co-founding Friends of the Earth Canada, attending regional and national environmental conferences, and inviting well-known environmental personalities to speak in New Brunswick, including Ursula Franklin, Amory Lovins (soft/alternative energy), Rosalie Bertell (environmental health), and George McRobie (sustainable development).[55] Silk was even very adept at navigating his way through all of the bureaucratic hoops and paperwork that came with the conserver-inspired government programs and grants.[56]

Silk's main accomplishment as head of the CCNB was providing the group with a centralized and professional institutional foundation through the hiring of staff and setting up of a permanent headquarters. Silk had been the voice for narrowing revitalization efforts to the provincial body in 1976, and so becoming president allowed him to guide the organization away from the now-defunct regional chapters and concentrate on the provincial body. The general administrative structure of the CCNB remained the same, while the classes of membership were increased to eight, with somewhat different titles, and membership prices went up for the first time in ten years.[57] As for staff and office space, the idea actually dated back to April 1977, when the fundraising committee offered the suggestion, to be achieved within three years, and the CCNB's board of directors passed a motion of acceptance.[58] One of the first people hired was Silk. He worked as the executive director of the New Brunswick division of the Community Planning Association of Canada from 1976 to 1979, but according to him, attending an environmental education conference in Toronto "was an eye-opener. . . . There were about 15 people from across the country and almost all of them worked more or less full-time on environmental issues, so it inspired me to join them." In 1980, Silk became the first executive director of the CCNB, a position he held until 1983.[59] The initial staff were Brian Harvey (researcher/coordinator), Janet Parkhill (researcher/coordinator and office manager), and Karen Hine (newsletter editor). They were hired for one year at minimum wage in the spring of 1979 through what was being referred to as the "Conserver Society Project," a Youth Job Corps–assisted venture to educate the public about conserver principles. Harvey, Parkhill, and Hine were then kept on as staff for at least one more year, working directly for the CCNB, and by the end of 1980, up to five people were working in the head office.[60]

Silk developed both short- and long-term options for headquarters. He contacted W. A. Waller, associate executive director of Fredericton's Chalmers Hospital, in March 1979, inquiring if the CCNB could "rent the old Personnel and Housekeeping Offices in the Victoria Public Hospital Building"; the rooms were eventually secured at a rental of $159.84 per month.[61] Silk also proposed a project called the "Conservation House," or "plans to retrofit an old house in Fredericton as a demonstration of the potential for incorporating the latest energy conservation technologies in the existing house stock," to the New Brunswick Energy Secretariat in February 1979. By that summer, Silk had arranged to lease a large house located at 180 St. John Street, known as the "old Press Club," from the provincial government for one dollar per year.[62] The deal was subsequently put on hold while the New Brunswick government negotiated a Conservation and Renewable Energy Demonstration Agreement (CREDA), a conserver-influenced granting program, with the federal government. The Canada–New Brunswick CREDA was signed on 16 January 1980, and the CCNB secured, at least according to the mid-term report, more than $350,000 over the next several years to "increase public awareness of conservation and renewable energy technologies, in particular those applicable to the residential sector, through the conservation and renewable energy retrofit of a century-old house and conversion of the house to a public information centre." Later renamed "Conserver House," the demonstration building at 180 St. John Street thereafter served as the CCNB's permanent headquarters, and received approximately 3,000 visitors per year, most of whom were from the Fredericton area, by 1982.[63]

The CCNB's overall productivity increased significantly during Silk's time as president and executive director. This is not to suggest that the organization was inactive from the decline of the regional chapters in the mid-1970s to the transfer of leadership from Tarn to Silk in late 1978. On the contrary, the provincial body remained committed to a number of environmental causes and projects during this period, everything from the mundane task of ensuring representation on government committees, to the educational role of publishing an on-again/off-again newsletter, to pioneering new initiatives like lobbying for the creation of wilderness areas in New Brunswick.[64] That said, there was a marked increase in the CCNB's productivity after Silk assumed the presidency, and particularly once he had become executive director, full-time staff had been hired, and office space had been established. An organization with an institutional foundation could simply dedicate more time to environmental activities than one run by volunteers, many of whom had full-time jobs not associated with the organization.

Silk and other members quickly discovered that there were limits on what they could potentially achieve. The sweeping influence of the concept of the conserver society had provided the CCNB with opportunities for revitalization and institutionalization, but it was much more complicated to follow through with the actualization of conserver principles. As Silk later recalled, "it was difficult for Maritimers to pursue the same concepts . . . as those from the big cities because our population base was much smaller and more dependent on natural resources. . . . We certainly enjoyed ourselves [at regional and national conferences] but it was all a bit Disneyland compared to our bread and butter issues back home."[65] The fact that New Brunswick was a highly resource-dependent province, and one with very limited financial resources, meant that, after the passage of some environmental legislation in the early 1970s, the provincial government was more interested in sponsoring resource-based industries than environmental regulation or encouraging widespread societal change. Indeed, in the mid to late 1970s the Hatfield government was busily promoting pulp and paper manufacturing and the large-scale use of industrial forest management on Crown lands as being central to social and economic modernization, with little attention being paid to environmental concerns, let alone conserver principles.[66] In spite of government indifference, there were attempts by the CCNB to spread the gospel of the conserver society, including setting up Conserver House as an energy-saving and renewable technologies demonstration building. In another instance, the CCNB applied for and received a grant through the New Brunswick Energy Secretariat to produce 1,500 copies of a "Welcome to the Conserver Society" poster, which highlighted energy-saving techniques that people could incorporate into their everyday lives.[67]

By and large, though, Silk and his contemporaries concentrated their efforts on various "bread and butter" issues, or those that had particular resonance within New Brunswick. One of the issues was energy. Silk had been involved with the anti-nuclear movement since the mid-1970s, and while the CCNB had had an energy committee for many years, energy issues became a more pressing concern once he was president/executive director. The organization was especially troubled by the Hatfield government's obsession with nuclear power development and perceived disregard for alternative energy sources and energy conservation.[68] And not surprisingly, the province's economic mainstay, forestry, was another issue pursued by the CCNB. Brian Harvey, a recent graduate from the University of New Brunswick's forestry program, sent a "questionnaire . . . to all the pulp and paper mills in the province [in June 1979] in the hope that a clear perspective on the industry might be obtained when all the information is in."[69] Later that fall, the CCNB celebrated its tenth anniversary by dedicating the organization's annual general meeting to a major conference on forest management, and issued invitations to representatives from government, industry, organized labour, woodlot owners' associations, and conservation and environmental groups.[70] Other issues of concern for the CCNB in the late 1970s and early 1980s, some of which were long-standing ones, were acid rain, land use management, recycling, and publication of the province's first environmental law handbook.[71]

The CCNB still spent much of its time engaging government officials, but under Silk's leadership it practised a more confrontational style of lobbying. Unlike many of the group's leading members in the early 1970s,

Silk and other CCNB staff were not civil servants, so they had the freedom to pursue environmental issues as aggressively as they wished. They were also well aware that the collaborative lobbying style used by the group earlier in the decade had achieved only limited gains. Silk thus believed that a less cozy and more direct and assertive approach might grab the attention of government officials, who were fixated on the promotion of resource-based industries, and eventually result in stronger environmental regulations. Of course, not all of the members appreciated the group's new confrontational style. Silk later noted that there was "a bit of a gap between the old guard and the younger, often rural group, who were implementing the Conserver Society in their own way."[72]

The CCNB's more confrontational lobbying style clearly irritated government officials. Probably the most contentious issue during Silk's time as head of the CCNB was the spruce budworm spraying program. In the second half of the 1970s, a wave of popular protest swept the province after revelations that fenitrothion, the main pesticide then used in the spraying program, and associated emulsifiers were linked to higher rates of Reye's syndrome among children in New Brunswick.[73] In its own way, the CCNB participated in this wave of protest; for example, it was Silk who appeared before the Pesticide Advisory Board in 1979 and criticized its mandate.[74] Silk and his contemporaries also engaged the provincial ministers of natural resources, health, and environment through extensive correspondence. They lobbied the ministers to enact stricter regulations to protect the environment and human health from what was perceived as widespread poisoning for the sake of corporate profiteering.[75] In letters exchanged in the spring of 1980, Minister of Natural Resources J. W. Bird and Brian Harvey debated the CCNB's criticisms of the Pesticide Advisory Board and other aspects of the spraying program. Bird ended the correspondence with the exasperated and somewhat passive-aggressive assessment that

> the obvious difference in our positions about the CCNB submission to the Pesticides Advisory Board is one of context, and I believe that further debate between us about the details of the situation would be fruitless.
>
> I would welcome future co-operation and open communication between our Department and the Conservation

Council. The best way for this to be achieved in my opinion, is to ensure that the communication is direct and specific. If your recommendations, criticisms and complaints are communicated in that manner, I can assure that they will receive serious consideration and substantive response.[76]

This sort of ministerial reaction to the CCNB's lobbying efforts was common in the late 1970s and early 1980s.

Unfortunately for the CCNB, the change in lobbying style did not yield better results. It appears that at the time New Brunswickers were prepared and willing to support increased regulatory action on a number of environmental issues. The CCNB conducted an extensive environmental survey of the province in 1980, and solid majorities of respondents believed the provincial government should do more to combat air and water pollution, while 48 percent (versus 41 percent) thought the spruce budworm spraying program could be reduced without economic damage. Sixty-nine percent of respondents also "felt there should be a greater emphasis on reducing our demand on non-renewable resources through conservation and the use of renewable resources like solar and wood power as opposed to increasing supply of non-renewable resources like oil, coal and nuclear power."[77] However, general support for conserver-related issues ran headlong into the "bread and butter" factor of which Silk and other CCNB members were so cognizant. This was the tension that Marilee Little had alluded to in her letter to the editor. Much of the New Brunswick populace might have recognized the possible benefits of the conserver society, but putting it into full practice was another matter entirely. As Silk later observed, "It's hard to persuade people who heat with wood because it's cheaper that they shouldn't aspire to heating with oil or electricity just because it's more convenient and cleaner."[78]

The circumvention of such tensions required the active participation of the state, but the Hatfield government, more interested in industrial promotion, had not implemented more than a minimal set of environmental regulations since coming to power in 1970. Subsequently, the CCNB's confrontational lobbying style in the late 1970s and early 1980s provoked government backlash and even some retrenchment. For Silk, the next step was obvious: "Although Richard Hatfield and I got along quite well personally, his government was not good for the environment, and when he got re-elected for the fourth time in 1982, I had alienated so many people in his government and bureaucracy that I thought it best to move on [in 1983]."[79]

The CCNB's experience of trying to engage government officials was typical of what many small Canadian groups went through during the formative years of modern environmentalism. Environmental organizations came up with a variety of novel approaches and strategies to convey their concerns, and yet more often than not encountered the political barrier of governments strongly committed to ongoing resource development schemes. Even though the CCNB adopted two different styles of lobbying, from a collaborative approach in the early 1970s to a more confrontational one later in the decade, its attempts to influence the state were only partially effective. This then raises questions about the notion of efficacy, one of the broader themes addressed by this edited collection, and how we have measured the effectiveness of the modern environmental movement in Canada. Indeed, perhaps we need to rethink our frame of reference, by moving the site at which judgments are rendered about the successes or failures of past environmental actions, or lack thereof, from the environmental groups to the level of the state. Rather than pondering how effectively environmental groups engaged with government officials, perhaps we need to ask why groups like the CCNB had to invest so much time and energy into trying to engage with the state in the first place. Why was it so difficult to convince governments that an environmental agenda was just as or even more valid than an economic one? Maybe by turning our analytical gazes to better understanding state obstructionism, like the type associated with the modernization schemes of the 1960s and 1970s, we would come up with compelling explanations for why some have perceived the Canadian environmental movement to have been largely ineffective or even an outright failure.

In turn, reframing how we think about the efficacy of the modern Canadian environmental movement draws our attention to the theme of scale. As noted, the end of the first wave of the Canadian environmental movement came about as groups supposedly struggled to make the successful transition from localized issues to larger, more abstract concerns in the mid-1970s. For example, national interest in alternatives to indiscriminate growth like the conserver society had offered some hope that serious and lasting change might be possible, but that proved fleeting. Nonetheless, many environmental groups took advantage of conserver-inspired government programs and grants to revitalize after the period of lost momentum in the mid-1970s, setting the stage for the second wave of the Canadian environmental movement in the 1980s.[80] With regard to the CCNB, Silk was able to provide the organization with a centralized and professional institutional foundation, which he later referred to as "my biggest contribution."[81] If the obstructionism of the state was truly as impenetrable as it seems during this period, then perhaps we need to recognize the transition in scale that many small Canadian environmental groups underwent, from the local to the provincial and beyond, as less of a story of logistical failure and more as a success in basic survival. Like the conserver society, the CCNB might have been "not an easy thing to implement," but owing to the organizational efforts of those early years it has been able to continue lobbying for stronger environmental regulatory frameworks in a resource-dependent province up to the present day.

Notes

A big thank you to the Conservation Council of New Brunswick for granting me permission to access their historical records. I also need to thank Andrew Secord for his help securing permission and contextualizing New Brunswick's environmental movement in the 1970s, Janice Harvey for agreeing to be interviewed, Dana Silk for conversing and answering all of my questions via email, and the anonymous reviewers for the excellent edits and suggestions. Thank you to Jonathan Clapperton and Liza Piper for their work as editors and organizing the Environmentalism from Below conference (Edmonton, Alberta, 7–9 August 2014), and to my fellow conference attendees for their helpful comments.

1   Brian Harvey to the editor of the *Daily Gleaner*, 23 April 1980, Conservation Council of New Brunswick fonds (hereafter CCNB fonds), MC1107, file MS1-5, Provincial Archives of New Brunswick (hereafter PANB).

2   *Daily Gleaner* (Fredericton), 22 April 1980.

3   B. Harvey to the editor of the *Daily Gleaner*, 23 April 1980, CCNB fonds, MC1107, file MS1-5, PANB. Harvey's letter to the editor was never published in the newspaper.

4   Matthew Farish and P. Whitney Lackenbauer, "High Modernism in the Arctic: Planning Frobisher Bay and Inuvik," *Journal of Historical Geography* 35, no. 3 (2009): 517–44; James L. Kenny and Andrew G. Secord, "Engineering Modernity:

Hydroelectric Development in New Brunswick, 1945–1970," *Acadiensis* 39, no. 1 (2010): 3–26; and Tina Loo, "People in the Way: Modernity, Environment, and Society on the Arrow Lakes," *BC Studies* 142/143 (2004): 161–96. In Atlantic Canada, the modernization ethos was in large part actualized through a series of federal-provincial regional economic development programs, such as the Atlantic Development Board (1962) and the Fund for Rural Economic Development (1966). See James Bickerton, *Nova Scotia, Ottawa, and the Politics of Regional Development* (Toronto: University of Toronto Press, 1990); and Donald J. Savoie, *Visiting Grandchildren: Economic Development in the Maritimes* (Toronto: University of Toronto Press, 2006).

5   See Janet Parkhill to Mellos, 16 June 1980, CCNB fonds, MC1107, file MS1-1-5, PANB.

6   Mark J. McLaughlin, "'Trees Are a Crop': Crown Lands, Labour, and the Environment in New Brunswick's Forest Industries, 1940–1982," (PhD diss., University of New Brunswick, 2013); McLaughlin, "Green Shoots: Aerial Insecticide Spraying and the Growth of Environmental Consciousness in New Brunswick, 1952–1973," *Acadiensis* 40, no. 1 (2011): 3–23; and McLaughlin, "'As Thick as Molasses': Water Pollution Regulation in New Brunswick, 1947–1974," in *Modern Canada: 1945 to Present*, ed. Catherine Briggs (Don Mills, ON: Oxford University Press, 2014), 369–82.

7   *Daily Gleaner*, 16 August 1969.

8   Audio recording of the Conservation Council of New Brunswick founding meeting, 18 October 1969, Fredericton, NB, recording in the CCNB's possession, Conserver House, Fredericton, NB; see also McLaughlin, "Green Shoots," 20–21.

9   CCNB Application for Incorporation, 1970, CCNB fonds, MC1107, file MS1-9, PANB.

10 Minutes of CCNB Annual General Meeting, 3 November 1973, including Article II of the attached CCNB constitution, CCNB fonds, MC1107, file MS1-4, PANB.

11 Minutes of CCNB Annual General Meeting, 3 November 1973, including the attached CCNB constitution, CCNB fonds, MC1107, file MS1-4, PANB.

12 Numerous examples of correspondence being addressed to the CCNB's presidents' homes or places of work can be found in CCNB fonds, MC1107, files MS1-1-1 and MS1-1-2, PANB.

13 Kenneth Langmaid to Donald J. Blackburn, 17 April 1972, CCNB fonds, MC1107, MS1-1-2, PANB.

14 Janice Harvey, interview by author, Fredericton, NB, June 2014. Janice Harvey joined the CCNB around 1980, and she was hired as the organization's executive director in 1983.

15 *Daily Gleaner*, 6 November 1970.

16 Langmaid to Richard Hatfield, 5 October 1970, and Hatfield to Langmaid, 20 October 1970, CCNB fonds, MC1107, file MS1-1-1, PANB. On the emergence of the environment as a political issue in New Brunswick, see McLaughlin, "'Trees Are a Crop,'" 247–310.

17 McLaughlin, "'Trees Are a Crop,'" 247–310. Hatfield was premier of New Brunswick from 1970 to 1987.

18 *Daily Gleaner*, 27 November 1969 and 6 November 1970.

19 George Gerald Shaw, *Report of the Pesticide Committee of the Conservation Council of New Brunswick* (Fredericton: 1970), McLaughlin, "Green Shoots," 21–22, and New Brunswick, *New Brunswick Acts* (1973), 136–50.

20 Langmaid to Blackburn, 17 April 1972, CCNB fonds, MC1107, file MS1-1-2, PANB; and New Brunswick, *New Brunswick Acts* (1971), 4–10. For a legal analysis of the Pesticides Control Act and the Clean Environment Act, see Hajo Versteeg, *Handbook on Environmental Law for New Brunswick* (Fredericton: Conservation Council of New Brunswick, 1983), 28–29.

21 In contrast, northern New Brunswick was less affluent and largely rural and Francophone, at once a reflection of the province's deep-rooted language divide but also lending credence to the argument put forward by some historians that environmentalism was often the domain of the middle class. For example, see Andrew Hurley, *Environmental Inequalities: Class, Race, and Industrial Pollution in Gary, Indiana, 1945–1980* (Chapel Hill: University of North Carolina Press, 1995). Mark Leeming (this volume) counters that "post-materialism," a concept used to encapsulate the middle-class condition in post–Second World War North America, is "a poor explanatory framework upon which to model a complex social movement" like environmentalism, preferring instead to focus on "ecological distribution conflicts."

22 Woodstock Chapter of the CCNB Annual Report, 1970–1971, CCNB fonds, MC1107, file MS1-15, PANB; J. Harvey, interview by author, Fredericton, NB, June 2014; and McLaughlin, "'As Thick as Molasses.'"

23 Saint John Chapter of the CCNB Annual Report, undated, CCNB fonds, MC1107, file MS1-15, PANB.

24 Anne Ottow, interview by author, Fredericton, NB, July 2010. On the anti-nuclear movement in the Maritimes, see Mark Leeming, "In Defence of Home Places: Environmental Activism in Nova Scotia, 1970–1985," (PhD diss., Dalhousie University, 2013); and Leeming, "The Creation of Radicalism: Anti-Nuclear Activism in Nova Scotia, c. 1972–1979," *Canadian Historical Review* 95, no. 2 (2014): 217–41. On Pollution Probe, see Ryan O'Connor, *The First Green Wave: Pollution Probe and the Origins of Environmental Activism in Ontario* (Vancouver: UBC Press, 2014).

25 Fredericton Chapter Report to the Annual Meeting of the CCNB, 30 October 1971, CCNB fonds, MC1107, file MS1-15, PANB.

26 Langmaid to Hatfield, 26 April 1971, CCNB fonds, file MS1-1-1, PANB.

27 *Minutes of the Pesticide Advisory Board Public Hearing* (1978), 52–63, and *Minutes of the Pesticide Advisory Board Public Hearing*, vol. 2 (1979), 30–48.

28 McLaughlin, "Rise of the Eco-Comics: The State, Environmental Education, and Canadian Comic Books, 1971–1975," *Material Culture Review* 77/78 (Spring/Fall 2013): 13.

29 McLaughlin, "'Trees Are a Crop,'" 116–78 and 311–80.

30 Minutes of the Directors Meeting of the CCNB, 7 December 1974 and 15 May 1976, file MS1-5-2 as well as Fredericton Chapter of the CCNB Annual Report, 1975, Woodstock Chapter of the CCNB Annual Report, 1975, and Saint John Chapter Report to the

CCNB's Board of Directors, 6 December 1975, CCNB fonds, MC1107, file MS1-15, PANB, and Anne Ottow, interview by author, Fredericton, NB, July 2010.

31 O'Connor, *The First Green Wave*, esp. the introduction and chap. 5; Robert Paehlke, "Eco-History: Two Waves in the Evolution of Environmentalism," *Alternatives* 19, no. 1 (1992): 18–23; and J. Harvey, interview by author, Fredericton, NB, June 2014.

32 Harold Hatheway to Terry Andrew, 4 December 1977, CCNB fonds, MC1107, file MS1-1-3, PANB.

33 President's Report to the Annual General Meeting of the Fredericton Chapter of the CCNB, 3 June 1974, CCNB fonds, MC1107, file MS1-15, PANB.

34 Richard Tarn to William Mackenzie, 24 October 1970, and Mackenzie to Tarn, 9 December 1970, CCNB fonds, MC1107, file MS2-4, PANB.

35 Memo from Hatheway to chapter secretaries, undated, file MS2-4, Minutes of CCNB Annual General Meeting, 3 November 1973, including the attached CCNB constitution, file MS1-4 as well as Woodstock Chapter of the CCNB Annual Report, 1975 and Saint John Chapter Report to the CCNB's Board of Directors, 6 December 1975, CCNB fonds, MC1107, file MS1-15, PANB.

36 O'Connor, *The First Green Wave*, and Jonathan Clapperton, "The Ebb and Flow of Local Environmentalist Action: The Society for Pollution and Environmental Control (SPEC), Vancouver, British Columbia" in this volume.

37 Minutes of the Directors Meeting of the CCNB, 15 May 1976, CCNB fonds, MC1107, file MS1-5-2, PANB; and Dana Silk's Curriculum Vitae, 2013, in possession of author.

38 Minutes of the Directors Meeting of the CCNB, 18 August 1976 and 5 February, 2 April, and 11 June 1977, CCNB fonds, MC1107, file MS1-5-2, PANB.

39 Minutes of the Directors Meeting of the CCNB, 5 February and 2 April 1977 and 11 March 1978, CCNB fonds, MC1107, file MS1-5-2, PANB.

40 Paul R. Ehrlich, *The Population Bomb* (New York: Ballantine Books, 1968); Donella H. Meadows, Dennis L. Meadows, Jørgen Randers, and William W. Behrens III, *The Limits to Growth* (New York: Universe Books, 1972).

41 Elisabetta Bini, Giuliano Garavini, and Federico Romero, eds., *Oil Shock: The 1973 Crisis and its Economic Legacy* (London: I. B. Tauris, 2016).

42 E. F. Schumacher, *Small is Beautiful: Economics as if People Mattered* (New York: Harper and Row, 1973).

43 O'Connor, *The First Green Wave*, esp. the introduction and chap. 5, and Paehlke, "Two Waves."

44 G. Brent Clowater, "Canadian Science Policy and the Retreat from Transformative Politics: The Final Years of the Science Council of Canada," *Scientia Canadensis* 35, nos. 1–2 (2012): 113–17; and Ursula Franklin (Chairperson), *Canada as a Conserver Society: Resource Uncertainties and the Need for New Technologies* (Ottawa: Science Council of Canada, Report No. 27, September 1977), 11–12.

45 Roger Gaudry (Chairperson), *Natural Resource Policy Issues in Canada* (Ottawa: Science Council of Canada, Report No. 19, January 1973), 39.

46 Franklin, *Canada as a Conserver Society*, 13–15, and Franklin (Chairperson), *Toward a Conserver Society: A Statement of Concern* (Ottawa: Science Council of Canada, February 1976), 2. The three other members of the committee were John Pollock, president of Electrohome Limited and acting chairperson during the transition from Cheesman to Franklin, Gabriel Filteau, associate dean of the Faculty of Science and Engineering at Laval University, and Ran Ide, chairperson of the Ontario Educational Communications Authority. Also, *Conserver Society Notes* was later taken over by the periodical *Alternatives*: see Piper, this volume.

47 Franklin, *Canada as a Conserver Society*, 15, and Ted Schrecker, *The Conserver Society Revisited: A Discussion Paper* (Ottawa: Science Council of Canada, May 1983), 5. As pointed out by Schrecker, "political and popular support for the idea of a Conserver Society, while widespread, is still limited to the minority of the population."

48 Lawrence Solomon, *The Conserver Solution* (Toronto: Doubleday Canada, 1978).

49 For an analysis of the Science Council's promotion of the conserver society concept as an exercise in economic nationalism and sustainable development, see Henry Trim, "Experts at Work: The Canadian State, North American Environmentalism, and Renewable Energy in an Era of Limits, 1968–1983" (PhD diss., University of British Columbia, 2014), esp. chap. 3; and Trim, "Planning the Future: The Conserver Society and Canadian Sustainability," *Canadian Historical Review* 96, no. 3 (2015): 375–404.

50 Franklin, *Canada as a Conserver Society*, 15. The committee made clear at various points in the report that its vision of the conserver society was not "anti-growth," "anti-technology," or "anti-industry."

51 Franklin, *Canada as a Conserver Society*, 23–37. Emphasis in original.

52 Franklin, *Canada as a Conserver Society*, 39–88. It is not surprising that much of the report dealt with energy issues, as it was conceived of, researched, and written in the shadow of the 1973–1974 oil crisis.

53 Trim, "Experts at Work," esp. chaps. 3, 5, and 6; Trim, "Planning the Future"; J. Harvey, interview by author, Fredericton, NB, June 2014; and Dana Silk, email message to author, 17 June 2014; quote from Trim, "Experts at Work," 147.

54 Dana Silk, email message to author, 17 June 2014; and Silk's curriculum vitae, 2013, in possession of author.

55 J. Harvey, interview by author, Fredericton, NB, June 2014; Silk, email message to author, 17 June 2014; and Silk to Ray Hnatyshyn, 20 June 1979, CCNB fonds, MC1107, file MS1-2, PANB.

56 J. Harvey, interview by author, Fredericton, NB, June 2014.

57 Silk to Jan Bonga, 5 January 1979, including attached membership renewal notice, CCNB fonds, MC1107, file MS1-3-1, PANB.

58 Minutes of the Directors Meeting of the CCNB, 2 April 1977, CCNB fonds, MC1107, file MS1-5-2, PANB.

59 Silk's curriculum vitae, 2013, in possession of author; and Silk, email message to author, 17 June 2014.

60   Minutes of the Directors Meeting of the CCNB, 11 May 1979 and 15 May 1980, file MS-1-5-2, as well as Saundra Hopper to the Atlantic Centre for the Environment, 10 November 1980, CCNB fonds, MC1107, file MS1-1-3, PANB.

61   Silk to W. A. Waller, 19 March 1979, Waller to Silk, 3 April 1979, and Silk to Waller, 12 April 1979, CCNB fonds, MC1107, file MS1-1-3, PANB.

62   Silk to John Williamson, 1 February 1979, file MS1-2, and Minutes of the Directors Meeting of the CCNB, 11 August 1979, CCNB fonds, MC1107, file MS-1-5-2, PANB.

63   Canadian Energy Development Systems International, Inc., *A Mid-Term Evaluation of the Canada/New Brunswick Conservation and Renewable Demonstration Agreement* (Ottawa: CEDSI, Inc., July 1983), i and B1-B5. For each Conservation and Renewable Demonstration Agreement, the federal government contributed 80 percent of the funding, while the province provided 20 percent. Also, Conserver House was inspired by Pollution Probe's Ecology House in Toronto and "community energy centres in Sweden."

64   On the CCNB's activities in the mid to late 1970s, see the various Minutes of the Directors Meeting of the CCNB in CCNB fonds, MC1107, file MS1-5-2, PANB.

65   Silk, email message to author, 17 June 2014.

66   McLaughlin, "'Trees Are a Crop,'" 311–80.

67   Minutes of the Directors Meeting of the CCNB, 15 May 1980, file MS1-5-2, Dan Clarke to Silk, 19 June 1980, file MS1-2, and B. Harvey to Miriam Murray, CCNB fonds, MC1107, file MS1-1-6, PANB. See file MS1-1-7 for a miniature version of the "Welcome to the Conserver Society" poster.

68   Silk to Hatfield, 15 June 1979, file MS1-2, as well as Silk to James D. McNiven, 3 July 1979, CCNB fonds, MC1107, MS1-1-3, PANB.

69   B. Harvey to H. J. O'Neill, 6 July 1979, and B. Harvey to the Ontario-Minnesota Pulp and Paper Co. Ltd., 27 June 1979, CCNB fonds, MC1107, file MS1-1-3, PANB. For most of the mills' responses to the questionnaire, see O'Neill to B. Harvey, 3 July 1979, Mark C. Trask to B. Harvey, 9 July 1979, D. W. Jebbink to B. Harvey, 25 July 1979, L. W. Sutherland to B. Harvey, 30 July 1979, G. L. Crozier to B. Harvey, 1 August 1979, J. C. Wig to B. Harvey, 2 August 1979, and Catherine Séguier to B. Harvey, 10 August 1979, CCNB fonds, MC1107, file MS1-1-3, PANB.

70   *Proceedings of the Conference on Forest Management in New Brunswick* (Fredericton: Conservation Council of New Brunswick, 1979), which can be found in the University of New Brunswick's Science Library.

71   See Koula Mellos to the CCNB, 12 May 1980, and Parkhill to Mellos, 16 June 1980, CCNB fonds, MC1107, file MS1-1-5, PANB, and Versteeg, *Handbook on Environmental Law*.

72   J. Harvey, interview by author, Fredericton, NB, June 2014, and Silk, email message to author, 17 June 2014.

73   Alan Miller, *Environmental Problem Solving: Psychosocial Barriers to Adaptive Change* (New York: Springer, 1999), 82–123; and Bert Deveaux, *"The Poison Mist": A Special*

Investigation into New Brunswick's Forest Spray Programme, CBC Radio, originally aired 3 January 1982 (transcript).

74   *Minutes of the Pesticide Advisory Board* (1979), 30–48.

75   For examples, see Silk to Brenda Robertson, 10 April 1979, Robertson to Silk, 7 May 1979, Silk to Robertson, 28 March 1980, Robertson to Silk, 25 April 1980, Silk to Robertson, 4 June 1980, Robertson to Silk, 10 July 1980, Silk to Eric Kipping, 15 August 1980, Kipping to Silk, 8 October 1980, Silk to Kipping, 8 April 1981, Kipping to Silk, 16 April 1981, Silk to Kipping, 22 July 1981, and Kipping to Silk, 15 June 1982, CCNB fonds, MC1107, file MS1-2, PANB.

76   J. W. Bird to Silk, 17 March 1980, B. Harvey to Bird, 23 April 1980, and Bird to B. Harvey, 26 May 1980, CCNB fonds, MC1107, file MS1-2, PANB; quote from letter dated 26 May 1980.

77   Neil Dickie to Bob Wilson, 6 August 1980, and Silk to Members of the Legislative Assembly, undated, file MS1-2, as well as CCNB Environmental Survey Press Release, undated, CCNB fonds, MC1107, file MS1-10, PANB; quote from press release. Out of the 1,300 questionnaires sent out by the CCNB, 718 were returned, for a response rate of 55 percent.

78   Silk, email message to author, 17 June 2014.

79   Silk, email message to author, 17 June 2014.

80   O'Connor, *The First Green Wave*, esp. the introduction; and Paehlke, "Two Waves."

81   Silk, email message to author, 17 June 2014.

The Ebb and Flow of Local Environmentalist Activism: The Society for Pollution and Environmental Control (SPEC), British Columbia

Jonathan Clapperton

As mentioned in this collection's introduction, over the past quarter-century a debate has simmered over why environmental organizations, and by extension the environmental movement, has failed to achieve the central goal of ecological sustainability. Most scholars and activists have attributed environmentalism's impotency to anti-environmentalist forces, a multi-faceted Goliath composed of capitalism, corporations, and the political right.[1] In contrast, more recent appraisals have blamed environmentalists themselves. Though such arguments have been formulated since the 1990s,[2] only in the past decade has the issue become hotly debated, sparked when environmental consultants Ted Nordhaus and Michael Shellenberger polemically announced the "death of environmentalism."[3] Fellow activist Adam Werbach, former US national president of the Sierra Club, then performed its autopsy. Cause of death: the failure of the environmental movement to both integrate its program with those of other progressive social movements and to narrate a compelling national vision.[4] Leaders of the country's top environmentalist organizations vehemently disagreed, arguing that signalling the demise of environmentalism was "preposterous and distracting from the real work ahead."[5] The dispute has remained at the forefront of discussion among scholars and activists within and beyond the United States; in 2012, even renowned Canadian environmentalist David Suzuki proclaimed that "environmentalism has failed."[6] The question remains contentious, polarized, and polarizing.[7]

Nonetheless, the debate Nordhaus et al. spurred has led to some serious and necessary reflection upon the circumstances under which environmentalist activities and groups succeed or fail. The only issue on which everyone participating in the debate seems to agree is that environmental activists need to create a new approach for the twenty-first century by reconfiguring their goals, strategies, and even core philosophies. Certainly, there is much evidence demonstrating that many strategies of the past—such as basing the movement's goals on the belief in a "wilderness" ideal—have hindered the environmental movement's efficacy.[8] But it is important not to jettison the past entirely. In fact, many of the practices that proponents point to as "new kinds" of environmentalism predicted to revitalize the environmental movement, such as the current push for urban civic sustainability or the buzz around "civic environmentalism,"[9] actually have some (often unrecognized) historical antecedents, originating most often in local and small-scale environmental non-governmental organizations, from which lessons can be imparted.[10]

Accordingly, this chapter focuses on one such organization: the Society Promoting Environmental Conservation (SPEC).[11] While not many outside of (but likely many within) the Vancouver area have heard of SPEC, it is British Columbia's oldest charitable environmental organization, it was once western Canada's largest environmental organization, and many of its members would become key players in the environmental movement.[12] Early on in his career David Suzuki served a stint as SPEC's vice-president, SPEC youth organizer Bill Darnell was the one to coin the name "Greenpeace," and Darnell joined Bob Hunter (a SPEC member and Greenpeace co-founder) on the famous fishing boat *Phyllis Cormack* to protest American nuclear tests in Alaska. Greenpeace's first office space was even located in SPEC's main building.[13]

This chapter analyzes the strategies and tactics that SPEC used to effect a material and cultural shift in civic society, such as the implementation of recycling programs, banning pesticide and herbicide use, and implementing widespread energy conservation. It also evaluates the extent to which these methods have succeeded or failed, contending that SPEC has been most effective in changing human-nature interactions when it has been able to strategically gain popular acceptance as a community "insider" to operate within, understand, and change the dynamics of civic environmental practices. When SPEC lost that identity and became perceived as an "outsider," the organization failed to repeat the successes it enjoyed in the local sphere and even came close to "dying."

The use of "insider" and "outsider" is influenced by discussions from anthropology, ethnohistory, and sociology; these fields have been chosen because of their focus on explaining and understanding cultures, and cultural shifts, as well as identity politics. Traditionally, the positions of insider and outsider have been seen as fixed: one was either an "outsider" who "thought to study Others whose alien cultural worlds they must painstakingly come to know," or one was, because of one's identity (as a member of that group, for example), an "insider" who was "believed to write about their own cultures from a position of intimate affinity," and who "share[d] an unspoken understanding with the people with whom" they work.[14] Over the past couple of decades these positions have come to be seen as far more fluid, hybrid, and involving a process of negotiation between the scholar and subject(s) of study.[15] In other words, just the fact that someone comes from a particular community or culture does not mean they will automatically be accepted as an "insider" and afforded with all the privileges and powers that such status grants. As that identity changes and fluctuates, it has implications for how the researcher is viewed and the degree to which the group will provide support, and it will ultimately determine the extent to which the researcher is "blocked" from accessing "insider" knowledge and support.[16] Approaches must therefore be established to overcome barriers to accessing an "insider" identity.[17] This theoretical discussion applies equally well to the desires of many social movement organizations, including SPEC. SPEC always prioritized public outreach spurring widespread civic activism, and therefore heavily relied upon overcoming the barriers in order to gain the influence that "insider" status provided.

The above is different from the definition of "insider" that Douglas Bevington, among others, uses to describe the strategy whereby environmental organizations attempt to effect change through conventional forms of participation in electoral politics—most often through lobbying—and thus primarily seek to gain privileged, "insider" access to the political system.[18] While SPEC certainly sought to influence politicians and other government officials, especially post-1970s, their principal strategies and tactics always revolved around engaging civic society and as portraying themselves, and seeking to receive recognition, as community insiders in the anthropological/ethnohistorical sense.

SPEC'S Formative Years and Rise to Prominence, 1969–71

The Pacific Northwest enjoys a well-deserved reputation as a hotbed of environmental (among other social) activism and it is arguably one of the modern environmental movement's epicentres. The province of British Columbia, Canada, specifically, is the birthplace of Greenpeace, includes many of the other largest and best-funded environmental organizations, it had at one point (if it does not still) the highest density of environmental activist organizations in the country, and it provided the first two elected Green Party members in Canada (one federal and one provincial).[19] Following the 2017 provincial election, the Green Party obtained nearly 17 percent of the popular vote, saw three of its members elected to the legislature, and secured significant power through its support of the minority NDP government. Yet there is a notable absence in the province's historiography regarding environmental activists pushing for change in urban environments, with most scholars (myself included) having paid more attention to the "wilderness" battles, colloquially referred to as the "war in the woods."[20]

Nonetheless, by the end of the 1960s, a rapidly growing proportion of British Columbia's population had become anxious, if also angry, about environmental deterioration in the province's urban spaces, notably the rapidly growing metropolitan centre of Vancouver. Unchecked resource and industrial development in the era of high modernism was pushed by the dominant Social Credit government, which was in power from 1952 to 1972.[21] Conservationists within the province, such as the renowned angler, nature enthusiast, and prolific writer Roderick Haig-Brown, called for a balance between development and preservation.[22] Moreover, urbanites in the province's most populated centre, Vancouver, were inspired to civic action by a growing North American environmental consciousness, epitomized and spurred by publications such as Rachel Carson's *Silent Spring* (1962) and Paul Ehrlich's *The Population Bomb* (1968), and events, such as an increasing backlash to nuclear bomb testing, especially in Alaska. Finally, Vancouver was a centre for generalized social activism in the 1960s, which created an atmosphere conducive to environmental activism.[23]

SPEC, first known as the Canadian Scientific Pollution and Environmental Control Society, then the Society for Pollution and Environmental Control, and finally the Society Promoting Environmental Conservation, was born into the above political, social, and cultural structure. SPEC began innocuously in the founders' basement in December 1968. Led by Derrick Mallard (1921–2001), a lecturer in the Department of Psychology at Simon Fraser University, and his wife Gwen (1917–1999), SPEC began with a broad ecological objective to: "preserve a healthy environment and promot[e] the *rational* use of natural resources."[24] Unlike Pollution Probe (which might be considered SPEC's counterpart in Toronto), founded in 1969 by students and supported by university professors, SPEC's executive was stocked with middle- to upper-class professionals: university professors, lawyers, journalists, and the like. SPEC targeted support from the same segment of "grassroots, middle-class" people, notably professionals, where SPEC's leadership felt "real power for change can be released."[25] The issues it tackled during its first few years, however, were quite similar to those of Pollution Probe and other "first wave" Canadian environmental groups: opposition to uranium mining, nuclear power generation, and atomic bomb testing; demands for better sewage and other effluent control for rivers; calls for sustainable logging and mining practices; an end to chemical pesticide and herbicide spraying; the implementation of a recycling program; and even steps to combat noise pollution.[26]

SPEC's strategies, again comparable to those of groups such as Pollution Probe, as well as other organizations addressed elsewhere in this volume, most notably the Conservation Council of New Brunswick (McLaughlin, this volume), were all designed to appeal to their target audience and to gain widespread recognition as insiders.[27] First, SPEC promoted a humanist ideology valuing science, rationality, and empiricism. Derrick Mallard described the "SPEC movement as an effort to make responsible presentation of facts."[28] At high modernism's peak, and as the ecological sciences grew in popularity, this strategy was a reflection of the founders' faith that science provided an objectivity and authority that politicians and corporations lacked. SPEC accordingly researched and wrote reports, which read like scientific papers but were worded in language suitable for the general public, submitted professional briefs at development hearings, and produced countless information pamphlets covering an array of environmental issues.

SPEC's second strategy was to infuse their humanist approach, which could come across as cold, emotionless, and elitist, with an equal amount of compassion. They hoped to promote themselves as a community-based and community-building organization that used their scientific research to solve social as well as environmental problems. For example, after SPEC released its ground-breaking, headline-grabbing *Fraser River Report* in 1970, industry and government criticized its findings for being amateurish, as much of the field work was carried out by students rather than professionals. SPEC countered with a defence of both its data and method—highlighting that the research had been overseen at all stages by experts—and with an emotional response, one that displayed SPECs local roots and engaged with the atmosphere of anxiety that permeated the middle class over youth employment and aimlessness:

> How often have people asked, 'What are young people doing for society?' Well here is a fine example. This last summer, 51 unemployed life science students, many with degrees, completed the first pollution survey of a major North American watershed—the Fraser River. Working in the field for 54 solid days. . . . [It was a] rugged and enlighten-

ing experience that also provided each student with $450 to further his [*sic*] education.[29]

As a result of this stance, SPEC received frequent praise for what one journalist termed its "particular attention to the HUMAN environmental needs of the present and future."[30]

Finally, and in line with its push to be rational, objective, and broadly appealing, SPEC's founders sought to pursue a non-radical strategy, one that ensured the organization's members would be identified as apolitical and mainstream rather than fringe "eco-freaks," Marxists, or militants. As one SPEC document explained, "The Society has neither courted nor acquired any political affiliation. It is considered that the objects of SPEC can best be advanced by avoiding identification with any single political group or economic interest."[31] In another instance, SPEC's President, Dr. Robin Harger, a zoologist working as a professor at the University of British Columbia, set SPEC in stark contrast to other social movements, asserting, "The 'do your own thing' line of modern thinking belongs properly to flower child cults and Trotsky radicalism where persuasive use of such thinking fosters dissolution of otherwise effective (non-Trotsky) social groups."[32]

In order to be perceived as insiders with mainstream society, SPEC made public outreach via education its principal tactic.[33] In its first few years of operation, SPEC's experts gave hundreds of public talks themselves, hosted guest speakers, and showed documentaries at schools, public venues, government offices, businesses, union meetings, and private events. Derek and Gwen Mallard, among other SPEC leaders, toured the province, met with local environmental groups and officials, discussed pollution problems, and recruited new members. SPEC boasted that in the society's first year of existence, "More than 30,000 school children have been exposed to our films and speakers throughout the Province. Over 50,000 adults have attended our public meetings, major shopping centre displays, etc. The Society's speaker's panel, composed of specialists, has fulfilled some 300 speaking engagements."[34] Alongside this public education initiative, media attention followed.

As with most social movement organizations, another of SPEC's tactics was to capture constant, favourable media attention, an outlet they rightly perceived as key to growth and success. SPEC's communications director, Jim Marunchak, consistently argued that SPEC needed to establish and maintain a "responsible relationship with the media through relevant and enlightening action."[35] SPEC was helped in no small part by the fact that journalists representing all of Vancouver's major newspapers held membership in the organization; accounts of SPEC's activities regularly appeared in all of the province's major, and many of the minor, publications.

Mainstream media offers, at best, unpredictable support. William Carroll and R. S. Ratner specifically argue that in the British Columbia context, "When organized dissent is given coverage, media accounts are usually commercially motivated and liable to reconstructions that mock or demonize the groups on which they report."[36] Yet for its first couple of years, SPEC largely avoided this type of negative attention, likely helped by their identity as "insiders" and the amount of social capital they were able to establish as a result of their many outreach activities, as well as their rational approach and staunch rejection of radicalism; for many, SPEC represented a clear choice over other social movement organizations such as Vancouver's far-left New Liberation Front. Even SPEC's hippie-like "Ecology Caravan," a scheme wherein a group of university students from Vancouver drove across the province in the summer of 1970 to drum up support and spread the group's message, received only media praise, though admittedly also some slight ridicule, pointing out, for instance, that the SPEC representatives were "scraggly looking" or that the caravan was "a large, gaudily coloured bus."[37]

Finally, any social movement organization that wanted to gain widespread support within British Columbia during the late 1960s and early 1970s needed to be tactical in gaining the support of organized labour. Environmental historians have noted that labour and environmentalist organizations generally cooperated during this period, but it appears that SPEC and labour were especially close allies.[38] Indeed, SPEC bridged the divide between labour and environmentalists with an ease that environmentalists over the past few decades have found frustratingly difficult to repeat. SPEC's success in this regard was achieved by focusing on the physical dangers that pollution caused to workers and their families, by supporting union calls for better labour standards, and by maintaining

Jonathan Clapperton

a non-radical position. Unions, in turn, demonstrated staunch support for SPEC. In one notable instance, about half the employees of a mining and construction company petitioned the provincial government to allow SPEC to present a brief at a Pollution Control Board (PCB) hearing. The employees' petition stated that the "men want to have SPEC's brief heard because it emphasizes the dangers of pollution created by the mine."[39] John McKnight, the petition committee chairman, stated he believed it was the first time that construction workers, in the process of building a mine, had ever taken part in this kind of petition. He continued that they were "violently opposed to the fact that the [PCB] denied SPEC the opportunity to present its brief. . . . We feel that there could be a danger of pollution to Rupert Inlet and the fact that the [PCB] refuses to hear SPEC's brief makes us feel this more strongly."[40] Other unions, when negotiating for new contracts, "put environment on the bargaining table, sacrificing part of pay increases to cover it."[41] Furthermore, once it expanded, SPEC branches emerged in many resource-dependent towns, labourers dependent upon the resource industry joined SPEC, and they even, though often anonymously, reported on their employers' environmental infractions. The insider-outsider demarcation separating labour and environmentalists thus ceased to exist.

Clearly, SPEC had found a winning formula and it produced tangible results. According to sociologists Jane Mansbridge and Katherine Flaster, social movements need to achieve success on two levels. One is to change policy at a variety of scales (e.g., local, regional, national, international) and structures (e.g., government, corporate, media).[42] SPEC was certainly involved in these efforts, and focused on, among its many campaigns, preventing nuclear power plants from being constructed in British Columbia, stymieing a number of developments that would have led to greater pollution of the Fraser River, and halting a city council scheme to widen streets and cut down trees. Second, social movements need to effect "everyday outcomes," or "changes in the realm of daily life."[43] Here, too, SPEC enjoyed many notable achievements, such as its anti-pesticide and herbicide campaign, likely the first of its kind in British Columbia, and its implementation of the first recycling depots in the province. SPEC also effected widespread citizen activism; these activists encouraged boycotts and called politicians to account. In one instance, Ray Williston, the provincial forest minister, singled out SPEC for causing a dramatic spike in the number of letters from concerned citizens, flooding his department with so many requests for information that the office staff could not respond to them all.[44]

Statistically speaking, SPEC was also a success. SPEC was similar to other environmental organizations (as Frank Zelko notes of Greenpeace in this volume) in measuring its efficacy by how "big" it could grow, both in its geographical spread and in terms of membership numbers. The organization's membership grew far larger and faster than its founders could have anticipated. Barely a year old, SPEC needed to amend its constitution in January 1970 to allow for the formation of branches in order to incorporate the many environmental groups that chose to join the burgeoning "SPEC Federation" (Figure 11.1). Over the next eight months, more than forty SPEC branches popped up across the province. As one of SPEC's newsletters reported,

> With such an incredible growth pattern SPEC has been barely able to cope with inter-branch needs let alone pursue environmental projects and activities with the knowledge and participation of the branches. Our growing pains have been many, but put in perspective with the tremendous progress made and impact we have had on industry, government and the general public, they have been mild indeed.[45]

Journalists commented upon this phenomenal growth, one pointing out that the appeal of SPEC's "approach has not been without results as SPEC has grown from a nucleus of five dedicated people to an active membership exceeding five thousand over the course of the last year."[46] By 1972, SPEC counted its membership in the tens of thousands.[47] Everyone was predicting that SPEC would quickly expand to become—if it was not already—Canada's largest and most powerful environmental organization.

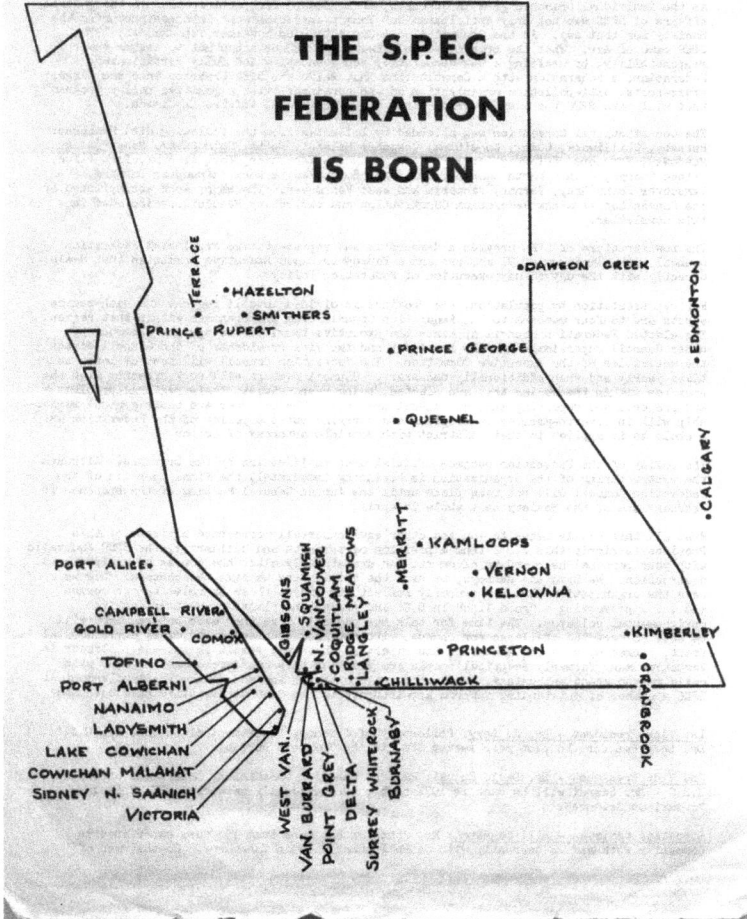

FIGURE 11.1: Map showing the branches of SPEC as of November 1970. City of Vancouver Archives, SPEC Fonds AM 1556, box 729-A-2, f. 10.

SPEC's Decline and Fall

Shockingly, given its dramatic ascent, by the mid-1970s SPEC's membership was bleeding out. It was (and would for years continue to be) on the verge of bankruptcy, its reputation tattered, and its near-hegemonic media attention notably lessened. This sudden, precipitous decline begs an explanation; the answer provides some broader insights into why social movement organizations succeed or fail, and specifically whether or not environmental organizations are to blame for the movement's failure. In SPEC's case, it was overwhelmingly forces within the organization that caused its downward spiral. These were twofold: a move toward radicalization, and the failure to manage exponential growth. Both contributed to SPEC's loss of community support, and with it their privileged insider identity, which was essential to SPEC's success, since it was not an environmental organization like Greenpeace that got "big" and stayed that way.

SPEC became embroiled in a widely publicized internal struggle over whether or not to adopt more confrontational—even radical—tactics, or to stay the course as a mainstream, "rational" society. Many of those who sought radicalization also hoped to turn SPEC into a political party. In 1971 SPEC launched an aggressive campaign against MacMillan Bloedel, the province's forest industry giant, which included a satirical poster printed in some newspapers depicting the company as a dinosaur run amok (Figure 11.2). While some members were "delighted that the real battle with industry had finally been joined," others were "afraid that it had smashed SPEC's middle class image."[48]

However, what marked a real turning point in SPEC's popularity and the beginnings of internal disunity was when the Burrard SPEC branch protested the annual meeting of the Council of BC Forest Industries, at the Bayshore Inn, on 16 April 16 1971. The demonstrators carried large papier-mâché eggs labelled with the names of major forestry firms, which were intended to represent the "pre-historic attitudes on the part of the industry to pollution." SPEC's former president, Robin Harger, and Gary Culhane, a past executive member, took the matter further, barging into the meeting with the intent to detonate "stink-bombs," which, according to Bayshore officials, failed to explode because of a faulty mechanism.[49] This action received exclusively negative press coverage as well as angering

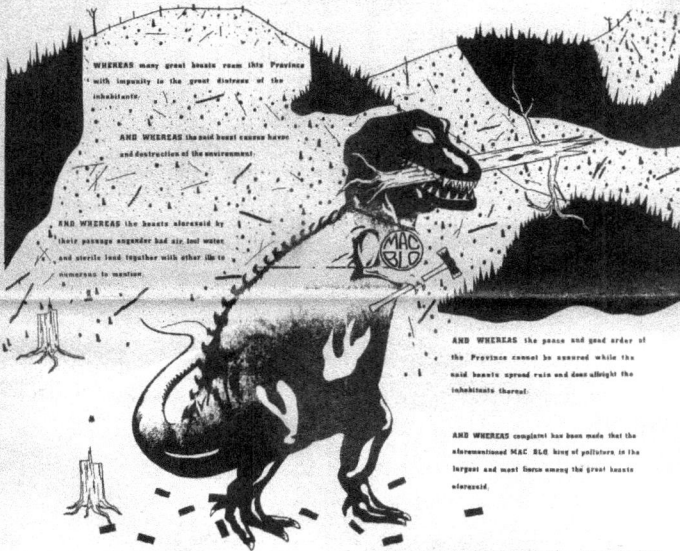

FIGURE 11.2 SPEC Anti-MacMillan Bloedel Poster, 1971. City of Vancouver Archives, SPEC Fonds AM 1556, box 729-F-7, f. 3.

many in SPEC. Mallard had to engage in damage control. He ultimately tried to explain away the protest as independent actions by individuals who did not represent the SPEC organization.[50]

Derrick Mallard and Robin Harger then engaged in a bitter rivalry for leadership of the society during its annual convention that same month. Harger argued for radicalization, claiming, "The traditional liberal approach would be great if we were selling toothpaste." He predicted that the rest of Vancouver would "catch up" to SPEC's radical tactics, and publicly stated that he was willing to risk the organization's future if he was wrong.[51] Mallard countered with his own prediction: "We have support from people of all parties, but if we become identified with any one political group, we would destroy SPEC as an effective anti-pollution, environmental organization."[52] Mallard also labelled Harger and his allies as "Marxist," a term he soon regretted using as it further cast an unappealing light on SPEC in general.[53] Harger and the "radical" faction ultimately lost, with Mallard being reappointed executive-director and many of the radicals resigning from their positions within SPEC.[54] Despite Mallard's victory, the damage had been done.

Media outlets, as William Carroll and Robert Hackett observe, are often agents of the hegemon and are after sponsorship, via advertising dollars, from large corporations, or are in fact owned by them.[55] Moreover, media relies far less on coverage of social movement organizations than these organizations rely upon media attention and support; the balance of power is clearly asymmetrical, and it was especially so at a time before social movements could turn to effective alternatives, such as online tools.[56] Social movements therefore needed to delicately balance utilizing the media while challenging its sponsors. As mentioned, SPEC walked this fine line very well when using the strategies and tactics described above. Once their attacks became too threatening to the media's interests, however, the media quickly turned on them. As evidenced in one *Vancouver Sun* editorial:

> [SPEC] that worthy organization (of which I am a sympathetic but deplorably inactive member) is suffering from pressures imposed by the Ecology Freaks. It was surely their influence that created the current tasteless and sophomoric

campaign against MacMillan Bloedel, the forestry firm. . . .
This isn't to say that anti-pollution groups shouldn't hit specific targets. They should—they must. But there's an effective way: *cool, tough, factual.* The smear posters and hi-jinks
against MacMillan Bloedel are self-defeating, alienating
even SPEC's own North Vancouver branch.[57]

Radicalization—or even the threat thereof—and disunity ultimately damaged SPEC's insider status, eroding public sympathy for the group, cur-
tailing SPEC's broad appeal across all political stripes and even resulting
in many members dropping their affiliation or simply failing to renew.

SPEC's aspirations for super-growth also proved antithetical to its
core strategy of appearing as an insider, inclusive, and mainstream movement, though at first SPEC's ambitions worked to its advantage. SPEC adopted an aggressive tactic of geographical and demographic expansion,
believing that a wider area of coverage and greater membership list would
result in increased power and popular support. Mallard hoped that SPEC
would cover the country and become Canada's largest environmental
organization, but he adjusted this aspiration to encompass only western
Canada once it became clear Canada's other leading anti-pollution group,
Pollution Probe, was growing in Toronto and expanding in eastern Canada.[58] By 1972 SPEC had expanded beyond the province, boasting branches
in the provinces of Alberta and Saskatchewan, as well as in the Yukon.[59]
SPEC helped to create other important organizations, such as the West
Coast Environmental Law Centre, and it founded the Recycle Council
of British Columbia. SPEC also took the lead in unifying anti-pollution
and other environmental groups throughout the province and, eventually, with similar groups in the rest of Canada and even into the United States.[60] This included, most notably, joining with Pollution Probe to
create an umbrella organization called the Canadian Association for the
Human Environment.[61]

SPEC's experience suggests that its incredible growth also led to internal fractures. Much of this tension, and the eventual decline in membership and loss of SPEC branches, arose from the disconnect felt between SPEC Central, where executive decisions were made, and the SPEC
branches. For example, the president and seven executive members of the

Nanaimo SPEC branch quit following a dispute with the central body's policies, with the branch's president stating that he was "no longer certain that all members of the SPEC central body still pursue the original aims and objectives of the society."[62] In another instance, SPEC Central publicly opposed the federal enactment of the Canadian War Measures Act in 1970 without consulting the other branches, and much to their ire.[63] Bob Hunter, at the time a *Vancouver Sun* columnist but better known for role in founding Greenpeace and, as Frank Zelko describes elsewhere in this volume, not well versed in how best to structure an environmental organization, nonetheless appraised the situation, writing,

> SPEC is at the most critical juncture. . . . On the one hand, its grandest organizational schemes stand on the verge of being realized. Within a month or two it will finally be hooked into a nationwide environmental and anti-pollution organization, a move which cannot help but work a transformation similar to the one worked on Clark Kent when he slipped into the telephone booth. . . . On the other hand, with . . . some branches at odds with the central executive, and the central executive itself split by clashes over tactics, the question which has to be asked is: Will SPEC survive?[64]

In response to such criticisms, Mallard and others sought to decentralize the organization by reducing the role of SPEC Central.[65] Such measures proved insufficient.

After SPEC's annual meeting in 1972, the organization remained "a divided organization [and] [i]t failed to reach accord during debate about its future and priorities." Many members argued SPEC had become too large, and others still sought to radicalize it. Some called for greater decentralization, while others wanted a central office to continue to closely coordinate the branches.[66] SPEC's internal problems became apparent when Derrick Mallard, along with Gwen, resigned from SPEC in April 1972, claiming he faced too much internal opposition to his moderate, decentralized approach.[67]

SPEC found itself adrift, internally fractured, and on the verge of collapse. As membership growth slowed, then declined, then plummeted, with it went funding. Such internal strife and bad press came at a poorly timed historical juncture, coinciding as it did with the energy crisis, beginning in October 1973 with the Organization of Arab Petroleum Exporting Countries (OAPEC) oil embargo, a key event that O'Connor and McLaughlin acknowledge as prompting the end of the "first wave" of the Canadian environmental movement.[68] As both government funding sources and, more importantly, individual contributions dried up throughout the 1970s, SPEC Central nearly went bankrupt a number of times, hitting its nadir in November 1976 with only $376 in the bank. Fortunately, it always managed to secure grants from various sources to stay alive, but other branches did not, and many folded.[69] In 1978, SPEC's president, Don Ellsay, stated the obvious, remarking that the organization's "credibility had fallen to an all-time low, as had membership."[70] By 1980 SPEC Central had no employees, only a handful of volunteers, a small, cramped office, and little funding; three years later, total SPEC membership had plummeted to 2,000.[71]

Revitalization, Reorganization, and Refocus

By the end of the 1970s, SPEC realized that the tactic of expansion was not working and that they could no longer claim to be a "mass citizens' movement."[72] No longer able to compete with the other dominant greens— eclipsed by Greenpeace in the 1970s and, later, the Western Canadian Wilderness Committee soon after its creation in 1980—the organization needed to find a niche if it hoped to survive. In short, they needed to regain their insider status as a grassroots, community-centric organization. SPEC therefore refocused on the local, narrowing its geographical purview largely to the province's lower mainland and targeting urban environmental issues, which no other environmental group in the 1980s was doing within British Columbia.[73]

While SPEC continued to maintain its roots in broader campaigns and a provincial outlook, it refocused on addressing "everyday" material change, notably its ongoing programs of recycling and opposition to pesticides and herbicides, as well as a number of new issues, such as home energy efficiency. The group also turned most of their efforts toward public education and away from confrontation, emphasizing collaboration with all interest groups, at all levels, including government—a strategy more generally termed "civic environmentalism," though one that scholars have not generally identified as existing prior to the 1990s.[74]

Public education and outreach within grade schools had proven popular and generated much community support in the first few years of SPEC's existence; accordingly, SPEC continued to focus much of its attention there. SPEC built upon its provincially unique "Environmental Education Program," which it had created in 1973–74 to fill the void in environmental education within the classroom, to include urban environmental issues, the need for conservation and the transition to renewable resources, and fostering an everyday "classroom conservation ethic," such as "more effectively using paper in the school office and classroom" and recycling.[75] SPEC received recognition for these programs from the Science Council of Canada, the British Columbia Energy Commission, and the Conserver City Committee of Vancouver City Council.[76]

SPEC also found some of its greatest vitality as the first environmental group in the province to implement a public education program on everyday energy conservation. SPEC's energy program included creating and distributing information packets that included tips for homeowners to reduce energy consumption, a vetted list of contractors who could renovate houses to be more energy efficient, and even a free "Energy Audit"—an innovative in-home energy analysis offered to homeowners in western Canada. SPEC's energy program proved incredibly popular and led to real change: according to SPEC, 90 percent (377) of the homeowners followed through with the inspectors' recommendations (such as caulking, weather-stripping, and pipe insulation), and 90 percent of them noticed a significant reduction in their energy bills.[77] SPEC also produced a number of education programs for adults. One, titled "Energy and Us," was so well researched and popular that it caught the attention of the federal Ministry of Energy, Mines & Resources, who contracted SPEC to transfer the program to 16mm film and distribute it throughout the province for public use.[78] SPEC's energy program also included a large push for improving everyday individual energy consumption between work and home, notably by encouraging an increase in bicycle traffic. SPEC lobbied the government for more bicycle lanes and better transit, as well as providing workshops on simple bicycle repairs and maintenance, parts and service, maps of bike outings and the best routes of travel, tips on clothing and bike accessories, basic sports medicine, and biking events.[79]

Collaboration—rather than confrontation—with multiple levels of government and industry also became one of SPEC's prime tactics. Perhaps the greatest achievement of this cooperation was the Vancouver Energy Information Centre, often referred to as the SPEC Conservation Centre, built in 1981. SPEC, in partnership with the City of Vancouver, the province, and the Canadian federal government, designed the centre as a much-needed resource building to educate the public about good energy practices. A renovated electrician's shop, the centre showcased sustainable building and living techniques that demonstrated how the typical home could save between 50 and 70 percent of its energy costs, served as a community meeting space, and had a resource library, an urban garden demonstration project (including a solar greenhouse), and a children's environmental education centre.[80] If SPEC had maintained its oppositional, if not radical, stance of earlier years, one can only speculate that such funding proposals, along with other activities in public institutions (such as schools) would have been much less forthcoming.

By the mid-1980s, SPEC had firmly re-established its sense of efficacy and presence in the community. Though it would still experience some periods of uncertainty, each time these occurred the organization displayed a maturity, a calmness, and an ability to weather the storm that was not displayed during its early life. Rather than measuring success by the number of members and expansive geographical reach beyond Vancouver, it refined its expectations, acknowledged its limitations, and maintained its insider status—which it had been unable to do in the 1970s.[81] During the last few years of the 1980s, for example, SPEC was once more faced with internal complaints of an ineffective board of directors and a declining membership.[82] However, the core group of members were confident in their product—expertise and community-based outreach—and this confidence showed in the organization's relatively quick turnaround. Indeed, by 1993 SPEC's president, Alice Coppard (according to SPEC's 1992–93 Annual Report, a founder of the Vancouver Raging Grannies activist group and a member of the City of Vancouver's Peace Committee), could boast that SPEC continued to offer community support through its Vancouver Environmental Information Centre, that it had the largest stand-alone environmental library in western Canada, which was used extensively by students and the public at large, and that SPEC staff were regarded as a community resource and an authority on all things environmental. "Very often," Coppard wrote, "members of the public, as well as government organizations, who have reached a dead end through the established channels rely on us to find answers to their problems. We help them find solutions, thereby providing a sense of community which is missing in other lower mainland jurisdictions."[83]

Indeed, arguably the most telling aspect of SPEC's success was (and is) its popularly accepted reputation as an expert on conservation and pollution control on the lower mainland. SPEC received countless in-person and mail requests from the general public, including a large number of grade school students, requesting information in the age before the Internet and Wikipedia, on a variety of environmental issues, such as how to start a recycling program, how to reduce energy use, and what alternatives to pesticides and herbicides existed. Students enrolled in environmental programs in high school or college, and others employed in the field, even wrote to SPEC asking if they could serve a stint with the organization as a volunteer to build up their qualifications.[84] One notable letter from a couple located in Germany asked for information on the state of the Fraser River environment and pollution. They explained they were planning to immigrate to the Lower Mainland but wanted to get information on the state of pollution before determining where to live.[85] In addition to this, SPEC representatives continued to be active on numerous environmental steering committees, working groups, and boards.

SPEC has maintained course through the twenty-first century, cognizant of the need to adapt to remain relevant, but also maintaining focus on the strategies, tactics, and issues that allowed them to stay alive. Today, their main campaigns are much the same as those they built up and refined in the late 1970s and through the 1980s. They continue to prioritize public education, community outreach, and providing up-to-date information. Their support is truly wide ranging—broader than its original founders likely envisioned—and comes from a diverse range of sponsors, from organic markets, to government bodies, to corporations such as The Home Depot.

With Hindsight

While many environmental organizations that start out relatively small and hope to expand to prominence fail to realize that goal, SPEC became one of the—if not *the*—fastest-growing environmental organizations in North America during its first few years of existence. Within eighteen months of its founding, SPEC had gained thousands of members and boasted branches across western Canada. SPEC's spectacular fall from prominence occurred equally as fast. SPEC membership, along with funding, plummeted, and SPEC Central very nearly "died" multiple times through the 1970s and into the 1980s; many of SPEC's regional branches did disappear. The approach SPEC eventually took to revitalize itself—focusing on the urban environment and educating the public through a variety of fora—provides useful lessons for environmental organizations struggling to find their way in a movement now saturated with environmental groups as well as within increasingly conservative, neoliberal political governance structures that extend from the municipal to the global levels. Many environmental groups have failed to remain relevant and stay "alive." Each time SPEC encountered setbacks—some of which appeared fatal—it found a way to reinvigorate itself and to make headway in creating both discursive and material progress toward environmental sustainability, proving that its time, like the environmental movement's, was far from passed.

Scholars of the environmental movement, and of social movements more generally, have tended to be attracted to, and emphasize the importance of, direct action and confrontation. Those who oppose dominant power structures via confrontational—if not radical—tactics, rather than seeking to work within them, are often applauded for their efforts if not also romanticized and valorized.[86] These radical actions and groups certainly have their place and purpose, and have produced results—or at least temporary ones—to protect the environment and to maintain the environmental movement's relevance. SPEC's turn to less confrontational tactics might be seen by those who are uncompromising in seeking a paradigm shift as a selling out or as "greenwashing"—or at least as being the foil for governments at all levels who are doing so. But what this study of SPEC reveals is that, at least when it comes to changing everyday civic environmental practices, confrontation and radicalism are not necessarily the only answer, and can—and did in SPEC's case—prove detrimental to these goals. Turning to confrontation and (at least toying with) radicalism in the 1970s meant that fewer people could relate to the organization, and thus SPEC found its insider status much diminished. In the environmental movement, then, there is ample room for confrontation and radicalism alongside collaboration and moderation.

Notes

1   See, for example: David Helvarg, *The War Against the Greens: The 'Wise-Use' Movement, the New Right and Anti-Environmental Violence* (San Francisco: Sierra Club Books, 1994); J. R. McNeill, *Something New Under the Sun: An Environmental History of the Twentieth Century World* (New York: W. W. Norton, 2000); Andrew Rowell, *Green Backlash: Global Subversion of the Environmental Movement* (New York: Routledge, 1996); Jacqueline Vaughn Switzer, *Green Backlash: The History and Politics of the Environmental Opposition in the U.S.* (Boulder, CO: Lynne Rienner Publishers, 1997).

2   See, for example: Mark Dowie, "American Environmentalism: A Movement Courting Irrelevance," *World Policy Journal* 9, no. 1 (1991/2): 67–92; and Mark Dowie, *Losing Ground: American Environmentalism at the Close of the Twentieth Century* (Cambridge, MA: MIT Press, 1996).

3   Ted Nordhaus and Michael Shellenberger, "The Death of Environmentalism: Global Warming Politics in a Post-Environmental World" (paper presented to the Environmental Grantmakers Association, October 2004). The points made in this paper were incorporated into a larger book, *Break Through: From the Death of Environmentalism to the Politics of Possibility* (New York: Houghton Mifflin, 2007). The second edition of this book was published as Ted Nordhaus and Michael Shellenberger, *Break Through: Why We Can't Leave Saving the Planet to Environmentalists* (New York: Houghton Mifflin, 2009).

4   Adam Werbach, "Is Environmentalism Dead?" (speech presented to the Commonwealth Club, San Francisco, December 2004).

5   Eileen Gauna, "El Dia De Los Muertos: The Death and Rebirth of the Environmental Movement," *Environmental Law* 38, no. 2 (2008): 457–72; and Amanda Little, "Over Our Dead Bodies: Green Leaders Say Rumors of Environmentalism's Death Are Greatly Exaggerated," *Grist*, 13 January 2005.

6   David Suzuki, "The Fundamental Failure of Environmentalism," David Suzuki Foundation, 3 May 2012, https://www.straight.com/article-674101/vancouver/david-suzuki-fundamental-failure-environmentalism.

7   For a representative sample of the ongoing debate, see: Terry Anderson, and Laura E. Huggins, *Greener Than Thou: Are You Really an Environmentalist?* (Stanford, CA:

Jonathan Clapperton

Hoover Institution Press, 2008); Douglas Bevington, *The Rebirth of Environmentalism: Grassroots Activism from the Spotted Owl to the Polar Bear* (Washington, DC: Island Press, 2009); Dave Foreman, "Take Back the Conservation Movement," *International Journal of Wilderness* 12, no. 1 (2006): 4–8; Timothy W. Luke, "The Death of Environmentalism or the Advent of Public Ecology?" *Organization and Environment* 18, no. 4 (2005): 489–94; John Meyer, "Does Environmentalism Have a Future?" *Dissent* 52, no. 2 (2005): 69–75; Gregory R. Singer, "Is it Time to Bury the Environmental Movement?" *Natural Resources and Environment* 20, no. 3 (2006): 56–58; Christopher D. Stone, "Is Environmentalism Dead?" *Environmental Law* 38 (2008): 19–45; Paul Wapner, *Living Through the End of Nature: The Future of American Environmentalism* (Cambridge, MA: MIT Press, 2010); and Stephen M. Meyer, *The End of the Wild* (Cambridge, MA: MIT Press, 2006).

8   See, for example: William Cronon, "The Trouble with Wilderness; or, Getting Back to the Wrong Nature," in *Uncommon Ground: Rethinking the Human Place in Nature*, ed. William Cronon (New York: W. W. Norton, 1995), 69–90; and Jonathan Clapperton, "Desolate Viewscapes: Sliammon First Nation, Desolation Sound Marine Park and Environmental Narratives," *Environment and History* 18, no. 4 (2012): 529–59.

9   See, for example: William A. Shutkin, *The Land that Could Be: Environmentalism and Democracy in the Twenty-First Century* (Cambridge, MA: MIT Press, 2001); Julian Agyeman and Briony Angus, "The Role of Civic Environmentalism in the Pursuit of Sustainable Communities," *Journal of Environmental Planning and Management* 46, no. 3 (2003): 345–63; Marc Landy and Charles Rubin, *Civic Environmentalism: A New Approach to Policy* (Washington, DC: George C. Marshall Institute, 2001); and Özgüç Orhan, "The Civic Environmental Approach," *The Good Society* 17, no. 2 (2008): 38–43.

10   While it is beyond the scope of this study, which considers postwar environmental activism, it is important to acknowledge that the many of these urban environmentalists were mimicking in many ways previous generations of activists such as urban sanitary and public health reformers and urban park proponents.

11   This organization has changed its name a number of times throughout its existence, and these names will be used as historically appropriate throughout the paper.

12   Arn Keeling is the only scholar who has made more than a passing reference to SPEC, and even his study pays relatively slight attention to the society. See Keeling, "The Effluent Society: Water Pollution and Environmental Politics in British Columbia, 1889–1980," (PhD diss., University of British Columbia, 2004).

13   Gary Gallon, "SPEC's Roots," *SPECTRUM*, Winter 1989, 5, in SPEC fonds AM 1556, box 729-A-3, f. 1 SPEC History, City of Vancouver Archives (hereafter CVA).

14   Kirin Narayan, "How Native is a 'Native' Anthropologist?" *American Anthropologist* 95, no. 3 (1993): 672, 674.

15   Narayan, "How Native," 672; and Narmala Halstead, "Ethnographic Encounters: Positionings Within and Outside the Insider Frame," *Social Anthropology* 9, no. 3 (2001): 307–8.

16   Bryan McKinley Brayboy and Donna Deyhle, "Insider-Outsider: Researchers in American Indian Communities," *Theory Into Practice* 39, no. 3 (2000): 163–69.

17   Brayboy and Deyhle, "Insider-Outsider," 165.

18   See also Michelle M. Betsill and Elisabeth Corell, "Analytical Framework: Assessing the Influence of NGO Diplomats," in *NGO Diplomacy: The Influence of Nongovernmental Organizations in International Environmental Negotiations*, ed. Michelle Betsill and Elisabeth Corell (Cambridge, MA: MIT Press, 2008), 19–41; and Sidney Tarrow, *The New Transnational Activism* (Cambridge: Cambridge University Press, 2005).

19   Donald K. Alper, "Transboundary Environmental Relations in British Columbia and the Pacific Northwest," *American Review of Canadian Studies* 27, no. 3 (1997): 359; Donald E. Blake, Neil Guppy, and Peter Urmetzer, "Canadian Public Opinion and Environmental Action: Evidence from British Columbia," *Canadian Journal of Political Science* 30, no. 3 (1997): 455.

20   Two notable exceptions are the work of Arn Keeling on water issues and Sean Kheraj on Stanley Park. See Arn Keeling, "Sink or Swim: Water Pollution and Environmental Politics in Vancouver, 1889–1975," *BC Studies* 142/143 (Summer 2004): 69–101; Arn Keeling, "Urban Waste Sinks as a Natural Resource: The Case of the Fraser River," *Urban History Review* 34, no. 1 (2005): 58–70; and Sean Kheraj, *Inventing Stanley Park: An Environmental History* (Vancouver: UBC Press, 2013).

21   The relationship between the Socred government and high modernism is discussed aptly in: Tina Loo, "People in the Way: Modernity, Environment, and Society on the Arrow Lakes," *BC Studies* 142/143 (Summer/Autumn 2004): 161–96; Christopher Dummitt, *The Manly Modern: Masculinity in Postwar Canada* (Vancouver: UBC Press, 2007); Jean Barman, *The West Beyond the West: A History of British Columbia,* 3rd ed. (Toronto: University of Toronto Press, 2007); and Philip Van Huizen, "Building a Green Dam: Environmental Modernism and the Canadian-American Libby Dam Project," *Pacific Historical Review* 79, no. 3 (2010): 418–53.

22   Haig-Brown would write twenty-eight books between 1931 and 1982. For further reading on his influence on environmental ethics in British Columbia, see Arn Keeling and Robert McDonald, "The Profligate Province: Roderick Haig-Brown and the Modernizing of British Columbia," *Journal of Canadian Studies* 36, no. 3 (2001): 7–23.

23   Frank Zelko, "Making Greenpeace: The Development of Direct Action Environmentalism in British Columbia," *BC Studies* 142/143 (Summer/Autumn 2004): 197–239; William K. Carroll and R. S. Ratner, "Old Unions and New Social Movements," *Labour / Le Travail* 35 (Spring 1995): 195–221; and Dominique Clément, "'I Believe in Human Rights, Not Women's Rights': Women and the Human Rights State, 1969–1984," *Radical History Review* 101 (Spring 2008): 107–29.

24   Emphasis added. "SPEC Report," 4 (December 1975). In SPEC fonds MS 1556, box 729-A-2, f. 7 SPEC Background 1970-80, CVA.

25   Jim Marunchak, Office Manager, Communications Director, to the Central Executive, April 1971, SPEC fonds AM 1556, box 729-A-2, f. 5 SPEC History, CVA (hereafter Marunchak to the Central Executive).

26   See Ryan O'Connor, *The First Green Wave: Pollution Probe and the Origins of Environmental Activism in Ontario* (Vancouver: UBC Press, 2014) for specific details of Pollution Probe's campaign issues.

27 Defined as the overall approach to achieving its main objective; strategies are distinguished from tactics, which are the means by which an organization exerts influence, such as litigation, direct action, protest, advocacy, or public outreach.

28 "Flyash Appals SPEC Chief," *Quesnel Cariboo Observer*, 15 July 1970, in SPEC fonds AM 1556, box 729-A-2, f. 7 SPEC Background 1970–80, CVA.

29 "Study Report," *Vancouver Sun*, 29 December 1970, in SPEC fonds AM 1556, box 729-A-2, f. 6 News Clippings 1970, CVA.

30 "The Canadian Conservation Scene," *Northwest Passage*, 23 March 1970, in SPEC fonds AM 1556, box 729-A-2, f. 6 News Clippings, CVA.

31 "Summary of SPEC—First year of operations," n.d., in SPEC fonds AM 1556, box 729-A-3, f. 1 SPEC History, CVA. See also "Our Union Allies," *PerSPECtive*, 8 March 1971, 2.

32 *PerSPECtive*, July 1970, in SPEC fonds AM 1556, box 729-A-2, f. 10 *PerSPECtive* 1969-1970, CVA.

33 In doing so, SPEC was certainly not unique. Dominique Clément, in his groundbreaking study of social movement organizations in Canada, notes that since these organizations lack face-to-face interaction with the majority of their potential supporters, they must prioritize public education campaigns or tools such as the media in order to spread their message. See Clément, *Canada's Rights Revolution: Social Movements and Social Change, 1937–1982* (Vancouver: UBC Press, 2009), 57.

34 "Summary of SPEC—First year of operations," n.d., in SPEC fonds AM 1556, box 729-A-3, f. 1 SPEC History, CVA.

35 Marunchak to the Central Executive, April 1971.

36 William K. Carroll and R. S. Ratner, "Social Movements and Counter-Hegemony: Lessons from the Field," *New Proposals: Journal of Marxism and Interdisciplinary Inquiry* 4, no. 1 (2010): 16.

37 "Spec Caravan Came," *Smithers Interior News*, 19 August 1970; and *PerSPECtive*, July 1970.

38 For further reading on the history of relationships between labour and environmentalist organizations see: Joan McFarland, "Labour and the Environment: Five Stories from New Brunswick Since the 1970s," *Labour / Le Travail* 74 (Fall 2014): 249–66; Katrin MacPhee, "Canadian Working-Class Environmentalism, 1965–1985," *Labour / Le Travail* 74 (Fall 2014): 123–49; Chad Montrie, "Expedient Environmentalism: Opposition to Coal Surface Mining in Appalachia and the United Mine Workers of America, 1945–1977," *Environmental History* 5, no. 1 (2000): 75–98; Robert Gordon, "'Shell no!': OCAW and the Labor-Environmental Alliance," *Environmental History* 3, no. 4 (1998): 460–87; Scott Dewey, "Working for the Environment: Organized Labor and the Origins of Environmentalism in the United States, 1948–1970," *Environmental History* 3, no. 1 (1998): 45–63; and Jean-Baptiste Velut, "A Brief History of the Relations between the U.S. Labor and Environmentalist Movements (1965-2010)," *Revue Française d'Etudes Americaines* 129, no. 3 (2011): 59–72.

39   "Workers Petition," *Vancouver Sun*, 23 November 1970, in SPEC fonds AM 1556, box 729-A-2, f. 6 News Clippings, CVA.

40   Ibid.

41   "Summary of SPEC—First year of operations," n.d., in SPEC fonds AM 1556, box 729-A-3, f. 1 SPEC History, CVA.

42   Jane Mansbridge and Katherine Flaster, "The Cultural Politics of Everyday Discourse: The Case of the 'Male Chauvinist,'" *Critical Sociology* 33, no. 4 (2007): 629.

43   Ibid.

44   "Letters Irk Williston," *Vancouver Sun*, 17 July 1970, in SPEC fonds AM 1556, box 729-A-2, f. 6 News Clippings, CVA. Williston was from the outset one of SPEC's most vocal opponents.

45   *PerSPECtive*, November 1970, in SPEC fonds, AM 1556, box 729-A-2, f. 10 PerSPECtive 1969–1970, CVA.

46   "The Canadian Conservation Scene," *Northwest Passage*, 23 March 1970, in SPEC fonds AM 1556, box 729-A-2, f. 6 News Clippings, CVA.

47   Gary Gallon, "SPEC's Roots," *SPECTRUM* (Winter 1989), 5, in SPEC fonds, box 729-A-3, f. 1, CVA.

48   Bob Hunter, "Survival-Crusaders Fight for Own Survival," *Vancouver Sun*, 1971, in SPEC fonds, AM 1556, box 729-A-2, f. 3 News Clippings, CVA.

49   According to Jim Marunchak, SPEC's Communications Director, Harger and Culhane chose not to set off the bombs because they would have created an "unfair and unnecessary nuisance to the entire hotel." Alex Young, "Leftist Spectre Haunts SPEC," 17 April 1971, in SPEC fonds AM 1556, box 729-A-2, f. 3 News Clippings, CVA.

50   Young, "Leftist Spectre."

51   Hunter, "Survival-crusaders Fight for Own Survival."

52   Young, "Leftist Spectre."

53   "Director Foils SPEC Revolt," *Vancouver Province*, 19 April 1971, 23.

54   *PerSPECtive*, November 1970.

55   William K. Carroll and Robert A. Hackett, "Democratic Media Activism through the Lens of Social Movement Theory," *Media, Culture & Society* 28, no. 1 (2006): 87.

56   Ibid.

57   Emphasis added. Trevor Lautens, "Editorial," *Vancouver Sun*, 28 July 1970, in SPEC fonds, AM 1556, box 729-A-2, f. 6 News Clippings, CVA.

58   Hunter, "Survival-Crusaders Fight for Own Survival." See also O'Connor, *The First Green Wave*; and Jennifer Read, "'Let Us Heed the Voice of Youth': Laundry Detergents, Phosphates and the Emergence of the Environmental Movement in Ontario," *Journal of the Canadian Historical Association* 7 no. 1 (1996): 227–50.

59   Gallon, "SPEC's Roots," 5.

60 Stephen Brown, "SPEC Leary [sic] of Socred-tainted Environmental Council," *Vancouver Free Press*, 17–24 December 1969, 14.

61 Gallon, "SPEC's Roots."

62 "Officials Quit SPEC," October 1970, in SPEC fonds, AM 1556, box 729-A-2, f. 11 News Clippings, CVA.

63 The War Measures Act was implemented during the "October Crisis," when members of the revolutionary separatist group Front de libération du Québec kidnapped British diplomat James Cross and Quebec provincial cabinet minister Pierre Laporte, the latter of whom was murdered. "Threats Denounced," *Vancouver Sun*, 7 December 1970, in SPEC fonds, AM 1556, box 729-A-2, f. 6 News Clippings, CVA.

64 Bob Hunter, "Survival-crusaders Fight for Own Survival," *Vancouver Sun*, 1971, in SPEC fonds, AM 1556, box 729-A-2, f. 3 News Clippings, CVA.

65 "Director Foils SPEC Revolt."

66 "SPEC Divided on its Future, Priorities," 1972, news clipping, in SPEC fonds, AM 1556, box 729-F-6, f. 3 News Clippings 1972–1992, CVA.

67 "SPEC Co-founder Breaks with Group," *Vancouver Province*, 24 April 1972, in SPEC fonds, AM 1556, box 729-F-6, f. 3 News Clippings 1972–1992, CVA.

68 O'Connor, *The First Green Wave*; and McLaughlin, this volume.

69 Gary Gallon, Executive Director, "Financial Status Report: SPEC Central," 13 November 1976, in SPEC fonds, AM 1556, box 729-F-6, f. 2 SPEC History 1976–1979, CVA.

70 "Minutes of the 1978 SPEC AGM," 3 June 1978, in SPEC fonds AM 1556, box 729-F-6, f. 2 SPEC History 1976–1979, CVA.

71 "SPEC Central Report, 1981," in SPEC fonds AM 1556, box 729-D-5, f. 6 SPEC Reports Concerning the Spetifore Development 1981, CVA.

72 Mide Jessen, president SPEC, to all SPEC federation council members and branch executive, "A brief capsule of SPEC activities," 4 January 1977, in SPEC fonds AM 729-F-6, f. 2 SPEC History, CVA.

73 Jill Saboe and Jacqueline Verkley, *SPEC Advertising and Marketing Report* (c. 1989), 1, in SPEC fonds AM 1556, box 729-D-5, f. 3 Education Courses Idea File 1973-1983, CVA.

74 "About S.P.E.C.," 1974, 4–5, in SPEC fonds, box 729-F-6, f. 1 Spec History, CVA. On the rise of civic activism, see John Dewitt, *Civic Environmentalism: Alternatives to Regulation in States and Communities* (Washington, DC: CQ Press, 1994).

75 SPEC, "Energy Education Programs: Schools," n.d., in SPEC fonds, AM 1556, box 729-D-5, f. 1 Education Course Idea File, CVA.

76 SPEC, "Our World of Energy," n.d., in SPEC fonds, AM 1556, box 729-D-5, f. 1 Education Course Idea File, CVA.

77 "SPEC Residential Energy Inspections Vancouver South," 1984–85, in SPEC fonds, AM 1556, box 729-D-5, f. 8 SPEC Energy Inspections, CVA.

78   Cliff Stainsby, Executive Director, SPEC, to Rafe Mair, 28 February 1979, in SPEC fonds, AM 1556, box 729-F-6, f. 2 SPEC History, CVA.

79   SPEC, "March 1983 Spring Program at Energy Information Centre," in SPEC fonds, AM 1556, box 729-D-5, f. 1 Education Courses Idea File, CVA.

80   SPEC counted the centre's creation as a huge victory, and continued to operate it through 2011 until it became outdated. SPEC, "Fostering Urban Sustainability Since 1969," last updated 2017, http://www.spec.bc.ca/since1969; and "New Centre to Give Advice on How to Cut Energy Bills," *Vancouver Sun*, 9 August 1981, in SPEC fonds AM 1556, box 729-F-6, f. 3 News Clippings 1972–1992, CVA.

81   The many definitions of "success" or "failure" are examined in further detail in the Afterword of this volume.

82   SPEC, "Minutes of the Meeting Called by the SPEC Membership," 15 December 1987, in SPEC fonds AM 1556, box 729-D-5, f. 16 Water for Tomorrow SPEC Campaign Planning, CVA.

83   Alice Coppard, "President's Report," 1992, in SPEC fonds, AM 1556, box 729-E-1, f. 11 SPEC History 1969-1993, CVA.

84   Many of these letters are available in SPEC fonds, AM 1556, box 729-E-6, f. 7 Correspondence in 1988–2005, CVA.

85   Andreas and Christine Mueller-Mettnau to SPEC, 13 March 1997, in SPEC fonds, AM 1556, box 729-E-6, f. 7 Correspondence in 1988–2005.

86   For example, see: Rik Scarce, *Eco-Warriors: Understanding the Radical Environmental Movement* (Chicago: The Noble Press, 1990); and Tzeporah Berman, *This Crazy Time: Living our Environmental Challenge* (Toronto: Knopf Canada, 2011).

From Social Movement to Environmental Behemoth: How Greenpeace Got Big

Frank Zelko

Three decades after he helped found Greenpeace, the countercultural journalist and charismatic environmentalist Bob Hunter had this to say about the organization: "It's big, but nowhere near big enough."[1] Hunter had hoped that Greenpeace would bring about a dramatic change in human consciousness in which a holistic ecological worldview would inform all politics and guide people's interactions with the rest of nature. Only by this measure could a Greenpeace founder be disappointed by the fact that the organization—created by a handful of American and Canadian activists in Vancouver's countercultural ghetto—had become a high-profile global NGO with offices in fifty countries and an annual budget of over 200 million dollars. But size, of course, is a relative concept. An environmental justice group toiling away on a toxics campaign in Louisiana could only dream of having the influence and resources of an NGO like Greenpeace. On the other hand, compared to global corporations and governments, Greenpeace looks positively puny. In terms of global political and economic influence, entities such as the US military and Exxon are the elephants. Greenpeace is just an annoying insect on their rump.

Nevertheless, among environmental NGOs, Greenpeace is clearly a whale. How did a small band of Vancouver-based anti-nuclear protestors—many of whom could be considered social misfits—create such a high-profile organization? In broad terms, the answer is simple: it was a combination of hard work, fortunate timing, and a willingness to compromise some of their core principles. However, a closer look at Greenpeace's history reveals a more complex story, one involving a good deal of contingency and many unexpected twists. Based on the vision and actions of its founders, Greenpeace could just as easily have become a social movement as a professional organization. For that matter, it could easily have disappeared after its first campaign. This chapter will examine some of the key moments in Greenpeace's growth in order to explain how the organization "got big." Unlike many small environmental groups that focused on local or regional issues, Greenpeace's founders set goals for themselves that could never be achieved merely through cultivating local renown and political influence. Entering the arena of what political scientist Paul Wapner calls "world civic politics" requires an ability to mobilize resources around the planet and attain recognition on a global scale.[2] Thus the imperative to get big was in a sense built into Greenpeace from the moment its founders decided to launch their first transnational protest campaign on the high seas.

Unlike, say, Friends of the Earth, which sprung fully formed from the mind of David Brower, Greenpeace's founding was more of a free-form process than an act of creation.[3] I have told this story in great detail elsewhere, but the short version goes something like this: In the late 1960s, numerous Americans found themselves living in Canada because of, in one way or another, various disagreements with their government's foreign policy. In addition to young draft evaders, there were older immigrants from the Second World War generation who wanted to ensure that their sons would not get drafted into the US military once they came of age. Others left because they found US preparations for nuclear war to be unconscionable. Quite a few were Quakers. In Vancouver, a fertile centre of the Canadian counterculture, these older Americans came into contact with numerous hippies and radical activists who shared their misgivings about issues such as nuclear warfare and the malign influence of the US military-industrial complex. Many were also concerned about issues such as pollution, while some of the Americans were Sierra Club members who were appalled by the BC government's utilitarian attitude toward the province's spectacular wilderness areas.[4]

This disparate array of anti-war activists, environmentalists, and the politically disaffected members of the counterculture were galvanized by one issue in particular: the US decision to conduct a series of nuclear weapons tests on Amchitka Island, a tiny speck of tundra in the faraway Aleutians. Apart from their general opposition to nuclear weapons, many feared that the tests—conducted in a geologically unstable area—could set off earthquakes and a tsunami that would, in Bob Hunter's dramatic description, "slam the lips of the Pacific Rim like a series of karate chops."[5] Between 1969 and 1971, the tests inspired much opposition and numerous protests. In 1969, for example, thousands of protesters descended on the US-Canadian border, disrupting the smooth flow of people and goods for the day. It was at one such protest on the BC-Washington border that the nucleus of the Greenpeace coalition was formed. It was here that two older American activists—Irving Stowe from Rhode Island and Jim Bohlen from Pennsylvania—met up with various student radicals and other young protest groups and decided to form an organization that would try to stop the next major nuclear test, scheduled for late 1971. They gave themselves the rather vivid, if somewhat clumsy moniker, the Don't Make a Wave Committee (DMWC), and began meeting regularly at Stowe's house in Vancouver. After many fruitless discussions, Bohlen came up with a plan: they would charter a boat and sail it into the nuclear test zone, thereby bearing witness to the ecological crime and putting political pressure on both the US and Canadian governments.

Bob Hunter, at the time a columnist for the *Vancouver Sun*, attended many of the meetings, as did Ben Metcalfe, a well-known CBC personality and journalist. Patrick Moore, a doctoral student in ecology at the University of British Columbia, was also a regular participant, and Paul Watson, at the time still a teenager, was also an active member of the group. At one point, as Irving Stowe was leaving a meeting, he flashed his usual V-sign and said "peace." Bill Darnell, a social worker and local activist, spontaneously replied, "Make it a green peace!" The group liked the sound of those two words together and decided that they would call their boat the *Greenpeace.* Thus the first Greenpeace action, in which a dozen activists tried to sail an old halibut seiner to Amchitka to protest the nuclear blast, was officially conducted by the DMWC. Only after this first campaign (the boat never made it to Amchitka but nonetheless garnered a lot of publicity in the attempt) did the group's members decide to officially register the "Greenpeace Foundation" (Hunter suggested the title) as a non-profit corporation in British Columbia in early 1972.

Although they were united in their overall environmental goals, there was considerable tension among the activists. The most obvious of these was the split between the older generation of peace movement protestors, who were inclined toward a sober and respectable form of scientific rationalism, and the younger activists, who embraced various countercultural beliefs and values. The participants labelled this dichotomy the "mechanics versus the mystics," and it would remain a fundamental cleavage within the organization throughout the 1970s. Regardless of their differences in lifestyle and outlook, however, those on board the *Greenpeace* recognized that their campaign had generated the embryonic stirrings of a broad international trans-political alliance. All agreed that such a possibility was too important to abandon, regardless of how amorphous the alliance or how difficult the task of mobilizing it might prove. And such feelings were not without justification. Despite their failure to reach their destination and the flakiness that characterized some aspects of the campaign, it was nonetheless a substantial achievement. Unlike the case with similar voyages of the past, such as the Quaker anti-nuclear protests of the 1950s, the *Greenpeace* managed to attract considerable media attention, in large part because of the presence of several experienced journalists among the crew. Furthermore, as well as employing the direct-action tactics of its predecessors, the campaign, which was almost two years in the making, made a genuine effort to unite two of the major social movements of the twentieth century—environmentalism and the peace movement. The DMWC managed to lay the groundwork for such an alliance in a deliberate and thoroughgoing way. Whereas previously the two movements had merely overlapped, now, at least among a certain segment of the Canadian population, the values and tactics of the peace and environmental movements, as well as their respective critiques of modernity, were on the way to being integrated.

The question for the DMWC, then, was what shape should the organization take in order to help give such an alliance a more concrete form?

According to Hunter, who from the beginning had possessed the grandest vision for the DMWC, the new organization needed to abandon the traditional revolutionary goal of replacing one political regime with another, which would only result in illusory change. Instead, it would have to focus all of its energy on bringing about a consciousness revolution on a world scale, using cameras, rather than guns, to fight a McLuhanesque war for the hearts and minds of the masses. The ultimate goal should be nothing less than the creation of a green version of the United Nations.[6] How exactly such an organization should be structured and managed was not precisely clear, but then again, organizational matters were never Hunter's strong suit.

CBC journalist Ben Metcalfe also had an essentially McLuhanesque vision for any new organization that might emerge from the DMWC, but it was one that was unencumbered by the kind of utopianism that characterized Hunter's thinking. Instead, the more cynical, elitist, and conspiratorial Metcalfe felt that the most useful thing that they could accomplish would be to create an organization that would do for ecology what Madison Avenue had done for corporate America. If brainwashing was the only way to save the earth from humanity, then so be it.[7] Bohlen, who had never really given much thought to the creation of an ongoing organization, was essentially satisfied with the DMWC as it stood, feeling that with some minor structural tinkering, it could be set up to run multiple campaigns based on direct action, scientific research, educational outreach, and solid media work.[8] For Irving Stowe, the DMWC had the potential to empower various disenfranchised social groups by acting as an organizer, facilitator, and funder of progressive social and political movements. The committee, he told the *Georgia Straight*, could use "its funds and influence, and speaking and organizing abilities [to help] those groups in the community which have a base for action to actually translate that concern into action." Students and women, Stowe felt, were particularly aware of the systemic problems of modern industrial societies, since they were among its victims. "My feeling is that the best expenditure that the people in the Don't Make a Wave Committee can do [sic] is to help these groups in whatever way they call upon us to become politically active, politically motivated, and take action."[9]

Clearly, right from the beginning, the founders were giving a good deal of thought to issues such as organizational form and growth. What was just as clear was that there were substantial differences between them on such questions, with the strongest cleavage represented by Bohlen's earnest Quakerism on one side and Hunter's grand countercultural vision on the other. In fact, the name "Greenpeace Foundation" was itself emblematic of the antagonism between Hunter and Bohlen and the worldviews they represented. For Bohlen, the word "foundation" described a non-profit organization interested in promoting research and funding campaigns and was synonymous with professionalism and respectability. Hunter, however, had specifically chosen the term as a reference to his all-time favorite work of science fiction, Isaac Asimov's *Foundation* trilogy. Asimov's novels described a Galactic Empire that, though corrupt and in decline, still clung to power at the expense of all the other creatures in the galaxy. Dissidents within the galaxy organized an oppositional force, called the Foundation, whose task would be to hasten the collapse of the Empire so that its brutal and destructive reign would only last another thousand years instead of the expected thirty thousand. In more than one sense, then, Hunter and Bohlen's conceptions of the new organization were worlds apart.[10]

The Greenpeace Foundation's first campaign was directed at French nuclear testing in the South Pacific. While the United States at least had the decency to explode its hydrogen bombs deep underground, the French were still detonating them in the air above coral atolls not too far from Tahiti. Jim Bohlen and Irving Stowe, the two Americans in their fifties, were exhausted after two years of working on the Amchitka campaign and were ready to pass the leadership baton to someone else. Bob Hunter was eager to grasp it, but Bohlen in particular found Hunter's countercultural proclivities difficult to stomach. Instead, they allowed Ben Metcalfe, who was also a Second World War vet, to take charge. Unlike the democratic, consensus-oriented approach favoured by Bohlen, Stowe, and Hunter, Metcalfe chose a kind of Wizard of Oz strategy to run the new organization, creating the impression that Greenpeace was a large movement when it was mostly just Metcalfe pressing buttons and pulling levers behind the curtain. Metcalfe's extensive experience with the media in the post–Second World War era had led him in the same intellectual direction as it had led Marshall McLuhan, who had been the first to articulate the concept of the "global village" in a systematic manner, creating a theory of media that resonated deeply with Metcalfe's experience. The idea of a world temporally and spatially compressed by a global media, combined with his Machiavellian view of society, led Metcalfe to adopt a condescending and cynical attitude. The media, he argued, was "fundamentally stupid." A hard-working, well-read reporter with common sense and a good nose for a story could easily manipulate the mass media and create pseudo-events virtually out of thin air. The secret was in the packaging of the stories as much as their content. So long as the clever journalist was able to manufacture a compelling narrative with the appropriate element of conflict, particularly of the David versus Goliath variety, the mass media would rise to it like a trout to a mayfly, regardless of the event's actual significance.[11]

According the Metcalfe, the Amchitka campaign could be characterized as "naïve bourgeois" because its organizers had announced its schedule and its limitations—the fact that they could only afford to stay on the boat for six weeks, for example—thereby providing the "enemy" with a huge tactical advantage.[12] Furthermore, they had been very distant from the centre of power in Washington, DC, which greatly reduced their visibility in the US media and their commensurate influence on American public opinion. To avoid a similar fate, the Mururoa campaign would need to be more cunning in order to keep the French guessing. It would also have to take the protest to France by conducting a direct action and a media event in Paris in order to alert the French population to the impact the nuclear tests were having in the South Pacific and to demonstrate the strength of international opinion against the *force de frappe*.[13]

Unlike the more open, consensus-oriented approach that had characterized the DMWC, the first Greenpeace Foundation campaign was planned and run as a virtual one-man show. Metcalfe would sit up late at night in his upstairs home office, which he self-mockingly referred to as the "Ego's Nest," developing ideas and strategies. To maintain an element of secrecy, he never informed anyone of more than part of his overall plan so that only he was aware of the big picture. When he needed something ratified by other members of the group he would "call meetings backwards;" that is, he would reach a decision unilaterally and then run the meeting in such a way that the majority would agree with him. Many of the meetings were held in Gastown, the funky, dilapidated countercultural quarter in inner city Vancouver, and were attended by dozens of hippies, street kids, and various social outcasts. This, Metcalfe knew, would alienate some of the older, "straighter" activists, such as the Stowes and the Bohlens, who would otherwise have been in a better position to challenge Metcalfe's authority.[14] Although Hunter, who had hoped to be the first Greenpeace leader, resented Metcalfe, he nevertheless admired the way he ran the campaign from his "media ivory tower" like a "beautiful one man, McLuhanesque show." Others, however, were alienated by his aloof and conspiratorial style, and Stowe in particular grew suspicious of Metcalfe and backed away from the campaign.[15]

Much to his subsequent regret, Metcalfe drafted a boom-and-bust Canadian businessman named David McTaggart into the organization. McTaggart, who had never so much as contemplated political activism in his forty years of life on the planet, was an unlikely candidate to lead a Greenpeace protest. Yet he would go on to exert greater influence over the organization than any other individual in its four-decade history. The scion of a conservative Vancouver family, McTaggart spent two tumultuous decades as a builder and developer of high-profile resorts. By 1971, he was in the midst of his third divorce, and his most recent venture—a ski resort and nightclub in California—had rendered him bankrupt and owing considerable debts. Without telling a soul, McTaggart took what little cash he had and boarded a plane for Tahiti, where he purchased a small yacht and spent the next several months aimlessly sailing around the South Pacific. By early 1972 he was in Auckland, where his new nineteen-year-old girlfriend alerted him to the fact that a group from his hometown was looking for a volunteer to sail a boat into the French nuclear test zone.[16]

McTaggart had never heard of Greenpeace and didn't have much interest in nuclear policy, or for that matter, politics in general. Nevertheless, with some helpful persuasion from his enthusiastic young girlfriend, he came to see the idea of such a voyage as an interesting adventure and a worthy challenge to his seamanship. He also grew increasingly irritated with the way the French were treating the South Pacific. So, in the southern winter of 1972, McTaggart led a small crew—including Metcalfe for part of the voyage—to Mururoa Atoll, where he attempted to enter the French nuclear testing zone and was rammed by a French destroyer for his troubles. He repeated the voyage in 1973. By this time, the French were thoroughly sick of him, and a group of commandos boarded his yacht and beat him to a pulp, almost blinding him in the process.[17]

While McTaggart was sailing across the South Pacific, Jim Bohlen and Patrick Moore were in New York, trying to raise awareness of Greenpeace's campaign at the United Nations. Other Greenpeace activists had flown to London and Paris to help organize marches and demonstrations. Without letting McTaggart or anyone else know, Metcalfe had arranged for a "decoy" boat to sail from Peru in order to keep the French navy on their toes.[18] He left McTaggart, who by then was well and truly fed up with his imperiousness and secretiveness, in Rarotonga, before flying on to Mexico City and then Rome, where he organized an audience with the Pope. The result was that Greenpeace became an increasing source of irritation to the French, particularly once photographs of McTaggart's beating and injuries appeared in newspapers throughout the world. In addition, McTaggart initiated a drawn-out legal case against the French military which kept the issue in the spotlight for several more years.

All of this frenzied campaigning by a few Vancouver-based activists helped make Greenpeace an increasingly household name in activist circles throughout Western Europe and Australasia. In Paris, for example, about 200 English and French Greenpeace supporters marched toward the Elysée Palace, leafleting along the way, before being rounded up by police and taken to the Opera police station.[19] In Bonn, a small group of West German peace activists and environmentalists gathered under a Greenpeace banner and marched through the capital's streets to the French Embassy to protest French nuclear testing in the South Pacific.[20] Another group of people using the Greenpeace label presented an anti-nuclear petition to the French government. Several Australians and New Zealanders among them demanded sanctuary in France, claiming that their own countries were being poisoned by radiation from the French tests.[21] In New Zealand, from where Greenpeace launched its protests against the French for three years in a row, a nascent Greenpeace group was formed.

At this stage the term "Greenpeace" could be used by anyone who supported the cause, without needing to ask the Vancouver Greenpeace Foundation for permission. While such a laissez-faire position had the advantage of encouraging widespread protest among like-minded activists, its results could sometimes be less than professional. For example, the efforts of a group of London activists to protest at the French tourist office in Piccadilly did not go quite to plan. "Sadly," the *Guardian* reported, "the demonstrators chose the wrong office for their demonstration and invaded and leafleted the Ceylon Airlines and Air Afrique offices by mistake. The French tourist office was next door. The man from Ceylon Airlines said: 'I quite agree with them.' The policemen outside the embassy applauded after the performance and said they had enjoyed the show. 'It gets chilly out here and this sort of thing passes the time.'"[22] It was a harmless enough farce, but too many such incidents would not do much for Greenpeace's credibility.

Unsurprisingly, all of this frenetic campaigning on a shoestring budget took its toll. By late 1973, less than two years after Ben Metcalfe had officially registered it as a legal non-profit group under the British Columbia Societies Act, the Greenpeace Foundation was in disarray. Fragmented, disorganized, and effectively leaderless, it was in danger of collapsing altogether. Metcalfe, despite being the group's official leader, was barely involved any more, and the group's meetings were poorly attended. McTaggart, who felt betrayed by Greenpeace's refusal (or rather, inability) to sue the French government for damages for ramming his boat and then boarding it and beating him, moved to Paris to fight the case on his own.[23] The divide between the older Quakers and peace activists on the one hand, and the countercultural ecology freaks on the other, was wider than ever, with each faction sometimes unaware of what the other was doing in the name of Greenpeace. In February 1973, for example, a group led by Hunter, Paul Watson, and a young activist named Rod Marining staged a protest against a pair of visiting French warships, an action that turned into something of a fiasco. The captain of the ship they had hired for the protest changed his mind at the last minute, prompting Hunter and Watson to rush off to Hunter's little yacht, which they sailed rather pathetically toward the approaching warships, while Marining stood atop a bridge dropping mushrooms and marshmallows on the bemused sailors, before being arrested for his troubles.[24] Marining's description of how the protest was conceived reflects the group's fragmentation and haphazard planning style: "There were six of us in a living room trying to figure out what to do about these French warships. That was two days before. It was just a little Greenpeace meeting. I had called everybody together but only six came."[25]

Despite the confusion and lack of planning, or perhaps because of it, the event still managed to attract plenty of local media attention. Even at this early stage, however, Marining was somewhat ambivalent about what press coverage alone could achieve: "The press picks up on all the sensational things. They say Greenpeace did this, Greenpeace did that. They make it look like there's thousands of people caring and bringing on the revolution, when there was really only about six of us. The rest is all myth. . . . All that Greenpeace Power is illusory. It looks like there's a lot of people worried about what's happening thousands of miles away in the South Pacific but they would really only be worried if it were happening in Squamish."[26]

As Marining's comments indicate, the number of committed Greenpeace activists was small. Despite this, the name had by this stage become quite recognizable throughout Canada and New Zealand, as well as among peace and environmental activists in numerous countries. Apart from denoting a Vancouver-based environmental organization, the term was also used to connote a particular form of non-violent direct action. It could be used as a noun or a verb (we "greenpeaced them"). And anyone who wanted to form a Greenpeace group was free to do so.[27] None of the Vancouver founders had any problems with this in 1973. In fact, given the organization's precarious state, most were happy that it seemed to be spreading without too much additional effort on their part. However, a few years later, as Greenpeace began to "get big," this loose, ad hoc model began to cause significant problems.

By 1974, Hunter still had high hopes for his original grand vision of Greenpeace. Nonetheless, he was beginning to grow weary of the anti-nuclear voyages, feeling that Greenpeace had gained all they could from them for now. Instead, he had become excited about a possible campaign against whaling. Over the previous year, Hunter had gotten to know Paul Spong, a scientist studying killer whales at the Vancouver Aquarium. Spong had come to the conclusion that whales were extraordinarily intelligent, complex, and wondrous animals, and was horrified by the fact that tens of thousands continued to be slaughtered each year. If any organization had the expertise to challenge whalers on the high seas, Spong felt, it was Greenpeace. Hunter needed little convincing, and the two of them came up with a plan that eventually led to the famous images of Greenpeace activists positioning their zodiac boats between harpoon guns and the whales.[28]

Despite several years of enthusiastic commitment to Greenpeace, Hunter was still perceived by the older Quakers and peaceniks—most of whom were Americans—as too unstable and eccentric for a leadership role. But the situation changed rapidly in mid-1974. Sadly, Irving Stowe died of stomach cancer, an unjust death for a teetotalling, non-smoking vegetarian. Jim Bohlen and his wife moved to an island off the coast of Vancouver Island, where they started the Greenpeace Experimental Farm, which they hoped would become a replicable model for sustainable living. And Ben Metcalfe had returned to his full-time career as a journalist. With nobody else desperate to take on the task—and Bohlen no longer in a position to stop him—Hunter finally became Greenpeace's leader. The torch, as Hunter saw it, passed from the mechanics to the mystics:

> There was no one left to resist any further Greenpeace's transformation from nuclear vigilantism to whale saving. And there was no one left to prevent us from dropping the hard brick-by-brick logic of the normal political world completely, seizing our *I Ching*s and allowing signs and visions to determine our course.[29]

Initially under Hunter's leadership, Greenpeace looked like a combination of a social movement, hippie commune, and insane asylum. Anyone, including some people with obvious mental illnesses, was welcome to join in and put in their two cents worth.[30] The meetings were now characterized by a tone of joyous celebration and chaotic good humour, a marked contrast to the "heavy atmosphere of moralistic purity," which, according to Hunter, had pervaded earlier Greenpeace meetings. As Patrick Moore recalled, the "sober suffering" of the Stowes and Bohlens was replaced by a joie de vivre, a fact that could partially be explained by the positive nature of the campaign. As long as Greenpeace's raison d'être had been to oppose nuclear weapons, there was little to celebrate. But now, in Hunter's words, "instead of fighting death, we were embracing life. It was not just that we wanted to save whales, we wanted to meet them, we wanted to engage them, encounter them, touch them, discover them. For the first time there was a transcendent element lying at the centre of the undertaking."[31]

By early 1975, Greenpeace still had no offices or employees. Far from operating as a professional organization, it straddled the line between a formal NGO and a social movement. Fundraising tended to be ad hoc and opportunistic rather than systematic. Hundreds of volunteers donated various amounts of time and goodwill to help prepare for the anti-whaling voyage, while the more committed activists, such as Hunter, Moore, Spong, and Watson, devoted their lives to the cause. In mid-1975, against all odds, Greenpeace's dilapidated old halibut seiner—the same boat that had tried to reach Amchitka in 1971—managed to track down the Soviet whaling fleet around 100 miles off the coast of northern California.[32] Activists leapt into their zodiacs and began harassing the whalers, while cameramen and photographers recorded the dramatic images. Two days later, they arrived in San Francisco to find a throng of reporters lined up along the Embarcadero to greet them. Immigration officials had to restrain the clamouring journalists, who leaned across the boat's gunwale with their cameras and microphones, impatient to talk to the heroic, if somewhat fanatical, environmentalists who had risked their lives to save the whales from the Soviet hunters. Hunter talked to virtually every TV and radio station in the Bay area, and the story, complete with dramatic photos and film footage, was printed and broadcast throughout the United States and the world. According to one study, the first whale campaign garnered more media coverage in the United States than all of Greenpeace's previous four years of anti-nuclear actions combined.[33] Walter Cronkite, the doyen of American newsreaders, introduced them to a massive TV audience on the CBS Evening News. The *New York Times* published a lengthy and overwhelmingly positive feature on the organization. As well as describing the clash with the whalers, the *Times* cited Spong's experiments with killer whales as proof of whales' unique intelligence, thereby adding scientific credibility to Greenpeace's list of virtues. As a media event, the campaign was successful beyond Hunter's wildest dreams.[34]

The crew spent a total of nine days in San Francisco, during which they were wined, dined, and generally celebrated by the local media and, to a lesser extent, local environmental organizations. After being cooped up in the claustrophobic confines of a fishing boat for the previous two months, the glamour and polish of the San Francisco media world, and the opulent houses of many of the city's environmentalists, proved to be something of a culture shock. A somewhat jaded Hunter recalled one of Ben Metcalfe's favorite aphorisms: "Fear success."[35] It was not long before the meaning of Metcalfe's words became clear. Less than twenty-four hours after their arrival, Hunter was contacted by the New York–based movie production company, Artists Entertainment Complex, the maker of such block-buster films as *Earthquake* and *The Godfather, Part II*. The next day, an AEC agent, Amy Ephron (sister of Nora), and a scriptwriter flew into San Francisco to meet with the crew in order to discuss a multi-million dollar movie about Greenpeace's exploits. Whatever tensions had existed on the halibut seiner paled into insignificance compared to the schism created by Ephron's visit. Her brusque New York style put most of the Greenpeacers off right from the start. She was prepared, she said, to offer them $25,000 for the movie rights to their story, with 10 percent down and a promise for the rest once the film was made. Although Hunter was no entrepreneur, he nonetheless knew the $25,000 was peanuts compared to the amount that Ephron's company stood to make from a successful film. Still, as far as Hunter was concerned, the objective was to raise "whale consciousness" around the world. The film, he felt, would contribute to this goal, as well as providing Greenpeace with a great deal of free publicity. Others, however, were deeply suspicious. Paul Watson was particularly upset and accused Hunter of being a "sell out." The contract required every crewmember to sign a release, giving the movie company the right to portray them as it saw fit. Watson refused to sign, which infuriated Hunter and Moore, who accused him of grandstanding. The division over the movie contract, according to Hunter, "was never to fully heal itself and was to lead to divisions that would plague us for years."[36]

The mixed feelings that emerged in San Francisco reflected the classical dilemma that many successful activist groups face: Should their progressive politics be reflected in their organizational structure or should ideology take a backseat to professionalization and efficiency? The anti-whaling campaign—which some of the older Quakers viewed as "soft" compared to the prospect of nuclear warfare—prompted numerous sympathetic environmentalists to set up Greenpeace groups throughout North America.

In addition to this spontaneous growth, Hunter also embarked on a deliberate campaign to foster the spread of the organization in Canada. In the fall of 1975, he and his wife Bobbi travelled throughout the country, visiting virtually every major university campus. Hunter would present a slide show and lecture about the Greenpeace whale campaign, while Bobbi would sit at the back selling T-shirts and buttons and signing people up for membership. After each show, they would be approached by at least a dozen volunteers interested in setting up a Greenpeace group. By Christmas of that year, there were approximately a dozen Greenpeace branches throughout Canada. Some of these were made up of merely a handful of people selling T-shirts, while others, such as those in Toronto and Montreal, were more substantial organizations that were soon contributing to Vancouver's campaigns, as well as mounting their own.[37]

The most important office outside Vancouver, however, was undoubtedly the one established in San Francisco in the fall of 1975. This was to be Greenpeace's American beachhead. While the various Canadian branches were largely left to themselves, Hunter and his cohorts set up the San Francisco office in a more deliberate fashion. It would be the focal point for Greenpeace activity in the United States, providing them with access to the American media and an ideal base from which to plan further whale campaigns, as well as placing them at the centre of California's lucrative fundraising market. While some locals would help to run the branch, it was clear to Hunter, Moore, and the others in Vancouver, that San Francisco was a subordinate office rather than an independent operation.[38]

Paradoxically, despite the fact that it was now run by unreconstructed hippies like Bob Hunter, Greenpeace was becoming more organized than it had been at any other stage in its five-year history and began to take on all the trappings of a traditionally run non-profit organization. The first, and perhaps most important step, was setting up an office in a small building on Fourth Avenue in the heart of Kitsilano. Such an apparently trivial event was a vital stage in Greenpeace's evolution. At last, there was an actual address where people could reach the organization, rather than having to contact individual members at their homes. Furthermore, there was a comforting sense of bourgeois legitimacy in the act of leaving home and going to an office. And despite the countercultural values adhered to by Greenpeace's inner circle, most of them came from backgrounds that were thoroughly middle class. Setting up an office also led to the adoption of the paraphernalia that one normally associates with offices: bookkeeping procedures, mailing lists, organized filing systems, in- and out-boxes, and letterhead stationery. The "buzz" created by groups of people working together in a shared space contributed to a general sense of comradeship and to a more inspired and efficient work ethic. Malingerers could be politely escorted from the premises.

Opening an office was the first—largely unintentional—step on the road to professionalization. Hunter and his fellow countercultural activists were ideologically committed to a grassroots structure with an openness that encouraged as much discussion and participation as possible. However, the months of unstructured meetings and consensus-based decision making that had preceded the first whale campaign had taken some of the shine off the grassroots model.[39] Although such a broad-based participatory structure had given everyone a voice, thereby encouraging goodwill and creativity, it had also led to endless and exhausting meetings and bureaucratic inefficiency. Furthermore, it tended to attract characters who were wacky even by Greenpeace's tolerant hippie standards. The 1975 save-the-whales campaign, while relying on a considerable amount of what could only be described as good luck, had also entailed a great deal of detailed planning and organization, as well as a level of secrecy and surreptitious research that would not have been out of place in the military. It became clear to Hunter that if Greenpeace was going to continue to carry out similar campaigns, they could no longer rely on the happy-go-lucky approach that had got them through so far. Paradoxically, therefore, the trappings of the traditional non-profit organization—Robert's Rules of Order, an executive, a board of directors, sensible financial planning—began to appear positively liberating. In short, the demands and pressures of running an outfit such as Greenpeace dictated a greater degree of professionalization.[40]

Not everyone, however, was entirely pleased with such developments. Some of the hard-core mystics and radicals began to worry that Greenpeace might become just another mainstream environmental organization rather than the fluid, unstructured social movement they envisioned. Just as they had refused to sign the film contract in San Francisco, several of these people grumbled about such unheroic notions as cash flows and bookkeeping. From their perspective, it was hard to see what the "eco-revolution" had to do with contracting T-shirts out to a distributor. Despite these murmurings of discontent, the situation remained, in Hunter's words, "within the bounds of acceptable comedy, because one of the worst of the flipped-out mystics—namely myself—was now the chief advocate of organization, fiscal responsibility, and the budget system itself."[41]

In 1976, Greenpeace embarked upon its next campaign, protesting the slaughter of harp seals in Newfoundland. Protecting adorable seal pups drew at least as much media interest and public sympathy as saving whales, and Greenpeace's fame continued to spread further afield, particularly in western Europe. David McTaggart, who was still in France while his case dawdled through the French court system, took advantage of this publicity to set up Greenpeace offices in Paris, London, and Amsterdam. McTaggart's attitude toward Greenpeace remained ambivalent: he was still embittered by the organization's refusal to adequately support his legal actions in France and, despite getting along well with Bob Hunter, had little respect for the rest of the countercultural crowd in Vancouver. Nevertheless, he was gradually coming around to the view that the core idea of Greenpeace—an international organization that relied on non-violent action and was not attached to any political party or ideology—had considerable potential if it could be run by hard-nosed professionals rather than hippies.[42] In other words, if *he* were at the helm, it might be possible to create a genuinely international organization that could effectively influence world opinion. It was not long before McTaggart had convinced most of the new European recruits that he had founded Greenpeace and that the Vancouver hippies were a bunch of incompetent fools who were destroying the organization he had fought so hard to establish.[43]

McTaggart, however, was not the only one who had visions of a more organized, professional international outfit. By late 1977, Bob Hunter, Patrick Moore, and others within the Vancouver group were beginning to see the need to establish a more formal set of ties between the various affiliates, as well as developing a chain of command that would facilitate a greater degree of efficiency in the decision-making process. With this in mind, Moore, who by then had succeeded Hunter as president, sent a letter headed "Greenpeace: Where Are We Going?" to the various groups scattered throughout North America. "We are faced with a problem," Moore began,

> that has baffled the best philosophers and politicians since the first federation of cave-people communities. Simply stated the problem is how can we achieve unity and cohesiveness as one organization and yet provide the individual and group autonomy necessary for creativity and initiative? Somehow we must be both centralized and decentralized at the same time. . . . Under the present structure, further growth is not possible without further confusion. There is a pressing and demanding need for organization.[44]

Moore suggested several organizational models, including General Motors, the United Nations, the Palestinian Liberation Organization, and the Sierra Club. However, he was particularly taken with the idea of a structure that was based on an ecosystem model. Diversity in ecosystems, he noted, in what many would now consider to be an outmoded theory, "tends to result in stability." While this was an argument for a decentralized structure, it was also important to remember that "each species has a well-defined niche or function that it must keep to in order to maintain that stability. . . . We must stick to those functions and we must demonstrate the capacity to carry them out."[45]

There was no doubt in Moore's mind that, hippie ideals aside, some degree of centralization would be necessary in order to ensure the smooth running of the organization, as well as preventing people from conducting unauthorized actions under the Greenpeace banner. To accomplish this, he drafted a document he called the "Declaration and Charter." It was a contract that carefully outlined the responsibilities that all the branches had to the Vancouver office in exchange for the use of the Greenpeace trademark. From mid-1978 onward, all new Greenpeace branches would have to sign this document. Moore also tried, with varying degrees of success, to force all the existing North American groups to sign the contract. Perhaps unsurprisingly, the most obstreperous affiliate was also the richest: Greenpeace San Francisco, a well-oiled fundraising machine, was not too keen to surrender its autonomy. In the process, it emboldened some of the smaller groups in the United States to take a similar stand.

Moore, Hunter, and others within the original Vancouver group spent over a year trying to convince the San Francisco group to sign the Declaration and Charter, but without success. So, in May 1979, with all other options exhausted, they filed a lawsuit. When word of this reached David McTaggart in Europe, he immediately boarded a plane and headed to San Francisco. If Vancouver won the suit, as they probably would, then McTaggart had no doubt that they would turn their attentions to the budding Greenpeace groups in Europe. Given McTaggart's fractious relationship with Vancouver, he was not about to sit quietly by while they tried to gain control of the promising European offices. The Americans and Europeans, he told the San Francisco board, "must come out unanimously to fight, and must work towards a democratic Greenpeace U.S." He suggested that the Americans offer Vancouver a settlement: in exchange for San Francisco paying off Vancouver's considerable debts, Vancouver would relinquish the rights to the name "Greenpeace" outside Canada. Prior to McTaggart's visit, the San Francisco board, pessimistic about its chances of winning, had been prepared to bow to Vancouver's demands. However, McTaggart managed to stiffen their resolve, and they decided they would fight Vancouver to the bitter end.[46]

Having accomplished what he set out to achieve in San Francisco, McTaggart then flew to Vancouver. He immediately organized a meeting with Hunter, the only person on the Vancouver board whom he respected. Patrick Moore, McTaggart insisted, was leading Greenpeace down the path to ruin. He also reported that the wealthy San Francisco office would fight Vancouver for as long as it took them to win their independence, though he failed to mention that he himself had played a large part in this decision. Couldn't Hunter convince Moore and the rest of the board to drop the lawsuit? Hunter replied that, although he was in general agreement with Moore's position, he might be able to talk him into toning down some of his inflammatory rhetoric, thereby creating a better environment for any potential compromise. Moore, however, was in no mood for compromise. When Hunter tried to talk him into examining possible settlement options, Moore felt he was being lectured by Greenpeace's elder statesman. In a fit of alcohol-induced pique, he told Hunter that he was a "washed up" environmentalist whose days of leading Greenpeace were well and truly over. He should butt out of the matter and allow Moore to run things as he saw fit. Deeply wounded by his old comrade's outburst, Hunter began to think that perhaps McTaggart was right. Maybe Moore was power-hungry and out of control.[47]

A few days later, McTaggart organized a meeting with the Vancouver board and their lawyers. With Hunter backing him up, McTaggart described his vision for the future of Greenpeace. Vancouver, he insisted, would have to drop the lawsuit and relinquish its rights to the Greenpeace name outside Canada. In exchange, a newly formed Greenpeace International would pay off Vancouver's debts. Once Moore realized that Hunter and several other board members were supporting McTaggart's plan, he eventually gave in. McTaggart's proposal, it was clear to Moore, was not so different from what he himself had had in mind. The main difference—though it was a significant one—was that Moore would clearly not be at the helm of McTaggart's new organization. Remarkably, in just a few short days, McTaggart had not only solved what had seemed an intractable problem but had succeeded in convincing Greenpeace's founders to effectively turn the organization over to him.[48]

With Vancouver's surrender notice in his hand, McTaggart flew triumphantly back to San Francisco, where he received a hero's welcome. The various American branches were so relieved and grateful that the lawsuit had been avoided that it became, in McTaggart's words, "an easy day's work to pull the twenty or so American offices together into Greenpeace USA. Somebody produces a map, and I draw nine different regions onto it. That's about it."[49] For McTaggart, the entire business was reminiscent of the kind of wheeling and dealing he had done on a weekly basis during his years in the building industry.

Several months later, McTaggart convened a meeting of Greenpeace delegates from around the world. At that meeting—held in Amsterdam—Greenpeace Europe agreed to change its name to "Greenpeace Council," and invited others to join the new organization. Greenpeace USA and Greenpeace Canada were immediately accepted as members but, in the process, had to accept the bylaws of Greenpeace Europe. All the national groups signed the Greenpeace Council accord, ceding their rights to the name "Greenpeace" in exchange for voting membership on the council.

Frank Zelko

Virtually overnight, the various Greenpeace tribes were merged together to create a European-dominated international organization with a large bureaucracy, a hierarchical, centralized structure, and with its headquarters based in Amsterdam. Not surprisingly, David McTaggart was voted in as the first chairman of the new international Greenpeace organization.[50]

Within a few months of the Amsterdam meeting, McTaggart's Greenpeace International developed a sophisticated management structure, with various legal, administrative, financial, and communications arms scattered throughout the world. It was not long before these offices were staffed by professionals with degrees in human resources, marketing, and accounting. In a short time, the organization's structure bore a remarkable similarity to the mainstream environmental organizations from which Greenpeace had differentiated itself in the early 1970s. The baton of radical environmentalism was soon passed to groups such as Earth First!, Sea Shepherd Conservation Society, and the Rainforest Action Network.

Despite its success, Greenpeace never became as big as Hunter had hoped it would: in other words, it did not become the leading apostle of a secular religion based on ecology.[51] It also did not develop into the kind of grassroots, participatory movement that Irving Stowe had hoped to build. Various aspects of Greenpeace's style and tactics—such as its inability to combine spectacular direct action protest with mass participation—compromised the development of such a movement. In contrast, we can look at groups such as the Clamshell Alliance and its west coast counterpart, the Abalone Alliance, as examples of 1970s movements that engaged in direct action environmentalism, such as protesting outside nuclear power plants and carrying out peaceful "invasions" of nuclear facilities, while also embodying their intensely progressive politics in their organizational structure. The Clamshell Alliance, unlike Greenpeace, remained decentralized, unhierarchical, participatory, and consensus-driven. It engaged in what Barbara Epstein calls "prefigurative politics": an attempt to convey their vision of an ecologically sustainable and egalitarian society not just through their rhetoric and protests but also in the structure of their organization and its day-to-day operations.[52]

Certain people within Greenpeace, such as Irving Stowe, may have wanted the organization to go in this direction. Their influence by the late 1970s, however, was not as paramount as that of Hunter, Moore, and

McTaggart. To one degree or another, these influential figures had come to accept the need for hierarchy and professionalism as a by-product of Greenpeace's modus operandi. However, we must beware of the false construction of purity: Greenpeace should not necessarily feel that it is incumbent upon it to develop organizational structures that reflect some distant, idealized future society. And while the Clamshell Alliance may have gone a considerable way toward achieving this, it did so only by renouncing the kind of political influence that groups such as Greenpeace have attained.

Naturally, Greenpeace, like any organization, was not entirely responsible for its own rapid growth. Opportunity structures are constantly shifting, often in unpredictable ways, and success always entails an element of good fortune—of being in the right place at the right time. Another structural factor that frequently affects organizational development is path dependency. The fact that Greenpeace's early campaigns involved sailing to difficult-to-reach areas in order to protest nuclear testing meant that it had the expertise and experience to protest against whaling, nuclear waste dumping, and other questionable activities on the high seas.[53] Thus in a sense, Greenpeace, if it was going to succeed, had to get big. Compare this to the Society for Pollution and Environmental Control (SPEC) discussed by Jonathan Clapperton in the previous chapter of this volume. SPEC sprung up in Vancouver at almost exactly the same time as Greenpeace and with overlapping membership. It was created in order to tackle local—and to a lesser extent regional—environmental problems, particularly urban pollution in Vancouver. Its self-conscious "localism" contrasts starkly with Greenpeace's "globalism." For SPEC, therefore, success could be measured by the degree of name recognition and policy influence the organization was able to achieve in Vancouver. Given the terms that Greenpeace set for itself, however, success required achieving such recognition and influence on a global scale, thereby engaging in Wapner's "world civic politics." Getting big was thus an organizational and existential imperative.[54]

To the extent that Greenpeace was in control of its own fate, its success was in no small part due to a willingness to compromise the grassroots democratic principles held by many of its founders and supporters. Professionalization enabled the organization to maintain tight control over its campaigns and fundraising throughout the world. However, the most efficient and logical means of achieving such control on a global scale was the rapid development of a centralized and hierarchical organization with a corporate-like structure. It is not, perhaps, what its founders envisioned, but in retrospect, it appears to have been the most likely path to realizing the goals they set for themselves. To paraphrase E. F. Schumacher, small can certainly be beautiful, and for many environmental organizations it makes sense to prioritize their commitment to a democratic participatory structure rather than growth. But given Greenpeace's global outlook, its frequent need for secrecy and detailed planning, and its desire to protest environmental crimes in some of the remotest parts of the planet, staying small was never a viable option.

Notes

1   Bob Hunter, interview by author, Toronto, ON, June 2000.

2   Paul Wapner, *Environmental Activism and World Civic Politics* (Albany: State University of New York Press, 1996).

3   Tom Turner, *David Brower: The Making of the Environmental Movement* (Berkeley: University of California Press, 2015).

4   Frank Zelko, *Make It a Green Peace! The Rise of Countercultural Environmentalism* (New York: Oxford University Press, 2013). For the history of Greenpeace from the perspective of an insider, see Rex Weyler, *Greenpeace: How a Group of Ecologists, Journalists, and Visionaries Changed the World* (Vancouver: Raincoast Books, 2004).

5   Bob Hunter, *Vancouver Sun*, 24 September 1969. Hunter had a regular column in the *Sun*.

6   Hunter interview.

7   Ben Metcalfe, interview by author, Shawnigan Lake, BC, June 2000. For an analysis of McLuhan's influence on Greenpeace, see Stephen Dale, *McLuhan's Children: The Greenpeace Message and the Media* (Toronto: Between the Lines Press, 1996).

8   Jim Bohlen, interview by author, Denman Island, BC, June 2000

9   *Georgia Straight*, 11–18 November 1971, 12

10   Bohlen and Hunter interviews.

11   Metcalfe interview.

12   *Vancouver Sun*, 4 January 1972.

13   Metcalfe interview.

14   Metcalfe interview.

15   Hunter and Bohlen interviews.

16   David McTaggart with Helen Slinger, *Shadow Warrior: The Autobiography of Greenpeace International Founder David McTaggart* (London: Orion, 2002).

17   David McTaggart, *Outrage! The Ordeal of Greenpeace III* (Vancouver: J. J. Douglas, 1973).

18   Metcalfe interview.

19   *Peace News*, 6 August 1973.

20   *Times* (London), 2 June 1973.

21   *Vancouver Sun*, 11 July 1973.

22   *Guardian*, 3 February 1973.

23   McTaggart and Slinger, *Shadow Warrior*.

24   *Vancouver Sun*, 13 February 1973.

25   Quoted in Brian Fortune, "Media Mellows Greenpeace," *Terminal City Express*, 23 February 1973, 5.

26   Fortune, "Media Mellows."

27   The British pacifist publication, *Peace News* (5 May 1973), for example, simply announced that there would be a "Greenpeace activity" in Dundee. Clearly, the editors felt no need to elaborate; their readers understood that this meant an anti-nuclear protest with an environmental focus. It did not imply that the action would be carried out by Greenpeace but, rather, in the style of Greenpeace.

28   Rex Weyler, *Song of the Whale: The Dramatic Story of Dr. Paul Spong—Founder of the Greenpeace Save-the-Whales Movement—and His Startling Discoveries About Whale Intelligence* (Garden City, NY: Anchor Press/Doubleday, 1986).

29   Bob Hunter, *Warriors of the Rainbow: A Chronicle of the Greenpeace Movement* (New York: Holt, Rinehart, and Winston, 1979), 149.

30   Hunter, *Warriors*, 150–51.

31   Patrick Moore, interview by author, Vancouver, BC, May 2000; Hunter, *Warriors*, 150.

32   For more details about how they managed this, see Weyler, *Song of the Whale*.

33   Sean Cassidy, *Mind Bombs and Whale Songs: Greenpeace and the News* (PhD diss., University of Oregon, 1992), 117

34   Charles Flowers, "Between the Harpoon and the Whale," *New York Times Magazine*, 24 August 1975; Weyler, *Song of the Whale*, 170; Hunter, *Warriors*, 231–32. In a letter to Hunter, Farley Mowat conveyed what was probably a widespread sense of surprise at the campaign's success: "I must frankly admit that, when you first announced your plans, I didn't give them a chance of success. Well, I was wrong. Happily wrong, I might add." Mowat to Hunter, 14 October 1975, file 1, box, 1R4377, Greenpeace fonds, Library and Archives Canada.

35   Hunter, *Warriors*, 232–33.

36   Weyler, *Song of the Whale*, 170; Hunter, *Warriors*, 233–34

37   Hunter, *Warriors*, 245–46; Hunter interview.

38   Hunter and Moore interviews.

39   Hunter interview.

40   Hunter interview.

41   Hunter, *Warriors*, 244.

42   McTaggart interview, Paciano, Italy, October 1999.

43   Remi Parmentier, interview by author, Amsterdam, NL, October 2000. Numerous people I interviewed corroborated Parmentier's story of how McTaggart tried to convince people that he was the true founder of Greenpeace. Some even thought that McTaggart had convinced himself that this was the case.

44   Moore to various Greenpeace offices, undated (though clearly late 1977). Patrick Moore's personal papers.

45   Moore to various Greenpeace offices, undated.

46   Greenpeace San Francisco, Minutes of the Meeting of the Board of Directors, 25 July 1979. David Tussman's personal papers.

47   McTaggart interview; Hunter interview.

48   McTaggart and Slinger, *Shadow Warrior*, 148–49; McTaggart interview; Hunter, Weyler, and Moore interviews

49   McTaggart and Slinger, *Shadow Warrior*, 149.

50   Minutes of the Greenpeace Council International Meeting, 16–20 November 1979, Amsterdam. Copy from Moore's personal papers.

51   Hunter interview

52   Barbara Epstein, *Political Protest and Cultural Revolution: Nonviolent Direct Action in the 1970s and 1980s* (Berkeley: University of California Press, 1991).

53   For more on this, see Frank Zelko, "Scaling Greenpeace: From Local Activism to Global Governance," *Historical Social Research*, 42, no. 2 (2017): 318–42.

54   Wapner, *Environmental Activism*.

Lessons and Directions from the Ground Up

Jonathan Clapperton & Liza Piper

Despite the stunning downturn in Alberta's economy caused by the plummet in oil prices beginning in 2014, anti–oil/tar sands protests remain strong. Decades of resistance on the part of the provincial Progressive Conservative government to implementing adequate environmental monitoring and protection measures, along with a decade of federal rule under former Canadian Prime Minister Stephen Harper in which hostility to environmentalists and environmental legislation became normalized, has made the current provincial government's job of selling Alberta oil as environmentally responsible nearly impossible. Alberta and the oil companies operating there are desperately working to build pipelines, aiming simultaneously south, west, and east. Along every step of the way, development hearings and initial construction work have been met by fierce resistance. While many of these protesters are members of the "Green Giants"— Greenpeace, for instance, playing a prominent role as usual—it appears to be small green and Indigenous activists who are the most active, and their successes to date are showing the continued power of such mobilization. The highly contentious and polarizing TransCanada Keystone XL pipeline, which would have run south from Alberta through Montana, South Dakota, and Nebraska, encountered a groundswell of localized resistance throughout each state from a diverse mixture of interests. President

Obama put an end to this odyssey when, in November 2015, he rejected TransCanada's application (although President Donald Trump reversed course and approved the project without any public consultation).[1] With hopes for the Keystone XL project temporarily dashed, oil executives and Canadian politicians turned their attention east with the proposed Energy East project, a 4,500-kilometre pipeline from Alberta to New Brunswick. Proponents and industry have met with powerful resistance by locals, who crashed National Energy Board hearings in Montreal, and who put enough pressure on the federal regulatory body so that it suspended all hearings and witnessed three of its panellists recuse themselves following complaints of conflict of interest accusations.[2] Enbridge's Northern Gateway Pipeline Proposal, which would run from Alberta through northern British Columbia to the port of Kitimat for shipping to international markets, received constant negative press as locals and Indigenous groups along the proposed route starkly stated that they would not allow a pipeline to pass. The Unist'ot'en (a clan of the Wet'suwet'en First Nation) set up a camp on their territory, which has been continually occupied for occupied for nearly a decade, in opposition to the Northern Gateway and other pipeline proposals. In July 2016, a Federal Court of Appeal decision halted the project on the grounds that the federal government had not met its duty to consult with First Nations.[3] The other west-facing pipeline—the Kinder Morgan Trans Mountain pipeline, ending in Burnaby, British Columbia—was approved by the federal government in November 2016. After facing staunch opposition from the communities in its path, Kinder Morgan threatened to cancel the project in April 2018. The Canadian federal government then purchased the pipeline and promised to get it built with taxpayer dollars, although, on 31 August 2018, the Federal Court of Appeal quashed that approval and sent the federal government back to the review phase to examine the impacts of tanker traffic and provide adequate consultation with First Nations.[4] Opposition to this project is, unsurprisingly, ongoing.[5]

In each instance above, proponents of these projects vastly underestimated the power and the persistence of small green and Indigenous activism; such perseverance, as demonstrated throughout this volume, is nothing new. Although small-scale organizations and environmentalist efforts may not all grow big in size, that does not mean that they have languished or stayed still. As the chapters in this collection highlight, taking

Jonathan Clapperton & Liza Piper

a historical perspective on late twentieth-century environmentalism, and drawing on diverse geographical locations across Canada, the United States, and beyond, clearly illuminates the many courses and consequences of small green activism.

One advantage of a historical perspective, particularly where it is articulated through narrative, is that it welcomes contingencies: the context, personalities, and unexpected twists can be as important to our understanding of the past as the theoretical perspectives that can connect divergent stories, and which many historians aim to reinforce. The place of contingency is highlighted in Zelko's account of the rise of Greenpeace, as it is in Clapperton's analysis of SPEC, where the turn to radicalization had unanticipated consequences for those organizations. Historical narratives are also often (if not always) inclined to look for even more distant roots. As several of our contributors asked: To what extent was the small-scale activism of the late twentieth century connected to earlier conservation, environmental, or other forms of activism? For Leeming, these roots could be found, for instance, in the role of the Women's Institutes as long-standing (if somewhat dated) venues for civic engagement and activism. In the pursuit of the histories of small green activism, several of the chapters in this collection nevertheless remind us to ask, whose narrative is this? Narrative is a powerful tool for communicating the character of past environmental activism, and as such it can be used to exclude certain perspectives and interpretations. DeWitt exposes such exclusions in the histories of state and provincial parks, as well as demonstrating the importance of including non-elites in arriving at more comprehensive histories of these sites. Welch's attention to the importance of sovereignty in the practice of heritage conservation at Fort Apache similarly speaks to the question, whose history is this? Welch, moreover, emphasizes the potency of this particular site "as an antidote to colonialism" through sovereignty-driven preservation because of "its early history as a hub for the imposition and enactment of non-Apache values and its recent history as the legal battleground between the Tribe and the United States." The conscious articulation of historical narratives connects the history of late twentieth-century small green activism to the antecedents that can then help us to frame the significance of these narratives.

Willow emphasizes the importance of imagining environmentalism "not just as a trajectory of movements and beliefs but also as a rich assemblage of tools and processes." So what are the "tools and processes" that our collective cross-context analysis has served to highlight? Grossman's study of Native/non-Native alliances illuminates the central importance of coalitions to many of the different chapters: from the provincial and regional coalitions that flourished in eastern Canada according to Leeming and McLaughlin, to the shared experiences, and thus support, among Indigenous activists Kinew describes in Ontario, to the cooperation at different levels that has been essential to the parks in Costa Rica, Brazil, Canada, and the United States, which Evans examines. Where local activists have been able to build broader networks, unsurprisingly, their efforts have had greater positive effects. This trend reverberates into the present: in September 2016, First Nations from Canada and the northern United States signed a treaty, formalizing an alliance to collectively fight against pipelines from the oil sands. Thus we see how local and Indigenous organizations grow through cooperation, even if they stay the same in size. Moreover, as Evans highlights, conservation itself has enabled greater state-Indigenous cooperation in the context of parks history. He, along with Grossman in particular, thus demonstrates that not only has cooperation enabled more effective environmental activism, but environmental activism has enabled greater cooperation between otherwise opposing groups.

The need for organizations to change with the times points to a second process: that of adaptation. The Conservation Council of New Brunswick's decision to professionalize enabled it to endure longer than many other small-scale environmental counterparts. SPEC's inability to maintain its "insider" status, as it grew in scale, can also be interpreted as failure of the organization to adapt to its growth and expansion in the 1970s—it was only by restoring that insider status, which involved staying small, that SPEC was able to endure. Greenpeace, as Zelko shows, compromised its founders' grassroots democratic principles in favour of a centralized, hierarchical structure to manage its phenomenal growth. Welch presents clearly how coming to terms with Indigenous sovereignty has been an essential adaptation to ensuring Fort Apache's long-term legacy, while Clapperton's chapter on Clayoquot Sound revealed the negative consequences for environmental organizations who merely paid lip service to First Nations' rights.

Lastly, the ways in which different small green organizations were able to integrate and deploy different kinds of knowledge—in particular scientific expertise—influenced their effectiveness. Local knowledge had to be legitimated in order to influence decision making; Piper's chapter shows how the magazine *Alternatives* sought to do just that by both turning scholarly research into community activism and legitimizing Indigenous knowledge. How such knowledge gained legitimacy is a process we see playing out across the case studies presented in this collection. In fact, this aspect of small green activism proved to be so persuasive and telling that the collaborators of this collection also simultaneously worked to produce a complementary special issue of the Rachel Carson Center's *Perspectives* journal, titled "Environmental Knowledge, Environmental Politics," which delves into this topic further than we do here.[6]

These "tools and processes," then, delineate how some forms of small-scale environmentalism succeeded. Did others fail? Ultimately, the best way to measure success or failure in these chapters is to understand the goals of the groups themselves. If the purpose of 1970s-era environmental activism was to grow (after the fashion of capitalist economies), with more participants, larger budgets, and wider reach, then histories of small green activism must become histories of the "Green Giants," as articulated by Zelko in this volume. But that was not necessarily the objective of all of these activists. For Bob Hunter of Greenpeace, yes, bigger was better. But DeWitt's actors more often wanted little more than to minimize conflict, protect special places, and ensure they could continue to make a living— worthy objectives, but not ones that required significant organizational capacity and institutional structures.

One of the core themes presented in the chapter by Leeming reverberates throughout this volume: the way in which attention to small green activism also draws attention back to the material issues at the core of such organizing. Throughout this volume we see economic concerns as powerfully intertwined with environmental activism and its legacies— whether it is McLaughlin, DeWitt, and Clapperton reflecting on the role of resource development objectives in shaping state, industry, and public responsiveness to small green agendas; or Evans showing that the potential for economic benefit from increased tourism has influenced governments in both protecting and promoting spaces important to Indigenous peoples; or, in contrast, Willow and Grossman showing how economic justifications served to keep Indigenous peoples out of other spaces. This emphasis, which shifts the character of late twentieth-century environmentalism away from the influence of "post-materialism," though without discounting it, not only serves to more effectively connect this period of activism with earlier antecedents but also resonates with the call, integral to Indigenous activism, to recognize how healthy environments sustain economic and cultural sovereignty.[7]

Further Directions

There remains important work to be done on the history of small green and Indigenous environmental activism that can extend some of what the authors in this collection have presented for consideration. Not least is the need for further sustained, rigorous research into the relationships between Indigenous activists and the "Green Giants," which would illuminate divergences and continuities in relationship building and successful (or failed) alliances between environmental activists working at different scales.

Gender is integral to the histories of the conservation and environmental movements, as scholars such as Maril Hazlett, Adam Rome, and Jocelyn Thorpe have shown.[8] Gender dynamics figure in several of the chapters presented here: in the evolving character of participation in rural environmental activism described by Leeming, and in the prominence of the Women's Institutes in particular; in the substance of Marilee Little's complaint that opens McLaughlin's chapter on the Conserver Society in New Brunswick; and in the exclusions of park "elites" that DeWitt describes. While gender was not a core element of our analysis in *Environmental Activism on the Ground*, the interrelationships between gender, women's and men's activism as it relates to environmentalism, the size of environmentalist organizations, and the strategies they deploy are, as Thorpe makes clear, key issues in the history of environmentalism, especially so in the underdeveloped literature on Indigenous peoples, gender, and environmentalism. These are essential themes in works that reflect on, for instance, the rich, growing body of work on ecofeminism, such as the ways in which maternal ideologies can inform the ability of particular individuals to speak on behalf of wider environmental issues; Lois Gibbs' effective advocacy in the Love Canal disaster is but one example.[9] Therefore, in thinking about histories of small-scale environmentalism in particular, the intersectionality of gender, race, and class dynamics should be foregrounded in future research.

The chapters, including those that focus on relationships between small green activism and the state—Evans, Welch, DeWitt, and McLaughlin—highlight the potential significance of further study into the role of law and legislation in shaping activist efforts and their successes or failures. The responsiveness of states, at different levels and at different times, to public pressure via litigation and legislation is integral to understanding the efficacy of those who have advocated on behalf of environmental issues in the past. Close examination of the kinds of legislation that small green organizing historically influenced, in contrast to the impact of "Green Giants" or state-based environmental measures, could discern patterns, across different contexts, that speak more directly to the issue of when and how "small green" activists have been able to have their voices heard. William Buzbee's recent *Fighting Westway: Environmental Law, Citizen Activism, and the Regulatory War that Transformed New York City* describes how a coalition of environmentalists, citizens, and their lawyers successfully opposed a highway project that was supported by presidents, senators, governors, business, and unions. *Fighting Westway* provides an excellent example of the promise a study of the law and small green activism might provide in reshaping the dominant perception of the legal system as a tool of the elite and those with the means to afford it, who then use the law to halt environmental (and other) activism.[10] Indeed, Paul Sabin's article "Environmental Law and the End of the New Deal Order" effectively conceptualizes "fledgling" public interest environmental law firms as small-scale activist groups along lines similar to how we do so throughout this collection, while Douglas Bevington, in *The Rebirth of Environmentalism*, sees litigation as a key tactic in small, grassroots biodiversity organizations having a "big" impact despite their meagre resources.[11] Indigenous groups, in particular, have been successful in using litigation to gain power over environmental use—from the landmark United

States v. Washington, or "Boldt," decision (1974) in Washington State over tribal fishing, to the recent (2016) Federal Court of Appeal decision in Canada to quash Enbridge's Northern Gateway pipeline certificates for failing in its constitutional duty to consult Indigenous peoples, as mentioned above.[12] Tribes in the United States have arguably greater leeway in this regard, possessing the legal and judicial sovereignty to set their own environmental standards, while First Nations in British Columbia have different political and strategic opportunities because of the lack of treaties in that province.[13] Moreover, over the past couple of decades, legal firms specializing in Indigenous and environmental law have sprung up across the continent, notably in the Pacific Northwest. Of course, the legal structure has been—and continues to be—used to exclude public involvement in environmental decision making, including, as Chris Tollefson, Joan Sherman, and Michael Gismondi describe, strategic lawsuits against public participation (or SLAPPs).

Social media is becoming increasingly vital for environmental organizations and activism. While few academic studies exist in this area, especially in North America, those that do exist have demonstrated some promising results for its application to Indigenous and small green organizing. For instance, Michael Dahlberg-Grundberg and Johan Örestig's analysis of social media use in an anti-mining struggle in Sweden argues that scholars must redirect their attention from large-scale campaigns to scrutinize the ways in which "geographically confined actors use social media to engage in protests." They further suggest that the combination of on-site resistance with social media strategies, such as through Facebook pages (sometimes referred to as "clicktivism") "added a translocal dimension to the . . . conflict. Media users were able to extend a locally and physically situated protest by linking it to a global contentious issue such as the mining boom and its consequences for indigenous populations."[14] Other international case studies provide equally important insights into the relationship between local activism and the broader geographical reach of social media.[15] In North America, Mark C. J. Stoddart and Laura MacDonald examine whether or not the "internet is a more open space than traditional media or activists to speak on behalf of nature," and they do so by analyzing the conflict over the proposed Jumbo Glacier ski resort in British Columbia.[16] A burgeoning body of work is also emerging that analyzes the extent to which Indigenous activism is both enhanced and limited by the use of digital media.[17] At Standing Rock, where Indigenous activists and their allies sought to halt the Dakota Access Pipeline through direct-action protest beginning in 2016, for example, social media was essential in coordinating strategy among activists in the field and creating a vast support network.[18] Another aspect of social media and environmental activism research includes the role and impact of "clicktivism." Many of the chapters in *Environmental Activism on the Ground* examine topics that do not consider the years when social media was available, or mainstream; if extended in temporal scope, however, they would certainly provide valuable insight into how tactics and strategies change or how they stay the same. Moreover, such studies could also test assertions that while non-profit organizations are frequently early adopters of new technology, environmental organizations lag behind.[19]

Lastly, further examples from other places will continue to refine our understanding of the diverse and interconnected character of small green organizing around the globe, and how any particular local context connects to broader regional or national trends.[20] Case studies are indispensable to deepening our understanding of the history of small green activism precisely because the scale of such activities can preclude larger analyses: the records available for study and individuals willing to be interviewed are, by definition, fewer and smaller in scope, where they exist at all. By pursuing more such localized research, we stand to better understand the interconnectedness of late twentieth-century activism, as well as the enduring importance of place.

Notes

1   Associated Press, "Barack Obama Rejects Keystone XL Pipeline Citing 'National Interest," *CBC News*, 6 November 2015, http://www.cbc.ca/news/business/keystone-xl-pipeline-obama-1.3307440. North Dakota, meanwhile, became the site of another protest event, with thousands of Indigenous people, along with their environmentalist allies, seeking to halt the Dakota Access Pipeline, which Obama halted, only for Trump to reverse this order as well.

2   Sabrina Marandola, "NEB Panel Members Step Down After Flurry of Criticism," *CBC News*, 9 September 2016, http://www.cbc.ca/news/canada/montreal/neb-panel-steps-down-1.3755872; and Canadian Press, "Energy East Pipeline Further in Doubt

After Panel Quits," *Toronto Star*, 12 September 2016, https://www.thestar.com/business/2016/09/12/energy-east-pipeline-further-in-doubt-after-panel-quits-analyst-says.html.

3   Jason Proctor, "Northern Gateway Pipeline Approval Overturned," *CBC News*, 30 June 2016, https://www.cbc.ca/news/canada/british-columbia/northern-gateway-pipeline-federal-court-of-appeal-1.3659561.

4   Laura Kane, "Court Ruling Quashes Approval of Trans Mountain," CTV News, 30 August 2018, https://www.ctvnews.ca/business/court-ruling-quashes-approval-of-trans-mountain-1.4073752; Canadian Press, "Feds restart Indigenous pipeline consultations, stoke caution from First Nations," CTV News, 3 October 2018, https://www.ctvnews.ca/politics/feds-restart-indigenous-pipeline-consultations-stoke-caution-from-first-nations-1.4119363; and Canadian Press, "National Energy Board ordered to redo Trans Mountain review in 22 weeks in bid to get pipeline approved," *Financial Post*, 21 September 2018, https://business.financialpost.com/commodities/energy/feds-launching-review-of-oil-tanker-traffic-in-bid-to-renew-pipeline-approval.

5   Krystalle Ramlakhan, "Protesters Haul Fake Pipeline to Parliament Hill as Trans Mountain Deadline Nears," *CBC News*, 21 July 2018, https://www.cbc.ca/news/canada/ottawa/trans-mountain-pipeline-kinder-morgan-deal-deadline-federal-liberal-government-justin-trudeau-canada-1.4756653.

6   Jonathan Clapperton and Liza Piper, eds., "Environmental Knowledge, Environmental Politics: Case Studies from Canada and Western Europe," *RCC Perspectives* 2016/4, http://www.environmentandsociety.org/perspectives/2016/4/environmental-knowledge-environmental-politics-case-studies-canada-and-western.

7   For an example of a turn toward this approach, see Kathleen Pickering Sherman, James Van Lanen, and Richard Sherman, "Practical Environmentalism on the Pine Ridge Reservation: Confronting Structural Constraints to Indigenous Stewardship," *Human Ecology* 38, no. 4 (2010): 507–20.

8   Maril Hazlett, "'Woman vs. Man vs. Bugs': Gender and Popular Culture in Early Reactions to Silent Spring," *Environmental History* 9, no. 4 (2004): 701–29; Adam Rome, "'Political Hermaphrodites': Gender and Environmental Reform in Progressive America," *Environmental History* 11, no. 3 (2006): 440–63; Jocelyn Thorpe, *Temagami's Tangled Wild: Race, Gender and the Making of Canadian Nature* (Vancouver: UBC Press, 2012).

9   For more on maternal feminism and ecofeminism, see Sherilyn MacGregor, *Beyond Mothering Earth: Ecological Citizenship and the Politics of Care* (Vancouver: UBC Press, 2006); and Stacy Alaimo, "Cyborg and Ecofeminist Interventions: Challenges for an Environmental Feminism," *Feminist Studies* 20, no. 1 (1994): 133–52. For further reading on ecofeminism and small green activism, see: Niamh Moore-Cherry's *The Changing Nature of Eco/Feminism: Telling Stories from Clayoquot Sound* (Vancouver: UBC Press, 2015); Mark Stoddard and David Tindall, "Feminism and Environmentalism: Perspectives on Gender in the BC Environmental Movement During the 1990s," *BC Studies* 165 (Spring 2010): 75–100; Clayton D. Smith, "Environmentalism, Feminism, and Gender," *Sociological Inquiry* 71, no. 3 (2001): 314–34; Cecile Jackson, "Women/Nature or Gender/History? A Critique of Ecofeminist

'Development,'" *Journal of Peasant Studies* 20, no. 3 (1993): 389–418; Susan A. Mann, "Pioneers of U.S. Ecofeminism and Environmental Justice," *Feminist Formations* 23, no. 2 (2011): 1–25; Rod Bantjes and Tanya Trussler, "Feminism and the Grass Roots: Women and Environmentalism in Nova Scotia, 1980–1983," *Canadian Review of Sociology & Anthropology* 36, no. 2 (1999): 179–97; Noël Sturgeon, *Ecofeminist Natures: Race, Gender, Feminist Theory, and Political Action* (New York: Routledge, 2016 [1997]); Greta Gaard, ed., *Ecofeminism: Women, Animals, Nature* (Philadelphia: Temple University Press, 1993); and Greta Gaard, "Ecofeminism Revisited: Rejecting Essentialism and Re-Placing Species in a Material Feminist Environmentalism," *Feminist Formations* 23, no. 2 (2011): 26–53.

10   William W. Buzbee, *Fighting Westway: Environmental Law, Citizen Activism, and the Regulatory War that Transformed New York City* (Ithaca, NY: Cornell University Press, 2014).

11   Paul Sabin, "Environmental Law and the End of the New Deal Order," *Law & History Review* 33, no. 4 (2015): 965–1003; and Douglas Bevington, *The Rebirth of Environmentalism: Grassroots Activism from the Spotted Owl to the Polar Bear* (Washington, DC: Island Press, 2009). For similar works showing how small-scale groups with limited resources used litigation as a means of empowerment, see: Christopher W. Wells, "From Freeway to Parkway: Federal Law, Grassroots Environmental Protest, and the Evolving Design of Interstate-35E in Saint Paul, Minnesota," *Journal of Planning History* 11, no. 1 (2012): 8–26; Darren Speece, "From Corporatism to Citizen Oversight: The Legal Fight Over California Redwoods, 1970–1996," *Environmental History* 14, no. 4 (2009): 705–36; and Darren F. Speece, *Defending Giants: The Redwood Wars and the Transformation of American Environmental Politics* (Seattle: University of Washington Press, 2016).

12   Gary Mason, "Northern Gateway Ruling a Reminder of Governments' Duty to Consult," *Globe and Mail*, 1 July 2016.

13   For more information on Native American sovereignty and the creation, or use, of environmental laws to protect their natural resources as a central feature of activism, see: Darren Ranco and Dean Suagee, "Tribal sovereignty and the Problem of Difference in Environmental Regulation: Observations on 'Measured Separatism' in Indian Country," *Antipode* 39, no. 4 (2007): 691–707; and Steven E. Silvern, "Reclaiming the Reservation: The Geopolitics of Wisconsin Anishinaabe Resource Rights," *American Indian Culture & Research Journal* 24, no. 3 (2000): 131–53. In British Columbia, First Nations without a treaty have used that status to contest numerous industrial projects on their traditional territories, perhaps oil and gas pipelines most of all.

14   Michael Dahlberg-Grundberg and Johan Örestig, "Extending the Local: Activist Types and Forms of Social Media Use in the Case of an Anti-Mining Struggle," *Social Movement Studies* 16, no. 3 (2017): 309–22. "Clicktivism" refers to activism conducted via the Internet, and current debates revolve around its effectiveness. While it has enabled issues to be circulated quickly regardless of borders, critics contend that it is a lazy form of activism ("slacktivism") and gives people who participate in it a false sense of accomplishment. For further reading see M. Butler, *Clicktivism, Slacktivism, or Real Activism: Cultural Codes of American Activism in the Internet Era* (Boulder: University of Colorado Press, 2011).

15   See, for examples: Natalie Pang and Pei Wen Law, "Retweeting #WorldEnvironmentDay: A Study of Content Features and Visual Rhetoric in an Environmental Movement," *Computers in Human Behavior* 69 (April 2017): 54–61; and Daniel Halpern, Andres Rosenberg, and Eduardo Arraiagada, "Who Are those Green Guys? Understanding Online Activism in Chile from a Communicational Perspective," *Palabra Clave* 16, no. 3 (2013): 729–59.

16   See Mark C. J. Stoddart and Laura MacDonald, "Media and the Internet as Sites for Environmental Movement Activism for Jumbo Pass, British Columbia," *Canadian Journal of Sociology* 36, no. 4 (2011): 313–36.

17   See, for examples: Tanja Dreher, Kerry McCallum, and Lisa Waller, "Indigenous Voices and Mediatized Policy-making in the Digital Age," *Information, Communication & Society* 19, no. 1 (2016): 23–39; Terria Smith and Vincent Medina, "Tribal Support Across the State for Standing Rock," *News from Native California* 30, no. 2 (2016/17): 8–11; Marie Alohalani, "Mauna Kea: Ho'omana Hawai'I and Protecting the Sacred," *Journal for the Study of Religion, Nature & Culture* 10, no. 2 (2016): 150–69; and Jane Bailey and Sara Shayan, "Missing and Murdered Indigenous Women Crisis: Technological Dimensions," *Canadian Journal of Women & the Law* 28, no. 2 (2016): 321–41.

18   Hayley Johnson, "#NoDAPL: Social Media, Empowerment, and Civic Participation at Standing Rock," *Library Trends* 66, no. 2 (2017): 155–75.

19   Stoddart and MacDonald, "Media and the Internet as Sites for Environmental Movement Activism," 317.

20   The promise of such case studies are exemplified in Marco Armiero and Lisa Sedrez, eds., *A History of Environmentalism: Local Struggles, Global Histories* (London: Bloomsbury, 2014).

BIBLIOGRAPHY

Archival Sources

APPA	Algonquin Provincial Park Archives
CCL	Cardinal Carter Library, King's University College, London, Ontario
CVA	City of Vancouver Archives
DUA-SC	Dalhousie University Archives and Special Collections
GA-CAC	Glenbow Archives, Coal Association of Canada Fonds
LUA-JGN	Laurier University Archives, James Gordon Nelson Fonds
LUA-GK	Laurier University Archives, Gerald Killan Fonds
LAC	Library and Archives Canada
PAA	Provincial Archives of Alberta
PANB-CCNB	Provincial Archives of New Brunswick, Conservation Council of New Brunswick Fonds
PANS-EAC	Public Archives of Nova Scotia, Ecology Action Centre Fonds
PANS-RCU	Public Archives of Nova Scotia, Royal Commission on Uranium Mining Fonds

Selected Published Material

Abreu-Ferreira, Darlene. "Oil and Lubicons Don't Mix: A Land Claim in Northern Alberta in Historical Perspective." *Canadian Journal of Native Studies* 12, no. 1 (1992): 1–35.

Adamson, Joni. *American Indian Literature, Environmental Justice, and Ecocriticism: The Middle Place.* Tucson: University of Arizona Press, 2001.

Agrawal, Arun. "Common Resources and Institutional Sustainability." In *The Drama of the Commons*, edited by Elinor Ostrom, Thomas Dietz, Nives Dolsak, Paul C. Stern, Susan Stonich, and Elke U. Weber, 41–86. Washington, DC: National Research Council, 2002.

Agyeman, Julian, and Briony Angus. "The Role of Civic Environmentalism in the Pursuit of Sustainable Communities." *Journal of Environmental Planning and Management* 46, no. 3 (2003): 345–63.

Agyeman, Julian, Peter Cole, Randolph Haluza-Delay, and Pay O'Riley, eds. *Environmental Justice in Canada*. Vancouver: UBC Press, 2009.

Alaimo, Stacy. "Cyborg and Ecofeminist Interventions: Challenges for an Environmental Feminism." *Feminist Studies* 20, no. 1 (1994): 133–52.

Alfred, Taiaiake, and Jeff Corntassel. "Being Indigenous: Resurgences against Contemporary Colonialism." *Government and Opposition* 40, no. 4 (2005): 597–614.

Alohalani, Marie. "Mauna Kea: Ho'omana Hawai'I and Protecting the Sacred." *Journal for the Study of Religion, Nature & Culture* 10, no. 2 (2016): 150–69.

Alper, Donald K. "Transboundary Environmental Relations in British Columbia and the Pacific Northwest." *American Review of Canadian Studies* 27, no. 3 (1997): 359–83.

Amend, Stephen, and Thora Amend eds. *¿Espacios sin Habitantes?: Parques Nacionales de América del Sur*. Caracas: Editorial Nueva Sociedad, 1992.

Anderson, Marnie. *Women of the West Coast: Stories of Clayoquot Sound Then and Now*. Sidney, BC: Sand Dollar Press, 2004.

Anderson, Terry, and Laura E. Huggins. *Greener Than Thou: Are You Really an Environmentalist?* Stanford, CA: Hoover Institution Press, 2008.

Armiero, Marco, and Lise Sedrez, eds. *A History of Environmentalism: Local Struggles, Global Histories*. London: Bloomsbury Academic, 2014.

Atleo (Umeek), E. Richard. *Principles of Tsawalk: An Indigenous Approach to a Global Crisis*. Vancouver: UBC Press, 2011.

———. *Tsawalk: A Nuu-chah-nulth Worldview*. Vancouver: UBC Press, 2004.

Bailey, Jane, and Sara Shayan. "Missing and Murdered Indigenous Women Crisis: Technological Dimensions." *Canadian Journal of Women & the Law* 28, no. 2 (2016): 321–41.

Bantjes, Rod, and Tanya Trussler. "Feminism and the Grass Roots: Women and Environmentalism in Nova Scotia, 1980–1983." *Canadian Review of Sociology & Anthropology* 36, no. 2 (1999): 179–97.

Barca, Stefania. "Laboring the Earth: Transnational Reflections on the Environmental History of Work." *Environmental History* 19, no.1 (2014): 1–25.

Becker, Egon. "Social-Ecological Systems as Epistemic Objects." In *Human-Nature Interactions in the Anthropocene*, edited by Marion Glaser, Gesche Krause, Beate Ratter, and Martin Welp, 37–50. New York: Routledge, 2012.

Berkes, Fikret. "Community-Based Conservation in a Globalized World." *Proceedings of the National Academy of Sciences* 104, no. 39 (2007): 15188–93.

———. "Rethinking Community-Based Conservation." *Conservation Biology* 18, no. 3 (2004): 621–30.

Berman, Tzeporah. *This Crazy Time: Living our Environmental Challenge*. Toronto: Knopf Canada, 2011.

Berman, Tzeporah, et al., *Clayoquot and Dissent*. Vancouver: Ronsdale Press, 1994.

Bess, Michael. *The Light-Green Society: Ecology and Technological Modernity in France, 1960-2000*. Chicago: University of Chicago Press, 2003.

Betsill, Michelle M., and Elisabeth Corell. "Analytical Framework: Assessing the Influence of NGO Diplomats." In *NGO Dipomacy: The Influence of Nongovernmental Organizations in International Environmental Negotiations*, edited by Michelle Betsill and Elisabeth Corell. Cambridge, MA: MIT Press, 2008, 19–41

Bevington, Douglas. *The Rebirth of Environmentalism: Grassroots Activism from the Spotted Owl to the Polar Bear*. Washington, DC: Island Press, 2009.

Bickerton, James. *Nova Scotia, Ottawa, and the Politics of Regional Development*. Toronto: University of Toronto Press, 1990.

Bini, Elisabetta, Giuliano Garavini, and Federico Romero, eds. *Oil Shock: The 1973 Crisis and its Economic Legacy*. London: I. B. Tauris, 2016.

Binnema, Theodore, and Melanie Niemi. "'Let the Line be Drawn Now': Wilderness, Conservation, and the Exclusion of Aboriginal People from Banff National Park in Canada." *Environmental History* 11, no. 4 (2006): 724–50.

Blake, Donald E., Neil Guppy, and Peter Urmetzer. "Canadian Public Opinion and Environmental Action: Evidence from British Columbia." *Canadian Journal of Political Science* 30, no. 3 (1997): 451–72.

Blomquist, Glenn C., and John C. Whitehead. "Existence Value, Contingent Valuation, and Natural Resources Damages Assessment." *Growth and Change* 26 (1995): 573–89.

Booth, Annie L., and Norm W. Skelton. "'We are Fighting for Ourselves': First Nations' Evaluation of British Columbia and Canadian Environmental Assessment Processes." *Journal of Environmental Assessment Policy and Management* 13, no. 3 (2011): 367–404.

———. "You Spoil Everything": Indigenous Peoples and the Consequences of Industrial Development in British Columbia." *Environment, Development and Sustainability* 13, no. 4 (2011): 685–702.

Boyd, David. *Unnatural Law: Rethinking Canadian Environmental Law and Policy*. Vancouver: UBC Press, 2003.

Bradley, Ben. "Manning Park and the Aesthetics of Automobile Accessibility in 1950s British Columbia." *BC Studies* 170 (2011): 41–65.

———. "Photographing the High and Low in British Columbia's Provincial Parks: A Photo Essay." *BC Studies* 170 (2012): 153–69.

Braun, Bruce. *The Intemperate Rainforest: Nature, Culture, and Power on Canada's West Coast*. Minneapolis: University of Minnesota Press, 2002.

Bray, David Barton, Leticia Merino-Pérez, and Deborah Barry, eds. *The Community Forests of Mexico: Managing for Sustainable Landscapes*. Austin: University of Texas Press, 2005.

Brayboy, Bryan McKinley, and Donna Deyhle. "Insider-Outsider: Researchers in American Indian Communities." *Theory Into Practice* 39, no. 3 (2000): 163–69.

Brockington, Dan. *Fortress Conservation: The Preservation of the Mkomazi Game Reserves, Tanzania*. Bloomington: Indiana University Press, 2002.

Brody, Hugh. *Maps and Dreams: Indians and the British Columbia Frontier*. Prospect Heights, IL: Waveland Press, 1981.

Brosius, J. Peter. "Endangered Forest, Endangered People: Environmentalist Representations of Indigenous Knowledge." *Human Ecology* 27, no. 1 (1997): 47–69.

Brosius, J. Peter, Anna Lowenhaupt Tsing, and Charles Zerner, eds. *Communities and Conservation: Histories and Politics of Community-Based Natural Resource Management*. Lanham, MD: AltaMira Books, 2005.

Bullard, Robert. *Dumping in Dixie: Race, Class, and Environmental Quality*. Boulder, CO: Westview Press, 1990.

Burke, Brian, and Boone Shear. "Introduction: Engaged Scholarship for Non-Capitalist Political Ecologies." *Journal of Political Ecology* 21 (2014): 127–44.

Burnham, Phillip. *Indian Country, God's Country: Native Americans and the National Parks*. Washington, DC: Island Press, 2000.

Buzbee, William W. *Fighting Westway: Environmental Law, Citizen Activism, and the Regulatory War that Transformed New York City*. Ithaca, NY: Cornell University Press, 2014.

Byrd, Jodi A., and Michael Rothberg. "Between Subalternity and Indigeneity: Critical Categories for Postcolonial Studies." *Interventions* 13, no. 1 (2011): 1–12.

Byrnes, W. Malcolm. "Climate Justice: Hurricane Katrina, and African American Environmentalism." *Journal of African American Studies* 18, no. 3 (2014): 305–14.

Campbell, Bruce, and Silvia López Ortíz, eds. *Integrating Agriculture, Conservation, and Ecotourism: Societal Influences*. New York: Springer, 2012.

Campbell, Claire E., ed. *A Century of Parks Canada, 1911–2011*. Calgary: University of Calgary Press, 2011.

Canadian Energy Development Systems International, Inc. *A Mid-Term Evaluation of the Canada/New Brunswick Conservation and Renewable Demonstration Agreement*. Ottawa: CEDSI Inc., July 1983.

Carlson, Hans. *Home is the Hunter: The James Bay Cree and Their Land*. Vancouver: UBC Press, 2008.

Carlson, Keith Thor, and Jonathan Clapperton. "Introduction: Special Places and Protected Spaces: Historical and Global Perspectives on Non-National Parks in Canada and Abroad." *Environment and History* 18 (2012): 475–96.

Carroll, William K., and Robert A. Hackett. "Democratic Media Activism through the Lens of Social Movement Theory." *Media, Culture & Society* 28, no. 1 (2006): 83–104.

Carroll, William K., and R. S. Ratner. "Old Unions and New Social Movements." *Labour/ Le Travail* 35 (Spring 1995): 195–221.

———. "Social Movements and Counter-Hegemony: Lessons from the Field." *New Proposals: Journal of Marxism and Interdisciplinary Inquiry* 4, no. 1 (2010): 7–22.

Carrus, G., M. Bonaiuto, and M. Bonnes. "Environmental Concern, Regional Identity, and Support for Protected Areas in Italy." *Environment and Behavior* 37, no. 2 (2005): 237–75.

Cassidy, Sean. "Mind Bombs and Whale Songs: Greenpeace and the News." PhD diss., University of Oregon, 1992.

Clapperton, Jonathan. "Desolate Viewscapes: Sliammon First Nation, Desolation Sound Marine Park and Environmental Narratives." *Environment and History* 18 (2012): 529–59.

———. "Stewards of the Earth? Aboriginal Peoples, Environmentalists and Historical Representation." PhD diss., University of Saskatchewan, 2012.

———. Entrenching the 'Ecological Indian': Aboriginal Peoples and Environmental Protest in James Bay, Northern Saskatchewan, and Clayoquot Sound." In *The History of Canada's Environmental Movement*, ed. by Owen Temby, Don Munton, Peter J. Stoett, and Ryan O'Connor. Calgary: University of Calgary Press (under review).

Clayton, Jenny. "'Human Beings Need Places Unchanged by Themselves': Defining and Debating Wilderness in the West Kootenays, 1969–74." *BC Studies* 170 (2011): 93–118.

Clément, Dominique. "'I Believe in Human Rights, Not Women's Rights': Women and the Human Rights State, 1969–1984." *Radical History Review* 101 (Spring 2008): 107–29.

Clowater, G. Brent. "Canadian Science Policy and the Retreat from Transformative Politics: The Final Years of the Science Council of Canada." *Scientia Canadensis* 35, no. 1–2 (2012): 113–17.

Clowe, Richmond L., and Imre Sutton, eds. *Trusteeship in Change: Toward Tribal Autonomy in Resource Management.* Boulder: University of Colorado Press, 2001.

Coates, Colin M., ed. *Canadian Countercultures and the Environment.* Calgary: University of Calgary Press, 2016.

Colchester, M. "Conservation Policy and Indigenous Peoples." *Environmental Science and Politics* 7, no. 3 (2004): 145–53.

Colpitts, George. *Fish Wars and Trout Travesties: Saving Southern Alberta's Coldwater Streams in the 1920s.* Edmonton: AU Press, 2018.

Conard, Rebecca. *Places of Quiet Beauty: Parks, Preserves, and Environmentalism.* Iowa City: University of Iowa Press, 1997.

Conklin, Beth A., and Laura R. Graham. "The Shifting Middle Ground: Amazonian Indians and Eco-Politics." *American Anthropologist* 97, no. 4 (1995): 695–710.

Conrad, Margaret. "The Atlantic Revolution of the 1950s." In *Beyond Anger and Longing: Community and Development in Atlantic Canada*, edited by Berkeley Fleming, 55–98. Fredericton: Acadiensis, 1988.

Costanza, R., et al. "The Value of the World's Ecosystem Services and Natural Capital." *Nature* 387 (15 May 1997): 253–60.

Cox, Thomas R. *The Park Builders: A History of State Parks in the Pacific Northwest.* Seattle: University of Washington Press, 1988.

Cronon, William. "Modes of Prophecy and Production: Placing Nature in History." *Journal of American History* 76, no. 4 (1990): 1122–31.

———, ed. *Uncommon Ground: Rethinking the Human Place in Nature.* New York: W. W. Norton, 1995.

Crosby, Alfred. *Ecological Imperialism: The Biological Expansion of Europe, 900–1900.* Cambridge: Cambridge University Press, 1986.

Crossley, Nick. *Making Sense of Social Movements.* Buckingham, UK: Open University Press, 2002.

Crutzen, Paul J. "Geology of Mankind." *Nature* 415, no. 6867 (2002): 23.

Dahlberg-Grundberg, Michael, and Johan Örestig. "Extending the Local: Activist Types and Forms of Social Media Use in the Case of an Anti-mining Struggle." *Social Movement Studies* 16, no. 3 (May 2017): 309–22.

Dale, Stephen. *McLuhan's Children: The Greenpeace Message and the Media.* Toronto: Between the Lines Press, 1996.

Dark, Alx. "Public Sphere Politics and Community Conflict over the Environment and Native Land Rights in Clayoquot Sound, British Columbia." PhD diss., New York University, 1998.

Davis, Rachel, and Daniel M. Franks. "Costs of Company-Community Conflict in the Extractive Sector." *Corporate Social Responsibility Initiative Report No. 66.* Cambridge, MA: Harvard Kennedy School, 2014. http://www.hks.harvard.edu/m-rcbg/CSRI/research/Costs%20of%20Conflict_Davis%20%20Franks.pdf.

Davisson, Lori. "Fort Apache, Arizona Territory: 1870–1922." *The Smoke Signal* 78. Tucson, AZ: Tucson Corral of Westerners, 2004.

Davisson, Lori, with Edgar Perry and the Original Staff of the White Mountain Apache Cultural Center. *Dispatches from the Fort Apache Scout: White Mountain and Cibecue Apache History Through 1881.* Edited by John R. Welch. Tucson: University of Arizona Press, 2016.

Dewey, Scott. "Working for the Environment: Organized Labor and the Origins of Environmentalism in the United States, 1948–1970." *Environmental History* 3, no. 1 (1998): 45–63.

DeWitt, Jessica. "A Convergence of Recreational and Conservation Ideals: The Cook Forest State Park Campaign, 1910–1928." Master's thesis, University of Rochester, 2011.

———. "A Lifestyle Off the Beaten Path: Cook Forest State Park and the Men and Women of Its Tourism Industry." Senior Thesis, Bethany College, 2008.

Dewitt, John. *Civic Environmentalism: Alternatives to Regulation in States and Communities*. Washington, DC: CQ Press, 1994.

Donovan, Richard. "Boscosa: Forest Conservation and Management through Local Institutions (Costa Rica)." In *Natural Connections: Perspectives on Community-Based Conservation*, edited by David Western, 215–33. Washington, DC: Island Press, 1994.

Dorst, Adrian, and Cameron Young, *Clayoquot: On the Wild Side*. Vancouver: Western Canadian Wilderness Committee, 1990.

Dowie, Mark. "American Environmentalism: A Movement Courting Irrelevance." *World Policy Journal* 9, no. 1 (1991/92): 67–92.

———. *Conservation Refugees: The Hundred-Year Conflict between Global Conservation and Native Peoples*. Cambridge, MA: MIT Press, 2009.

———. *Losing Ground: American Environmentalism at the Close of the Twentieth Century*. Cambridge, MA: MIT Press, 1996.

Dreher, Tanja, Kerry McCallum, and Lisa Waller. "Indigenous Voices and Mediatized Policy-making in the Digital Age." *Information, Communication & Society* 19, no. 1 (January 2016): 23–39.

Drissen, Paul. *Eco-Imperialism: Green Power, Black Death*. Bellevue, WA: Free Enterprise Press, 2003.

Dunaway, Finis. *Seeing Green: The Use and Abuse of American Environmental Images*. Chicago: University of Chicago Press, 2015.

Early, Frances. "'A Grandly Subversive Time': The Halifax Branch of the Voice of Women in the 1960s." In *Mothers of the Municipality: Women, Work, and Social Policy in Post-1945 Halifax*, edited by Judith Fingard and Janet Guildford, 253–80. Toronto: University of Toronto Press, 2005.

Egbers, Adrian. "Going Nuclear: The Origins of New Brunswick's Nuclear Industry, 1950–1983." MA thesis, Dalhousie University, 2008.

Ehrlich, Paul R. *The Population Bomb*. New York: Ballantine Books, 1968.

Eisinger, Peter. "The Conditions of Protest in American Cities." *American Political Science Review* 67, no. 1 (1973): 11–28.

Embry, Jessie L., ed. *Oral History, Community, and Work in the American West*. Tucson: University of Arizona Press, 2013.

Epstein, Barbara. *Political Protest and Cultural Revolution: Nonviolent Direct Action in the 1970s and 1980s*. Berkeley: University of California Press, 1991.

Evans, Sterling, ed. *American Indians in American History, 1870–2001: A Companion Reader*. Greenport, CT: Praeger Press, 2001.

———. "Badlands and Bones: Towards a Conservation and Social History of Dinosaur Provincial Park, Alberta." In *Place and Replace: Essays on Western Canada*, edited by Adele Perry, Esyllt W. Jones, and Leah Morton. Winnipeg: University of Manitoba Press, 2012.

———. *The Green Republic: A Conservation History of Costa Rica*. Austin: University of Texas Press, 1999.

Farish, Matthew, and P. Whitney Lackenbauer. "High Modernism in the Arctic: Planning Frobisher Bay and Inuvik." *Journal of Historical Geography* 35, no. 3 (2009): 517–44.

Finney, Carolyn. *Black Faces, White Spaces: Reimagining the Relationship of African Americans to the Great Outdoors*. Chapel Hill: University of North Carolina Press, 2014.

Fisher, William H. "Megadevelopment, Environmentalism, and Resistance: The Institutional Context of Kayapó Indigenous Politics in Central Brazil." *Human Organization* 53, no. 3 (1994): 220–32.

Forbes, Ernest. *The Maritime Rights Movement 1919–1927: A Study in Canadian Regionalism*. Montreal: McGill-Queen's University Press, 1979.

Foreman, Dave. *Confessions of an Eco-Warrior*. New York: Crown Trade Paperbacks, 1991.

———. "Take Back the Conservation Movement." *International Journal of Wilderness* 12, no. 1 (2006): 4–8.

Foreman, Dave, and Bill Haywood, eds. *Ecodefense: A Field Guide to Monkeywrenching*. 3rd ed. Chico, CA: Abbzug Press, 2002.

Franks, D. M., R. Davis, A. J. Bebbington, S. H. Ali, D. Kemp, and M. Scurrah. "Conflict Translates Environmental and Social risk into Business Costs." *Proceedings of the National Academy of Sciences* (2014). http://www.pnas.org/cgi/doi/10.1073/pnas.1405135111.

Frey, Patrice. "Making the Case: Historic Preservation as Sustainable Development." Washington, DC: National Trust for Historic Preservation, 2007.

Fumoleau, René. *As Long as This Land Shall Last: A History of Treaty 8 and Treaty 11, 1870–1939*. Calgary: University of Calgary Press, 2004, first published 1975.

Gaard, Greta. "Ecofeminism Revisited: Rejecting Essentialism and Re-Placing Species in a Material Feminist Environmentalism." *Feminist Formations* 23, no. 2 (2011): 26–53.

———, ed. *Ecofeminism: Women, Animals, Nature*. Philadelphia: Temple University Press, 1993.

Gauna, Eileen. "El Dia De Los Muertos: The Death and Rebirth of the Environmental Movement." *Environmental Law* 38, no. 2 (2008): 457–72.

George, Paul. *Big Trees Not Big Stumps: 25 Years of Campaigning to Save Wilderness with the Wilderness Committee*. Vancouver: Western Canadian Wilderness Committee, 2006.

Ghoghaie, Nahal. "Native/non-Native Watershed Management in an Era of Climate Change: Freshwater Storage in the Snohomish Basin." MA thesis, The Evergreen State College, 2011.

Gibson-Graham, J. K., and Gerda Roelvink, "An Economic Ethics for the Anthropocene." *Antipode* 41, S1 (2009): 320–346.

Gissibl, Bernhard, Sabine Höhler, and Patrick Kupper, eds. *Civilizing Nature: National Parks in Global Historical Perspective.* New York: Berghahn Books, 2012.

Goetze, Tara C. "Empowered Co-Management: Towards Power-Sharing and Indigenous Rights in Clayoquot Sound, BC." *Anthropologica* 47, no. 2 (2005): 247–65.

Gordon, Robert. "'Shell no!': OCAW and the Labor-Environmental Alliance." *Environmental History* 3, no. 4 (1998): 460–87.

Gosine, Andil. *Environmental Justice and Racism in Canada: An Introduction.* Toronto: Emond Montgomery, 2008.

Gottlieb, Robert. *Forcing the Spring: The Transformation of the American Environmental Movement.* Washington, DC: Island Press, 1993.

Grele, Ronald J. "Oral History as Evidence." In *History of Oral History: Foundations and Methodology,* edited by Thomas L. Charlton, Lois E. Myers, and Rebecca Sharpless, 33–91. Toronto: AltaMira Press, 2007.

Grossman, Zoltán. *Unlikely Alliances: Native Nations and White Communities Join to Defend Rural Lands.* Seattle: University of Washington Press, 2017.

———. "Unlikely Alliances: Treaty Conflicts and Environmental Cooperation between Native American and Rural White Communities." *American Indian Culture and Research Journal* 29, no. 4 (2005): 21–43.

Grossman, Zoltán, and Alan Parker. *Asserting Native Resilience: Pacific Rim Indigenous Nations Face the Climate Crisis.* Corvalis, OR: Oregon State University Press, 2012.

Guha, Ramachandra. *How Much Should a Person Consume? Environmentalism in India and the United States.* Los Angeles: University of California Press, 2006.

———. "Radical American Environmentalism and Wilderness Preservation: A Third World Critique." *Environmental Ethics* 11, no. 1 (1989): 71–83.

———. *The Unquiet Woods: Ecological Change and Peasant Resistance in the Himalaya,* 2nd ed. Oxford: Oxford University Press, 1989.

Guha, Ramachandra, and Juan Martinez-Alier. *Varieties of Environmentalism: Essays North and South.* London: Earthscan, 2006.

Habermas, Jurgen. "New Social Movements." *Telos* 49 (1981): 33–37.

Halder, Bornali. "Ecocide and Genocide: Explorations of Environmental Justice in Lakota Sioux Country." In *Ethnographies of Conservation: Environmentalism and the Distribution of Privilege,* edited by David Anderson and Eva Berglund, 101–18. New York: Bergham Books, 2003.

Hall, Carolyn. *Costa Rica: A Geographical Interpretation in Historical Review.* Boulder, CO: Westview Press, 1985.

Halpern, Daniel, Andres Rosenberg, and Eduardo Arraiagada. "Who Are those Green Guys? Understanding Online Activism in Chile from a Communicational Perspective." *Palabra Clave* 16, no. 3 (December 2013): 729–59.

Halstead, Narmala. "Ethnographic Encounters: Positionings Within and Outside the Insider Frame." *Social Anthropology* 9, no. 3 (2001): 307–8.

Harding, Jim. *Canada's Deadly Secret: Saskatchewan Uranium and the Global Nuclear System*. Halifax: Fernwood, 2007.

Harkin, Michael Eugene, and David Rich Lewis, eds. *Native Americans and the Environment: Perspectives on the Ecological Indian*. Lincoln: University of Nebraska Press, 2007.

Harris, Douglas C. "A Court Between: Aboriginal and Treaty Rights in the British Columbia Court of Appeal." *BC Studies* 162 (Summer 2009): 137–64.

Hartley, Emery. "Tribal Parks: Thirty Years and Counting." *Friends of Clayoquot Sound*. Summer 2014.

Hassan, Rashid, Robert Scholes, and Neville Ash, eds. *Millennium Ecosystem Assessment, Ecosystems and Human Well-being, Vol. 1: Current State and Trends*. Washington, DC: Island Press, 2005.

Hays, Samuel P. *Beauty, Health, and Permanence: Environmental Politics in the United States, 1955–1985*. Cambridge: Cambridge University Press, 1987.

———. *Conservation and the Gospel of Efficiency: The Progressive Conservation Movement, 1890–1920*. Pittsburgh: University of Pittsburgh Press, 1999. First published 1959 by Harvard University Press.

Hayter, Roger. "The Contested Restructuring qua Remapping of BC's Forest Economy: Reflections on the Crossroads and War in the Woods Metaphors." *Canadian Journal of Regional Science* 27 (2004): 395–414.

———. "'The War in the Woods': Post-Fordist Restructuring, Globalization, and the Contested Remapping of British Columbia's Forest Economy." *Annals of the Association of American Geographers* 93, no. 3 (September 2003): 706–29.

Hazlett, Maril. "'Woman vs. Man vs. Bugs': Gender and Popular Culture in Early Reactions to Silent Spring." *Environmental History* 9, no. 4 (2004): 701–29.

Head, Suzanne, and Robert Heinzman, eds. *Lessons of the Rainforest*. San Francisco: Sierra Club Books, 1990.

Hébert, Martin, and Michael Gabriel Rosen. "Community Forestry and the Paradoxes of Citizenship in Mexico: The Cases of Oaxaca and Guerrero." *Canadian Journal of Latin American and Caribbean Studies* 32, no. 63 (2007): 9–44.

Helvarg, David. *The War Against the Greens: The 'Wise-Use' Movement, the New Right and Anti-Environmental Violence*. San Francisco: Sierra Club Books, 1994.

Hermer, Joe. *Regulating Eden: The Nature of Order in North American Parks*. Toronto: University of Toronto Press, 2002.

Hildyard, Nicholas, Pandurang Hegde, Paul Wolvekamp, and Somasekhare Reddy. "Pluralism, Participation and Power: Joint Forest Management in India." In *Participation: The New Tyranny?*, edited by Bill Cooke and Uma Kothari, 56–71. London: Zed Books, 2001.

Hoerig, Karl A., John R. Welch, T. J. Ferguson, and Gabriella Soto. "Expanding Toolkits for Heritage Perpetuation: The Western Apache Ethnography and Geographic Information Science Research Experience for Undergraduates." *International Journal of Applied Geospatial Research* 6 (2015): 60–77.

Hoover, Elizabeth, et al., "Indigenous Peoples of North America: Environmental Exposures and Reproductive Justice." *Environmental Health Perspectives* (2012). http://dx.doi.org/10.1289/ehp.1205422.

Horsfield, Margaret, and Ian Kennedy. *Tofino and Clayoquot Sound: A History.* Madeira Park, BC: Harbour Publishing, 2014.

Howitt, Richard, and Sandra Suchet-Pearson. "Rethinking the Building Blocks: Ontological Pluralism and the Idea of 'Management.'" *Geografiska Annaler* 88, no. 3 (2006): 323–35.

Hunter, Bob. *Warriors of the Rainbow: A Chronicle of the Greenpeace Movement.* New York: Holt, Rinehart, and Winston, 1979.

Hurley, Andrew. *Environmental Inequalities: Class, Race, and Industrial Pollution in Gary, Indiana, 1945–1980.* Chapel Hill, NC: University of North Carolina Press, 1995.

Hynes, Patricia H. "Ellen Swallow, Lois Gibbs and Rachel Carson: Catalysts of the American Environmental Movement." *Women's Studies International Forum* 8, no. 4 (1984): 291–98.

Igoe, Jim. *Conservation and Globalization: A Study of National Parks and Indigenous Communities from East Africa to South Dakota.* Belmont, CA: Thompson and Wadsworth, 2004.

Inglehart, Ronald. *The Silent Revolution: Changing Values and Political Styles Among Western Publics.* Princeton, NJ: Princeton University Press, 1977.

Inglehart, Ronald, and Jacques Rene-Rabier. "Political Realignment in Advanced Industrial Society: From Class-based Politics to Quality-of-Life Politics." *Government and Opposition* 21, no. 4 (1986): 456–79.

Jackson, Cecile. "Women/Nature or Gender/History? A Critique of Ecofeminist 'Development.'" *Journal of Peasant Studies* 20, no. 3 (1993): 389–418.

Jacobs, Jane. *The Death and Life of Great American Cities.* New York: Random House, 1961.

Jacoby, Karl. *Crimes Against Nature: Squatters, Poachers, and the Hidden History of American Conservation.* Berkeley: University of California Press, 2001.

Jenkins, Craig. "Resource Mobilization Theory and the Study of Social Movements." *Annual Review of Sociology* 9 (1983): 527–53.

Johnson, Hayley. "#NoDAPL: Social Media, Empowerment, and Civic Participation at Standing Rock." *Library Trends* 66, no. 2 (2017): 155–75.

Karan, Pradyumna, and Unryu Suganuma. *Local Environmental Movements: A Comparative Study of the United States and Japan.* Lexington: University Press of Kentucky, 2008.

Keeling, Arn. "The Effluent Society: Water Pollution and Environmental Politics in British Columbia, 1889–1980." PhD diss., University of British Columbia, 2004.

———. "Sink or Swim: Water Pollution and Environmental Politics in Vancouver, 1889–1975." *BC Studies* 142/143 (Summer 2004): 69–101.

———. "Urban Waste Sinks as a Natural Resource: The Case of the Fraser River." *Urban History Review* 34, no. 1 (2005): 58–70.

Keeling, Arn, and John Sandlos. "Environmental Justice Goes Underground? Historical Notes from Canada's Northern Mining Frontier." *Environmental Justice* 2, no. 3 (2009): 117–25.

Keeling, Arn, and Robert McDonald. "The Profligate Province: Roderick Haig-Brown and the Modernizing of British Columbia." *Journal of Canadian Studies* 36, no. 3 (2001): 7–23.

Keller, Jr., Robert H., and Michael F. Turek. *American Indians and National Parks.* Tucson: University of Arizona Press, 1998.

Kenny, James L., and Andrew G. Secord. "Engineering Modernity: Hydroelectric Development in New Brunswick, 1945–1970." *Acadiensis* 39, no. 1 (2010): 3–26.

Kent, Jim. "Managing Bison in the Badlands South Unit." *Classical* 24 (South Dakota Public Broadcasting, 16 May 2014). www.listen.sdpd.org/post/managing-bison-badlands-south-unit.

Keyser, James D., and Michael A. Klassen. *Plains Indian Rock Art.* Seattle: University of Washington Press, 2001.

Kheraj, Sean. *Inventing Stanley Park: An Environmental History.* Vancouver: UBC Press, 2013.

Killan, Gerald. *Protected Places: A History of Ontario's Provincial Parks System.* Toronto: Dundurn Press, 1993.

Klein, Naomi. *This Changes Everything: Capitalism vs. the Climate.* New York: Simon & Schuster, 2014.

Kline, Benjamin. *First Along the River: A Brief History of the U.S. Environmental Movement.* Lanham, MD: Rowman & Littlefield, 2007.

Krech, Shepard, III. *The Ecological Indian: Myth and History.* New York: W. W. Norton, 1999.

Landorf, Chris. "A Framework for Sustainable Heritage Management: A Study of UK Industrial Heritage Sites." *International Journal of Heritage Studies* 15, no. 6 (2009): 494–510.

Landrum, Ney C. *The State Park Movement in American: A Critical Review.* Columbia: University of Missouri Press, 2004.

Landy, Marc, and Charles Rubin. *Civic Environmentalism: A New Approach to Policy.* Washington, DC: George C. Marshall Institute, 2001.

Leal, Claudia. "Conservation Memories: Vicissitudes of a Biodiversity Conservation Project in the Rainforests of Colombia, 1992–1998." *Environmental History* 20, no. 3 (2015): 368–95.

Leddy, Lianne C. "Intersections on Indigenous and Environmental History in Canada." *Canadian Historical Review* 98, no. 1 (2017): 83–95.

Leeming, Mark. "The Creation of Radicalism: Anti-Nuclear Activism in Nova Scotia, c.1972–1979." *Canadian Historical Review* 95, no. 2 (2014): 217–41.

———. *In Defence of Home Places: Environmental Activism in Nova Scotia.* Vancouver: UBC Press, 2017.

Leonard, David. *Delayed Frontier: The Peace River Country to 1909.* Calgary: Detselig Enterprises, 1995.

Lewis, David Rich. "Skull Valley Goshutes and the Politics of Nuclear Waste." In *Native Americans and the Environment: Perspectives on the Ecological Indian*, edited by Michael E. Harkin and David Rich Lewis, 304–42. Lincoln: University of Nebraska Press, 2007.

Lifset, Robert D. *Power on the Hudson: Storm King Mountain and the Emergence of Modern American Environmentalism.* Pittsburgh: University of Pittsburgh Press, 2014.

Limerick, Patricia N. *Legacy of Conquest: The Unbroken Past of the American West.* New York: W. W. Norton, 1987.

Loo, Tina. "People in the Way: Modernity, Environment, and Society on the Arrow Lakes." *BC Studies* 142/143 (Summer/Autumn 2004): 161–96.

———. *States of Nature: Conserving Canada's Wildlife in the Twentieth Century.* Vancouver: UBC Press, 2006.

Lowenthal, David. *George Perkins Marsh: Prophet of Conservation.* Seattle: University of Washington Press, 2015.

Luke, Timothy W. "The Death of Environmentalism or the Advent of Public Ecology?" *Organization and Environment* 18, no. 4 (2005): 489–94.

Lundell, Liz. *Algonquin: The Park and Its People.* Toronto: McClelland & Stewart, 1993.

Lytle, Mark Hamilton. *The Gentle Subversive: Rachel Carson,* Silent Spring, *and the Rise of the Environmental Movement.* New York: Oxford University Press, 2007.

MacEachern, Alan. *The Institute of Man and Resources: An Environmental Fable.* Charlottetown: Island Studies Press, 2003.

MacGregor, Sherilyn. *Beyond Mothering Earth: Ecological Citizenship and the Politics of Care.* Vancouver: UBC Press, 2006.

MacIsaac, Ronald, and Anne Champagne. *Clayoquot Mass Trials: Defending the Rainforest.* Gabriola Island, BC: New Society Publishers, 1994.

MacPhee, Katrin. "Canadian Working-Class Environmentalism, 1965–1985." *Labour / Le Travail* 74 (Fall 2014): 123–49.

MacRaild, Donald M., and Avram Taylor. *Social Theory and Social History*. New York: Palgrave Macmillan, 2004.

Magnusson, Warren, and Karena Shaw, eds. *Political Space: Reading the Global Through Clayoquot Sound*. Minneapolis: University of Minnesota Press, 2002.

Maher, Neil M. *Nature's New Deal: The Civilian Conservation Corps and the Roots of American Environmental Movement*. Oxford: Oxford University Press, 2008.

Mann, Susan A. "Pioneers of US Ecofeminism and Environmental Justice." *Feminist Formations* 23, no. 2 (2011): 1–25.

Mansbridge, Jane, and Katherine Flaster. "The Cultural Politics of Everyday Discourse: The Case of the 'Male Chauvinist.'" *Critical Sociology* 33 no. 4 (2007): 627–60.

Martinez, Dennis. "Protected Areas, Indigenous Peoples, and the Western Idea of Nature." In *People, Places, and Parks: Proceedings of the 2005 George Wright Society Conference on Parks, Protected Areas, and Cultural Sites*, edited by David Harmon, 214–18. Hancock, MI: The George Wright Society, 2006.

Martinez-Alier, Juan. *Ecological Economics: Energy, Environment, and Society*. Oxford: Basil Blackwell, 1990.

——. *The Environmentalism of the Poor: A Study of Ecological Conflicts and Valuation*. Northampton, UK: Edward Elgar, 2002.

McFarland, Joan. "Labour and the Environment: Five Stories from New Brunswick Since the 1970s." *Labour / Le Travail* 74 (Fall 2014): 249–66.

McGurty, Eileen. *Transforming Environmentalism: Warren County, PCBs, and the Origins of Environmental Justice*. New Brunswick, NJ: Rutgers University Press, 2007.

McLaughlin, Mark. "'As Thick as Molasses': Water Pollution Regulation in New Brunswick, 1947–1974." In *Modern Canada: 1945 to Present*, edited by Catherine Briggs, 369–382. Don Mills, ON: Oxford University Press, 2014.

——. "Green Shoots: Aerial Insecticide Spraying and the Growth of Environmental Consciousness in New Brunswick, 1952–1973." *Acadiensis* 40, no. 1 (2011): 3–23.

——. "Rise of the Eco-Comics: The State, Environmental Education, and Canadian Comic Books, 1971–1975." *Material Culture Review* 77/78 (Spring/Fall 2013): 9–20.

——. "'Trees Are a Crop': Crown Lands, Labour, and the Environment in New Brunswick's Forest Industries, 1940–1982." PhD diss., University of New Brunswick, 2013.

McNab, David T. "Remembering an Intellectual Wilderness: A Captivity Narrative at Queen's Park in 1988-9." In *Blockades and Resistance: Studies in Actions of Peace and the Temagami Blockade of 1988–89*, edited by Bruce Hodgin, Ute Lischke, and David T. McNab, 31–53. Waterloo, ON: Wilfred Laurier University Press, 2003.

McNeill, J. R. *Something New Under the Sun: An Environmental History of the Twentieth Century World*. New York: W. W. Norton, 2000.

McTaggart, David. *Outrage!: The Ordeal of Greenpeace III*. Vancouver: J. J. Douglas, 1973.

McTaggart, David, with Helen Slinger. *Shadow Warrior: The Autobiography of Greenpeace International Founder David McTaggart*. London: Orion, 2002.

Meadows, Donella H., Dennis L. Meadows, Jørgen Randers, and William W. Behrens III, *The Limits to Growth*. New York: Universe Books, 1972.

Meffe, Gary, Larry Nielson, Richard L. Knight, and Dennis Schenborn, eds. *Ecosystem Management: Adaption, Community-Based Conservation*. Washington, DC: Island Press, 2002.

Merino, Leonardo. "Zonas de Influencia Cultural en la Costa Rica Indígena y sus Relaciones con el Medio Ambiente." *Ilé: Anuario Ecológico, Cultura y Sociedad* 5, no. 5 (2005): 143–53.

Meyer, John. "Does Environmentalism Have a Future?" *Dissent* 52, no. 2 (2005): 69–75.

Meyer, Stephen M. *The End of the Wild*. Cambridge, MA: MIT Press, 2006.

Miller, Alan. *Environmental Problem Solving: Psychosocial Barriers to Adaptive Change*. New York: Springer, 1999.

Montrie, Chad. "Expedient Environmentalism: Opposition to Coal Surface Mining in Appalachia and the United Mine Workers of America, 1945–1977." *Environmental History* 5, no. 1(January 2000): 75–98.

———. *A People's History of Environmentalism in the United States*. New York: Continuum, 2011.

Moore, Niamh. *The Changing Nature of Eco/Feminism: Telling Stories from Clayoquot Sound*. Vancouver: UBC Press, 2015.

Moranda, Scott. "The Emergence of an Environmental History of Tourism." *Journal of Tourism History* 7, no. 3 (2015): 268–89.

Mosley, Stephen. "Integrating Social and Environmental History." *Journal of Social History* 39, no. 3 (2006): 915–33.

Muir, Bruce R., and Annie L. Booth. "An Environmental Justice Analysis of Caribou Recovery Planning, Protection of an Indigenous Culture, and Coal Mining Development of Northeast British Columbia, Canada." *Environment, Development, and Sustainability* 14 (2012): 455–76.

Murphree, Marshall W. "Protected Areas and the Commons." *Common Property Resource Digest* 60 (2002): 1–3.

Nadasdy, Paul. "The Anti-Politics of TEK: The Institutionalization of Co-Management Discourse and Practice." *Anthropologica* 47, no. 2 (2005): 215–32.

———. *Hunters and Bureaucrats: Power, Knowledge, and Aboriginal-State Relations in the Southwest Yukon*. Vancouver: UBC Press, 2003.

———. "Transcending the Debate over the Ecologically Noble Indian: Indigenous Peoples and Environmentalism." *Ethnohistory* 52, no. 2 (2005): 291–331.

Narayan, Kirin. "How Native Is a 'Native' Anthropologist?" *American Anthropologist* 95, no. 3 (1993): 671–86.

Natcher, David C., Susan Davis, and Clifford G. Hickey. "Co-Management: Managing Relationships, Not Resources." *Human Organization* 64, no. 3 (2005): 240–50.

National Wild and Scenic Rivers System. "Clarion River and Mill Creek Wild and Scenic River Eligibility Report." March 1996.

Nesper, Larry, Anna J. Willow, and Thomas F. King. *The Mushgigagamongsebe District: A Traditional Cultural Property of the Sokaogon Ojibwe Community*. Mole Lake, WI: Sokaogon Chippewa Community, 2002.

Nicholas, George P., John R. Welch, and Eldon C. Yellowhorn. "Collaborative Encounters." In *Archaeological Practice: Engaging Descendant Communities*, edited by Chip Colwell-Chanthaphonh, and T. J. Ferguson, 273–98. Walnut Creek, CA: AltaMira Press, 2007.

Noezke, Claudia. *Aboriginal Peoples and Natural Resources in Canada*. Concord, ON: Captus Press, 1994.

Nordhaus, Ted, and Michael Shellenberger. *Break Through: From the Death of Environmentalism to the Politics of Possibility*. New York: Houghton Mifflin, 2007.

Norton, Michael. *The Everyday Activist: 365 Ways to Change the World*. Oxford: Pan Macmillan, 2007.

O'Brien, William E. *Landscapes of Exclusion: State Parks and Jim Crow in the American South*. Amherst: University of Massachusetts Press, 2015.

O'Connor, Ryan. *The First Green Wave: Pollution Probe and the Origins of Environmental Activism in Ontario*. Vancouver: UBC Press, 2014.

Orhan, Özgüç. "The Civic Environmental Approach." *The Good Society* 17, no. 2 (2008): 38–43.

Pang, Natalie, and Pei Wen Law. "Retweeting #WorldEnvironmentDay: A Study of Content Features and Visual Rhetoric in an Environmental Movement." *Computers in Human Behavior* 69 (April 2017): 54–61.

Parr, Joy. "Smells Like?: Sources of Uncertainty in the History of the Great Lakes Environment." *Environmental History* 11, no. 2 (2006): 269–99.

Pavel, M. Paloma, ed. *Breakthrough Communities: Sustainability and Justice in the Next American Metropolis*. Cambridge, MA: MIT Press, 2009.

Pennsylvania Department of Health. "Industrial Waste Survey of the Clarion River Basin." In *Tenth Annual Report of the Commissioner of Health of the Commonwealth of Pennsylvania*, 1915: 1279–1316.

Pierotti, Raymond. *Indigenous Knowledge, Ecology, and Evolutionary Biology*. New York: Routledge, 2011.

Pinkerton, Evelyn W. "Coastal Marine Systems: Conserving Fish and Sustaining Community Livelihoods with Co-Management." In *Principles of Ecosystem Stewardship: Resilience-Based Natural Resource Management in a Changing World*, edited by F. Stuart Chapin, III, Gary P. Kofinas, and Carl Folke, 241–58. New York: Springer-Verlag, 2009.

Pinkerton, Evelyn W., and Leonard John. "Creating Local Management Legitimacy: Building a Local System of Clam Management in a Northwest Coast Community." *Marine Policy* 32, no. 4 (2008): 680–91.

Portier, Dimitri. "The Meares Island Case: Nuu-chah-nulth vs. the Logging Industry." *Native American Studies* 14, no. 1 (2000): 31–37.

Posey, Darrell A. "Diachronic Ecotones and Anthropogenic Landscapes in Amazonia." In *Advances in Historical Ecology*, edited by William Balée, 104–18. New York: Columbia University Press, 1998.

Pratt, Mary Louise. *Imperial Eyes: Travel Writing and Transculturation*. New York: Routledge, 1992.

Premauer, Julia. "Rights, Conservation, and Governance: Indigenous Peoples-National Parks Collaboration in Makuira, Colombia." PhD diss., University of Manitoba, 2013.

Rainforest Action Network. "American Dream, Native Nightmare: A Report on Weyerhaeuser." 2006. http://ran.org/sites/default/files/weyerhauser_report.pdf.

———. "Catalyzing A Movement," *Greatest Hits, 1985–2010: Rainforest Action Network 2010 Annual Report*. San Francisco: Rainforest Action Network, 2010.

Ranco, Darren, and Dean Suagee. "Tribal Sovereignty and the Problem of Difference in Environmental Regulation: Observations on 'Measured Separatism' in Indian Country." *Antipode* 39, no. 4 (2007): 691–707.

Rangarajan, Mahesh. *Fencing the Forest: Conservation and Ecological Change in India's Central Provinces 1860–1914*. Delhi: Oxford University Press, 1996.

Rashkow, Ezra D. "Idealizing Inhabited Wilderness: A Revision to the History of Indigenous Peoples and National Parks." *History Compass* 12 (2014): 818–32.

Read, Jennifer. "'Let Us Heed the Voice of Youth': Laundry Detergents, Phosphates and the Emergence of the Environmental Movement in Ontario." *Journal of the Canadian Historical Association* 7 no. 1 (1996): 227–50.

Richland, Justin B. "Beyond Listening: Lessons for Native/American Collaborations from the Creation of the Nakwatsvewat Institute." *American Indian Culture and Research Journal* 35 (2011): 101–11.

Ridington, Robin, and Jillian Ridington. *Where Happiness Dwells: A History of the Dane-zaa First Nations*. Vancouver: UBC Press, 2013.

Rippelmeyer, Kay. *Giant City State Park and the Civilian Conservation Corps: A History in Words and Pictures*. Carbondale: Southern Illinois University Press, 2010.

Rome, Adam. *The Genius of Earth Day: How a 1970s Teach-In Unexpectedly Made the First Green Generation*. New York: Hill & Wang, 2014.

———. "'Political Hermaphrodites': Gender and Environmental Reform in Progressive America." *Environmental History* 11, no. 3 (2006): 440–63.

Rossiter, David A. "The Nature of a Blockade: Environmental Politics and the Haida Action on Lyell Island, British Columbia." In *Blockades or Breakthroughs:*

Aboriginal Peoples Confront the Canadian State, edited by Yale D. Belanger and Whitney Lackenbauer, 70–89. Montreal: McGill-Queen's University Press, 2014.

Rothman, Hal K. *America's National Monuments: The Politics of Preservation.* Lawrence: University Press of Kansas, 1994.

———. *The Greening of a Nation? Environmentalism in the United States Since 1945.* New York: Harcourt Brace, 1998.

Rothman, Hal K., and Char Miller. *Death Valley National Park: A History.* Reno: University of Nevada Press, 2013.

Rowell, Andrew. *Green Backlash: Global Subversion of the Environmental Movement.* New York: Routledge, 1996.

Sabin, Paul. *The Bet: Paul Ehrlich, Julian Simon, and Our Gamble over Earth's Future.* New Haven, CT: Yale University Press, 2013.

———. "Environmental Law and the End of the New Deal Order." *Law & History Review* 33, no. 4 (2015): 965–1003.

Sale, Kirkpatrick. *The Green Revolution: The American Environmental Movement 1962–1992.* New York: Hill & Wang, 1993.

Sandler, Ronald D., and Phaedra C. Pezzullo. *Environmental Justice and Environmentalism: The Social Justice Challenge to the Environmental Movement.* Cambridge, MA: MIT Press, 2007.

Sandlos, John, and Arn Keeling. "Claiming the New North: Development and Colonialism at the Pine Point Mine, Northwest Territories, Canada." *Environment and History* 18, no. 1 (2012): 5–34.

Savoie, Donald J. *Visiting Grandchildren: Economic Development in the Maritimes.* Toronto: University of Toronto Press, 2006.

Scarce, Rik. *Eco-Warriors: Understanding the Radical Environmental Movement.* Updated ed. Walnut Creek, CA: Left Coast Press, 2006.

Schumacher, E. F. *Small is Beautiful: Economics as if People Mattered.* New York: Harper & Row, 1973.

Scott, James C. *Two Cheers for Anarchism.* Princeton, NJ: Princeton University Press, 2012.

Sellers, Christopher. *Crabgrass Crucible: Suburban Nature and the Rise of Environmentalism in Twentieth-Century America.* Chapel Hill: University of North Carolina Press, 2012.

Shabecoff, Philip. *A Fierce Green Fire: The American Environmental Movement.* New York: Hill & Wang, 1993.

Shapiro, Aaron. *The Lure of the North Woods: Cultivating Tourism in the Upper Midwest.* Minneapolis: University of Minnesota Press, 2013.

Shaw, Karena. "Encountering Clayoquot, Reading the Political." In *A Political Space: Reading the Global through Clayoquot Sound*, edited by Warren Magnusson and Karena Shaw, 25–66. Minneapolis: University of Minnesota Press, 2003.

Shellenberger, Michael, and Ted Nordhaus. "The Death of Environmentalism: Global Warming Politics in a Post-Environmental World." *Geopolitics, History, and International Relations* 1 (2009): 121–63.

Sherman, Kathleen Pickering, James Van Lanen, and Richard Sherman. "Practical Environmentalism on the Pine Ridge Reservation: Confronting Structural Constraints to Indigenous Stewardship." *Human Ecology* 38, no. 4 (2010): 507–20.

Sherry, Erin E. "Protected Areas and Aboriginal Interests: At Home in the Canadian Arctic Wilderness." *International Journal of Wilderness* 5, no. 1 (1999): 17–20.

Sherry, John W. *Land, Wind, and Hard Words: A Story of Navajo Activism.* Albuquerque: University of New Mexico Press, 2002.

Shkilnyk, Anastasia M. *A Poison Stronger than Love: The Destruction of an Ojibwa Community.* New Haven, CT: Yale University Press, 1985.

Shutkin, William A. *The Land that Could Be: Environmentalism and Democracy in the Twenty-First Century.* Cambridge, MA: MIT Press, 2001.

Silvern, Steven E. "Reclaiming the Reservation: The Geopolitics of Wisconsin Anishinaabe Resource Rights." *American Indian Culture & Research Journal* 24, no. 3 (2000): 131–153.

Simpson, Audra. *Mohawk Interruptus: Political Life Across the Borders of Settler States.* Durham, NC: Duke University Press, 2014.

Simpson, Leanne Betasamosake, ed. *Lighting the Eighth Fire: The Liberation, Resurgence, and Protection of Indigenous Nations.* Winnipeg: Arbeiter Ring, 2008.

Sims, Daniel. "Ware's Waldo: Hydroelectric Development and the Creation of the Other in British Columbia." In *Sustaining the West: Cultural Responses to Canadian Environments*, edited by Liza Piper and Lisa Szabo-Jones, 303–24. Waterloo, ON: Wilfrid Laurier University Press, 2015.

Singer, Gregory R. "Is it Time to Bury the Environmental Movement?" *Natural Resources and Environment* 20, no. 3 (2006): 56–58.

Singleton, Sara. *Constructing Cooperation: The Evolution of Institutions of Comanagement.* Ann Arbor: University of Michigan Press, 1998.

Smith, Clayton D. "Environmentalism, Feminism, and Gender." *Sociological Inquiry* 71, no. 3 (2001): 314–34.

Smith, Jennifer. "Intergovernmental Relations, Legitimacy, and the Atlantic Accords." *Constitutional Forum* 17, no. 3 (2008): 81–98.

Smith, Terria, and Vincent Medina. "Tribal Support Across the State for Standing Rock." *News from Native California* 30, no. 2 (Winter 2016/17): 8–11.

Snow, David, Louis Zurcher, and Sheldon Ekland-Olson. "Social Networks and Social Movements." *American Sociological Review* 45, no. 5 (1980): 787–801.

Snow, Donald, ed. *Voices from the Environmental Movement: Perspectives for a New Era.* Washington, DC: Island Press, 1992.

Solomon, Lawrence. *The Conserver Solution.* Toronto: Doubleday Canada, 1978.

Speakman, Joseph M. *At Work in Penn's Woods: The Civilian Conservation Corps in Pennsylvania*. University Park: Pennsylvania State University Press, 2006.

Speece, Darren. *Defending Giants: The Redwood Wars and the Transformation of American Environmental Politics*. Seattle: University of Washington Press, 2016.

———. "From Corporatism to Citizen Oversight: The Legal Fight Over California Redwoods, 1970–1996." *Environmental History* 14, no. 4 (2009): 705–36.

Spence, Mark. *Dispossessing the Wilderness: Indian Removal and the Making of National Parks*. New York: Oxford University Press, 1999.

Spielmann, Roger, and Marina Unger. "Towards a Model of Co-Management of Provincial Parks in Ontario." *Canadian Journal of Native Studies* 20, no. 2 (2000): 455–86.

Stearns, Peter R. "The New Social History: An Overview." In *Ordinary People and Everyday Life: Perspectives on the New Social History*, edited by James B. Gardner and George Rollie Adams, 3–21. Nashville, TN: American Association for State and Local History, 1983.

Stefanik, Lorna. "Baby Stumpy and the War in the Woods: Competing Frames of British Columbia Forests." *BC Studies* 130 (Summer 2001): 41–68.

Steffen, Will, Paul J. Crutzen, and John R. McNeill, "The Anthropocene: Are Humans Now Overwhelming the Great Forces of Nature?" *Ambio: A Journal of the Human Environment* 36, no. 8 (2007): 614–21.

Stevens, Stan, ed. *Conservation through Cultural Survival: Indigenous Peoples and Protected Areas*. Washington, DC: Island Press, 1997.

———, ed. *Indigenous Peoples, National Parks, and Protected Areas*. Tucson: University of Arizona Press, 2014.

Stoddard, Mark, and David Tindall. "Feminism and Environmentalism: Perspectives on Gender in the BC Environmental Movement During the 1990s." *BC Studies* 165 (Spring 2010): 75–100.

Stoddard, Mark, and Laura MacDonald. "Media and the Internet as Sites for Environmental Movement Activism for Jumbo Pass, British Columbia." *Canadian Journal of Sociology* 36, no. 4 (Fall 2011): 313–36.

Stone, Christopher D. "Is Environmentalism Dead?" *Environmental Law* 38 (2008): 19–45.

Sturgeon, Noël. *Ecofeminist Natures: Race, Gender, Feminist Theory, and Political Action*. New York: Routledge, 2016 [1997].

———. *Environmentalism in Popular Culture: Gender, Race, Sexuality, and the Politics of the Natural*. Tucson: University of Arizona Press, 2009.

Switzer, Jacqueline Vaughn. *Green Backlash: The History and Politics of the Environmental Opposition in the U.S.* Boulder, CO: Lynne Rienner Publishers, 1997.

TallBear, Kimberly. "Shepard Krech's The Ecological Indian: One Indian's Perspective." *International Institute for Indigenous Resource Management* (2000): 1–5, http://www.iiirm.org/publications/Book%20Reviews/Reviews/Krech001.pdf, last accessed 6 June 2017.

Tarrow, Sidney. *The New Transnational Activism*. Cambridge: Cambridge University Press, 2005.

Taylor, Alan. "Unnatural Inequalities: Social and Environmental Histories." *Environmental History* 1 no. 4 (1996): 8.

Teale, Phelps Bondaroff, and Danita Catherine Burke. "Bridging Troubled Waters: History as Political Opportunity Structure." *Journal of Civil Society* 10, no. 2 (2014): 165–83.

Thompson, E. P. *Customs in Common*. London: Merlin Press, 1991.

Thorpe, Jocelyn. "Temagami's Tangled Wild: The Making of Race, Nature, and Nation in Early-Twentieth-Century Ontario." In *Rethinking the Great White North: Race, Nature, and the Historical Geographies of Whiteness in Canada*, edited by Andrew Baldwin, Laura Cameron, and Audrey Kobayashi, 193–210. Vancouver: UBC Press, 2011.

———. *Temagami's Tangled Wild: Race, Gender, and the Making of Canadian Nature*. Vancouver: UBC Press, 2012.

Torras, Mariano. "The Total Economic Value of Amazonian Deforestation, 1978–1993." *Ecological Economics* 33, no. 2 (2000): 283–97.

Trim, Henry. "Experts at Work: The Canadian State, North American Environmentalism, and Renewable Energy in an Era of Limits, 1968–1983." PhD diss., University of British Columbia, 2014.

———. "Planning the Future: The Conserver Society and Canadian Sustainability." *Canadian Historical Review* 96, no. 3 (2015): 375–404.

Turner, Tom. *David Brower: The Making of the Environmental Movement*. Berkeley: University of California Press, 2015.

Ulloa, Astrid. *La Construcción del Nativo Ecológico: Complejidades, Paradojas, y Dilemas de la Relación entre los Movimientos Indígenas y el Ambientalismo en Colombia*. Bogotá: Instituto Colombiano de Antropología e Historia-Colciencias, 2004.

United States National Park Service and Oglala Sioux Tribe Parks and Recreational Authority. "South Unit, Badlands National Park: Final General Management Plan and Environmental Impact Statement." US Department of the Interior, National Park Service, April 2012.

Van Huizen, Philip. "Building a Green Dam: Environmental Modernism and the Canadian-American Libby Dam Project." *Pacific Historical Review* 79, no. 3 (2010): 418–53.

———. "'Panic Park': Environmental Protest and the Politics of Parks in British Columbia's Skagit Valley." *BC Studies* 170 (2011): 67–92.

Vaughan, Jacqueline, and Hanna J. Cortner. *Philanthropy and the National Park Service*. New York: Palgrave Macmillan, 2013.

Velut, Jean-Baptiste. "A Brief History of the Relations between the U.S. Labor and Environmentalist Movements (1965–2010)." *Revue Francaise d'Etudes Americaines* 129 (2012): 59–72.

Vizenor, Gerald. *Survivance: Narratives of Native Presence.* Lincoln: University of Nebraska Press, 2008.

Voggesser, Garrit. "When History Matters: The National Wildlife Federation's Conservation Partnership with Tribes." *Western Historical Quarterly* 40, no. 3 (2009): 349–57.

Wakild, Emily. *Revolutionary Parks: Conservation, Social Justice, and Mexico's National Parks, 1910–1940.* Tucson: University of Arizona Press, 2011.

Wall, Sharon. *The Nurture of Nature: Childhood, Antimodernism, and Ontario Summer Camps, 1920–55.* Vancouver: UBC Press, 2009.

Wapner, Paul. *Environmental Activism and World Civic Politics.* Albany: State University of New York Press, 1996.

———. *Living Through the End of Nature: The Future of American Environmentalism.* Cambridge, MA: MIT Press, 2010.

Warecki, George. *Protecting Ontario's Wilderness: A History of Changing Concepts and Preservation Politics, 1927–1973.* New York: Peter Lang, 2000.

Welch, John R. "National Historic Landmark Nomination for Fort Apache and Theodore Roosevelt School." Washington, DC: National Park Service, 2011.

Welch, John R., and Robert C. Brauchli. "'Subject to the Right of the Secretary of the Interior': The White Mountain Apache Reclamation of the Fort Apache and Theodore Roosevelt School Historic District." *Wicazo Sa Review* 25, no. 1 (2010): 47–73.

Welch, John R., Dana Lepofsky, Megan Caldwell, Georgia Combes, and Craig Rust. "Treasure Bearers: Personal Foundations for Effective Leadership in Northern Coast Salish Heritage Stewardship." *Heritage and Society* 4, no. 1 (2011): 83–114.

Welch, John R., and Ramon Riley. "Reclaiming Land and Spirit in the Western Apache Homeland." *American Indian Quarterly* 25, no. 1 (2001): 5–12.

Wells, Christopher W. "From Freeway to Parkway: Federal Law, Grassroots Environmental Protest, and the Evolving Design of Interstate-35E in Saint Paul, Minnesota." *Journal of Planning History* 11, no. 1 (2012): 8–26.

Wendt, Mathias. "The Importance of *Death and Life of Great American Cities* (1961) by Jane Jacobs to the Profession of Urban Planning." *New Visions for Public Affairs* 1 (Spring 2009): 1–24.

Wenzel, George. *Animal Rights, Human Rights: Ecology, Economy and Ideology in the Canadian Arctic.* Toronto: University of Toronto Press, 1991.

West Moberly First Nations Land Use Department. *I Want to Eat Caribou before I Die.* Initial Submissions for the Proposed Mining Activity at First Coal Corporation's Goodrich Property (2009).

West, Patrick C., and Steven R. Brechin, eds. *Resident Peoples and National Parks: Social Dilemmas and Strategies in International Conservation.* Tucson: University of Arizona Press, 1991.

Western, David, ed. *Natural Connections: Perspectives on Community-Based Conservation.* Washington, DC: Island Press, 1994.

Western, David, and R. Michael Wright. "The Background to Community-Based Conservation." In *Natural Connections: Perspectives on Community-Based Conservation*, edited by David Western, 1–12. Washington, DC: Island Press, 1994.

Weyler, Rex. *Song of the Whale: The Dramatic Story of Dr. Paul Spong—Founder of the Greenpeace Save-the-Whales Movement—and His Startling Discoveries About Whale Intelligence.* Garden City, NY: Anchor Press/Doubleday, 1986.

Wildcat, Daniel. *Red Alert!: Saving the Plant with Indigenous Knowledge.* Golden, CO: Fulcrum, 2009.

Willow, Anna J. "Collaborative Conservation and Contexts of Resistance: New (and Enduring) Strategies for Survival." *American Indian Culture & Research Journal* 39, no. 2 (2015): 29–52.

———. "Doing Sovereignty in Native North America: Anishinaabe Counter-Mapping and the Struggle for Land-Based Self-Determination." *Human Ecology* 41 (2013): 871–84.

———. "Re(con)figuring Alliances: Place Membership, Environmental Justice, and the Remaking of Indigenous-Environmentalist Relationships in Canada's Boreal Forest." *Human Organization* 71, no. 4 (2012): 371–82.

———. *Strong Hearts, Native Lands: Anti-Clearcutting Activism at Grassy Narrows First Nation.* Winnipeg: University of Manitoba Press, 2012.

Wolfley, Jeanette. "Reclaiming a Presence in Ancestral Lands: The Return of Native People to the National Parks." *Natural Resources Journal* 56 (Winter 2016): 55–80.

Wray, Jacilee, Alexa Roberts, Allison Peña, and Shirley J. Fiske. "Creating Policy for the National Park Service: Addressing Native Americans and Other Traditionally Associated Peoples." *The George Wright Forum* 26, no. 3 (2009): 43–50.

Yohan, Ariffin. "On the Scope and Limits of Green Imperialism." *Peace Review: A Journal of Social Justice* 22, no. 4 (2010): 373–81.

Yuen, Eddie. "The Politics of Failure Have Failed: The Environmental Movement and Catastrophism." In *Catastrophism: The Apocalyptic Politics of Collapse and Rebirth*, edited by Sasha Lilley, David McNally, and Eddie Yuen, 15–43. Oakland, CA: PM Press, 2012.

Zelko, Frank. *Make it a Green Peace!: The Rise of Countercultural Environmentalism.* New York: Oxford University Press, 2013.

———. "Making Greenpeace: The Development of Direct Action Environmentalism in British Columbia." *BC Studies* 142/3 (Summer/Autumn 2004): 197–239.

———. "Scaling Greenpeace: From Local Activism to Global Governance." *Historical Social Research* 42, no. 2 (2017): 318–42.

Zimring, Carl. *Clean and White: A History of Environmental Racism in the United States.* New York: New York University Press, 2015.

LIST OF CONTRIBUTORS

JONATHAN CLAPPERTON is an adjunct professor in the Department of History at the University of Victoria.

JESSICA M. DEWITT is a PhD candidate in the Department of History at the University of Saskatchewan.

STERLING EVANS is retired from the University of Oklahoma, where he held the Louise Welsh Chair in the Department of History.

ZOLTÁN GROSSMAN is a professor of Geography and Native Studies at The Evergreen State College.

TOBASONAKWUT PETER KINEW (1936–2012) served as Grand Chief of Grand Council Treaty 3, as the first Ontario regional chief for the Assembly of First Nations, and several terms as Chief of the Ojibways of Onigaming.

MARK LEEMING is the Learning Skills Coordinator, Student Success Centre, at St. Francis Xavier University.

MARK J. MCLAUGHLIN is an assistant professor of History and Canadian Studies at the University of Maine.

LIZA PIPER is an associate professor in the Department of History and Classics at the University of Alberta.

JOHN R. WELCH is a professor and director of the Professional Master's Program in Heritage Resource Management in the Department of Archaeology and School of Resource and Environmental Management at Simon Fraser University.

ANNA J. WILLOW is an associate professor in the Department of Anthropology at the Ohio State University.

FRANK ZELKO is an associate professor of History and Environmental Studies at the University of Vermont.

INDEX

Note: Page numbers in bold refer to illustrations.

A

forestry industry, 181, 196–97, 234, 249, 272

forests, 35, 103–4, 120, 186–87

Fort Apache
  history, 75–77, 79
  management, 80–82
  preservation activities, 73–74, **78**, 79–80
  vision and value of, 90–91

Fort Apache and Theodore Roosevelt School
  National Historic Landmark, 75–80

Fort Apache Heritage Foundation (FAHF),
  80–82, 86–91

Fort Berthold Indian Reservation, 57, 63

fossil fuel industry, 47–48, 51, 53, 57–60, 59

Foundation trilogy (Asimov), 294

FPP. *See* Friends of Pinery Park (FPP)

fracking, 30, 57, 61, 63

France and Greenpeace, 294–98

Francis, Louis, 214

Francis, Raymond, 214

Frank, Billy Jr., 47, 58

Frank, Francis, 194

Franklin, Ursula, 243

Franklin report (*Canada as a Conserver
  Society*), 244–45

Franks, David, 51

Fraser River Report (SPEC), 266

Fredericton, New Brunswick CCNB Chapter,
  238–42

Friends of Algonquin Park (FOAP), 138–39

Friends of Clayoquot Sound (FOCS), 119,
  181, 185–86, 189–90, 197, 200

Friends of Pinery Park (FPP), 138–39

funding
  community-based conservation, 102
  environmental groups, 233, 242, 245, 277,
    304–5
  Friends groups, 139
  government programs, 212, 215
  heritage and tourism, 79–81, 111
  Indigenous activism, 187–88

G

gender dynamics, 103, 320–21

George, Annie, 196

Gibbs, Lois, 321

Gismondi, Michael, 322

global vs. local environmentalism, 93–94,
  290, 310

Goetze, Tara C., 194

Gómez-Pompa, Arturo, 101

Gottlieb, Robert, 6

governments
  engagement with, 211–12, 232, 234
  lobbying to, 236–37, 252–53

governments. *See also* Canadian
  government; *specific provinces*

Grassy Narrows First Nation, 24, 26–29, 34,
  162, 172, 177

Grays Harbor, Washington, 58, 60

"Green Giants", 4, 10, 315, 319, 320. *See also*
  "Big Green" organizations

Green Party, 264

Greenpeace. *See also* Don't Make a Wave
  Committee (DMWC)
  anti-logging protests, 181, 190, 195, 200
  anti-whaling campaigns, 299–300
  Bob Hunter's leadership of, 300–305
  and drilling rigs, 51
  formation, 289–94
  growth, 309–11
  international, 297–99
  Mururoa (South Pacific) campaign,
    294–97
  organizational change, 305–9, 318
  scholarly treatment, 13–14
  and SPEC, 262

Greenpeace (boat), 291–92

Guatemala parks, 120

Guha, Ramachandra, 209–10

Gwich'in, 116

H

Habermas, Jürgen, 210

Hackett, Robert, 274

Haig-Brown, Roderick, 265

Hall, Carolyn, 114

Hanson, W. H. (Wally), 2

Hants County, Nova Scotia, 220–21

Harcourt government, 188, 193–95, 197

Harger, Robin, 156, 267, 272, 274

Harris, Douglas, 186

Hartley, Emery, 119

revitalization, 277–82, 318
scholarly treatment, 13
Sokaogon Chippewa Community, 24
Solomon, Lawrence, 244
South Shore Environmental Protection
    Association (SSEPA), 212, 217–19
sovereignty
    Fort Apache Heritage Foundation
        initiatives, 73–74, 86–89, 317–18
    and Native-park relations, 120–21
SPEC. *See* Society Promoting Environmental
    Conservation (SPEC)
SPEC Conservation Centre, 279
Spong, Paul, 299–300
Sport, Willie, 196
Spotted Eagle, Faith, 61
Sprague, Roger, 55–56
spruce budworm spraying program, 234, 250
SSEPA. *See* South Shore Environmental
    Protection Association (SSEPA)
Standing Rock, 323
Starblanket, Noel, 160
state parks. *See* provincial and state parks;
    specific parks
Stevens, Stan, 102
Stoddard Island nuclear project, 216
Stoddart, Mark C. J., 322
STOP: Save Tomorrow, Oppose Pollution,
    1–2
Stowe, Irving, 291, 293–94, 296, 300, 309
Sudbury, Ontario, 174
sulphur dioxide (SO_2) emissions, 163, 172–75,
    177
surveys and questionnaires, 140, 220–21,
    249, 251
Suzuki, David, 262
Swift, Louise, 1
Swinomish Tribe, 64

T

Tabajara, 108–9
Tarn, Richard, 239, 241–42
Tataryn, Lloyd, 160–61
Térraba, 114
Theodore Roosevelt School (T.R. School),
    76–77, 80–81

thermal pollution, 217
Thevik, Larry, 59
Thorpe, Jocelyn, 320
Thunder Bay environmental meetings, 178
Tielemen, William, 186
Timbisha Homeland Act, 113
Timbisha Shoshone Band, 112–13
Tla-o-qui-aht First Nation, 119, 183, 185
Tlingit, 116
Tofino, British Columbia, 184–86, 188
Tollefson, Chris, 322
tourism
    economic opportunities, 133–34
    and environmental restoration, 135–37
    Indigenous involvement with, 79, 81, 107,
        109, 115–16, 187
    and park policies, 100, 111
    research focus, 130
T.R. School. *See* Theodore Roosevelt School
    (T.R. School)
trail networks, 186–87
trains opposition, 58
treaties (international), 53
Treaty 3, 28, 161, 164, 172–75, 177–78
Treaty 3 Chiefs Council, 12, 154, 159, 162–63,
    172. *See also* Kinew, Tobasonakwut
    Peter
Treaty 8, 30–31
treaty rights, 49, 52, 55–57, 62–63, 65, 159
tree-spiking, 186, 200
Tulalip Tribes, 64
Two Bulls, Krystal, 56

U

Ucluelet, 183, 197
Uintah and Ouray Reservation, 63
Umatilla Tribe, 53
UNESCO, 101–3, 107
unions and environmentalism, 54, 268–69
Unist'ot'en Clan, 316
United Mine Workers of America (UMW),
    132
United States
    draft evaders, 290
    federal court decisions, 56
    Fort Apache management, 75–77, 80, 84

www.ingramcontent.com/pod-product-compliance
Lightning Source LLC
Chambersburg PA
CBHW040146270326
41929CB00025B/3390